U.S. COUNTERTERRORIST FORCES

U.S. COUNTERTERRORIST FORCES

Fred J. Pushies, Terry Griswold,
D. M. Giangreco, and S.F. Tomajczyk

MBI Publishing Company

First published in 2002 by MBI Publishing Company, Galtier Plaza, Suite 200, 380 Jackson Street, St. Paul, MN 55101-3885 USA

U.S. ARMY SPECIAL FORCES © Fred J.Pushies, 2001
DELTA © Terry Griswold & D. M. Giangreco, 1993
U.S. ELITE COUNTERTERRORIST FORCES © S. F. Tomajczyk, 1997

The information in this book is true and complete to the best of our knowledge. All recommendations are made without any guarantee on the part of the author or Publisher, who also disclaim any liability incurred in connection with the use of this data or specific details.

We recognize that some words, model names and designations, for example, mentioned herein are the property of the trademark holder. We use them for identification purposes only. This is not an official publication.

MBI Publishing Company books are also available at discounts in bulk quantity for industrial or sales-promotional use. For details write to Special Sales Manager at Motorbooks International Wholesalers & Distributors, Galtier Plaza, Suite 200, 380 Jackson Street, St. Paul, MN 55101-3885 USA.

Library of Congress Cataloging-in-Publication Data available

ISBN:0-7603-1363-6

On the front cover: SEAL Team One engages in CBR (Chemical, Biological, Radiation) attack training at Coronado, California. The gas mask shown here is current issue for Special Operations Forces only. *S. F. Tomajczyk*

On the back cover: A member of the U.S. Marshals Service's elite Special Operations Group points a 9mm Colt SMG at his intended target. Known as the "Shadow Stalkers," the SOG focuses on vanquishing the horrors of an ever-changing criminal element, including the threat of terrorists within our borders. *S. F. Tomajczyk*

On the title page: Members of the 3rd Special Forces Group (Airborne) perform a Rubber Duck operation from an MH-47E helicopter. Immediately after the Zodiac raft has cleared the ramp, the Special Forces team will follow it out, load in, and continue their insertion to the target area. *Fred J. Pushies*

Photo on page 5 by Fred J. Pushies
Photo on page 7 by S. F. Tomajczyk

Printed in China

CONTENTS

U.S. Army Special Forces

DELTA: America's Elite Counterterrorist Force

U.S. Elite Counterterrorist Forces

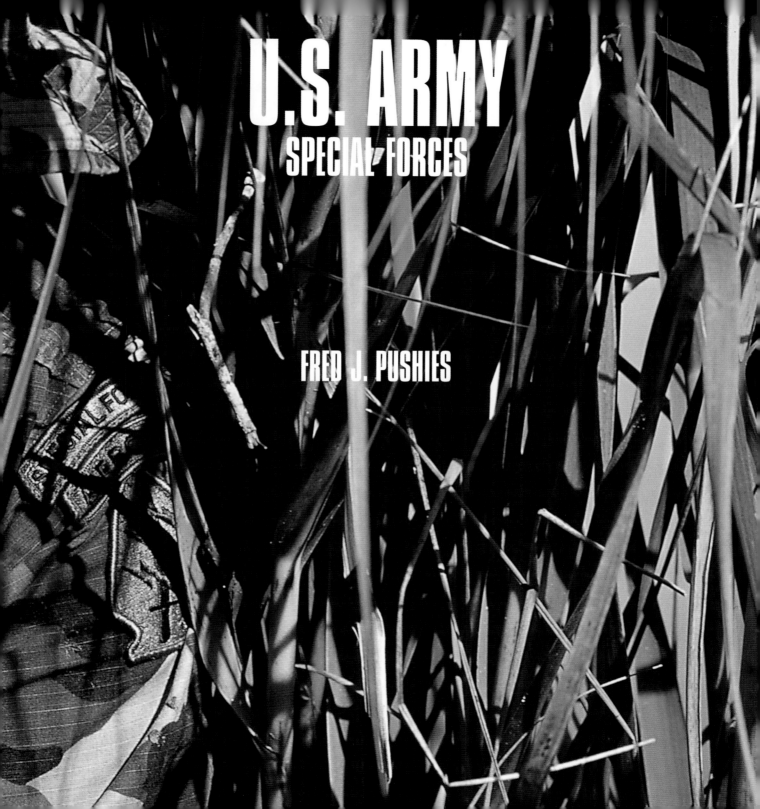

U.S. ARMY
SPECIAL FORCES

FRED J. PUSHIES

Foreword

This book pays tribute to a special breed of man, a special breed of Americans, and a special breed of warrior. Special Forces soldiers, commonly referred to as the "Green Berets," are unique—not only due to the types of missions they undertake, the rigorous training they undergo, or the equipment they use, but also because of their character, spirit, and dedication. They are men who step away from conventional methods and conventional thinking to undertake tasks that many experts would deem impossible. They are men who can be ruthless in their quest to accomplish a mission, yet selfless and compassionate, caring for people who are in desperate need of a helping hand. I know this from first-hand experience. I will always be grateful to have had the opportunity to serve alongside, and to be associated with, such courageous and awe-inspiring men.

Although officially only 49 years old, the Green Berets can trace their proud lineage back to the daring and courage of Americans serving in the Revolutionary War. Since the Special Forces inception in 1952, the Green Berets have been at the forefront of nearly every operation involving America's military, from Korea to Vietnam, from Grenada and Panama to Iraq, and from Somalia and Haiti to the Balkans. Often the Green Berets are the United States' only military presence in a number of countries around the world. They stand as both America's vanguard and its good-will ambassadors. The renaissance men of warfare, Special Forces stand ready to undertake any mission, from unconventional warfare, direct action, and rescue missions to peace operations and humanitarian assistance. Our Special Forces provide unique capabilities that are essential to the United States' national security strategy and its ability to provide leadership in an uncertain and troubled world.

Since the creation of the Special Operations Command in 1987, a unified command with headquarters at MacDill Air Force Base in Tampa, Florida, Special Forces has become a vital element of joint and combined military operations. Each regional Commander in Chief (CinC), which includes European Command, Pacific Command, Southern Command, Central Command, and Joint Forces Command, has a Special Operations component manned with Special Forces soldiers. The Green Berets provide forces to conduct operations across the spectrum of conflict as well as the staff expertise to better integrate their unique capabilities and talents into joint and combined operations around the world.

The trend to greater integration is important. The men of the Green Berets and their colleagues in the Special Operations community are recognized not only for their ability to conduct missions for which they are uniquely qualified, but also as a great combat multiplier during conventional military operations.

The future of Special Forces will be tied to its ability to continue to attract and develop quality personnel, as well as maintain its standards of excellence. The United States relies on its technological prowess to stay ahead of potential adversaries—and Special Forces will leverage that technology. But it is the spirit, ingenuity, and professionalism of each individual who wears the Green Beret that maintains the force's vital core, ensuring its long-term efficacy. They are extraordinary men whom we ask to accomplish what others would often consider impossible. As this book underscores, it is the extraordinary caliber of the individual Green Berets that has been the constant source of strength for this incomparable organization. The men who constitute its ranks will continue to be the underlying and undying strength of the Special Forces as it meets the challenges of the new millennium.

De Oppresso Liber!

—*General Henry H. Shelton*
Chairman of the Joint Chiefs of Staff

Acknowledgments

First and foremost, I must acknowledge my thanks to God for His guidance and wisdom in this project. To Michael Haenggi, editor at Motorbooks International; General Henry H. Shelton, Chairman of the Joint Chiefs of Staff; Lt. Colonel Thomas Rheinlander, Carol Darby, Barbara Ashley, SFC Amanda Glenn, Specialist John Creese, U.S. Army Special Operations Command -Public Affairs Office, Ft. Bragg; Major Tom McCollum, Captain Andrew "Dutch" Franz, Major Jonathan B. Withington, Special Forces - PAO, Ft. Bragg; Major Rich Patterson, Special Warfare Center - PAO, Ft. Bragg; Randy Action, President & CEO, U.S. Cavalry; Lt. Colonel Mike Nagata, Major Jack Jensen, Major Patrick Eberhart, Major Douglas Robertson, Command Sergeant Major Melvin Lyles, Staff Sergeant Peter Simchuk, Training Cadre - 1st Special Warfare Training Group; Command Sergeant Major Richard Fitzgerald - Non-Commissioned Officers Academy; Lt. Colonel Clifford C. Cloonan, MC, U.S. Army; Commander Michael Wilkinson, MSC, U.S. Navy; Captain Steve Ellison, MC, U.S. Army Joint Special Operations Medical Training Center; Major Kimm Rowe - Range 37; Mr. Donald Strassburg, Special Forces Arms Facility; Major Thomas Hartzel; CWO4 "Bulldog" Balwanz; Roxanne Merritt - JFKSWC Museum Curator; Mr. Joe Lupyak, CSM (ret.); Mr. David Clarke, CSM (ret.); Cadre 1st SWTG, Colonels "Daniels, Ranger & Mosby" G-Chiefs of Pineland; ODA 914 & ODA 916; Mrs. Catherine Bank; Mr. Noel Corby - Operations - National Training Center, Ft. Irwin; Gordon Sims, President, 1st Special Service Force Association; Colonel Mike Jones - Commander; Major Jeff Kent; Major Craig Johnson; C Company 3rd Battalion: Colonel Jack Zeigler; Major Ken Cobb; Captain Brent Jorgenson; Captain Mike Irvine; ODA-391, ODA-392, & ODA-395, MSgt. Gary Kenitzer, 3rd Special Forces Group (Airborne); CWO2 Michael Roth; MSG Sam Wright; SSG J. DeVerteuil; ODA-774, 7th Special Forces Group (Airborne) A Company 3rd Battalion; ODA-581, Colonel Gary Danley Commander 3rd Battalion, 5th Special Forces Group (Airborne); ODA-052, ODA-055, & ODA-065, Lt. Colonel David Alegre 10th Special Forces Group (Airborne) Company C, 2nd Battalion; Lt. Colonel Daniel Moore G7 Force Integration - USASFC(A); Major Richard Steiner, S-3, 2nd Battalion, 3rd Special Forces Group (Airborne); Captain Drew Bayliss, CWO2 Ken Hodges, SFC David A. Harrington, and ODA-363; SOTIC instructors, NCOIC - MSG Bill Olson, SFC Ron Woolett, SFC George Simmons, SFC Jim Wallace, SFC Dave Garner, Rick Boucher, MSgt. (ret.), Cpl. George Bundy, 2nd Rangers and SSgt. Clifford Richardson, 5th Special Forces Group (Airborne) ODA-546; Captain Brent Epperson - Assistant S-3, Sgt. Mark Williams, Multimedia, NCOIC, 7th Special Forces Group (Airborne); Mr. Emit B. Hutsman, Curator, Ft. Clark Museum - Indian Scouts; Colonel Robert S. Sumner USA (ret.) Alamo Scouts, 6th Army; Robert E. Passanisi, Historian, Merrill's Marauder Association; Mr. Richard Sanne; Mary Scott Smith, Vice President, Barret Firearms Manufacturing, Inc.; Michael J. Winey, Curator, U.S. Army Military History Institute; John W. Goldtrap, Rebe Phillips, General Atomics Aeronautical Systems, Inc.; Kathy Vinson, Defense Visual Information Center; Steve Harrigan, Johnson Controls World Service, Inc. Also Darren Proctor, Robert Bentley Jr., and my family.

Special Thanks to "The Sea Pigs": Captain Brian Ebert, CW2 Tony Bonnell, MSG B.F. Burnham, SFC Mikel Chapman, SSG Jason Clark, SSG Jeremy Jemmett, Sgt. Joe Ferris, SSG Jason Perkins, SSG Doug Peterson, and SFC Greg Green of ODA-173, 1st Special Forces Group (Airborne).

Introduction

Unconventional warfare is nothing new. The Old Testament recounts the story of Gideon, whom God told to do battle with the Midianites approximately 5,500 years ago. The Midianites, an enemy of Israel, had a force so large their numbers were uncountable. Gideon began his campaign with 32,000 men, but twice God told him to reduce the ranks of his troops. Finally, when Gideon's force numbered only 300, God gave him a plan and set the attack in motion.

Gideon divided the 300 men into three companies of 100 each. He armed them each with a trumpet, an empty pitcher and a lamp, which was placed inside the pitcher. During the night the three companies secretly took up preordained positions, surrounding the enemy. Just around midnight, when the Midianites had placed the first watch, Gideon and his men blew their trumpets, broke the pitchers, and raised their lamps. In the ensuing confusion that befell the enemy, the Midianites turned their swords on one another, as Gideon and his band disappeared into the night. This encounter foreshadowed future unconventional methods: employ psychological warfare, stealth, and lightening hit-and-run tactics.

Some 5,000 years later, in 218 BC, a young commander named Hannibal employed yet another facet of unconventional warfare. Hannibal marched his men, roughly 35,000 troops, over the Italian Alps. While such a movement is not unusual, what was unexpected and well out of the ordinary was the fact that Hannibal's invasion force included elephants. To move huge equatorial animals through the frozen expanses of the mountains would be unthinkable today—and it was unthinkable then. Hannibal added more principles for unconventional warfare: Do the unexpected, tackle the impossible, and succeed at all costs.

Unconventional warfare has been with mankind since the beginning of time. In Greek mythology the Greek warriors feigned retreat and sailed away, leaving behind a large wooden horse. The Trojans believed it was an offering to the goddess Athena, and brought it into the city for luck. Unbeknownst to the jubilant Trojans, the Greeks were hidden inside. As the city slept, the Greeks slipped from the horse, now within the enemy's fortress, opened the city's gates to the returning sailors, and decimated the Trojan forces.

The legendary Trojan Horse was featured on the beret crest when the U.S. Army Special Forces troops carried out postwar activities in 1952 Germany. It was used again in the formation of U.S. Special Operations Command in the 1980s. Currently, the representation of the Trojan Horse embodied in the knight piece can be found on the beret crest of the U.S. Army Special Warfare Center/School. A symbol of unconventional warfare from ancient times, it continues in the heraldry of the modern Special Forces warrior.

From its humble beginnings as a handful of men roaming the Bavarian Alps of post–World War II Germany, the Special Forces has evolved into a critical component of U.S. military operations. Whether performing civic actions and training with the indigenous populace or carrying out clandestine activities in denied territory, these men epitomize the term *warriors*, and bring unconventional warfare to a new level. This is their story—where they have come from, and where they are heading in the new millennium. These are the men of the U.S. Army Special Forces, "The Quiet Professionals."

CHAPTER 1

Special Forces Lineage

The lineage of today's Special Forces soldier begins some two centuries ago in an emerging country called America. It was here during the French and Indian War (1754–1763) that colonists would serve with British forces. In 1756, Major Robert Rogers recruited these Americans into a unit that would number nine companies of men. Although Maj. Rogers did not invent the unconventional warfare techniques, he did

The forerunner of the current Special Forces, Francis Marion, was known as the "Swamp Fox." He and his men brought unconventional warfare tactics to the Revolutionary War, making guerrilla raids against the British. *South Caroliniana Library*

exploit the tactics and establish them into Ranger doctrine. He is credited by some with writing the first Ranger Manual.

The newly founded Ranger companies would learn to assimilate these techniques. Following Rogers' command, they would strike where the enemy least expected them to hit, and they would traverse terrain conventional forces would avoid. The Rangers employed stealth and secrecy in their movements on the enemy. Once in position they would spring the attack and, like a North American rattlesnake, hit fast and hit hard. Major Rogers instituted a plan of action to train his Rangers and personally watched over its execution. He set strict orders for his troops to follow, stressing operational security, readiness, and tactics.

Rogers' tactics contained more than two dozen paragraphs detailing the Rangers' operational techniques. Over the years these techniques have been summarized in what has come to be known as the "Standing Orders—Rogers' Rangers." They are:

1. Don't forget nothing.

2. Have your musket clean as a whistle, hatchet scoured, sixty rounds powder and ball, and be ready to march at a minute's warning.

3. When you're on the march, act the way you would if you was sneaking up on a deer. See the enemy first.

4. Tell the truth about what you see and what you do. There is an army depending on us for correct information. You can lie all you please

when you tell other folks about the Rangers, but don't never lie to a Ranger of office.

5. Don't never take a chance you don't have to.

6. When we're on the march we march single file, far enough apart so one shot can't go through two men.

7. If we strike swamps, or soft ground, we spread out abreast, so it's hard to track us.

8. When we march, we keep moving till dark, so as to give the enemy the least possible chance at us.

9. When we camp, half the party stays awake while the other half sleeps.

10. If we take prisoners, we keep 'em separate till we have had time to examine them, so they can't cook up a story between 'em.

11. Don't ever march home the same way. Take a different route so you won't be ambushed.

12. No matter whether we travel in big parties or little ones, each party has to keep a scout 20 yards ahead, 20 yards on each flank, and 20 yards in the rear so the main body can't be surprised and wiped out.

13. Every night you'll be told where to meet if surrounded by a superior force.

14. Don't sit down to eat without posting sentries.

15. Don't sleep beyond dawn. Dawn's when the French and Indians attack.

16. Don't cross a river by a regular ford.

17. If somebody's trailing you, make a circle, come back onto your own track, and ambush the folks that aim to ambush you.

18. Don't stand up when the enemy's coming against you. Kneel down, lie down, hide behind a tree.

19. Let the enemy come till he's almost close enough to touch, then let him have it and jump out and finish him up with your hatchet.

Rogers' Rangers and these rules lay the groundwork for future generations of Special Operations Forces of the United States.

The tradition of the Rangers continued when the time came for the colonists to fight for their independence during the American Revolution. Active during the Revolutionary War were Dan Morgan's "Corps of Rangers," formed under orders from George Washington, and the Connecticut Rangers, under the leadership of Thomas Knowlton. While Morgan's men were considered expert marksmen, Knowlton's Rangers, a force of hand-picked men, were skilled in reconnaissance techniques.

It was Francis Marion, however, who would bring guerrilla war to the British and establish a firm position in the Special Forces lineage. Born and raised in South Carolina, Francis Marion fought the Cherokee Indians in 1760 as a lieutenant in the militia. During the Cherokee War, Marion learned the fighting techniques of the Indians, how they would initiate a surprise attack and then fade away as quickly as they had begun the assault. After the war Marion retired from service to take up the quiet, peaceful life of a farmer.

The war for independence changed these plans. Due to his past experience fighting the Cherokee, Marion received a commission as captain in the Continental Army and took up arms in the fight for freedom. Eventually, Marion would be promoted to the rank of General.

When Charleston fell to the British, Marion escaped capture and, like the Cherokee Indians he had fought, headed into the South Carolina swamps. Once in the swamp he established his base camp and with 150 men formed what would become known as Marion's Brigade. As the war progressed Marion and his men carried out

The U.S. Scouts, or Indian Scouts, were the first to employ the crossed arrows for their unit insignia in August 1890. Later, in World War II, the 1st Special Service Force would adopt the insignia. The crossed arrows continued their appearance in the SF beret crest and became the ensign of the U.S. Army Special Forces when the Army designated them as a separate branch in 1987. *Ft. Clark Museum*

unconventional warfare tactics against the British. They would ambush British troops, attack their supply lines, and perform hit-and-run raids on the enemy's camps; when done they would fade away into the dark forbidding recesses of the swamps. Try as they might, the British found it futile to attempt to follow these guerrillas into their safe haven of the swamp. A British colonel dubbed Marion the Swamp Fox.

Guerilla and unconventional war tactics reappeared in the U.S. Civil War. Mean's Rangers of the Union Army and Ashby's Rangers of the Confederacy were specialists in scouting, harassing, and raiding. Each did its best to hamper the efforts of the other side. Yet the best-known unconventional warfare troops of this war undeniably were the Confederate Army's Mosby's Rangers. Under the command of Colonel John Singleton Mosby of Virginia, Mosby's Rangers operated behind Union lines, just south of the Potomac. Col. Mosby began with a three-man scout element in

1862. By 1865, Mosby's Rangers had evolved into a force of eight companies of guerrillas.

Col. Mosby was a firm believer in the use of reconnaissance, aggressive action, and surprise attacks. Mosby and his Rangers cut off Union communications and supply lines, wrecked railroads, and raided base camps behind enemy lines. One of their greatest feats was to capture Union General Edwin H. Stoughton by bluffing their way into, and removing him from, his own house. Due to his stealth and uncanny ability to avoid capture, Mosby earned the nickname the Gray Ghost. Mosby's Rangers were well trained and well disciplined, setting a standard for future unconventional warfare forces.

In the years following the Civil War, American "Horse Soldiers" fought in the Great Plains Wars of the Southwest. Aware that hostile forces could not be tracked down by the cavalry alone, the U.S. Army created a new special operations force, known as the Indian Scouts. Drawn primarily from Pawnee, Navajo, and Seminole tribes, they were deployed at length all through the West. The Indian Scouts aided General G. Crook in capturing Geronimo.

With attributes comparable to today's Special Forces soldiers, these Indians Scouts were renowned in such military traits as tracking, field craft, physical courage, and boldness. The language skills, cultural appreciation, and civic action that characterized these forces are quite similar to today's Army Special Forces. The heritage of the Indian Scouts continued in the Crossed Arrows insignia that was adopted by the 1st Special Service Force during World War II.

The history of the U.S. Army Special Forces may be traced to the pre–Revolutionary War time period; however, a more direct lineage and organizational relationship follows from the elite U.S. military forces operating during World War II. Special operations units were active in all theaters of operations, from the jungles of Pacific islands,

Burma, and China, to the expanses of European mountains, woodlands, and towns.

The Second World War added the term Army Rangers to the annals of military history, and to the pages of Special Forces heraldry. Major General Lucian K. Truscott, the U.S. Army liaison to the British General Staff, submitted the idea of an American unit similar to the British Commandos to General George Marshall. The War Department responded with cables to Truscott and Major General Russell P. Hartle, commander of all Army forces in Northern Ireland, authorizing formation of the special unit.

General Truscott liked the term "commandos," but it was a British name and he desired something more American. Looking back on the history of unconventional warfare, Truscott found American troops that met the highest standards of courage, motivation, tenacity, fighting spirit, and ruggedness. The group that inspired him was that commanded by Major Rogers, and a new name was added to the U.S. military—Army Rangers.

General Hartle picked Captain William O. Darby, who had been serving as his aide-de-camp, to recruit, select, and organize the newly formed unit. Darby, a West Point graduate, was intelligent and enthusiastic, demonstrating the capacity to gain the confidence of his superiors and the loyalty of his men. Promoted to Major, Darby took on the task in hand. Major Darby and his hand-picked staff officers interviewed volunteers from the 1st Armored Division, the 34th Infantry Division, and other units from the area.

Within a few weeks, the first unit of Army Rangers was selected. On 19 June 1942, in Carrickfergus, Ireland, the 1st U.S. Army Ranger Battalion was activated under the command of Major William O. Darby. This unit would come to be known as Darby's Rangers.

Major Darby and his Rangers would spend three months at the Commando Training Center at Achnacarry, Scotland. Here, under the tutelage of combat-seasoned British Commandos, the American Rangers learned the basics of unconventional warfare. Out of 600 men that began the training with Darby, 500 remained.

Darby's Rangers fought throughout Western Europe, but they achieved their greatest recognition on D-Day, 6 June 1944. The Rangers would scale the cliffs of Pointe du Hoc as part of the Allied invasion of Normandy.

The 1st Special Service Force was officially established at Fort William Henry Harrison, Montana, on 9 July 1942. These unconventional warfare troops comprised both American and Canadian soldiers under the command of Colonel Robert T. Frederick. The 1st SSF was a

Portrait of Brigadier General Robert T. Frederick, commander of the 1st Special Service Force. Known as the "Devil's Brigade," these unconventional warfare troops were constituted of both American and Canadian soldiers. *JFK Special Warfare Museum*

March 1944, at Laganga/Walawbum area, Burma. One of the 5307th's Battalion's I & R (Intelligence & Reconnaissance) Platoons, patrolling the area before the attack at Walawbum. (The 3rd Battalion consisted of two Combat Teams, Orange and Khaki, each with its own I & R Platoon.) Note the men are not carrying their field packs, so they can move about and conceal themselves more easily. *Lt. David Lubin Merrill's Marauders Association*

force of three battalion-size units, with 60 percent of the men coming from the ranks of the American military. Volunteers were sought out from various units; in some cases commanders eagerly "volunteered" some of their troublesome soldiers and sent them out to Montana. Col. Frederick weeded out men who arrived less than highly motivated, from which one could argue he was responsible for instituting the first Special Forces Assessment and Selection (SFAS). As Gordon Sims, president of the 1st Special Service Force Association, relates, "Many people think the American soldiers were roughnecks and yard birds. The truth was, some of these men were more at home in the field than in garrison. What regular Army commanders saw as troublesome actually turned out to be some of the best operators."

Col. Frederick formulated a training schedule for his men that would stress physical conditioning, hand-to-hand combat, weapons training, demolitions, infantry tactics, and mountain work. The soldiers of the 1st SSF were also airborne trained, and schooled in skiing and winter operations. Their specialty was close-quarter combat against numerically superior forces.

The 1st Special Service Force would see combat against the Japanese in the Aleutians and with the Germans in Italy and France. It was in Europe that the 1st SSF got its nickname, the Devil's Brigade. The crossed arrows and distinctive unit insignia of the present-day Special Forces was first authorized to be worn by the 1st SSF by the Secretary of War.

While Darby's Rangers and the Devil's Brigade were conducting their operations in Europe, another group of men was writing its lessons into the journal of unconventional warfare in the Pacific. Here the men of the 5307th Composite Unit (Provisional), under the leadership of Brigadier General Frank Merrill, brought the war to the Japanese in the jungles of Burma.

Organized in 1943, this unit of 3,000 men, all volunteers, was tasked with the mission of long-range infiltration behind Japanese lines. Their objective was to destroy the enemies "jugular"—their communications and supply lines. Furthermore, they were to harass and attack the Japanese at will. This unit would come to be known as Merrill's Marauders.

One of the Marauders' greatest undertakings was the seizure of the Myitkyina Airfield. Merrill and his men infiltrated through the hot, humid, insect- and disease-ridden Burmese jungle. And that was the good news. These unconventional warriors were constantly outnumbered by the enemy, and support was almost nonexistent. Merrill's Marauders' accomplishments are legendary and inspirational, even by today's standards.

Another unconventional raiding force operating in the Pacific was the Alamo Scouts. This unit of highly skilled soldiers was created by Lt. General Walter Krueger, commanding General of the U.S. Sixth Army. Those who volunteered for assignment to this force went through six weeks of arduous training and field exercises encompassing land navigation, hand-to-hand combat, weapons, communications, survival, small boat operations, and advance patrolling techniques. Those who graduated from the training were selected to become Alamo Scouts and formed into small teams, usually one officer and six or seven enlisted men.

These teams would infiltrate the numerous Japanese-held islands throughout the South Pacific, emerging from PT boats and rubber rafts to perform their missions. Their primary mission was originally reconnaissance, but their skills and the demands of war led them to greater challenges. In one of their foremost missions, the Scouts led U.S. Rangers and Filipino guerrillas in an attack on a Japanese prison camp at Cabantuan, freeing all 511 Allied prisoners there. Never numbering more than 70 men, the Alamo Scouts

Team leaders of the Alamo Scouts, left to right: Lt. Bill Nellist, Lt. Tom Roonsaville, Lt. Robert "Red" Sumner, Lt. Jack Dove. Leyte, Philippine Islands, January 1945. In more than 100 missions, the Alamo Scouts never lost a man. *Alamo Scout Association*

conducted more than a hundred missions without the loss of a single soldier.

These unconventional units of World War II were indeed U.S. Army elites. They took the principles founded by Rogers' Rangers and gave them a twentieth-century application, thus establishing a basis for modern special operations forces. Their mission was simple: Hit the enemy, hit them hard with lightning attacks, and disappear into the countryside, whether the mountains and woodlands of Europe, or the jungles of Burma. In addition to units employing lightning raids on the enemy, World War II produced another kind of unconventional warrior—a soldier who could adapt and integrate the types of methods employed by the Swamp Fox and Col. Mosby. This force would combine these principles with new techniques of airborne and guerrilla fighting.

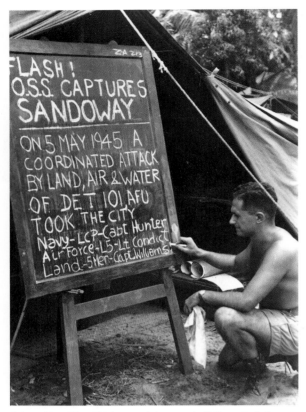

Private First Class Edeleanu prints news bulletin on bulletin board outside Intelligence tent of Kyaukpyu Camp, the day before Office of Strategic Services (OSS), AFU, departure via convoy for Rangoon. Detachment 101, Ramree Island, Burma. *National Archive*

They were know as Shadow Warriors. Their organization would become known as the Office of Strategic Service, or OSS.

Prior to the United States becoming involved in World War II, President Franklin D. Roosevelt realized the need for the collection of intelligence and special operation capabilities. He authorized creation of the Office of the Coordinator of Information (COI), formed under the leadership of William "Wild Bill" Donovan in 1941. The COI

flourished, establishing operations sites in England, North Africa, India, Burma, and China.

When the United States entered World War II in December 1941, the COI agency was renamed the Office of Strategic Services. The OSS was instrumental in gathering intelligence and conducting sabotage raids in occupied Europe. It also worked with the French resistance fighting against the Nazis.

In April of 1942, Detachment 101 of the OSS was activated for service in Burma. Under the command of General "Vinegar Joe" Stillwell, this unit conducted operations behind the Japanese line in Burma. Detachment 101 consisted of nearly 11,000 Kachin tribesmen. Starting from scratch, these guerrillas were responsible for killing 10,000 Japanese, while losing only 206 of their own.

On 23 December 1942, the Joint Chiefs of Staff authorized the formation of multi-national Operation Groups (OGs), for which Donovan had been the principal advocate. The OGs were French, Greek, German, Italian, Norwegian, and Yugoslavian. These units included specially selected, trained, and disciplined U.S. Army soldiers who were proficient in conducting operations behind enemy lines. An Operation Group comprised 30 enlisted men and three officers, further split into two 15-man sections. OGs were the forerunners of the Operational Detachments-Alpha (ODAs), or A-teams, of today's Special Forces.

The mission of the OGs was to infiltrate by parachute or sometimes by sea into enemy territory. There they would meet up with existing guerrilla forces and support them in conducting unconventional warfare. Like current ODAs, the OGs were self-sufficient and had the ability to train and coordinate guerrilla operations. Such operations included, but were not limited to, direct sabotage, rescue of downed Allied pilots, and collection of intelligence. Although efforts were made to coordinate their action with the

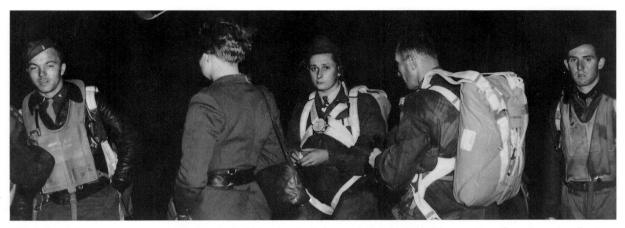

OSS Jedburgh team members prepare to board a B-24 bomber for their parachute drop behind German lines. Operating primarily at night, B-24s of the 801st Bombardment Group, known as the Carpetbaggers, supported missions the same as today's Combat Talons—penetrate enemy airspace and infiltrate special operations teams. *National Archive*

Resistance, the OGs could, and did, conduct raids and operations without any partisan support.

In the early part of 1944, in preparation of the D-Day invasion of France, the OSS began the creation of the first of the Jedburgh Teams, which eventually numbered 96. The name Jedburgh came from the area of Scotland where the Scots carried on a guerrilla war against the British invaders in the twelfth century.

The typical Jedburgh Team consisted of three men—two officers and one enlisted radio operator. These individuals were trained in demolitions, weapons, knife fighting, hand-to-hand combat, infiltration and exfiltration techniques, small units tactics, survival, and a multitude of other unconventional warfare skills to assure them success in their missions behind the German lines.

The mission of the Jedburgh Teams was to infiltrate, via parachute primarily, occupied France, Belgium, and Holland prior to the D-Day invasion. There they would organize guerrillas and conduct unconventional warfare against the Nazis, providing the resistance fighters with supplies and weapons. Operations began on D-Day to ambush German convoys, disrupt communications, destroy railways, bridges, and roadways and to delay enemy reinforcements from reaching the beachhead at Normandy.

At the conclusion of World War II, President Harry S. Truman deactivated the OSS, yet its legacy lives on today. The intelligence branch of the service is considered the father of the current Central Intelligence Agency (CIA), formed in September 1947. The first directors of the agency were former OSS veterans.

Special Forces thus drew inspiration and tactics from many sources throughout U.S. history and before our nation was formed. With each new conflict, the leaders of unconventional warfare drew on the proven techniques of the past, and added to them with resources and techniques of the time. World War II provided a pressing international stage on which to hone unconventional warfare techniques, and the lessons learned in that conflict have been extended and refined to the present day.

The Birth of the U.S. Army Special Forces

Two OSS operatives, Col. Aaron Bank and Col. Russell Volckmann, remained in service with the U.S. Army. These two officers had been assigned to the Army Psychological Warfare Staff at the end of World War II, commanded by Brigadier General Robert McClure. Gen. McClure had been the director of information in the U.S.-occupied area of West Germany. A strong advocate of psychological warfare, he would take

The original beret crest of the U.S. Army Special Forces—the Trojan Horse centered in a shield with a lightning bolt in the background, resting on a pair of airborne wings. This crest can still be seen in use today at the headquarters of the 10th Special Forces Group (Airborne) at Fort Carson, Colorado, and in Germany.

command of the Office of the Chief of Psychological Warfare (OCPW) on 15 January 1950. The OCPW was divided into three branches, PsyWar, covert deception, and Special Operations.

Working for the OCPW, Cols. Bank and Volckmann developed plans for organizing and training a special operations unit. They worked diligently to convince the Army Chiefs that the post–World War II world held numerous sites of potential conflict that would not be open to conventional warfare, but were prime targets for unconventional warfare tactics and guerrilla fighting. One such area was Eastern Europe, now occupied and dominated by the Soviets. Intelligence indicated that a substantial potential for guerrilla and covert Unconventional Warfare (UW) operations existed in the area.

Special operations units as envisioned by the two colonels, and Banks in particular, would be a force multiplier. Based on the OSS Jedburgh Teams, with striking similarities to today's Special Forces A-Detachments, these small teams could operate behind the enemy's lines and raise havoc and confusion within its ranks. It would be possible for a handful of men to effectively hamper, disrupt, and paralyze a much larger conventional force, e.g., the Soviets.

This was daring and innovative thinking that went against the grain of traditional, conventional concepts. However bold the idea, by 1952 the U.S. Army was at last ready to commence a new era of unconventional warfare.

The new organization would be referred to as "Special Forces," a name derived from the OGs fielded by the OSS in 1944. The Army allocated

2,300 personnel slots for the unit and assigned it to Fort Bragg, North Carolina.

In the spring of 1952, Col. Bank headed to Fort Bragg to choose the location for a Psychological Warfare/Special Forces Center. The area he selected is still the home of Special Forces, located at the corner of Reilly Road and Ardennes. This area was, and remains to this day, Smoke Bomb Hill. Although a remote location at Fort Bragg in 1952, within a decade it would become one of the busiest areas in the U.S. Army.

At this time Col. Bank began bringing together selected officers and NCOs who would serve as the nucleus of the new organization. These men would act as the training cadre to fill in the ranks of the fledgling unit. Col. Bank did

The father of the U.S. Army Special Forces, Colonel Aaron Bank. He was the first Special Forces Commander, commanding the 10th Special Forces Group (Airborne) as it was organized in June 1952 at Smoke Bomb Hill, Ft. Bragg, North Carolina. *JFK Special Warfare Museum*

not want any inexperienced soldiers; from the inception of Special Forces, only the best troops were sought, and Banks got them. Among the ranks assembled in the newly formed organization were former OSS officers, airborne troops, Ranger troops, and combat veterans from World War II and Korea.

The individuals who volunteered for service with the newly formed Special Forces were unique, highly motivated men looking for new challenges—the tougher the better! Virtually all the soldiers were fluent in at least two languages, had the minimum rank of sergeant and were trained in infantry and airborne skills. They were all volunteers who were willing to work behind enemy lines. They further agreed to operate in civilian

When first organized in 1952, members of the Special Forces wore the Glider and Parachute airborne patch. Subsequently, it would be replaced with the Arrowhead patch, which is the current shoulder patch of the SF soldiers.

clothes as necessary. This in itself would be dangerous, since soldiers in civilian clothes were no longer protected under the Geneva Convention and most likely would be executed if captured.

But the men who volunteered did not worry about the risks. Mr. Joe Lupyak SF-CSM (ret.) relates that "most of the early SF troops were foreigners." Indeed, many of the early troopers were from Eastern Europe, and had lived through their share of communist tyranny and Nazi rule. They had fled to America after the end of World War II under the provisions of the Lodge Bill, a law that allowed immigrants from politically persecuted countries to become U.S. citizens by serving in the United States armed forces.

Because of their backgrounds and motivation, the men of the first Special Forces organization were ideally suited for guerrilla operations in Eastern Europe. This was precisely the geographical area Bank had in mind when he designed the

Members of the 10th Special Forces Group (Airborne) take a break in the Bavarian mountainside. A number of the early SF soldiers were not from the United States. They joined under the Lodge Bill, a legislative act designed to allow immigrants from politically persecuted countries to become U.S. citizens by serving in the U.S. armed forces. The soldier on the left is armed with a Czechoslovakian submachine gun. *JFK Special Warfare Museum*

Members of the 10th Special Forces Group (Airborne) during mountain training, seen here wearing the forbidden green berets. In the early years the beret was often worn in the field, but rarely, if ever, worn in garrison. Note the glider and parachute shoulder patch worn by the original SF units. *JFK Special Warfare Museum*

group. Not only were they fluent with the language of the targeted areas, they were also familiar with the local customs, political sentiments, police, and industrial structure, as well as the overall geography.

After months of concentrated preparation, the new unit was ready. On 19 June 1952, the 10th Special Forces Group (Airborne) was activated, under the command of Col. Aaron Bank. On the day of its activation, the 10th SFG (A) had a total complement of ten soldiers—Col. Bank, one warrant officer, and eight enlisted men. This fledgling organization would soon flourish into a formidable force.

Within months of its activation, hundreds of the first volunteers reported to Smoke Bomb Hill as they completed the initial phase of their Special Forces training. As the group grew in size, it was divided into a compilation of three types of detachments or teams: A-teams, B-Teams, and C-Teams.

Students from the Special Warfare Center go through their final exercises in the National Forest area near Ft. Bragg, North Carolina. This exercise, known as Robin Sage, will pit the newly trained SF students against a larger conventional "enemy" force. Uniform of the day is "guerrilla casual" so they can blend in with the locals. *JFK Special Warfare Museum*

The basic operational unit of Special Forces was the A-detachment or A-team. The A-team consisted of twelve men—two officers and ten enlisted men—and was commanded by a captain. The A-team was the core of the new Special Forces. They were the soldiers who would be on the ground deep inside enemy territory. Their job was to make contact with the local resistance leaders and develop the indigenous population into a cohesive guerrilla force. The A-team had two operations and intelligence sergeants, two medical sergeants, two communications sergeants, two weapons sergeants, and two demolition/engineer sergeants. This configuration would allow the A-team to operate in two six-man teams or "split A-teams" if necessary. It was standard operating procedure that

each member of the A-team was crossed-trained in the SF skills. A-team soldiers were highly trained in unconventional warfare and spoke at least one foreign language. To this day the A-team remains the basis of Special Forces operations.

The functions of the B- and C-teams were more organizational. B-teams coordinated the actions of numerous A-teams assigned to specific areas in a designated country. C-teams were at the top of the Special Forces hierarchy. They worked with top leaders of indigenous guerrilla movements, and provided overall guidance to other SF teams in the area.

As soon as the 10th group was large enough, Banks started training his soldiers in the most advanced unconventional warfare techniques. The initial mission of the 10th Special Forces Group was to infiltrate designated areas of enemy territory by land, sea, or air and establish and train indigenous forces to conduct Special Forces operations, with an emphasis on guerrilla warfare. There were also secondary missions, including deep-penetration raids, intelligence-gathering assignments, and counter-insurgency operations. Special Forces operations demanded a commitment to professionalism and excellence unparalleled in the history of America's military, but the men of the 10th Special Forces Group (Airborne) were up to the challenge.

Like today's Special Forces soldier, the men under Col. Banks' newly formed organization were Airborne qualified and many of them had undergone Ranger training as well. Familiar with tough training, volunteers for Special Forces quickly realized this was not a mere review of Ranger tactics. As Banks put the men through their paces, they would learn many more skills, undergo more intense training, practice different mission profiles, and master more complex operations.

The Ranger units of World War II and the Korean War had been created to perform as shock troops and carry out light infantry raids—to hit and run and wait for follow-on forces. Special Forces troops, by contrast, were expected to remain behind enemy lines for months on end, perhaps even years. They would be self-sufficient experts in survival, capable of living off the land. And they would speak the language of the indigenous populace in their area of operation.

The Special Forces soldier would learn all of these skills and many more. Operating as a full Special Forces Group for less than 18 months, the men of the 10th Special Forces demonstrated to the Army that they were masters of these unconventional and very useful skills.

With the political climate heating up in East Germany, half of the 10th Special Forces Group was re-deployed on 11 November 1953 to Bad Tolz, West Germany. These A-teams would be on call to provide support to any resistance movements, if necessary, in Soviet-occupied Europe. The other half of the group would remain at Fort Bragg and was redesignated the 77th Special Forces Group. This split was significant, as it demonstrated that Special Forces had established itself as a vital unit of the U.S. Army.

During the balance of the 1950s, Special Forces would continue to grow, slowly but consistently, into a formidable organization. Special Forces was surveying its interest in the Far East, moving beyond their previous European focus. In April 1956 the 14th Special Forces Detachment (Area) (Airborne) was secretly activated at Fort Bragg; two months later they would deploy to Hawaii, and subsequently to Thailand, Taiwan, and Vietnam.

This detachment of 16 SF soldiers taken from the 77th SFG was tasked with the mission of leading Asian resistance against any communist thrust into Indo-China, Malaya, South Korea, and the surrounding area. Operations in Korea were not new to Special Forces personnel. Near the end of 1952, Special Forces troops had been operating behind enemy lines and had been deployed on classified missions. Special Forces soldiers assisted anti-communist guerrillas who had joined the United Nation Partisan Forces-Korea or UNPFK. These guerrillas were often referred to as "donkeys," from the Korean word for liberty, dong-il. The guerrillas, operating from small islands off the Korean coast, would conduct raids, rescue downed airmen, provide gunnery spotting, and maintain electronic facilities. This would be the first time that U.S. Army Special Forces would operate with guerrilla troops behind enemy lines.

Shortly after the activation of the 14th SFOD, three additional operational detachments, the 12th, 13th, and 16th, were designated for service in Asia and the Pacific. These three SFOD were

President Kennedy speaks with Brigadier General William P. Yarborough at Fort Bragg, 12 October 1961. President Kennedy would later comment that the green beret was "a symbol of excellence, a badge of courage, a mark of distinction in the fight for freedom." *JFK Library*

By 1961 there were three active Special Forces groups securely established in the U.S. Army—the 1st Special Forces Group (Airborne), the 7th Special Forces Group (Airborne) (re-designated from the 77th on 6 June 1960), and the original 10th Special Forces Group (Airborne).

The Cold War produced increased demand for unconventional tactics and soldiers. The Special Forces were in Berlin when the Berlin wall was erected. Special Forces personnel would conduct cross-border operations, some of these missions still classified today. These soldiers were assigned to a unit known simply as detachment "A." When in garrison, they would not wear the SF patches or berets; they would blend in with other conventional troops wearing the Berlin brigade patch. As their Office of Strategic Services (OSS) predecessors, when these soldiers would go out to roam around Germany, they would do so in civilian clothes. The clothes they wore, the shoes on their feet, their rucksacks, and even their underwear were of German origin. There would be nothing to trace them to the United States if they were compromised.

Other missions given to the Special Forces during this time included training Cuban expatriates. Special Forces teams were sent to Guatemala to train soldiers for the possible invasion of Cuba again in October of 1962 during the Cuban Missile Crisis, when the Soviets placed offensive nuclear missiles in Cuba. The U.S. military was put on full alert, including Special Forces teams placed on standby, should the call for their insertion be sent.

If Col. Aaron Bank was the father of the Special Forces, then President John F. Kennedy was to become their godfather. President Kennedy, a military scholar with more than a mere interest in counterinsurgency, recognized the need for a counter-guerrilla force. He referred to this as "another type of war, new in its intensity, ancient in its origins—war by guerrillas, subversives,

eventually combined into the 8231st Army Special Operations Detachment. On 17 June 1957 the 14th and 8231st united to form the 1st Special Forces Group (Airborne) based out of Okinawa and responsible for the Far Eastern area of operation. In the summer of 1959, Special Forces training teams would be inserted covertly into Laos to train soldiers of the Royal Lao Army. These SF teams were designated "White Star" mobile training teams, or MTT. Working under the direction of the Central Intelligence Agency (CIA), the Special Forces MTTs were also used to train Meo tribesmen as a guerrilla force.

insurgents, assassins; war by ambush instead of by combat; by infiltration instead of aggression, seeking victory by eroding and exhausting the enemy instead of engaging him." This, he continued, would require "a whole new kind of strategy, a wholly different kind of force."

During his visit to Ft. Bragg in 1961, President Kennedy found such a force as he reviewed the men of the U.S. Army Special Forces. These dedicated soldiers were what the President was looking for to thwart the spreading threat of communist insurgents around the world. President Kennedy also liked the green beret headgear. These men had a special mission; it was only fitting they have a special symbol to set that mission apart. As the ranks of the Special Forces grew, the green beret became synonymous with Special Forces.

With the support of the President, the Special Forces grew, and additional SF groups were formed. On 21 September 1961, the 5th Special Forces Group (Airborne) was activated, followed by the 8th SFG(A) on 1 April 1963, the 6th SFG(A) on 1 May 1963, and finally the 3rd SFG(A) on 5 December 1963. Members of the Special Forces would also find themselves in Army Reserve and National Guard units with the formation of the 11th and 12th SFG(A)—Reserve and 19th and 20th SFG(A)—National Guard, in 1966.

Nineteen-sixty-three would see the death of the U.S. Army Special Forces' greatest proponent, President John F. Kennedy. He had given them a

On 29 May 1965, the United States Army John F. Kennedy Center for Special Warfare was dedicated. The ceremony was held in front of the first completed building of the Center, John F. Kennedy Hall. John F. Kennedy Hall would be a hub of activity for Special Forces operations during the Vietnam War.

"Bronze Bruce" stands as a memorial to the Special Forces soldier. Depicted as a Sergeant First Class, he is armed with an M16 rifle signifying his readiness to do battle. Yet his other hand is open and outstretched, indicating his willingness to help and provide comfort.

mission, had given them the "green beret," and had set a course for the Special Forces soldier. On 29 May 1965, the date that would have been the president's 48th birthday, the United States Army John F. Kennedy Center for Special Warfare was dedicated. The ceremony was held in front of the first completed building of the Center, John F. Kennedy Hall.

The mission of the Special Warfare Center was to instruct selected U.S. military personnel, civilians, and eligible foreign offices; develop tactics and techniques for the Special Forces soldier in the field—e.g., infiltration methods, target analysis, operations and intelligence, communications, weapons, medical and engineering; prepare training documents in support of instructional programs and special unit training; coordinate with other armed forces and civilian agencies and support training activities of the U.S. Continental Army Command, USCONARC.

Special Warfare was defined at this time as the application of three associated activities as carried out by highly trained soldiers to achieve the nation's objective, whether in cold, limited, or general war. Those three areas were Counterinsurgency Operations, Unconventional Warfare, and Psychological Operations.

Counterinsurgency Operations would include any and all military, political, and economic actions taken to eliminate subversive insurgency. Subversive insurgency, e.g., wars of liberation, had received increased support by the communists as a primary course of action to extend communist control. Counterinsurgency Operations required the integration and coordination of all military and non-military resources to achieve the necessary results.

Unconventional Warfare encompassed guerrilla warfare, evasion and escape, and sabotage against hostile forces. UW operations would be conducted within enemy territory or enemy-controlled areas by establishing, training, and supporting the indigenous personnel in carrying out these missions.

Psychological Operations included PsyWar (psychological warfare) and covered the political, military, economic, and ideological actions necessary to create in enemy, neutral, or friendly forces the emotions, attitudes, or behaviors to support the national objectives.

Throughout the early 1960s soldiers of the Special Forces participated in more than six major exercises and more than 74 smaller FTXs (Field Training Exercises) ranging from Exercise Polar Strike in Alaska to Quick Kick VII conducted in the Caribbean. Soldiers from SF groups would be included in counter-guerrilla and counterinsurgency warfare training with assorted conventional units located in the continental United States.

Many Special Forces soldiers with distinct capabilities as teachers were assigned to Army Special Action Forces (SAF). These units would be tasked with civil affairs, engineer, intelligence, military police, and psychological operations units. Five such units were active: one for Asia, one for Latin America, one for Europe, and two for Africa and the Middle East. SAF instruction in medicine, sanitation, agricultural techniques, local government administrations, communications, and basic commerce was a direct deterrent to the spread of communism.

Simultaneous with these other activities, the Special Forces soldiers and groups constantly prepared for the UW task of infiltrating deep into enemy-controlled territory to contact, organize, train, equip, and advise the local partisans for guerrilla warfare against a common enemy.

During this time Special Forces soldiers were sent all over the globe in MTT. In 1965, for example, 25 MTT were deployed to 14 different countries. These countries included Argentina, Bolivia, Brazil, Ethiopia, Iran, Iraq, Jordan, Mali, Nepal, Nigeria, Pakistan, Peru, the Philippines, and the Republic of the Congo.

The missions of these teams varied by country, but would include aerial delivery methods, communications, engineering/demolition, language interpretation, medical instruction, and other tactical training. Lt. General William P. Yarborough called the Special Forces soldiers "the finest representatives that the United States Army has ever had." These MTT missions assisting friendly foreign countries expanded the role of the SF soldier from unconventional warfare and counterinsurgency to one of today's important SF functions, Foreign Internal Defense.

With the growing success of its teams and their missions, the Special Forces had soldiers who had seen action all over the world. Not all of the missions were benign in nature. While the public's and military's primary attention was directed to the area of Southeast Asia, SF teams were quite active in Latin America. Members of the 8th Special Forces Group (Airborne) operating out of Fort Guick, in the Panama Canal Zone, were involved in operations against communist-backed guerrillas in Latin America. Special Forces soldiers would be involved in the pursuit and capture of Ernesto "Che" Guevara, a known Cuban revolutionary in the mountainous terrain in the country of Bolivia in 1968.

Special Forces was originally created to provide an unconventional warfare force in the event of Soviet aggression in Europe. It would not be the massing of Soviet armor funneling through the Fulda Gap, however, that would give Special Forces the action they were trained to carry out. The small wars of liberation referred to by President Kennedy would be where the Special Forces would come of age. They were the watershed for soldiers of the green beret.

CHAPTER 3

Baptism by Fire: Vietnam

While many people believe America's involvement in Vietnam was initiated by President Kennedy, it was actually President Dwight D. Eisenhower who first committed U.S. troops to southeast Asia. The French debacle at Dien Bien Phu in 1954 left a void in the region, opening it to the spread of communism.

Special Forces soldiers were among the first U.S. advisers sent to the Republic of Vietnam. Here members of the 5th Special Forces Group (Airborne) are armed with M1 Garand rifles, carbines, and BARs (Browning Automatic Rifles) and wear an assortment of uniforms, from early issue jungle fatigues to the "duck hunter" camouflage. Note the SF Captain, (kneeling, left) is holding a newly issued AR-15 rifle, the predecessor to the M-16. *U.S. Army Photo*

At this time President Eisenhower promised direct aid to the government of South Vietnam. In 1957 the first U.S. Army Special Forces soldiers actually arrived in Vietnam. That summer members of the 1st SFG(A) would train members of the Vietnamese Army at the Commando Training Center located at Nha Trang. This began the official involvement of U.S. Army Special Forces in Vietnam, which would last for 14 years until their withdrawal in February 1971.

During the time period of 1959–1960, South Vietnamese insurgents referred to as Viet Cong (Vietnamese communists) were growing in numbers and in power. The VC, as they came to be called, would move through villages spreading terror, torture, and destruction among the people. Thirty Special Forces soldiers were sent to South Vietnam in May 1960 to set up a training program for the army of Vietnam. It was on 21 September 1961 that the new president, John F. Kennedy, made good his inaugural address, "we shall support any friend, oppose any foe." His deep concern over the communist insurgents in South Vietnam drew the president to the Special Forces and their capability. The 5th Special Forces Group, 1st Special Forces, were made responsible for conduct of all SF missions in Vietnam.

To the average American citizen, places such as Nam Dong, Plei Mei, Kontum, Lang Vei, Dak To, and Bu Brang were unknown locations on a map. To the men of the Special Forces they were home, fortresses where they took a stand for freedom. These names meant camps where SF soldiers labored to build a future for liberty, bunkers where they spilled their blood, and a handful of dirt where some gave the ultimate sacrifice for what they believed in: "De Oppresso Liber." (SF motto: To Free the Oppressed.)

In the early part of U.S. involvement in Vietnam, Special Forces soldiers carried out missions to train a guerrilla force. According to intelligence from the CIA, the SF teams were deployed to the central highlands of South Vietnam to begin training the Montagnards (a French term defined as "mountain people"). The Montagnards numbered more than 500,000 in South Vietnam and came from approximately 20 different tribes. The agency had recognized the Montagnards as a possible ally in the war against the communists.

Special Forces began a program with mountain people that would become known as CIDG, or Civilian Irregular Defense Group. The organization and training of this paramilitary group became the primary mission for Special Forces in Vietnam. From 1961 to 1965 more than eight CIDG camps were built in the isolated countryside of South Vietnam. Each of these outposts was self-contained and manned by a CIDG Strike Force, a complement of South Vietnamese Special Forces and a U.S. Special Forces A-team. The primary role of the A-detachments took a turn from their origins in 1952. Instead of training a guerrilla force to interdict conventional army troops, they were now training indigenous tribesmen to conduct actions against other guerrillas, the Viet Cong.

Over the course of the war more than 250 outposts of A-Camps would be established throughout South Vietnam. Scattered along the Laos and Cambodian boarders, these strategically located outposts of freedom would become a considerable thorn in the side of the Viet Cong and later the North Vietnamese Army.

One such camp was Nam Dong, commanded by SF Captain Roger H. Donlon. Located some 32 miles west of Da Nang, the camp was distinctly in enemy territory. Established 15 miles from the Laotian border, it was placed strategically to inter-

"Green Beret" Staff Sergeant Arthur Fletcher assisted two members of the Vietnamese Special Forces in the repair of a 30-caliber machine gun. *U.S. Army Photo*

dict and harass the VC coming down the Ho Chi Minh from the North. Nam Dong was not like any other A-Camp design the SF soldiers had seen at Ft. Bragg—e.g., Plei Mei was triangular, Dak To circular, Lang Vei a diamond, and so on. This plot of real estate measured approximately 80 yards by 120 yards, looking more like a West Virginia ham than a formidable fortress. Beyond the camp perimeter was another area 350 yards long and 250 yards wide. Here is where the Vietnamese strike force lived, in about a dozen hootches. In addition to the "strikers," there was a contingent of 60 Nungs. (The Nungs were ethnic Chinese mercenaries who fought bravely, and were dedicated to the Special Forces soldiers they fought alongside.) Just beyond the outer fence line there lay a jungle airstrip, courtesy of the U.S. Navy Seabees.

Approximately 5,000 Katu tribesmen live in the area of the Nam Dong Valley. The SF Camp would provide them with medical attention and protection, and hopefully be a source of aggravation for the VC. The team medical specialists, Sgt. Thomas L. Gregg and Sgt. Terrance D. Terrin, would become the "popular" members of the team with the locals, as oftentime happened among the camps.

Nam Dong would be home for the Special Forces soldiers of A-726 (A-team-7th SFG(A)Team #26). What team A-726 did not know was that this civic action mission would turn into a life-or-death battle before they would leave.

At 0226 Monday 6 July 1964, the VC began their attack of Camp Nam Dong. Mortar rounds, grenades, and small arms fire erupted from every direction. The Special Forces soldiers were surrounded. SSG Keith Daniels, shaken out of bed by the first explosion, was now on the camp's radio. He made contact with Da Nang and requested a flare ship and air strike. Hearing explosions coming closer to his position, he knew the communications shed was next. He grabbed his AR-15 and hit the door. Just as he left, the building exploded behind him.

By now the Nungs and South Vietnamese had moved to their fighting positions, and the SF were manning the mortar pits. A typical mortar pit was approximately eight feet around, with sandbags stacked around the edge to provide some protection from small arms fire and flying fragments. Located at the rear of the pit was a cement bunker housing 300 rounds of assorted ammunition for the tube—high explosive (HE) and white phosphorous, either 60mm or 81mm, accordingly.

President Kennedy had referred to the green beret as a "symbol of excellence, a badge of courage, a mark of distinction in the fight for freedom." The men of team A-726 put their training and experience to work that morning. From bunkers, mortar pits, or behind debris piles, the Special Forces soldiers were returning fire

The Son Tay Raid

By the spring of 1970, more than 350 U.S. pilots had been captured and held in prison camps in North Vietnam. These pilots and aircrews were exposed to appalling living conditions and subjected to frequent beatings and torture. The majority of American captives in the North were not even allowed contact with other prisoners or the outside world.

In May of 1970, reconnaissance photographs revealed the existence of two prison camps west of Hanoi. At Son Tay, one of the recce photos showed a large letter "K" drawn in the dirt. This was a code for "come get us."

Brigadier General Donald D. Blackburn, who had trained Filipino guerrillas during World War II, recommended that a small hand-picked group of Special Forces volunteers be assembled to mount a rescue operation to liberate these prisoners. For this operation, he choose Lt. Colonel Arthur D. "Bull" Simons to lead the force.

Since the prison compound was located more than 20 miles west of Hanoi, operation planners believed Son Tay was isolated enough to enable a small group to land, rescue the prisoners, and withdraw. A full-scale replica of the prison compound was constructed at Eglin Air Force Base, Florida. Here a select group of Special Forces soldiers trained at night for the mission. The mock compound was dismantled during the day to avoid detection by Soviet satellites. A model of the camp was built that would allow the raiders to view the camp under various light to duplicate moonlight, flares, night vision, and so on. The replica was named "Barbara." To be successful, the troops needed to be prepared, yet time was running out. Evidence, although inconclusive, showed that Son Tay may have been empty.

On 18 November 1970 Col. Simons moved his raiders to Takhli, Thailand, to begin staging for the mission. Only Col. Simons and three others knew what the final mission would be. Five hours before takeoff, 20 November, Col. Simons informed his force of 59 men, "We are going to rescue 70 American prisoners of war, maybe more, from a camp called Son Tay. This is something American prisoners have a right to expect from their fellow soldiers. The target is 23 miles west of Hanoi." As Col. Simons left the room the solders broke into applause.

Approximately 0215, Hanoi time, on 21 November 1970, the raid began. An Air Force C-130 flare ship illuminated the area with flares, and the HH-53 began firing on the guard towers with its twin Gatling guns. The U.S. Navy also provided diversionary fire. The raiders now had less than 30 minutes to land and complete their mission before they would have to face North Vietnamese reinforcements. The only problem was, the helicopter mistakenly set down at another site. Instead of being just outside the prison compound, the support group was some 400 meters away at what was referred to as a 'secondary school' on the maps. This building was a barracks that housed Chinese and Soviet advisers and a large number of NVA troops. The raiders took this force under fire and eliminated them from reinforcing the prison.

After this brief encounter, Col. Simons and the support group re-loaded his HH-53 and moved to the prison compound. Nine minutes into the raid, Col. Simons was outside the prison wall. There, he and the support element augmented the assault and security elements and eliminated approximately 60 guards. However, as they searched from building to building the hard facts begin to sink in, there were no American prisoners. There were no prisoners whatsoever. The Son Tay raid ended after 27 minutes and the raiders were once again airborne. The force had not lost a single man, and al-

The Son Tay Raid Patch

though there were no prisoners to rescue, the planning and execution itself were flawless. To this day the Son Tay raid is often referred to as a "textbook" mission.

"Outpost of Freedom." This aerial photo shows a good overview of an SF camp. Scattered throughout South Vietnam, these fighting camps would serve as bases of operations against the Viet Cong and later the North Vietnamese Army troops. Numerous layouts and plans were tried; this plan, referred to as a star pattern, was one of the later designs. Each tip of the star is a fighting bunker, and as you move in toward the core of the camp you can see additional motor pits or machine gun emplacements. This also is where the "Green Berets" would set up their Tactical Operations Center. *JFK Special Warfare Museum*

toward the rushing horde of VC guerrillas. As the courageous troops fought to defend their camp, the VC kept coming. Two reinforced VC battalions, more than 800 guerrillas, had managed to encircle the camp. They had already penetrated the outer perimeter and were now bearing down on team A-726.

After five hours of intense fighting, the defenders of the camp successfully thwarted the VC attack. Camp Nam Dong had survived, but not without a cost: 55 of the camp's defenders had been killed. Among them, MSgt. Gabriel R. Alamo and Sgt. John Houston, members of A-726, and

an Australian Warrant Officer, Kevin Conway. The body count showed that more than 200 VC had died in the failed attack.

On 5 December 1964, President Lyndon B. Johnson awarded the Medal of Honor to Captain Roger Donlon, who had particularly distinguished himself. The text of the citation explains that "Captain Roger C. Donlon, 7th Special Forces Group (Airborne), 1st Special Forces, distinguished himself on 6 July 1964, while commanding Special Forces Detachment A-726 at Nam Dong, republic of Vietnam. On 6 July, the camp was assaulted in a pre-dawn attack by a reinforced Viet

Cong battalion. During the violent five-hour battle, resulting in numerous causalities on both sides, Captain Donlon directed the overall defense of the camp. He swiftly marshaled his forces and ordered the removal of needed ammunition from a blazing building hit by the initial assault. He then dashed through a hail of small arms and exploding hand grenade fire to a breach of the main gate where he detected and annihilated an enemy three-man demolition team. Exposed to an intense attack and sustaining a severe stomach wound, he succeeded in reaching the 60mm mortar pit. Discovering most of the men in the gun pit were wounded, Captain Donlon disregarding his own injury, risked his own life by remaining in the pit and returning the enemy fire, allowing

Captain Roger H. Donlon returns to the Special Forces camp at Nam Dong, where he was the Officer in Charge when the camp was attacked by the Viet Cong on 6 July 1964 by a force estimated to be of battalion size. He inspects what is left of the mess hall. Captain Donlon was the first soldier to be awarded the Medal of Honor during the Vietnam War. By the end of the conflict, Special Forces soldiers would bring home 17 Medals of Honor, our nation's highest award for gallantry above and beyond the call of duty. *National Archive*

the men to withdraw. While dragging his team sergeant out of the gun pit, an enemy mortar round exploded, hitting Captain Donlon's left shoulder. Suffering from multiple wounds, he carried the 60mm mortar to a new location 30 meters away where he found another three wounded defenders. After administering first aid and encouragement to these men, he left the weapon with them and then raced toward another location, retrieving a 57mm recoilless rifle. With great courage under fire, he returned to the abandoned gun pit, evacuated ammunition for the weapons and crawling and dragging back the urgently needed ammunition, received a third wound on his leg. Despite his critical condition, he crawled 175 meters to an 81mm mortar position and began directing firing operations, which protected the east sector of the camp. Until daylight brought defeat of the enemy forces, Captain Donlon moved from position to position around the beleaguered perimeter, hurling grenades at the enemy and inspiring his men to superhuman effort. Captain Donlon's conspicuous gallantry, extraordinary heroism and intrepidity at the risk

Special Forces with I Field Force Vietnam, Ban Me Thout. Assisted by U.S. Special Forces and indigenous personnel, the people of Buen Tor 1, some 10 miles south of Ban Me Thuot, evacuated their former homes. *U.S. Army Photo*

of his life above and beyond the call are in the highest tradition of the military service, reflecting the utmost credit upon himself, the Special Forces and the United States Army."

At the award ceremony, Captain Donlon said the award belonged to the entire team—to the valiant men of Special Forces Detachment A-726.

This was the first Medal of Honor to be awarded in the Vietnam war, but it would not be the last earned by the Special Forces. Sixteen of the nation's highest award, the MOH, would go to Special Forces soldiers: SFC Eugene Ashley, Jr.*, Detachment A-101, 5th SFG(A)—Lang Vei; Sgt. Gary B. Beikirch, Detachment B-24, 5th SFG(A)—Dak Seang; SSgt. Ray P. Benavidez, Detachment B-56, 5th SFG(A)—Loc Ninh; SFC William M. Bryant*, 5th SFG(A)—Long Khanh Province; Sgt. Brian L. Buker*, Detachment B-55, 5th SFG(A)—Chau Doc Province; SSgt. Jon R. Cavaiani—U.S. Army Vietnam Advisory Group; SSgt. Drew D. Dix—Chau Doc Province; 1st Lt. Loren D. Hagen*—U.S. Army Vietnam Advisory Group; SSgt. Charles E. Hosking, Jr.*, Detachment A-302, 5th SFG(A) Phuoc Long Province; SFC Robert L. Howard, 5th SFG(A); Specialist Fifth Class John J. Kedenburg*, Command and Control Detachment North, 5th SFG(A); SSgt. Franklin D. Miller, 5th SFG(A); 1st Lt. George K. Sissler*, 5th SFG(A); 1st Lt. Charles Q. Williams, 5th SFG(A)—Dong Xoai; Sgt. Gordon D. Yntema*, Detachment A-431, 5th SFG(A)—Cai Cai; SSgt. Fred W. Zabitosky, SOG.

The battle for Nam Dong was not an anomaly. In fact the Special Forces Camps were such a barb in the side of the VC that the communists would sacrifice thousands of their troops to try to dislodge a team or overrun a camp. Occasionally they did succeed, but only after the SF team extracted a heavy toll. If you go to a map of South Vietnam and pick a camp, there will be story for each one—Plei Mei in 1965, a battle so intense it would mark a major turn in U.S. involvement to the ground war in Vietnam; Lang Vei in 1968, where the communists had to employ Soviet-supplied PT-76 tanks in order to overrun the camp; Ben Het, where the NVA laid siege to the isolated post for two months, never taking it over; Dak To, Dak Pek, Dak Seang, Bu Brang, the list goes on. Strange names on a tactical map, hundreds of camps, and a thousand acts of heroism by Special Forces soldiers.

In addition to the tenacity of the SF teams located in these camps demonstrated, they had the versatility to employ various methods of turning the tide in their favor should the proverbial "hit the fan." The U.S. Air Force, Air Commandos flew AC-47 Gunships, "Spooky" and "Puff the Magic Dragon," that were often on call. TAC air, whether A-1E "Spads" or the fast movers, F-4 Phantoms, could be overhead in minutes. There were even times when B-52 bombers would rain down terror to break the assault on a camp in trouble. While all these sources provided outstanding assistance, the Special Forces also had an ace up their sleeves. Organic to the Special Forces, it was a group the camps called in when they were in danger of being overrun: the MIKE Force.

The MIKE Forces were Mobile Strike Forces. Each force consisted of three companies of soldiers, giving them a strength of 600 men. These units comprised elite CIDGs that would act as quick reaction forces to support the SF camps. Because of their loyalty and aggressiveness, Nungs were often well represented in the MIKE Forces. Highly trained in airborne and helicopter operations, the MIKE Forces could be called in to reinforce a camp and turn the tide in favor of the Special Forces soldiers on the ground.

Unlike other assets in theater, the MIKE Force was under direct control of the U.S. Special Forces and commanded by SF soldiers. Under the control of the "C" detachment commander, by 1968 there were five Mobile Strike Force Commands in Vietnam, numbering approximately 2,000 men per command. These forces were highly responsive and

*(* awarded posthumously)*

could be placed into action at a moment's notice. For this reason, members of the MIKE Force seldom had the luxury of sitting around garrison. They would return from an engagement often with only enough time to resupply and load up on the helicopters for the next run. The soldiers of the MIKE Force were the "cavalry" in Huey's, and many a besieged SF camp owes its survival to this group of courageous soldiers, both American and indigenous. By the end of 1966 the 5th Special Forces Group (Airborne) had an operational strength of 2,400 men, with strike forces numbering 33,400 indigenous troops and supported by 2,400 MIKE Force soldiers.

Special Forces soldiers leading indigenous troops were also employed at this time by the Central Intelligence Agency (CIA) to conduct reconnaissance operations. Reconnaissance teams, or RTs, usually consisted of two SF soldiers and four indigenous personnel. These early CIA-sponsored operations were referred to as PROJECT DELTA and filled Military Assistance Command Vietnam (MACV) intelligence requirements across the entire country. The capability of these small teams proved so valuable that subsequent recce missions were formed in the operations known as Projects, GAMMA, SIGMA, and OMEGA.

These small teams were extremely vulnerable to the larger communist forces they were sent to study. Helicopters were regularly called in to extract an RT from a "hot" (enemy engaged) landing zone (LZ). For the times when the helicopters could not land, the RT could be extracted with the use of the McGuire rig, named after Special Forces Sergeant Major Charles McGuire, who invented it. The McGuire rig was a simple rope 100 feet long with a canvas sling attached; it would be lowered to the ground from a hovering helicopter. The team member on the ground could quickly place himself in the sling and hold on, to be snatched from grasp of the enemy as the helicopter pulled him out. Four of these rigs could be fitted on a helicopter at one time.

In addition to providing special reconnaissance, 5th SFG(A) established the MACV Renaissance/Commando School in September 1966, located in Nha Trang, South Vietnam. Known as the "Recondo" School, this three-week course trained the indigenous forces in helicopter insertions techniques, survival, evasion and escape (E&E), communications, weapons (U.S. and enemy), intelligence gathering methods, and other subjects pertaining to Special Forces operations. Non-airborne soldiers would also receive parachute training. Members of U.S. Long Range Reconnaissance Patrols (LRRPs) and recon troop from Vietnam, Korea, and other allied countries also attended the Recondo School.

Because of the many successes of the CIDG program, in addition to the U.S. buildup of conventional troops in Vietnam during 1965–1966, the Special Forces–led CIDG units shifted to more offensive operations. In late 1966, Colonel Francis "Blackjack" Kelly, then commander of 5th SFG(A), presented the plan for the formation of the Mobile Guerrilla Force (MGF). Col. Kelly envisioned a company-size force that would operate in the same method as Merrill's Marauders operated in Burma during World War II.

The MGF was to be a small, self-contained unit; there would be no artillery support or reinforcements flown in to fill in for casualties. The only support that would be provided would come from a lone Forward Air Control aircraft. Resupply of the MGF would be done not by transport or helicopter but by fighter planes. In order not to compromise the troop's location, A-1E Skyraiders flown by the U.S. Air Commandos would drop napalm canisters, fitted with parachutes, filled with up 400 pounds of food, ammunition, and other supplies. The purpose of the MGF would be to drop in the middle of a known enemy's area of operation and create havoc. Col. Kelly was putting the VC on notice—SF was in town and they were going hunting! Hunting was good. The MGF

A captain from the 6th Special Forces Group (Airborne) goes over a mission plan with his A-team. Planning, rehearsing, and evaluating the mission are all part of the Special Forces operations. Every possible contingency they can think of is discussed and alternate measures developed. Very few things happen that have not been discussed in mission planning. Special Forces are successful because they "sweat the small stuff"! *U.S. Army Photo*

would be engaged in more than 50 battles, called in on countless air strikes against the enemy and involved in assaults on numerous company- and battalion-strength base camps. Mobile Guerrilla Force - Detachment A-303 was also responsible for recovering a highly sensitive "black box" from a U-2 aircraft operating with the SAC, Strategic Reconnaissance Wing, that had crashed.

The MIKE Force and MGF missions were highly successful. These units were large, however, and there was a need for a smaller, more covert unit. In February 1964 the commander of the MACV, General Paul D. Harkins, authorized the creation of

SOG. Officially the name stood for Studies and Observation Group; unofficially, and more exactly, it stood for Special Operations Group. While SOG did engage members of the other services, e.g., Navy SEALs, Air Commandos, and even USMC Force Recon, the majority of personnel came from the 5th Special Forces Group (Airborne).

The purpose of SOG was to conduct covert missions on "the other side of the fence." This meant the insertion of teams into North Vietnam, Laos (codename: Prairie Fire), and Cambodia (codename: Daniel Boone). SOG missions could include guerrilla warfare, direct action, sabotage, psychological operations, E&E nets, and other operations that are still classified. SOG was broken down into three operational areas: Command and Control North (CCN) with forward operating bases (FOB) located in the area of Hue and operating in North Vietnam and Laos; Command and Control Central (CCC), FOB in Kontum, operating in Laos and northeastern Cambodia; and Command and Control South (CCS), FOB located in Ban Me Thout and Quan Loi, operating in Cambodia.

A former SOG member reports that SOG teams would load M-16 cartridges with "pet," a high explosive. "We would wait until we got into a fire-fight with a [NVA] unit. We would begin our withdrawal and as we left, we'd drop magazines with these doctored rounds. They would be in for quite a surprise when they used them in their captured weapons." The "pet" round would blow up when the enemy tried to fire the weapon. A similar method was used in mortar rounds. A SOG team would infiltrate an enemy base camp and locate its ammunition supply. Instead of rigging it with explosives, the SOG members would plant these "special rounds" in the ammo boxes, and exfiltrate. Again, when the enemy would drop a round into the tube, it would explode. This had a marked psychological effect on the enemy concerning the quality of the ammunition they were receiving.

Although SOG forces regularly overcame overwhelming odds, not every mission dreamed up for them was realistic. One SOG veteran relates that as he was getting ready to go on R&R, he was called into the commander's office. There were rumors floating around that the Soviets had introduced tanks into the south and SOG wanted confirmation of this information. He had been chosen, since he had a background in armor and knew how to drive a tank. His mission was to be inserted "across the fence," locate one such tank, affix a white flag to its antenna and drive it back to friendly lines in the south. His eyes widened at the prospect of such a mission. He was also told that the tank was at a base camp deep inside enemy territory and had a regiment protecting it. This veteran continues, "Even some missions were just too wild for SOG. I said, thanks, then grabbed my bag and headed for R&R." (MACV/SOG would get its verification of the tanks some months later when 11 PT-76 tanks overran Lang Vie Special Forces camp.)

SOG teams took extremely high casualties. Often teams would have to run for their lives moving from one LZ to another hoping the Hueys could get them out in time. It was during the SOG missions that the STABO rig was developed. The name STABO was derived by the three SF soldiers from the Recondo School that developed the device: Major Robert Stevens, Captain John Knabb, and Sergeant First Class Clifford Roberts. For this device the soldier wore a specially designed web harness in place of his normal web gear. When the need for extraction came, the soldier would undo two straps from the back of the harness, secure them around his legs, then attach himself to the STABO yoke via carabiners at each shoulder. This harness differed from the McGuire rig in that it provided a more secure connection and allowed the user to keep his hands free to operate weapons as he flew through the air and out of harm's way.

Another method for extracting special operations personnel from the ground was the Fulton Surface-To-Air Recovery (STAR) system, known as "Skyhook." The STAR device consists of two containers that can be air-dropped to special forces units operating in a covert operation. Upon opening the canisters the soldiers on the ground would find a balloon, two helium inflation bottles, and an insulated flight suit and harness. When inflated, the balloon measured eight feet in diameter by 23 feet in length. Attached to the balloon would be a 500-foot nylon line equipped with marker flags for daylight extractions and strobe lights for nighttime operations. The individual to be extracted puts on the insulated flight suit and harness, hooks himself to the balloon's lines, and then sits facing the oncoming plane as the balloon is released and heads skyward.

A specially equipped MC-130 Combat Talon from the 90th Special Operations Squadron was also part of the Skyhook system. As the aircraft approached the recovery area, the yoke arms or "whiskers" were extended. These arms snagged the line in a locking device. The balloon would break away and the line would be fed into an attached hydraulic power winch in the rear of the

MACV-SOG (Military Assistance Command Vietnam–Studies and Observation Group) ran three AOs, or areas of operations. Command and Control North (CCN) operated in North Vietnam and Laos, Command and Control Central (CCC) operated in Laos and northeastern Cambodia, and Command and Control South (CCS) operated in Cambodia.

aircraft. The individual was then reeled into the ramp door. Along with personnel, the STAR system could also recover up to 500 pounds of equipment or material, if needed.

The soldiers of SOG were tasked with some of the most dangerous missions of the war. Reconnaissance teams became known as Spike Teams. Hatchet Teams, similar to a MIKE Force, would be ready to swoop in on any target the Spike Team exposed. The acronym for their missions said it all: SLAM—Search, Locate, Annihilate Mission. What more can you add? These were the types of missions assigned to SOG. Of the Medals of Honor given to SF soldiers in Vietnam, two went to SOG members.

Whatever the results of the Vietnam War, the men of the U.S. Army Special Forces emerged from the conflict with a permanent place in the history of the U.S. Army. They were highly adaptable in their fighting techniques. Introduced in the unconventional warfare role, they adjusted remarkably well to counter-insurgency, as well as dealing with conventional warfare and civilian irregulars. Whether building and defending an isolated CIDG camp, serving with larger MGFs, or operating on a small SOG team, Special Forces soldiers were highly motivated and determined to accomplish their missions at all costs.

When the Special Forces departed Vietnam, they accounted for 17 Medals of Honor, one Distinguished Service Medal, 60 Distinguished Service Crosses, 814 Silver Stars, 13,234 Bronze Stars, 235 Legions of Merit, 46 Distinguished Flying Crosses, 232 Soldier's Medals, 4,891 Air Medals, 6,908 Army Commendation Medals, and 2,658 Purple Hearts.

Mission after mission these warriors demonstrated their courage and tenacity to tackle the impossible and come out victorious. The men of the U.S. Army Special Forces, known to many as the "Green Berets," did their duty and departed from Southeast Asia with honor.

Special Forces Beyond Vietnam

This modified version of the HUMMV for desert operations during Desert Shield/Storm was dubbed the DUMMV. Currently it's referred to as a Ground Mobility Vehicle (GMV). The ultimate 4x4 vehicle, it allowed SF soldiers to execute their mission at long range, or serve as a Mission Support Site (MSS), from which ODAs operate in their AO. This particular GMV is armed with a Mark 19, 40mm Grenade Machine gun, and is loaded with fuel cans, water, ammunition, and other mission-essential equipment. Attached to the rear of the vehicle is camouflage netting that may be deployed by the team to conceal its MSS.

In the years following the Vietnam war the Special Forces saw a dramatic downsizing. The 1st, 3rd, 6th, and 8th Special Forces Groups were deactivated or consolidated into other groups. Conventional commanders were trying to distance themselves from the war in Southeast Asia and cast their attention anew on the verdant valleys of "cold-war" Europe. Beset by conventional commanders, Special Forces soldiers fought the Army mindset for mere survival. The Special Forces soldier had become an anachronism, and many people considered becoming a member to be a dead-end career path. During the early 1970s, the Army was placing more emphasis on the Rangers, and some of the SF missions were being incorporated into the two newly formed Ranger battalions. In January 1969 the JFK Institute for Special Warfare was renamed the U.S. Army JFK Institute for Military Assistance. (IMA)

In an attempt to maintain their capabilities, Special Forces commanders formulated the SPARTAN program. SPARTAN stood for Special Proficiency at Rugged Training and Nation Building. This program was created to demonstrate the many skills of the Special Forces soldier. It also proved that SF troops were not outdated merely because the United States was no longer engaged in active warfare.

The SPARTAN program sent soldiers from the 5th SFG(A) and 7th SFG(A) to various states throughout the United States, such as Florida, Arizona, and Montana, to work on American Indian reservations. Here the SF soldiers applied their talents on American soil, building roads, schools, medical facilities. They provided medical treatment to the poverty-stricken areas of Hoke and Anson counties in North Carolina. To this day, you can still find SF soldiers working among the American Indian population. Major Tom McCollum, SF-PAO, said, "going to these locations, our soldiers get the feel for real Third World conditions." As honorable as this program was, civic actions were not the primary purpose Special Forces had been intended to serve. Special Forces was created for unconventional warfare, and with the lessons learned in the Vietnam War, Special Forces missions would be broadened beyond Unconventional Warfare (UW) to include direct action in a guerrilla war. They would not have to wait too long for the opportunity to serve this role.

In November 1979 the U.S. Embassy in Teheran, Iran, was captured and its staff taken hostage. While alternate venues were discussed, President Jimmy Carter, after six months, authorized the military option, and Operation Eagle Claw commenced.

What began as an extraordinary attempt by the U.S. Special Operations Forces ended in tragedy in the darkness of an Iranian desert. It was April 1980 when Special Forces Operation Detachment - Delta, better known as "Delta Force," along with supporting Air Force and Marine aircraft and aircrews, met with disaster. Operation Eagle Claw had failed. It resulted in the loss of eight courageous troops and damaged the honor of the United States of America and the credibility of U.S. Special Operations.

Following the disaster at Desert One, a review committee known as the Holloway Commission convened to look into problems within U.S. Special Operations. At the conclusion of its review, the Commission made two major recommendations. First, the Department of Defense should establish a Counterterrorism Joint Task Force (CTJTF) as a field organization of the Joint Chiefs of Staff (JCS) with a permanently assigned staff and forces. The JCS would plan, train for, and conduct

Two members of Company C, 2nd Battalion, 7th SFG(A). Staff Sergeant John Anchex and Sergeant Rodney Allen (left to right) rappel down an icy mountain during Exercise Brim Frost, 1981. Rappelling skills are still used today when necessary to maneuver down a mountain slope, or down the side of a building as in SFAUC. *Defense Visual Information Center Photo*

operations to counter terrorist activities directed against the United States. The CTJTF would employ military forces in the counterterrorism (CT) role. These forces could range in size from small units of highly specialized personnel to larger integrated forces. Second, the JCS should consider the formation of a Special Operations Advisory Panel (SOAP). This panel would consist of high-ranking officers to be drawn from both active service and retired personnel. To be selected a soldier needed a background in special operations or service at a CinC or JCS level with proficient knowledge of special operations or defense policy.

With the election of President Ronald W. Reagan in 1980, the U.S. military would get a much-needed revitalization. The defense policy of the new administration, along with the emergence of anti-Leninist guerrillas in Nicaragua, Angola, Mozambique, and Afghanistan, compelled the United States to take a more dynamic role in combating communism. These situations also heightened the awareness of deficiencies in U.S. Special Operation Forces. A new focus came into being: Low Intensity Conflict, and the Army Special Forces in particular would benefit from this new attention.

On 1 June 1982, the Center for Military Assistance was redesignated the 1st Special Operations Command (Airborne) (SOCOM), and assigned to U.S. Army Forces Command (FORSCOM). FORSCOM was responsible for all activities of Special Operations Forces units. In June 1983 the IMA

During Exercise Team Spirit 1986 a member of the 1st Special Forces Groups (Airborne) assumes a prone firing position to provide security for his team as they secure the perimeter of the Pohang DZ (drop zone). Using his rucksack for cover, he aims his M-16 and watches for any OpFor (Opposition Force) soldiers. *Defense Visual Information Center Photo*

Kuwaiti soldiers from the 2nd Infantry Battalion, 15th Brigade, fire M-16 rifles on the firing line while being supervised by a U.S. Army Special Forces Sergeant First Class. Special Forces troops conducted live fire training with the Kuwaitis and instructed them on the use and care of M-16s and assorted small arms. They were part of the coalition forces who fought in Desert Storm. The working relationship and cultural experience the SF soldiers possess made the members of the SF ODAs (Operational Detachments-Alpha) "the glue that held the coalition together," per General Norman Schwarzkopf. *Defense Visual Information Center Photo*

was again named the U.S. Army John F. Kennedy Special Warfare Center. The qualification course for Special Forces was lengthened and toughened, so only the highest quality soldiers would make it to the SF A-teams. The A-teams were also slightly modified, with the executive officer changed from a lieutenant to a warrant officer. The A-teams remained the backbone of Special Forces. In October 1984 the Army established a separate career management field (CMF 18) for Special Forces soldiers. The warrant officer career

management field (CMF 180) was introduced shortly thereafter on 9 April 1987.

In October 1983 the United States mounted Operation Urgent Fury to rescue American medical students and suppress pro-communist insurgents on the island of Grenada. All the services, consisting fully of volunteer forces, wanted to show what they could do. Within two days of landing on the island on 15 October 1983, the island was secure. U.S. forces were victorious, but

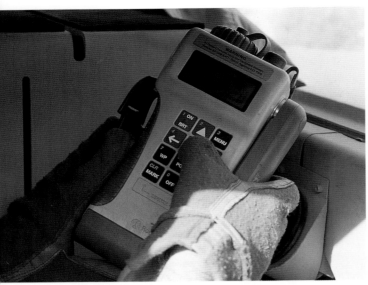

Using the Global Positioning System (GPS) unit, SF teams were able to determine their positions accurately as they performed SR, DA, and other missions across the wasteland of the Iraqi desert during the Gulf War.

it appeared special operations units still needed better coordination.

In 1984 the 1st Special Forces Group (Airborne) was reactivated at Fort Lewis, Washington. On 9 April 1987 the chief of staff of the Army established the Special Forces as a separate office career branch of the service. Special Forces officers would now wear the Crossed Arrow insignia on their uniform collars and Jungle Green was designated as the Special Forces Branch color.

As the Reagan policy unfolded, Special Forces detachments were deployed to numerous countries around the world. Their main mission was Foreign Internal Defense (FID). Other missions included training allied armed forces to defend their countries, humanitarian assistance, medical care, and construction of roads and buildings in various Third World countries. Special Forces played a pivotal role in El Salvador and Honduras, preventing a civil war in Nicaragua from spilling over the borders.

In May 1986, Congressmen William Cohen and Sam Nunn introduced a Senate bill to amend the 1986 Defense Authorizations Bill. The following month, Congressman Dan Daniel introduced a similar bill in the House of Representatives. This bill, signed into law in October 1986, in part directed the formation of a unified command responsible for special operations. In April 1987, the U.S. Special Operations Command (USSOCOM) was established at MacDill AFB, Florida, and Army General James J. Lindsay assumed command.

In June 1988 the SF training program was increased from approximately 21 weeks to a full six months. This increase included a three-week Special Forces Assessment and Selection. SFAS also changed assignment from a PCS (permanent change of station) to TDY (temporary duty); this created a more fluid flow of soldiers who volunteered for Special Forces. This new assessment tested the candidates both psychologically and physically. Consequently, any unsuitable candidate could be removed from the program before ever entering the SF training. Field time was lengthened from 63 to 100 days.

Another milestone for Special Forces came on 1 December 1989, when the U.S. Army Special Operations Command (Airborne) was created under USSOCOM. USASOC, commanded by a three-star general, would be responsible for all Army Special Operations Forces. This would include the Rangers, the 160th Special Operations Aviation Regiment and, of course, the Special Forces.

This new command would have its effectiveness battle-tested when President George Bush ordered the execution of Operation Just Cause in Panama in December 1989. Special Forces would play a proactive part in the invasion, which lasted less than 24 hours.

Members of the 7th SFG(A), Company A, 3rd Battalion under the command of Major Kevin Higgins, secured and held the Pacora River Bridge, a vital crossing point. Special Forces soldiers, along with conventional troops, blocked a Panamanian Defense Forces (PDF) vehicle convoy from bringing reinforcements across the bridge. As they held the convoy, using LAW and AT-4 anti-tank weapons, an AC-130H Spectre gunship orbiting overhead employed precision fire, halting any further PDF movement.

In another part of the country, members of the 7th SFG(A) were tasked with the surgical mission of disabling a television repeater facility at Cero Azul. As Operation Just Cause began on 19 December 1989, two MH-60 helicopters lifted off for their target. Aboard these two aircraft was an 18-man element of Special Forces soldiers, augmented with members of the 1109th Signal Battalion.

Once on site, they fast-roped to the ground and, using explosives, neutralized the target. While the signalmen went to work on the electronics equipment, the SF soldiers swept the building, making sure it was secure, and conducted patrols in the local area. With the mission complete without taking any enemy fire, they extracted by MH-60 Blackhawks.

A year later, U.S. Army Special Forces Command (USASFC), which assumed command of all SF units, was established as a Major Subordinate Command, or MSC. A second MSC, USACAPOC (U.S. Army Civil Affairs and Psychological Operations Command), would be included under USASOC. USACAPOC included all PsyWar and civil affairs units. In June 1990 USASOC also took over command of the JFK Institute and School from TRADOC (Training and Doctrine Command). All of the capabilities and components of the Army Special Operations Forces were now under U.S. Army Special Operations Command (Airborne), or USASOC.

In the beginning of 1991, USASOC and the Special Forces would be called to war again in the vast desert wasteland of Southwest Asia. Operation Desert Shield was launched after Iraq invaded the neighboring country of Kuwait. National Command Authority (NCA) immediately deployed members of the 3rd, 5th, and 10th Special Forces Groups (Airborne), along with Civil Affairs and Psychological Operations units, to the Persian Gulf region. Special Operations Command Central, or SOCCENT, was responsible for the area abutting the Iraqi border, some 60,000 square miles of desert. Unlike their Panamanian mission, when U.S. Special Operations Forces went to war this time, they operated with a new set of parameters: Is this an appropriate SOF mission? Does it support the CinC's campaign plan? Is it operationally feasible? Are the required resources available to execute? Does the expected outcome justify the risk?

The primary mission of the Special Forces soldiers as Operation Desert Shield began was to work with their FID skills in the formation of a defensive posture among the newly formed Coalition Forces. The 5th Special Forces Group's mission of Coalition Assistance came to the forefront at this time. Due to its constant deployment into the theater and working relationship with the local military, the 5th SFG(A) was familiar with the areas, languages, and cultures of these soldiers. They also knew the abilities of these forces and how they operated in this region. This mission also included members of 10th Special Forces Group, who interacted with coalition members from Europe, e.g., British, French, Czech, and so on. Because of the SF soldiers' expertise, they worked with almost every level of Coalition Forces, 109 battalions in total. They were instrumental in establishing working relations with the Saudi, Egyptian, and Syrian military.

Under camouflage netting, the GMVs are well hidden in the MSS. Captain Steve Warman of ODA581 receives a communication over the SatCom radio. While the team leader sends in a situation report, or SitRep, Commo Sergeant Christopher Spence provides security, keeping a watchful eye on the terrain.

During Operation Desert Storm, Special Forces ODAs (Operational Detachments-Alpha) would conduct deep reconnaissance in Saudi Arabia, Iraq, and Kuwait. These recon missions not only provided up-to-the-minute intel on the Iraqi forces, but included analyzing soil conditions to ascertain whether it would support the heavy weight of armored vehicles. In addition to the special reconnaissance (SR) mission, the ODAs would perform direct action (DA) missions, e.g., sabotaging lines of communication, raids, ambushes, and destroying command and control targets. They also assisted in Combat Search

and Rescue (CSAR) missions and supported the Kuwaiti resistance.

As the air war began, SF teams were tasked with behind-the-lines intelligence-gathering missions. One such SR mission was carried out by ODA-525 of the 5th SFG(A), under the command of CWO2 John "Bulldog" Balwanz. Chief Balwanz relates that 5th SFG-Desert Shield basically started with coalition work, beginning with border recon on Saudi and Kuwaiti borders. The group was using DUMMVs—HUMMVs modified for desert operations. They were on the border between Saudi and Kuwait; they were the eyes of the command. ODA-525 was located at the King Fahad airport, along with the 1st Battalion of the 5th SFGF and SOCCENT. This underground command center was known as the "Bat Cave."

Balwanz had his team running training missions—cross country movement, long range movements, including areas in the Northwest portion of Saudi, near the Jordan border. They also began rehearsing such things as building hide sites. There was no SOP for desert hide sites, so in the tradition of good SF soldiers the team scrounged and scavenged material. King Fahad airport was under construction at this time, so procurement was not a problem. Soon the SF troopers had assorted lengths of metal conduit on hand to fabricate their hide site. The basic hide site consisted of a hole, approximately nine feet square and five feet deep dug into the desert. Up from the hole came the center stand, which was an umbrella-like device with arms that stretched over the hole. The whole assembly was then covered with plastic, then burlap, then topped off with sand, making the hide site blend into the terrain. This whole assembly would then be broken down and carried in the soldiers' rucksacks. An average hide site kit could weigh more than 100 pounds.

Finally, the word came down that ODA-525 had its SR mission. Chief Balwanz and his team were moved from King Fahad airport to King Khalid Military City (KKMC), which was the staging area for the 5th Special Forces group. During Isolation, all details of the mission were gone over, and the list of needed equipment was decided upon by the team. When the team inserted into Iraq, each man's rucksack, including the hide site kit, weighed over 175 pounds. Chief Balwanz relates that "Along with the kit, there was 5 gallons of water per man, ammunition, food, shovels, extra batteries, redundant radio systems. We had two SatCom systems, a system to talk with the aircraft, and even a PRC-104 radio for emergencies." In addition to all this equipment, four of the team members carried M-16A2 rifles, two carried M-16s outfitted with M-203 grenade launchers, the last two carried the HK MP5 SD3 suppressed 9mm submachine guns; all members of the team also carried the M-9, 9mm Beretta as a sidearm.

On the morning of 23 February 1991, Chief Balwanz and the men of ODA-525 loaded onto two MH-60 Blackhawks of the 160th Special Operations Aviation Regiment (Airborne)—the "Night Stalkers." This would be the first time in the history of the Army that a warrant officer would lead a team into combat. The team was prepared to stay on the ground for four days. At the end of four days, they would be extracted, or if the ground war had begun by this time, they would link up with the ground force as the corps passed through their position. (They did not know when they loaded the helicopters that the ground war was scheduled to begin the next morning.) Chief Balwanz relates a conversation with Chief Warrant Officer 3 Kenny Collier. CWO3 Collier was a former SF soldier, now a helicopter pilot with the 160th SOAR. He would be piloting one of the MH-60s that would be inserting ODA-525. "Kenny," Chief Balwanz said, "I know you'll get me in . . . [my] concern is you coming back for me." With a smile on his face

Chief Collier assured his friend and fellow warrior, "I tell you, dog . . . you call, we'll haul!"

"Our mission called for us to go about 150 miles into Iraq," says Balwanz. "We wanted to put eyes on a major highway, Highway 7. It ran from Baghdad to Nasiriyah, then cut over to Basara." This put them in the right spot to provide "hard" intel to the corps commander once the ground war began. Were the Iraqis sending in reinforcements, or were they withdrawing their troops? They would locate their hide site in the area of the Euphrates River. Since there would be some vegetation, the SF soldiers opted to wear standard issue woodland BDUs (battle dress uniforms), rather than the desert "chocolate chip" or three-color desert camouflage patterns.

They flew from KKMC to Rahfa, just inside the Iraqi boarder, to refuel the Blawkhawks. Fuel would be a critical factor in inserting the SR team. Mission planners had determined that infil and exfil would be done with only 10 minutes of fuel to spare. This also meant that if ODA-525 hit a hot LZ, they had less than 10 minutes to get the helicopters back out. Timing was also critical because the team needed to be on the ground a certain number of hours to build their hide sites before the sun came up. The plan called for a departure at 2000 hours, refuel at 2200, and getting on site with six hours before first light.

As the two helicopters flew into the Iraqi night, the pilots got word that the mission had been aborted, and they returned toward Rahfa. As they landed in Rahfa, they were told that it was on again. While there is a lot of speculation as to why this happened, no one ever gave clear reason. With the mission back on, the MH-60 needed to refuel. This ate up valuable darkness time and placed the team behind schedule for the insertion.

Fuel tanks now topped off, and the insertion window getting smaller, the MH-60s took off. The pilots were flying on NVGs (night vision goggles) approximately 20 feet above the desert at

During Operation Uphold Democracy, Brigadier General Meade studies maps and aerial photos with a group of Special Forces soldiers. The general is being briefed by the SF members after a grenade attack in Port au Prince, Haiti, that killed five people and wounded another 25. *Defense Visual Information Center Photo*

more than 120 knots. It was hazardous moving so low and fast, and all of a sudden the Blackhawk jerked up. Chief Balwanz, wearing a head set, inquired what had happened. Chief Collier calmly responded, "We just hit a sand dune, probably tore off the rear landing gear."

Well hell, thought Bulldog, if Kenny isn't worried, then I'm not going to worry about it, either.

Shortly thereafter, a flock of ducks flew up from a lake or pond and one got sucked into one of the engines, shutting it down. This still did not deter the pilots of the 160th.

As they got close to their target site, they performed a couple of false insertions. They would intentionally get picked up on enemy radar, then sit down on the ground 10–15 seconds, then move to another site. As they neared their predetermined site, another snag arose. Due to the recall, they had lost global position system (GPS) satellite coverage, so the pilots went to alternate navigational systems that are not as accurate.

As the two Blackhawks touched down, the eight-man SF team—four men from each helicopter—jumped to the ground and assumed a defensive position on the desert surface. They had been told there would be no dogs, but moments after landing the air filled with barking. They removed their PVS7 NVGs and let their eyes acclimate to the night and their surroundings. By now the GPS was back online, and the team found out it was about a mile from its planned insertion spot. The men broke out the map and a compass, hoisted their 175-pound packs, and headed to the spot they had selected for their hide sites.

After moving about 3/4 mile, they stopped to cache the PRC-104, an FM radio capable of Morse code. If everything went south, they could get to the radio and E&E out of the area. Each member of the team had the GPS location of the site; there was also a small palm tree at the position so it would be easy for them to locate.

The team members moved on, finally reaching the canal where they planned to establish their hide sites. When they rehearsed digging hide sites in Saudi, the soil was soft loam, but here the ground was rock hard. There was no way the team would be able to replicate the Saudi-style hide site in the allotted time before daylight. They decided to dig into the side of the canal where the earth was softer. One team set up a hasty hide site in the canal, while the other dropped back a little where the ground was looser. From the highway either site would be invisible.

The team split, digging two separate hide sites 150 meters apart and approximately 300–400 meters from the highways. One group would watch the northbound traffic, the other the southbound. They needed to be close to the road so they could identify "signature items," pieces of equipment that are specific to a particular division or type of unit. As Chief Balwanz explained, "If you could ID the equipment, then you could ID the unit." Close proximity also allowed them to identify whether a tank was a Soviet T-72 or a T-55.

As the sun rose, the men in the hide site heard the sound of children playing. The children came closer to the site and looked inside, seeing team member SSgt. James Weatherford. Startled, the children ran away. Immediately, the team medic, Sgt. Daniel Kostrzebski, and weapons specialist, SFC Robert Degroff, were out the rear of the hide site with their weapons sighted on the fleeing children. They asked Chief Balwanz what they should do. Knowing full well that if the children made it back to their homes, the team would be compromised, he told his men not to shoot. The team gathered in the canal and via the SatCom contacted XVIII Airborne Corps, informing them they had been compromised and requesting immediate exfiltration.

The hide sites being compromised, Chief Balwanz instructed his team sergeants to stay in the canal and once it became dark, they would move to a new location and continue their mission. All was going well, until just after noon. At this time, CWO2 Balwanz was leaning on the parapet of the canal, observing the highway with his binoculars, when another group of children discovered them. A sheepherder also saw them and began heading quickly back to the village. The team again contacted base, requesting an exfil and possibly close air support (CAS). They were told that emergency exfiltration would be mobilized and that CAS was 20 minutes out.

A group of Bedouins came out looking for the team, and shortly afterward, four or five trucks, a Toyota Land Cruiser, and a bus stopped on the highway. An estimated 150 Iraqi soldiers armed with weapons poured from the vehicles and began to move toward the ODA-525's canal site. Sensing an imminent firefight, Chief Balwanz put into effect their emergency destruct plan: All the team's classified crypto gear, radios, and burst equipment were stuffed into one of the rucksacks and rigged with a block of C4 explosive that was then set with a one minute timer. The team piled the rest of their rucksacks on top of it. Carrying only their weapons, load-bearing equipment (LBE), with ammunition and water, and one LST-5 SatCom radio, the SF soldiers ran down the canal. The Iraqis, plus the Bedouins, began maneuvering around the eight-man SF team. As the team tried to put some distance between themselves and the enemy, they heard the C4 explode and the screams of Iraqi soldiers. This meant that the Iraqis were about a minute behind them.

Their pursuers began firing and were trying to outflank them. Chief Balwanz ordered his two M-203 gunners (SFCs Degroff and Hovermale) to start laying down fire. The team was now located in an "elbow' of the canal, with nowhere else to run. Fortunately, the troops closing in on the Americans were not aware they had stumbled on an SF team; perhaps they thought it was just a downed aircrew. Secondly, these were not Republican Guards, they were more militia-type soldiers. They tended to bunch up and walk upright, firing on the SF soldiers. When the 40mm HE rounds went off, these bunches became history. In the first minute of the firefight Chief Balwanz and his men took out almost 40 of the enemy. Another advantage for ODA-525 was that five of its eight men were school-trained snipers. They did not have any sniper rifles, but at 300 to 500 meters, their training made a real difference in the fight. Precise shooting also allowed the team to conserve its ammunition.

Finally, over the LST-5 they could hear the Forward Air Controller calling for the team. Unfortunately, in their haste to destroy the radio gear, the VHF whip antennae for the LST-5 had been left behind. Although the team could hear the aircraft, they could not communicate with them. As a last resort, SFC Degroff pulled his PRC-90 survival radio out and tried to make contact with any coalition aircraft. After a number of attempts, he got a response from an AWACS, which then passed the team's frequency on to the U.S. Air Force F-16s there to provide CAS.

While the Falcon pilots had yet to establish the actual location of the team, their mere presence caused many of the Iraqis to run away from the beleaguered SF team. At last the flight detected the team's position. The first request from the team was to take care of the vehicle and the people on the highway. The F-16s made their run dropping cluster bomb units (CBU). One minute there were vehicles, the next there was nothing but burning scrap metal. Now the attention of the CAS was directed at those enemy soldiers closing in on the team. Flying at 20,000 feet, the F-16 pilots were dropping CBU approximately 200 meters, or "danger close" to the SF soldiers. A total of 16 sorties were flown in support of ODA-525 that day.

As daylight faded, the team fought back down the canal and the fight died down. The helicopters were now inbound. The team returned to the cached PRC-90 radio, which was equipped with a beacon. They turned the unit to beacon mode and after a couple of minutes, two MH-60s descended almost right on top of the team. In less than ten seconds the team was on board. The helicopters lifted into the night sky and headed back to KKMC. Chief Balwanz was awarded the Silver Star, and the balance of the team was awarded the Bronze Star with V-device. The Blackhawk pilots received the Distinguished Flying Cross, and their crew members were awarded Air Medals.

Special Forces ODAs continued to perform similar missions even deeper as Operation Desert Storm began the ground phase of the war. SF teams shadowed the Iraqi Republican Guard, and every move they made was immediately reported to General Schwarzkopf's command center. This gave the CinC the vital, up-to-the minute information he required to mount the offensive that would decimate the Iraqi forces. In one of his briefings, General Schwarzkopf acknowledged that the Special Forces teams "let us know what was going on out there, and they were the eyes out there."

In summation, the ODAs of the U.S. Army Special Forces put their principles of coalition warfare into reality, combining the synergy of three allied corps into a united force that liberated Kuwait. General Schwarzkopf would say of the Special Forces, "They were the glue that held the coalition together."

After the Gulf War, in April 1991, members of the 1st Battalion, 10th Special Forces Groups (Airborne), were deployed to southeast Turkey and northern Iraq to participate in Operation Provide Comfort. Here the SF soldiers were involved in humanitarian operations with more than a half-million Kurdish refugees. As the month wore on, the 2nd and finally the 3rd Battalion would join in the operation, resulting in the deployment of the entire 10th group. The SF teams were instrumental in saving these refugees, as they provided direction, overall ground relief, and security for the operational activities.

As the missions wound down in the Persian Gulf region, Special Forces teams found themselves occupied with training schedules and new missions to carry out, as the latest operations unveiled themselves. Members of the 2nd Battalion, 5th SFG(A), were involved in Operation Restore Hope and Provide Comfort on the continent of Africa. They were placed under the command of the Joint Special Operations Forces, a component command of the Unified Task Force. When the detachment deployed to Somalia, the men established an Advance Operations Base (AOB) and began their initial mission of border surveillance along the Ethiopian boarder. Their mission was to locate and identify members of Somalian factions and bandits using Ethiopia as sanctuary while they carried out raids into Somalia.

In January of 1993, the SF forward operating base, or FOB, deployed to Mogadishu and assumed command and control of Joint Special

The United States leads de-mining operations around the world. Members of the SF are instrumental in teaching host nations' troops the proper methods of safely dealing with the plethora of mines scattered across the battlefields. Here a soldier from the 10th SFG(A) buries an inert land mine, which will be used to teach students the finer points of probing. *Defense Visual Information Center Photo*

Operation – Somalia (JSOFOR). JSOFOR organized and conducted Special Operations in Somalia in support of the UNITAF humanitarian relief efforts.

JSOFOR originated with a small force of one Operational Detachment B, or ODB, five ODA operating out of Belet Uen, and one ODA in Bardera. These forces supported operations under the UNITAF area of responsibility ranging from the Indian Ocean in the South to the Ethiopian boarder in the North. This area was subsequently divided into nine sections referred to as Humanitarian Relief Sectors (HRS); SF would be employed in four of the nine sectors.

The SF ODA units proved themselves a valuable asset to the task force. On one occasion SF soldiers made contact with an Ethiopian boarder post after 10 days of diplomatic efforts had failed. Making this connection with the post created a relationship that would provide valuable intelligence regarding the movement of Somali factions along the border.

While Operation Restore Hope did have some success in Somalia, any benefits these SF soldiers contributed in carrying out their missions faded into the background. Somalia will be remembered by the firefight in October 1993 involving Task Force Ranger, resulting in 18 U.S. soldiers killed and more than 30 wounded; enemy losses were estimated at more than 1,000.

On the other side of the globe, SF soldiers were participating in Operation Uphold Democracy on the island of Haiti. Members of the 3rd SFG(A) were sent to Haiti to establish an FOB, while the bulk of conventional troops of the 10th Mountain Division and later the 25th Infantry secured the city in Port au Prince. SF ODAs would deploy to the FOB and then fan out into the countryside in order to stabilize the remainder of the island.

During Haitian operations, a Special Forces captain and his men were making their way through a village. Three women approached him pleading for their assistance. The women told the SF captain that the local "witch" had placed a curse on their children and they wanted the American officers to help them. The so-called witch in question just sat there glaring at the soldiers. This was definitely something out of the ordinary for these men.

The captain slung his M-4 carbine over his shoulder and pondered the situation. Had the women told him there were rebels in the hills, he could call in helicopters; had he been informed that armored cars were attacking civilians, he had Spectre gunships at hand; but a "witch" was well beyond the scope of normal mission parameters.

As he deliberated over the predicament, the captain stuck his hand in the pocket of his BDU. There he found a small chemical light stick. Secretly he snapped the stick, allowing the chemicals to mix, thus creating a soft glow. Shielding the light from view, he pulled the light stick out of his pocket and held it behind his thumb. With the other hand he removed his combat knife from its sheath. In a deliberate and careful move he cut what appeared to be the tip of his thumb, in reality the top of the chemlight. As the light mixture started to ooze out, the SF captain gently rubbed a small mark on the forehead of each of the children. All eyes, now wide with awe, were on the captain. He told the women this would protect their children from any curses or spells. Then he told the "witch" that she was to leave these mothers and children alone, or he would return. This is exactly what Special Forces soldiers are trained to do, to think "outside the box."

Operational Tempo, or OpTempo, as it is called, remained continually high for members of the Special Forces, as the United States committed more than 20,000 American soldiers to the country of Bosnia. In December 1995, a joint NATO (North Atlantic Treaty Organization) force would deploy to this war-torn country to partake in Operation Joint Endeavor as the military elements of the Dayton Peace Accords. The first of the U.S. units to enter Bosnia-Herzegovina would come from the 10th SFG(A). Further operations in this region would find the SF soldiers of the 3rd & 10th groups involved in Operations Joint Guard and Joint Forge.

Additionally, the 10th SFG(A) would be active in Operation Joint Guardian in Kosovo. As members of the Kosovo Forces (KFOR), SF teams

Staff Sergeant Gary Koenitzer of ODA-126, 1st Special Force Group (Airborne), takes a break with his students in southern Thailand. These Thai troops are being instructed in patrolling, small unit, and unconventional warfare tactics. *Courtesy MSgt. Gary Koenitzer*

employed their unique skills and cultural abilities in this region. During the early stages of American involvement, NATO planes began an air campaign over the skies of Kosovo in spring of 1999. When a U.S. Air Force F-117 Nighthawk was downed, members of the 10th SFG(A) who were on alert for possible CSAR (Combat Search And Rescue) missions were loaded onto waiting helicopters within 10 minutes of getting the information.

Members of the 3rd, 10th SFG(A), and selected SF National Guard units participated in all major operations in the Balkans. Special Forces teams were instrumental in the peacekeeping efforts in this region, and provided SF liaison control elements to the NATO allies and coalition partners. As of this writing, ODAs from the 10th SFG(A) are still active in Bosnia and Kosovo. The 5th SFG(A) has teams active in Kuwait. SF soldiers of the 3rd SFG(A) are conducting missions throughout the continent of Africa as part of the African Crisis Response Initiative (ACRI). ODAs from the 7th SFG(A) are performing FID and Counter-Drug (CD) training for national police and military forces in the jungles of Colombia, and members of the 1st SFG(A) carry out their missions in the Asia-Pacific region. Whether they are part of a larger operation or a single A-Detachment—perhaps the only U.S. military presence in a country—the sun never sets on the U.S. Army Special Forces.

CHAPTER 5

Special Forces Organization and Missions

Today's Special Forces is founded on a rich heritage and warrior lineage. The modern SF soldiers draw their combat skills from the proud tradition of their special warfare predecessors—the "Swamp Fox," the Office of Strategic Service (OSS) Jedburg teams, 1st Special Service Forces, and others. Members of the U.S. Army Special Forces still espouse the ensign held up by President John F. Kennedy. Kennedy gave the men of the Special Forces more than the green beret; he gave them a mission: to uphold democracy at all costs. Over the past five decades this standard has been carried into various conflicts, and the men of the Special Forces have paid the price. At the height of the Vietnam War there were more than a dozen Special Forces Groups, including active, Army Reserve, and National Guard units.

Today, under the command of Brigadier General Frank J. Toney Jr., the U.S. Army Special Forces Command (Airborne), USASFC(A), commands seven major subordinate units (or groups), each commanded by a colonel. The mission statement of the SF Command is "To organize, equip, train, validate and prepare forces for deployment to conduct worldwide special operations, across the range of military operations, in support of regional combatant commanders, American ambassadors and other agencies as directed."

Special Forces units are oriented to specific areas around the world. By concentrating on specific regions, the SF soldiers gain experience in the regional culture and languages of their assigned countries. This also gives them the opportunity to form a bond with the foreign mil-

itary forces and a working relationship with the indigenous population. There are five active SF groups: the 1st SFG(A), 3rd SFG(A), 5th SFG(A), 7th SFG(A), and 10th SFG(A). In addition to these active units, there are two National Guard SF groups, the 19th SFG(A) and 20th SFG(A). In addition to the Special Forces Groups, USASFC(A)

The modern SF soldiers draw their combat skills from the proud tradition of their special warfare predecessors. As with the OSS Jedburgh teams of World War II, airborne insertion is a hallmark trait of the Special Forces soldier. This SF team prepares for an over-the-water insertion via parachute. They wait in the cavernous fuselage of the C-130 for the signal to jump. The red lights allow their eyes to adjust to the darkness.

The SF soldiers may find themselves operating in a variety of environments, from the tropical rain forest of South America to the desert sands of the Middle East; from the jungles of Africa to the snow-covered mountainsides of Europe and the Balkans. Natural surroundings may pose as much danger as any foe. Fortunately, SF soldiers are proficient at dealing with both circumstances.

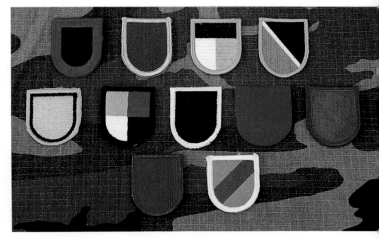

Beret Flashes of the U.S. Army Special Operations (Left to Right) Top Row: U.S. Army Special Operations Command (Airborne), U.S. Army Special Forces Command (Airborne), U.S. Army John F. Kennedy Special Warfare Center & School (Airborne), and U.S. Army Special Warfare Training Group (Airborne). Middle Row (Active): 1st Special Forces Group (Airborne), 3rd Special Forces Group (Airborne), 5th Special Forces Group (Airborne), 7th Special Forces Group (Airborne), and 10th Special Forces Group (Airborne). Bottom Row (National Guard): 19th Special Forces Group (Airborne) and 20th Special Forces Group (Airborne).

also has two active duty and two reserve chemical recon detachments (not SF personnel) and a 13-man SF detachment, assigned to 1st SFG(A) to support theater war-planning requirements on the Korean peninsula, known as Detachment K or Det-K.

The 1st Special Forces Group (Airborne) has its headquarters in Ft. Lewis, Washington. Their motto is "Warriors First—First in Asia." Under the authority of PACOM (Pacific command) this group has a pre-deployed battalion or ODB stationed on the island of Okinawa. Additionally,

the 1st SFG(A) provides soldiers for Detachment K in Korea. Their area of responsibility (AOR) is the Pacific rim and Asia, which includes all the islands up through India, Manchuria, and China. Also, due to its size, part of Russia also falls under their AOR. The 1st Group maintains a high state of preparedness to carry out special operations in support of USCINCPAC (U.S. Commander In Chief Pacific) in a major theater war.

The 3rd SFG(A) is based at Ft. Bragg, North Carolina, and is assigned to EUCOM (European Command), concentrating mainly on the continent of Africa, excluding the Horn of Africa. Third Group also has one battalion that is on line to support CENTCOM (Central Command), which is

The Special Forces soldier is often the eyes and the ears of a theater commander. Members of the SF teams hold a minimum grade of E-5 sergeant. Each soldier is a mature, physically rugged, morally straight, thoroughly lethal, and highly skilled individual who brings a new level of professionalism to an already elite military unit.

The team leader of the SF ODA (Operational Detachment-Alpha) is a captain. He will spend two years as a detachment commander before he moves on to other assignments within the Special Operations Forces (SOF) community. Occasionally, a team leader will get an additional rotation with the teams; however, this is the exception rather than the rule. Unique in their operations from a conventional infantry commander, the SF captain team leaders take on missions and encounter obstacles that not only require unconventional military measures, but also require unorthodox thinking.

responsible for the Middle East. One of the major missions involving the 3rd SFG(A) is the African Crisis Response Initiative, or ACRI. This is a prime example of an SF collateral mission, that of security assistance. ACRI is a U.S. Department of State-supported program intended to enhance the security and peace in selected countries on the continent of Africa. SF ODAs (Operational Detachments-Alpha) will train soldiers from these countries into highly effective and rapid-deployable peacekeeping units. With this training, the local forces can be used as peacekeeping forces, thus limiting or perhaps even eliminating the need for large U.S. involvement.

Next is 5th SFG(A), located in Ft. Campbell, Kentucky. It is the lead Group under CENTCOM. Their AOR is from the Horn of Africa up through the Central Asia Republics of Kazakhstan, Turkmenistan, and Tajikistan. While it does not have

a forward deployed battalion, like the 1st Group, the 5th SFG(A) does regularly rotate an ODA through the Middle East, maintaining a constant presence in Kuwait. The exploits of the 5th Group are legendary. From the jungles of Vietnam to the desert wastelands in Iraq, the men of 5th SFG(A) have set a benchmark in Special Forces operations.

If you travel north on Ft. Bragg's Yadin Road and hang a right at 77th SFG Way, you'll locate the HQ for the 7th SFG(A). Its motto is "Lo Que Sera, Cuando Sera, Donde Sera" (Anything, Anytime, Anyplace). They operate the SOUTHCOM (South Command) AOR in Central and South America and the Caribbean. One company of the 7th SFG(A) is forward based in Puerto Rico, at Roosevelt Roads Naval Station, or "Roosey Roads," as it is called. Additionally, members of the 7th have been selected to participate in the Army WarFighter Experiment exercises, to test new SF doctrine, organization, and equipment.

Finally, under EUCOM, is the 10th Special Forces Group (Airborne) based out of Ft. Carson, Colorado. It also has a forward deployed battalion in Panzer Kaserne, Boeblingen, Germany. This AOR for the 10th Group comprises Europe and countries of the former Soviet Union, including Russia (except for the part handled by 1st SFG(A)). The 10th Group holds the honor of being the original SF Group. If that seems confusing, it was meant to be. The Special Forces were created in the early 1950s to prepare a specialized force in the event of a World War III. They were to conduct guerrilla operations behind enemy lines, should the Soviets invade Europe. The U.S. Army only had one Special Forces unit at this time, but it did not want the Soviets to realize this—hence, this Special Forces Group was designated the 10th. The 10th SFG(A) was stationed in Bad Tolz, Germany, during the Cold War, and subsequently relocated to the Stuttgart area in July 1991. While the 10th Group encompasses all of the SF doctrinal missions, its ODAs hone their skills in unconventional warfare (UW), and they remain the premier mountain and winter troops among the U.S. Army Special Forces.

In November 1990, the Reserve SF Groups were deactivated, leaving only the National Guard Groups. The 19th SFG(A), a National Guard outfit with headquarters in Salt Lake City, Utah, has units spread throughout the western United States. The 19th group is a "jack of all trades." It operates in the Pacific, it has the ability to operate one battalion in Central Command, and it performs duties around Europe. The other Guard

If the SF team is the eyes and the ears of the CinC, then the eyes and ears of the SF ODA are the Operations and Intelligence Sergeants. These senior non-commissioned officers (NCOs) "run" the teams. They are the quintessential SF soldier. They thrive on ambiguity and uncertainty, thinking the unconventional and daring the uncommon. They see obstacles as something to be overcome, surroundings as environments to be adapted to, and tasks as opportunities for improvisation. A team sergeant will immerse himself in the art, science, and history of war.

outfit is the 20th SFG(A) with headquarters in Birmingham, Alabama, and units throughout the eastern United States. The 20th operates mostly in the Caribbean and Central and South America.

When you look around the world, you do not see large armored or infantry divisions in all places, yet Special Forces has a constant presence. So valuable are the SF groups that the CinC of EUCOM recently requested two additional SF Groups for his AOR.

The purpose of the SF Group is to establish, support, and operate a Special Forces Operational

The SF Weapons sergeants are responsible for the employment of weapons using conventional and UW tactics and techniques. They will serve as the detachment armorer. Here can be seen both light arms, M4A1 carbine, and heavier weapons, the AT-4 anti-tank weapon. The weapons sergeant will be an expert on both U.S. and foreign weapons systems and the best way to employ them.

Base, SFOB, and Forward Operational Base, FOB, to provide special operation command and control units to conventional headquarters. The SF Group is responsible for training and preparing the SF ODA for deployment, and directing, supporting, and sustaining those ODA once deployed. Under each of these Groups, you'll find a Headquarters/Headquarters Company (HHC), a Support unit, and three SF Battalions.

The HHC plans, coordinates, and directs SF operations, either separately or as part of a larger force. This includes training and preparing SF teams for deployment, providing command and

staff personnel to operate an SFOB, and providing advice, coordination, and staff assistance on the employment of SF assets to a joint Special Operations Command (SOC), Joint Special Operations Task Force (JSOTF), or other major headquarters. The Support Company will provide military intelligence, signal support, and general aviation support. Each of these Battalions in turn comprises a Headquarters and three SF Companies.

The SF Battalion operates like the Group on a smaller scale. It conducts and supports any special operation in any operational environment, whether in peace, conflict, or war. The SF Company, also referred to as SFODB (Special Forces Operational Detachment-B or B-Team), consists of five ODAs or A-teams. SFODB has the capability to plan and carry out SF missions; train and prepare ODA for deployment; infiltrate and exfiltrate by air, land, or sea; conduct operations in remote areas and hostile environments for extended periods; and organize, equip, and train indigenous troops up to a regimental size. When you total all the personnel, you end up with approximately 1,200 people per SF Group, or 10,000 worldwide.

Each SF battalion will have one HALO (High Altitude Low Opening) team, schooled in Military Free Fall, MFF; one SCUBA (Self-Contained Underwater Breathing Apparatus) team, trained as Combat Swimmers; and one CT or Counterterrorist team. The balance of the teams are referred to as ruck teams, and they use the "low impact" method of insertion—by foot.

The A-team

The ODA remains the essence of the U.S. Army Special Forces. Here is where the "rucksack meets the ground," where missions are carried out. No matter how you got to that point, HALO, SCUBA, Ground Mobility Vehicle (GMV), Zodiac, or Helicopter, here is where the planning is put into action. The ODA is specifically designed

Without a doubt the **green beret** headgear sets the U.S. Army Special Forces soldier apart from other troopers. It has become part of American folk history like the coonskin hat and cowboy hat. The hat was first sported by the members of the 10th SFG(A) in the Bavarian mountain ranges. The men would order the berets from a woolen company in Canada at their own expense, usually $7 to $8, in 1955. According to Mr. Joe Lupyak SF-CSM-ret., "The berets were only worn in the field, during exercises. [The Army] would not allow the wearing of the berets in garrison."

The green beret was originally designated in 1953 by Special Forces Major Herbert Brucker, a veteran of the OSS. Later that year, 1st Lt. Roger Pezelle adopted the beret as the unofficial headgear for his A-team, Operational Detachment FA32. Soon it spread throughout all of the Special Forces troops—much to the dismay of the U.S. Army and conventional commanders.

In 1961, President John F. Kennedy planned to visit Fort Bragg. He sent word to Brigadier General William P. Yarborough, the commander of the Special Warfare Center, that all Special Forces soldiers were to wear the green berets for this visit. President Kennedy felt that since they had a special mission, Special Forces should have something to set them apart from the rest of the conventional troops. Coincidentally, even before the presidential request came, the Department of the Army had reversed its objections to the headgear and sent a message to the center authorizing the green beret as part of the Special Forces uniform.

When President Kennedy arrived at Fort Bragg on 12 October 1961, Brigadier General William P. Yarborough wore his green beret to greet the commander-in-chief. The president said, "Those are nice. How do you like the green beret?" Yarborough responded, "They're fine, sir. We've wanted them a long time."

President Kennedy sent a message to General Yarborough, stating, "My congratulations to you personally for your part in the presentation today . . . The challenge of this old but new form of operations is a real one and I know that you and the members of your command will carry on for us and the free world in a manner which is both worthy and inspiring. I am sure that the green beret will be a mark of distinction in the trying times ahead."

On 11 April 1962, in a White House memorandum for the United States Army, President Kennedy showed his continued support for the Special Forces, calling the green beret, "a symbol of excellence, a badge of courage, a mark of distinction in the fight for freedom."

Over the years, the custom of the green beret changed in Special Forces. When the first Special Forces wore the berets, they would only wear them in the field and never in garrison. Today, 50 years later, the green berets are worn only in garrison and rarely, if ever, are they worn in the field or on operations. There are a few exceptions to this rule. When meeting foreign military for the first time, the SF captain or sergeant may wear his green beret to receive instant credibility. Also, an NCOIC, or Non-Commissioned Officer In Charge, who is training local troops might wear the beret for immediate recognition by the indigenous troops.

Talk to some SF soldiers and they will tell you it is just a headgear, while others will explain that the green beret is the quickest way of identifying a member of the U.S. Army Special Forces, when starting to discuss Special Operation Forces. Either way, when an SF soldier places that green beret on his head, he walks a little straighter, and stands a little taller.

The **arrowhead** patch is worn by members of the Special Forces around the world. Drawing from the heritage of American Indians, the arrowhead depicts the field craft, stealth, and tactics of these tenacious warriors. The upturned dagger is symbolic of the nature of Special Forces unconventional warfare missions. The three lightning bolts represent the three methods of infiltration—land, sea, and air. Lightning is also characteristic of

intense speed and strength. The color gold exemplifies fortitude and inspiration, and the teal blue background represents the Special Forces' encompassing of all branch assignments.

The distinctive **Special Forces crest** is black and silver, emblazoned with the Special Forces motto: De Oppresso Liber. This Latin phrase translates into To Free the Oppressed. A fighting knife is upturned and placed over two crossed arrows. The arrow symbolizes the Special Forces' role in unconventional warfare, and the knife reflects the attributes of a Special Forces soldier, straight and true. Both arrow and knife were silent weapons employed by the American Indians, thus providing a further link to the warrior spirit of this great nation.

In April of 1987 a new and separate branch of the Army was created for Special Forces officers. Prior to this time, officers assigned to Special Forces would wear the symbol for their branch of service on their collars, e.g. infantry, engineers, etc. With the creation of a separate branch, the crossed arrows were designated for the Special Forces officers. The Special Forces officer branch inherited this insignia from the Indian scouts, several of whom were awarded Medals of Honor for their actions with U.S. forces. The **crossed arrows** were also used by the 1st Special Service Force in World War II. During the 1960s, it was not uncommon to see SF officers sporting the crossed arrows on their uniform collars.

In July of 1983 the **Special Forces Tab** was authorized to be worn by SF qualified personnel. Upon completion of SF training the soldier is authorized to wear the tab on the left shoulder. This tab is worn above the Airborne tab and SF arrowhead. If an individual is also Ranger qualified, he may wear the Ranger tab as well. It would be located between the SF tab and the Airborne tab.

SF Insignias

Special Forces engineer sergeants are just as skilled in building bridges as demolishing them. As part of their mission, they may do "nation building" with a hammer and saw as well as C4 and Det-cord. The ODA engineer sergeants perform and instruct in all aspects of combat engineering, light construction, and demolitions techniques. Here an SF engineer sergeant prepares a charge of military dynamite for a training mission. It should be noted that dynamite is not the first explosive of choice; however, SF are taught to use what they have, and in a Third World setting or UW role, this may be the only explosive material available.

to organize, train, advise, direct, and support indigenous military or paramilitary forces in UW and FID operations. The units are capable of training a force up to a battalion in size. Unlike a conventional unit, which will deploy with its full chain of command, staff officers, and support and logistics units, SF does not. The 82nd does not send an infantry squad out on a mission and say, "By the way, sergeant, it's all yours." On the other hand, that is exactly how an SF ODA deploys; often the SF team is the only U.S. military presence in a country.

The Special Forces ODA is commanded by a captain (18A00). He may also command or advise

Call him "Doc" or "18-Delta," the SF medical sergeant is one of the most capable medical specialists in the U.S. military. He is trained in first aid, trauma care, dentistry, and veterinary skills. He functions as an independent medical care practitioner in a remote environment, and takes care of the A-team's medical needs as well as those of any indigenous personnel. Although he is a medical specialist, the SF 18D is also a combatant. He not only knows how to perform a tracheotomy, he can perform a CAS strike or take out an enemy sentry with the same precision. When the other members of the team head out on a patrol with their LBE and loads, he will also be carrying a medical pack or trauma bag filled with assorted medical supplies.

concert with conventional forces in large-scale operations. As the team leader, he is accountable for everything that happens on that team, right or wrong. He is tasked with mission planning—working with the team specialist to establish the best possible strategy for mission success. As Captain Steve Warman, of ODA-581, 5th SFG(A) sums it up, the team leader "is responsible for the men and their equipment, and makes sure that everything happens the way it is supposed to happen."

When you look at the difference between an SF captain and the captain of a conventional unit,

The two Communications "Commo" Sergeants of the ODA advise the detachment commander on communications matters. They install, operate, and maintain FM, AM, HF, VHF, and SHF radio communications in voice, CW, and burst radio nets. Here SFC Greg Green of the 1st Special Forces Group (Airborne) performs a communications check. He is using an AN/PSC-5 Multi-band, Multi-mission communications terminal, with SatCom antennae.

up to a battalion-size group of indigenous combat troops. He is proficient in those tasks that support the detachment's mission-essential task list, or METL, with knowledge of a broad spectrum of common and special operations tasks. Not only must the SF captain know the skills that will make him mission-capable during independent special operations, he must also be able to operate in

A Special Forces sergeant takes aim with his M4A1/M203. He will be ready to provide cover fire for his team members as they move stealthily through the wooded marsh.

you see the vast chasm in their operational capabilities. A typical infantry, airborne, or armor captain will operate usually within 10 kilometers of his command and control. He'll have full logistical support and medical facilities nearby, and his operations will be in concert with other larger units. His need for E&E skills is limited, and he will normally fight within range of artillery support. Conversely, the SF captain will operate in isolated areas, often over 100 kilometers from his headquarters. Logistical support will be little, if any, and often he'll live off the land; availability for MedEvac is limited and will depend on the team medical specialist. ODAs will operate independently of other units. The need for survival and E&E skills

is high, and the SF captain will rarely operate within the range of friendly fire support.

The executive officer of the ODA is the detachment technician, a warrant officer (WO) (180A0). He serves as second in command, ensuring that the detachment commander's decisions are implemented. His tasks also include administrative and logistical aspects of area studies, briefbacks and operational plans (OPLANs), and operational orders (OPORDs). He will assist in the recruitment of indigenous troops and the subsequent training of these combat forces up to and including a battalion size. In the event the mission requires the ODA to run a "split team op," the WO would command one of these teams.

What makes SF soldiers special? An SF sergeant summed it up best when he said, "You look at his shoulder, that tells you his Quals [Qualifications, e.g. Airborne, Ranger, Special Forces tabs]. You look at his chest, that tells you his schools [e.g. Air Assault, Airborne, EIB (Expert Infantry Badge),etc.]. You look in his eyes, that tells you what kind of a man he is."

The next man on the team is the operations sergeant (18Z50), the "team sergeant." He is the senior NCO on the detachment. A master sergeant, he advises the ODA commander on all training and operational matters. His job also entails providing the team with tactical and technical guidance and support. He will prepare the operations and training portion of the area studies, briefbacks and OPLANs, and OPORDs. In the absence of the WO, the "team sergeant" will fill in this position.

Directing the ODA's intelligence training, collections, analysis and dissemination is the assistant operations and intelligence sergeant (18F40), a sergeant first class (SFC). As the name implies, he assists the operations sergeant in preparing area studies, briefbacks, and so on. He is also responsible for field interrogation of enemy prisoners. He briefs and debriefs SF and indigenous patrols, and will fill in for the ops sgt. when necessary.

The operations and intelligence sergeant comes from the ranks of Special Forces. He will have been on an ODA for some time and will have attended the Advanced Non-Commissioned Officers Course at the NCO Academy, USAJFK-SWC/S at Ft. Bragg.

Next on the team are the two weapons sergeants (18B40) and (18B30), an SFC and staff sergeant (SSG) respectively. They are responsible for the employment of weapons using conventional and UW tactics and techniques. They will train the indigenous troops as well as other team members in the use of small arms (e.g., pistols, rifles, assault weapons), crew-served weapons (e.g., machine guns, mortars), anti-aircraft (e.g., stingers) and anti-tank weapons (e.g., LAW, AT-4). They may assist the operations sergeant, and they can organize, train, advise, and command up to a company-size indigenous force.

Two engineer sergeants (18C40) SFC and (18C30) SSG supervise, lead, plan, perform, and instruct all aspects of combat engineering and light construction. They are knowledgeable in demolitions and improvised munitions. They will plan and perform sabotage operations. As the weapons sergeants, they can organize, train, advise, and command an indigenous force up to a company size.

Two medical sergeants (18D40) SFC and (18D30) SG provide emergency, routine, and long-term medical treatment for the ODA and associated allied or indigenous forces. They will train, advise, and direct detachment members and indigs in emergency medicine and preventive medical care. In the event of a prolonged mission, they will establish a medical facility and are also trained in veterinary care. They are considered physician substitutes and can provide emergency, routine, and long-term medical care for the ODA, allied forces, and host nation personnel. One other unique capability of the SF medical sergeant is that he is fully schooled in the SF skills and is a combatant. As are the other team members, he is capable of training and commanding up to a company-size force.

Finally, the last two members of the ODA are the communications sergeants (18E40) SFC and (18E30) SSG. These two soldiers advise the detachment commander on communications matters. They install, operate, and maintain FM, AM, HF, VHF, and SHF radio communications in voice, CW, and burst radio nets. They prepare the communications portion of briefbacks, OPLANs, and OPORDs. They will train members of the ODA and indigenous personnel in the use and maintenance of the communication equipment. They can advise, train, and command indigenous forces up to a company in size.

According to Major Tom McCullom, SF-PAO, "A SF soldier is a highly skilled, extremely capable soldier, there is very little he as an individual cannot figure out how to do; but as a team, the team is unstoppable, because each SF soldier builds off the others' strengths. The commo sergeant may know everything to know about commo, but may be weak in demolitions; meanwhile the team has an engineering sergeant that knows everything there is to know about demolitions. And he can help out the commo sergeant. . . . A good team does not just do their job and go home at the end of the day, they socialize together, they know each other. Special Forces are a type A personality times three! SF soldiers have a lot of initiative, [and] the ability to think on their own. They've got to be mature enough that when they are on their own they will be making the right decisions."

While conducting an SR mission, the SF soldier may use a ghillie suit to camouflage his position. He will report his observations using the SALUTE method—Size, Activity, Location, Unit, Time, and Equipment. Special Forces also include their proximity to the target. High command will determine what ordnance to use against the target and whether the SF team's position is considered Danger Close.

Members of the 5th Special Forces Groups (Airborne) practice their lethal trade. Here the Ground Mobility Vehicle (GMV) has pulled off the road into a partial defilade position. While the team sergeant mans the Mark 19, 40mm Grenade Machine Gun, other members of the ODA provide 360 degrees of cover fire, if necessary.

Special Forces Missions

Originally created to train and maintain a guerrilla force against communist aggression in Europe, their primary mission in 1952 was that of unconventional warfare. Over the years the geopolitical world has changed and so has the mission of the Special Forces soldier and ODA. Today, the Special Forces comprises five core missions, and while UW is one of them, they are prepared to conduct and execute any of them. These core missions are the following:

Special Reconnaissance (SR), is defined as the reconnaissance and surveillance activity conducted by Special Operations Forces (SOF). Performed by SF teams, this covers the area of HUMINT (HUMan INTelligence), placing U.S. "eyes on target" in hostile, denied, or politically sensitive territory. An SF team could be tasked to conduct these missions. This means putting warm bodies on the ground in a specific location to accomplish what no satellite can do. An ODA performing an SR mission will be infiltrated into enemy area to report back to their commanders necessary information needed to carry out ongoing attacks. Special Forces teams may be utilized to acquire or verify, by visual observation or other methods available, information concerning the capabilities, intentions, and activities of an enemy force. SR may also include the placement of remote sensor equipment in enemy territory. Special Reconnaissance includes recording meteorological, hydrographic, and geographic characteristics of the objective area. Additionally, SR comprises target acquisition, bomb damage assessment, and post-strike reconnaissance. Reconnaissance provides the CinC with intelligence needed to conduct operations.

SR provides intelligence that is *strategic*—data that is required by national decision makers in formulating national or foreign defense policies, *operational*—details and reports used by theater level commanders to plan and conduct their campaigns, and *tactical*—information that commanders need for fighting battles.

Direct Action (DA), involves small-scale offensive actions, normally of a short-term duration conducted by SF teams. Such actions include seizure, destroying, capture of enemy personnel—any action that would inflict damage on enemy personnel or material. Direct action missions may also include the recovery of sensitive items or isolated personnel—e.g., POWs. SF units are highly trained and may employ raids, ambushes, and

Qatar soldiers listen to a class given by SFC Tim Keck of the 5th Special Forces Group (Airborne), on the proper procedures for clearing enemy forces from buildings. *DOD Photo*

71

A SF captain from ODA 052, 10th Special Forces Group (Airborne) pauses to check his map. Wearing snow camouflage, he blends in well with his surroundings. While some units still have the three-color snow camo, he is wearing the newly issued "All White" camo.

Foreign Internal Defense (FID) is a primary means of providing U.S. military SOF's expertise to other governments in support of their internal defense and developmental efforts. FID is one of the SF's primary peacetime tasks. By providing such training, SOF may eliminate the need to deploy conventional forces in a particular region of the world. Yet by employing SF ODAs in this mission, teams stay prepared for their role as combat advisers in the event of war. FID missions have included basic static line parachute training, MFF, and jumpmaster training; light infantry tactics, encompassing counterinsurgency operations, advance patrolling, urban combat, and advance marksmanship/sniper training; water operations, including riverine ops, small boat ops, and scout swimming; and engineering and communications training. Medical and veterinary training are also incorporated in the SF FID missions.

Unconventional Warfare (UW), the origin of SF, encompasses guerrilla warfare, the use of irregular forces—normally indigenous personnel operating in enemy-held territory—and other direct offensive, low visibility, covert, or clandestine operations. Incorporated in the UW mission are the indirect activities of subversion, sabotage, intelligence gathering, and evasion and escape nets. Armed rebellion against an established force or occupying power is often within the scope of UW. In wartime, Special Forces may be tasked with directly supporting any resistance or guerrilla force. This is commonly accomplished by infiltrating operational detachments or A-teams into denied or sensitive areas for the purpose of training, equipping and advising, or directing indigenous forces.

Counterterrorism (CT) consists of the offensive actions taken to prevent, deter, and respond to terrorism; this includes intelligence gathering and threat analysis. SF troops are ideal for engaging in antiterrorism and counterterrorism missions. Such assets could be on station in the rapidly changing environment of a CT operation,

other small unit tactics in the pursuit of these mission goals. They may employ mines and other demolitions or conduct attacks by employing fire support from air, ground, or sea assets. Direct action may employ stand-off weapons, such as a sniper team or an SF team with a SOFLAM (Special Operation Force Laser Acquisition Marker) who lase a target for terminal guidance ordnance—e.g., precision-guided "smart bombs."

Although one of the five core missions of Special Forces, CT, or Counterterrorism, is not talked about openly by USASOC. They do not want to give the terrorist any edge. This member of a CT team is "armed for bear"; he carries the M4A1 carbine with dual magazine, vertical grip and sight, a Berretta M9 pistol, flash-bang grenades, and numerous ammo magazines at the ready. He wears special head and eye protection.

greatly enhancing flexibility in meeting the critical demands of the situation. The CT mission could include training of host nation counterterrorist forces, conducting hostage rescues, recovering sensitive material from terrorists, or performing DA on the terrorist infrastructure to reduce the effects of international or state-sponsored terrorist activities.

Collateral Missions

Due to the nature of SF soldiers, who can adapt, overcome, and improvise according to ever-changing missions and environments, they are frequently called upon to perform Collateral Activities, in addition to the five core missions.

These activities include **Humanitarian Assistance**, as in Operation Provide Comfort (the highly trained medical specialists in SF are often called for such missions); **Security Assistance**, training and advisory roles; Personnel Recovery, from **Combat Search and Rescue** (CSAR) to **Non-Combatant Operations** (NEOs), such as Operation Assure Lift in Sierra Leone, where members of 3rd SFG(A) extracted Ambassador Ann Wright from her embassy in 1997; **Counter-Drug (CD)** efforts, supporting counter drug operations inside the United States in cooperation with JTF-6 and in various locations OCONUS (OutsideCONtinental US); and **Counter Mine**, conducting several de-mining initiatives worldwide. The United States is the world leader in removing mines, and the SOF and SF lead this initiative. Finally, there is the area of **Special Activities**, which is classified.

6 Selection and Training

In addition to the active and National Guard SF groups, two additional groups come under the command of USASOC. They are the U.S. Army John F. Kennedy Special Warfare Center and School (Airborne) and U.S. Army Special Warfare Training Group (Airborne). These two groups are tasked with the training of the Special Forces soldiers. Their mission is to assess, select, train, and qualify Special Forces soldiers in preparation

for assignment to an Operational Detachment-Alpha, or ODA.

The JFK Special Warfare Center and School is responsible for special operations training, leader development, doctrine, and personnel advocacy. The center and school's training group conduct the full spectrum of training in special operations. The 1st Battalion administers Special Forces Assessment and Selection (SFAS) and the SF Qualification Course, or Q-Course. The 2nd Battalion is responsible for advanced SF skills, military free fall (MFF); combat diving (SCUBA); the SERE (Survival, Escape, Resistance, and Evasion) course; Special Operations Target Interdiction course; Special Forces Advanced Reconnaissance, Target Analysis & Exploitation Techniques course, and Advanced Special Operations Techniques. The 3rd Battalion teaches civil affairs, psychological operations, Special Forces warrant officers, language training, and regional area studies.

What makes an SF soldier special? What makes him stand head and shoulders above any other soldier in the world? He is in a class by himself. He is a mature, highly skilled, outstandingly trained individual, and without a doubt the finest unconventional warfare expert in the world, bar none. He is a teacher, a fighter, and oftentimes a diplomat. And a warrior of uncommon physical and mental caliber, ready to serve at a moment's notice anywhere his mission may take him. An SF sergeant summed it up best when he said, "You look at his shoulder, that tells you his QUALs [Qualifications, e.g. Airborne, Ranger, Special Forces tabs]. You look at his chest, that tells you his schools [e.g., MFF, SCUBA,

Land navigation is an essential skill for SF soldiers. While they are well versed in the use of high tech gear, like the Global Positioning System (GPS), they are just as comfortable with a map and compass. The SF soldier will use whatever means are available, even if that means navigating from the stars.

The subdued patch of the John F. Kennedy Special Warfare Center and School. This instructor is also Ranger and SF qualified.

"Airborne, All The Way!" All members of the U.S. Army Special Forces are Airborne qualified. This training takes place at the U.S. Army Airborne School, Ft. Benning, Georgia. Upon successful completion, a soldier is awarded the "Silver Wings" and is no longer considered a Low Energy Ground soldier, or "LEG."

Pathfinder, and so on]. You look in his eyes, that tells you what kind of a man he is."

One of the unique characteristics making the Special Forces "special" is the fact that soldiers who make it into this branch of the Army are triple volunteers. First, an individual must volunteer for service with the U.S. Army. Second, they volunteer for Airborne training. Then, after serving in their Military Occupational Specialty (MOS), they volunteer for Special Forces. When the time comes for the SFAS, the soldier has a couple years under his belt. This ensures that SF

soldiers are well grounded in conventional Army tactics before undergoing Special Forces training.

During the 1970s and early 1980s, an individual could enlist directly into the SF field. He would go through Basic Combat Training, Advanced Individual Training, Airborne School and then go on for Special Forces training. Today, the SF "direct" enlistment option is no longer available. Special Forces is a "non-accession" branch of the Army, which means SF does not accept entry-level personnel. Any male soldier may volunteer for SFAS. At this point he

Where the journey into SF begins—the Special Forces Assessment and Selection phase at Camp MacKall. The purpose of SFAS is to identify soldiers who have the potential for Special Forces training.

The SF weapons sergeants are trained on more than 80 weapons—U.S. and foreign, friend and foe, old and new. You never know what weapons the host nation will be using, so you train up on everything you can get your hands on. Brass flies into the air as two members of ODA-173, "The Sea Pigs," send some .45 caliber rounds down range using the M3 submachine gun, also known as the "Grease Gun." A World War II–era weapon, it is still in use today.

may not be Airborne qualified. If he makes it through SFAS, he will have to go through Airborne training before entering the Qualification Course.

To join Special Forces the soldier must be a proven performer, having risen to the rank of captain or sergeant. Warrant officers come out of the SF senior NCO ranks. Here is the training progression, beginning with Airborne, SFAS, and then the Q-Course.

Airborne

The separation of the SF trooper from his fellow soldiers begins in the hot Georgia sun. Airborne training for the prospective Special Forces trooper is conducted at the U.S. Army Airborne School at Ft. Benning, Georgia. For the next three weeks he will be at the mercy of the Army's "Black Hats," the Airborne instructors of the 1st Battalion (Airborne), 507th Parachute Infantry Regiment, who will convert a "leg" into an "Airborne" trooper. He will learn what it takes to hurl oneself out of an airplane for the purpose of infiltrating into his mission drop zone (DZ). And he will run.

He will also learn a new mantra, which he will repeat over and over during the three weeks at Ft. Benning. He will shout out, "Motivated!

Motivated!! Motivated!!! Airborne!" and he will run. He will repeat the mantra, "Fired up! Fired up!! Fired up!!! Airborne!" and when his body is aching and cannot move another inch, he will run some more. These veteran Airborne qualified instructors wearing the "Black Hats" ensure these potential Green Berets are indeed motivated and fired up! This is far more than an evolution. This is Airborne!

Basic airborne training is broken into segments of a week each: Ground, Tower, and Jump Week.

SF Engineers receive extensive training in building and construction. Often, nation building is accomplished with a hammer and saw rather than an M4A1 and Claymore. There are times, of course, when what has gone up must now come down. It has been said that most problems can be solved with the proper amount of high explosives. Here an SF engineer sergeant is preparing a timing fuse for an explosive charge.

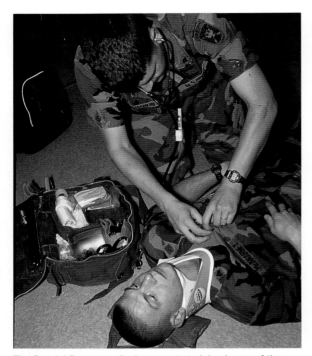

The Special Forces medical sergeants training is one of the most exhaustive training programs in the SF/SOF arena. Very often the SF medic will be the only source of medical care to which the team or indigenous personnel have access. He is trained and capable of serving as a physician substitute in the austere environments where the Operational Detachment-Alpha (ODA) operate.

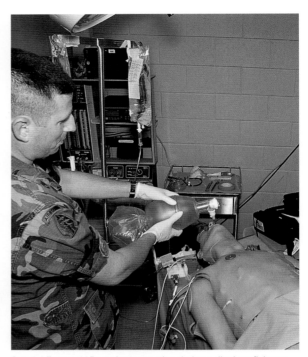

Special Forces 18D students practice their medical proficiency on the Human Patient Simulator. This highly sophisticated simulator, in use at the JSOMTC, is capable of producing normal and abnormal physiological responses to myriad anesthetic, medical, and surgical events. Lungs fill with and empty of air, eyes can become fixed and dilated, and so on. The benefit of the simulator is that these conditions are repeatable, thus removing a variable in the restoration or demise of the patient. By using the patient simulator, there is no risk to live patients during this phase of training.

During Ground Week, our trainee will start an intensive program of instruction designed to prepare the trooper to complete his parachute jump. He will learn how to execute a flawless parachute landing fall (PLF) to land safely in the landing zone (LZ). The PLF uses five points of contact designed to absorb the shock of landing and distribute it across the balls of the feet, calves, thighs, buttocks, and the push-up muscles of the back. He will learn the proper way to exit an aircraft using mockups of a C-130 and a C-141. He will climb

up a 34-foot tower, where he will be connected to the lateral drift apparatus and upon command will assume door position and jump. Proper body position will be evaluated, and he'll do it over and over until the "Black Hats" are happy; and he will run.

Next comes Tower Week. Now that our trainee has learned how to exit, position, and land, he will have this second week to refine those skills. Using a training device known as the swing landing tower (SLT), where he is hooked up to a parachute harness, he jumps from a 12-foot-high elevated platform. The apparatus provides downward motion and oscillation to simulate an actual parachute jump. To make things more challenging for the student, the instructors have control of the SLT and can determine if they want to land him hard or soft. As one student rushes toward the ground, hands clinging to his harness, the instructor yells at him, "Hazard left!" and leans into the rope controlling the drop. He watches as the airborne trainee hits the ground, and he had better land in a manner to avoid the imaginary obstacle, or the "airborne sergeant" will have a few choice words for him and a number of pushups, too. During week two the student gets to ride the "tower." The tower is designed to give the student practice in controlling his parachute during the descent from 250 feet, and in executing a PLF upon landing. He will learn how to handle parachute malfunctions, and he will run.

Finally, week three, Jump Week. The potential SF trooper will perform five parachute jumps. First, an individual jump with a T-10B parachute. Next a mass exit with equipment and T-10B chute; then another individual exit with MC1-1B parachute and tactical assembly. His fourth jump will be a mass exit at night with a T-10B and tactical equipment. And finally the fifth jump is either an individual jump with an MV1-1B, or a mass jump with a T-10B parachute.

The United States Army's "Guide for Airborne Students" states, "Airborne training is a rite of passage for the warrior." Upon graduation he will be awarded the coveted Silver Wings and is now qualified as an airborne trooper.

Special Forces Assessment and Selection (SFAS)

What is SFAS? The purpose of SFAS is to identify soldiers who have the potential for Special Forces training. The career management

Adapt, Overcome, and Improvise is the hallmark of an SF soldier. The SF Commo Sergeant is instructed in numerous communications devices, from the basic Morse code to high-tech satellite communications. Here is an improvised radio antenna. It has been built with branches, 550 cord, spoons from a Meal Ready to Eat (MRE) and commo wire. It may seem crude, but it works. Want to be more creative? One ODA has practiced using a kite get an antenna aloft; now that is thinking outside the box!

field (CMF) 18 includes positions concerned with the employment of highly specialized elements to accomplish specifically directed missions in times of peace and war. Many of these missions are conducted at times when employment of conventional military forces is not feasible or is not considered in the best interests of the United States. Training for and participation in these missions is strenuous, somewhat hazardous, and often sensitive in nature. For these reasons it is a prerequisite that every prospective Special Forces soldier successfully complete the 24-day SFAS program. SFAS is conducted by the 1st Battalion, 1st SWTG(A) at Rowe Training Facility, Camp MacKall, approximately an hour's drive from Ft. Bragg.

The SFAS program assesses and selects soldiers for attendance at the Special Forces Qualification Course (SFQC). This program allows SF an opportunity to assess each soldier's capabilities by testing his physical, emotional, and mental stamina. SFAS also allows each soldier the opportunity to make a meaningful and educated decision about SF and his career plan. Any male soldier may volunteer for SFAS. A normal progression will see a number of RANGERs volunteer; however, a large portion comes from soldiers with varying MOSs.

Applicants volunteering for SFAS must meet the following criteria: male soldier in rank of E-4 to E-7; U.S. citizen with a high school diploma or GED (General Education Development certificate); airborne qualified, or a volunteer for airborne training (candidates not airborne qualified will be scheduled for airborne training at the completion of SFAS); able to swim 50 meters wearing boots and battle dress uniform (BDU); meeting Special Forces fitness standards; eligible for a "Secret" security clearance; and not a prior Airborne or SF voluntary terminee.

All candidates participate in a variety of activities designed to place them under various forms

of physical and mental stress. The training assesses potential and qualities through behavioral observation, and analysis of performance measures and recorded data. All tasks are performed with limited information and no performance feedback. What this means is no praise, no encouragement, no harassment; tasks are assigned and rated, period. SFAS assesses a candidate's potential for being independent, yet a team player and a leader. Instructors look for the soldiers to demonstrate the following individual attributes: motivation, accountability, maturity, stability, teamwork, intelligence, physical fitness and trustworthiness. Leadership traits include communications, influence, judgment, decisiveness, and responsibility.

The SFAS program has two phases. Phase one assesses physical fitness, motivations, and the ability to cope with stress. Activities during this phase include psychological tests, physical fitness and swim tests, runs, obstacle course, basic First Aid, land navigation, ruckmarches, and military orienteering exercises. An evaluation board meets after the first phase to determine which of the candidates will be allowed to continue the program. The second phase assesses leadership and teamwork skills. SFAS not only serves to select the proper soldier for Special Forces training, it screens out those individuals who are lacking the qualities and potential to complete training. Only those soldiers who have demonstrated the potential to complete Special Forces training successfully are allowed to continue. At the end of the 24 days, another board meets to select those soldiers who may attend the SFQC. Fewer than 50 percent of the soldiers that start SFAS are selected for Special Forces training.

After a soldier is selected through SFAS, he will return to his unit and wait for his slot in the SFQC. This process may take several months before the soldier will actually begin SF training. Those soldiers selected for MOS 18B (weapons) and MOS 18C (engineer) report directly to Ft. Bragg to begin their training. Soldiers selected for MOS 18E (communications) will first complete a course in Advance International Morse Code (AIMC) before attending the SFQC.

SFQC and SFDOQC (Special Forces Detachment Officer Qualification Course)

Each branch of service that produces special operations personnel has its own unique training. This specialized training not only emphasizes physical prowess and military skills, but also serves to bring about teamwork, unit cohesiveness, and esprit de corps. For the U.S. Air Force's Special Tactics Teams, it is accomplished with Indoctrination and the Pipeline; for the U.S. Navy SEALs it is achieved with BUD/S and "Hell Week." For the Special Forces soldier it is the "Q-Course."

The SFQC/SFDOQC teaches and develops the skills necessary for effective use of the SF soldier. Duties in CMF 18 primarily involve participation in Special Operations interrelated fields of unconventional warfare. These include foreign internal defense and direct action missions as part of a small operations team or ODA. Duties at other levels involve command, control, and support functions. Frequently, duties require regional orientation, including foreign language training and in-country experience. SF emphasizes not only unconventional tactics, but also knowledge of nations in waterborne, desert, jungle, mountain, or Arctic operations.

The CMF 18 is subdivided into five accession MOS: detachment commander -18A; SF weapons sergeant - 18B; SF engineer sergeant - 18C; SF medical sergeant - 18D; and SF communications sergeant - 18E. Each SF volunteer receives extensive training in a specialty, which prepares him for his future assignment in an SF unit. SF units are designed to operate either unilaterally or in support of and combined with native military and paramilitary forces. Levels of employment for Special Operations Forces include advising and assisting host governments, involvement in continental United States–based training, and direct participation in combat operations.

After successful completion of SFAS, officers who have not already attended their Advance Course will attend either the Infantry or Armor Officer Advance Course. For the enlisted soldier, the SFQC is currently divided into three phases. Phase I is Individual Skills, Phase II is MOS Qualification, and Phase III is Collective Training. The enlisted applicant's SFQC training will be scheduled upon successful completion of SFAS.

Phase I—Individual Skills

During this time, soldiers in process are trained on common skills for CMF 18, skill level three. Training is 40 days long and is taught at the Camp Rowe Training Facility. The training covered during this phase includes land navigation (cross-country) and small unit tactics. This phase culminates with a special operations overview.

Phase II—MOS (Military Operation Specialty) Qualification

For the enlisted soldier, the decision on which of the four specialties he will receive training in will be made based upon his background, aptitude, and desire, and the needs of Special Forces. Training for this phase is 65 days and culminates with a mission planning cycle. During this phase, soldiers are trained in their different specialties:

18A - SF detachment commander. Training includes teaching the officer student the planning and leadership skills he will need to direct and employ other members of his detachment. He will be trained in escape and recovery; infiltration (Infil) and extraction (Exfil) techniques; SF weapons, engineering, medical and communications skills; Military Decision Making Process, MDMP; terrain analysis; Direct Action; Special

Reconnaissance; Foreign Internal Defense; and Unconventional Warfare. Training is conducted at Fort Bragg, North Carolina, and is 24 weeks long. The culmination of this training is an FTX called the Troy Trek, held in the Pisgah National Forest or at Ft. A.P. Hill.

18B - SF weapons sergeant. Training includes learning the characteristics and capabilities of more than 89 types of U.S. and foreign light weapons—e.g., handguns, submachine guns, rifles, machine guns, mortars, anti-tank weapons, and man-portable air defense weapons. The trainee will learn range planning, tactics, indirect fire operations, weapons emplacement, and integrated combined arms fire control planning. He will learn how to teach marksmanship and the employment of weapons to others. Training is conducted at Fort Bragg, North Carolina, for 24 weeks.

18C - SF engineer sergeant. Training includes planning and constructing buildings, bridges, and field fortifications, as well as the use of demolitions for their destruction. The trainee learns how to read blueprints, as well as developing carpentry, electrician, and plumbing skills. Training also includes target analysis and demolitions techniques, including electric and non-electric firing systems. He will be taught the latest demolitions techniques and how to improvise with substitutes for ammunition and explosives. Training also includes land mine warfare and de-mining techniques. The program is conducted at Fort Bragg, North Carolina, for 24 weeks.

18D - SF medical sergeant. This course also includes U.S. Navy SEAL corpsmen, U.S. Army Ranger medics, and U.S. Air Force pararescuemen. The medical training is divided into two portions. First, trainees go through the Special Operations Combat Medic course (SOMC). Upon successful completion of this program, they move on to the more advanced Special Forces Medical Sergeants course.

At the SOMC, which lasts 24 weeks, the soldiers undergo a curriculum of concentrated medical training specifically designed for special operations medical personnel. They receive emergency medical technician-basic (EMT-B) and paramedic (EMT-P) training and certification. They also get certified by the American Heart Association in basic life support and advanced cardiac life support. SOMC training teaches students how to manage trauma patients prior to evacuation and provide them with medical treatment. This includes minor field surgery, pharmacology, combat trauma management, advanced airway treatment, and military evacuation procedures. Students will actually be assigned to hands-on patient care both in emergency and hospital settings as part of their training. This is conducted during a four-week assignment in one of the country's largest metropolitan areas, New York City.

The second major phase of this program is the Special Forces Medical Sergeants Course Training. This course provides skills in trauma management, infectious disease, cardiac care, life support, basic dentistry, basic Veterinary skills, X-ray, anesthesia, surgical procedures, team medical care, and indigenous population care. Training is conducted at the Joint Special Operations Medical Training Center located at Fort Bragg, North Carolina. Training takes approximately 57 weeks.

18E - SF communications sergeant. The purpose of this course is to train and qualify the SF soldier in the basic skills and knowledge required to perform duties as the SF communications sergeant on a Special Forces ODA. Training includes AIMC—encompassing instruction in radio telegraph procedures, military block printing, and exercises in transmitting and receiving Morse code; cryptographic systems; burst outstation systems; and common radios found throughout the Army. Students become familiar with antenna theory and radio wave propagation

continued on page 86

Just east of John F. Kennedy Hall, Fort Bragg, North Carolina, behind a tall fence topped with barbed wire, is the U.S. Army Joint Special Operations Medical Training Center (JSOMTC). Here, the 18-Deltas, or Special Forces Medics, learn their trade. This facility is responsible for the training of all enlisted medical personnel within the United States Special Operations Command. Over a decade in development, the JSOMTC is the result of an effort to create a single medical training facility for all Special Operations Forces (SOF) enlisted medical personnel. The JSOMTC was created for the centralized training of Special Forces medics, the Special Forces Medical Sergeants Course (SFMSC), and a new training program for all non-SF SOF medics, called the Special Operations Combat Medic Course (SOCM). With all SOF enlisted medical personnel now training at a single site, and with all becoming certified EMT-Paramedics, the level of medical training and of medical interoperability within SOF has been significantly enhanced.

According to LTC. Clifford Cloonan of JSOMTC, this Department of Defense (DOD) training center was established to consolidate and standardize medical training among all DOD SOF, while continuing a mission to provide first-class medical training to U.S. Army Special Forces (SF) medics (18D). Beginning in 1986, in an effort to consolidate enlisted medical training for all DOD SOF, the headquarters of the United States Special Operations Command (USSOCOM) and the U.S. Army Medical Department Center and School, began preliminary discussions on the feasibility of integrating Special Operations medical training in a single facility at Fort Bragg, North Carolina. The training of Special Forces medics had formerly been divided between programs at

Fort Sam Houston and Fort Bragg and there existed no specialized advanced medical training for non-SF special operations medics, e.g. Rangers, SEALS, and USAF Para-rescue. In 1996 the JSOMTC was open for business.

The expected benefits were improved training for non-SF SOF medical personnel (who were formerly trained only to the conventional force standard), reduced training costs, and standardization of all SOF medical training leading to enhanced interoperability. Early in the process of designing the joint SOF medic training program to be taught at this new facility, it was decided that training and certification as a paramedic to National Registry EMT-Paramedic standards would be an integral and requisite part of the course.

This new training center uses the latest training techniques and technological advances to impart medical skills and knowledge to SOF medical personnel. The JSOMTC is designed to support the training of multiple classes simultaneously. Located on 9.6 acres of land, the 74,000-square-foot main building houses the offices, classrooms, and ancillary facilities necessary to support training. There are 17 large and small classrooms available for small group sessions and lecture, the largest of these capable of seating 200 students. Additionally, there are more than two acres of enclosed woodlands on the grounds of the JSOMTC to support training in simulated field environments.

A barracks facility constructed near the JSOMTC houses 140 single and unaccompanied students and an identical barracks is currently under construction immediately adjacent to the existing barracks. Upon completion of the second barracks all single and unaccompanied students will reside within immediate proximity to the JSOMTC.

A host of other facilities dedicated to instruction for the SF & SOF medical specialist are located within the JSOMTC. Ten operative procedure rooms modeled after modern hospital operating rooms are equipped for instruction in surgical techniques. Two 800-square-foot laboratory classrooms are available for student instruction and can accommodate up to 48 students each. These laboratories would be the envy of contemporary university facilities, each having a five-headed microscope with mounted digital camera. A modern anatomy and physiology teaching laboratory is well equipped for instruction. A dedicated x-ray suite is available for teaching radiological techniques with field x-ray equipment. These specialized areas are supported by a large medical logistics division complete with instrument sterilization equipment and supply storage areas. Between five and eight cadaver specimens are available for each class through arrangement with a local university. In addition to the "specimens," JSOMTC has a state-of-the-art patient simulator. This sophisticated computer patient can be programmed with an assortment of maladies that the student must identify and treat properly. It simulates all the correct body responses—eyes dilate, chest rises and falls, it can be intubated, IVs can be administered to it, or it can be charged "back to life."

Funding obtained from USSOCOM in 1998 allowed for the creation, within the JSOMTC, of an SOF-focused medical library and a student computer lab. The JSOMTC currently has holdings of more than 700 titles covering a wide range of topics of relevance to SOF medicine. In addition to books, the library subscribes to a variety of medical journals of SOF relevance, and has videotapes that can be viewed in the library. The 1,300-square-foot library allows for approximately 40 patrons to sit and study. Students can facilitate their learning on interactive CDs and via the Internet at 44 state-of-the-art computer work stations located in the library and in a separate computer lab. Access to MEDLINE and other full-text databases allows patrons to read the latest journals in the field and search for relevant articles of interest.

Special Forces medical specialists often have to deal with animals of the region. For this purpose there is also a 9,000-square-foot veterinary facility that supports veterinary and medical skills training. Complete with automated feeding equipment and air exchange mechanisms, this facility incorporates the newest animal care provisions and emulates the finest facilities of this type in the country. The latest in computer, electronic, and fiber optic technology has been incorporated into the design of the JSOMTC.

Instruction at the JSOMTC is provided by a skilled and experienced group of permanently assigned officers and enlisted personnel from all branches of the military. Dean of the JSOMTC is a colonel army physician with a special operations background. The Navy and the Air Force each provide an assistant dean with medical, educational, and special operations training and experience. Day-to-day operation of the facility is the responsibility of the Special Operations Medical Training Battalion, which is commanded by a lieutenant colonel Special Forces branch officer. Included in the staff are officers selected for their professional expertise and special operations experience from the Medical, Dental, Veterinary, Nursing, and Physician Assistant branches. Enlisted instructors are assigned from SOF in the Army, Navy, and Air Force. Enlisted technicians specializing in pharmacy, radiology, laboratory diagnostics, surgery, animal care, and logistics and personnel management provide additional support. A group of civilian employees with backgrounds in education, personnel management, information management, and pre-hospital emergency medical care complete the staff of the JSOMTC.

U.S. Army Special Forces students attend the 46-week Special Forces Medical Sergeants (SFMS) course, which is Phase II of a three-phase, 58-week-long Special Forces Qualification Course conducted at Ft. Bragg. Students in this course must successfully complete the 24-week SOCM curriculum before continuing on for an additional 22 weeks of specialized training in medical, surgical, dental, veterinary, and preventive medicine subjects. Upon completion of this course, students are qualified to function as independent health care providers. USN personnel qualified for this advanced training attend a similar course of instruction at the JSOMTC, known as the Advanced Special Operations Combat Medic course (ADSOCM), which is also 22 weeks in length. Upon completion of this course, the Navy awards these students the title of Independent Duty Corpsman (IDC).

Joint Special Operations Medical Training Center, Ft. Bragg, North Carolina.

In addition to the four weeks of clinical training provided during the SOCM portion of their training, U.S. Army SFMS and USN ADSOCM students receive another four weeks of clinical experience (called Special Operations Clinical Training, or SOCT) at selected military health care facilities throughout the eastern and central United States. During this rotation, the students will perform ride-alongs with city EMS units and serve in the emergency rooms of various metropolitan hospitals.

The JSOMTC participates in the continuing medical education or medical sustenance training of SOF medical personnel in numerous ways. Qualified Special Forces Medical sergeants receive two weeks of medical instruction at the JSOMTC as part of their Advanced Non-Commissioned Officers Course. Advanced Cardiac Life Support Instructor certification is available to qualified personnel through JSOMTC-taught instruction. Qualified SOF medical personnel may also attend Advanced Trauma Life Support courses that are conducted periodically by the Defense Medical Readiness Training Institute using JSOMTC facilities. In addition, a number of initiatives are being pursued that will provide JSOMTC instruction via distance learning to SOF medical personnel worldwide. In the near future, SOF personnel will be able to continue their medical education or receive support in the field by logging on to a JSOMTC World Wide Web home page via the Internet.

Currently, the JSOMTC is tasked with the execution of two complete courses of instruction, the SFMS, and the SOCM. Also provided is instruction for two modular courses, the USAF EMT-I course for Air Force Pararescue (PJs) not assigned to a special operations unit, and the USN ADSOCM for senior SEAL corpsmen. In addition, portions of two other Special Warfare Center and School Courses, the 18D Special Forces Medic Advanced Non-Commissioned Officer Course and the Special Forces officer orientation course, are also taught at the JSOMTC.

and learn how to teach these skills to others. They will be taught how to install, operate, and maintain FM, AM, HF, VHF, UHF, and SHF communications in voice, continuous wave, and burst radio nets, and learn SF communication operations procedures and techniques. Training culminates with an around-the-world communications field training exercise called Maxgain. Training is conducted at Ft. Bragg, North Carolina, and Camp Gruber, Oklahoma, and lasts 32 weeks.

Phase III - Collective Training

The third and final phase of the SFQC is a 38-day training period conducted at Camp MacKall. Soldiers are instructed in Special Operations, Direct Action, Isolation, Mission Planning, Air Operations (LZ/DZ, MPU, Resupply), and Unconventional Warfare (UW) training. In collective training all the instruction, hard work, and preparation come together. This field training exercise combines and strengthens both the specialty training and common skills. Soldiers from each of the SF skills areas and a detachment commander will put their training to the test. Approximately 160–170 students form 10–12 "A-teams," or ODAs. These ODAs will vary in size ranging from as few as eight to as many as 15 students.

The ODAs will be deployed as separate teams throughout the Uwaharrie National Forest for a UW exercise. Each of the ODAs will have a Training Group cadre member who will be their evaluator for their "final exam." This exercise comes complete with some 120 opposing force (Op Force) soldiers, a guerrilla force (Gs) numbering around 200, and a civilian auxiliary. The students will have to work with the guerrilla force just as they would in a real-world situation. While the SF and Gs are learning to deal with each other, they are being hunted and often attacked by OpForce troopers. This exercise will last for two weeks and is known as Robin Sage.

Robin Sage

The Robin Sage exercise takes place in the fictional country of Pineland on the continent of Atlantica, located in the Atlantic Ocean between America and Europe. Surrounding Pineland are OpForLand, DozerLand, and NeutraState. Pineland is of strategic importance to the United States. For this reason, members of the 9th Special Forces Group (Airborne), also a fictitious unit, have been tasked to provide military assistance. The guerrilla forces have been fighting for some time. The ODA-914 of 9th Group will be sent in to establish a link with these forces and train them in UW techniques.

Depending on their mission profiles, the student ODAs will be inserted by helicopter, parachute, boat, or truck. Regardless of how the team infils, it will ultimately be humping a ruck through some of the roughest terrain in the state of North Carolina, that is, Pineland.

After a day or two, depending on the scenario and how good the team is, the men will make contact with the guerrilla force. If they thought humping an 80–100 pound rucksack for a day or so was rough, it's nothing compared to the task ahead, meeting the guerrilla chief.

The G chief is played by an experienced SF soldier, usually a senior NCO, or perhaps a retired SF soldier brought in to test the mettle of these students who seek to join their ranks. These people know their business and will not spare the fledgling team, or their detachment commander. Whereas the Navy Seals' BUD/S "Hell Week" involves a week of sleep deprivation and 90 percent physical effort, Robin Sage is a thinking man's game.

The ODAs will meet and have to deal with a number of different scenarios and the G's. During their initial meeting, the guerrillas and their leaders are instructed to give the A-team a hard time, to be aloof, stand-offish, perhaps even a little hostile or threatening. One guerrilla comments to

Phase III—Robin Sage. Here is where all the training comes together. The SF students are matched up into functional A–teams, or ODAs, and sent into Pineland. Here they will put to use the skills set they have learned, and discover whether they have what it takes to wear the green beret.

the student, "We have been fighting for years. How much combat do you have? None? How can you tell me how to fight?" One of the G chiefs does not like officers, so he will only deal with the senior NCO of the team. This throws a definite curve to the team and can be unsettling to a detachment commander with too big an ego. When another team meets the G's, the chief's right-hand man is not happy with the situation and tries to convince the ODA to overthrow the chief. These are the types of mind games the G chief and the Gs will force upon the team—and some of these G's take this role-playing very seriously. This sense of realism adds to the intensity of the exercise, and an ODA only has to spend a few days in the base camp before beginning to believe that he really is in Pineland.

Time is a factor, however, since Robin Sage lasts only two weeks. Unless the team really

The team leader of ODA914 converses with the resident guerrilla chief. The G Chief is played by an SF sergeant with many years of experience under his belt. He will ensure that the young captain and his team receive the "Pineland" experience.

Five-Star accommodations, à la SF. While running the Phase III-Robin Sage exercise, this is about as good as it gets—a poncho on the ground and one hanging overhead. "Hey, where is the concierge? My MRE is cold!"

messes up, the Gs will eventually warm to them. Now the team will place into action what they have learned. The weapons specialist will teach the guerrillas how to establish a defensive perimeter around the base camp, the medics will teach hygiene and first aid. The engineers will teach the Gs how to build, and how to take down a target with a very large boom, while the commo specialist provides instruction on radio equipment and procedures. The trainees teach the guerillas small unit tactics, raids, and ambushes. By teaching and doing, the students will learn the hallmarks of a successful raid: Surprise, Speed, and Violence of Action.

Slowly the Gs will evolve from a ragtag bunch of individuals into an organized fighting force. Missions will be planned and executed, all under the watchful eye of the Training Group evaluator. This evaluator is a cadre member of the 1st Special Warfare Training Groups (Airborne). After one such mission, an assault on an OpForce position, the evaluator will sit down with the student and go over his performance. Did you perform the proper Warning Order? It's 98 degrees out here, why didn't you instruct your squad to carry more water? Did you do a recon of the target? Why didn't you wear any face camo? Did you have an alternate plan if you got compromised?

Q-Course student goes over a mission plan with one of the Gs. The hallmarks of a successful raid are surprise, speed, and violence of action on the target. The prospective SF soldier will explain these traits to this guerrilla prior to an assault.

On and on the questions go, and the evaluator will mark the progress or lack of progress of a student. All of these evaluations will go into a leadership assessment that will be used to determine whether the student has what it takes to be a member of the Special Forces.

Trainees must also respect and employ the skills of others on the "island." The OpForce includes soldiers from active military units who have been tasked to assault or engage the team from time to time. The Gs usually possess a modest form of infantry skills, as well as those of clerks, cooks, truck drivers, and so on. The third group who makes up the population of Pineland

During the two weeks of Robin Sage, the SF students get numerous opportunities to apply their skills and exercise their talents. Here a medical sergeant student administers an IV to one of the Gs suffering from heat exhaustion.

89

Engineer Sergeant student Joe Ferris prepares timing fuses for a future mission. Note that in training, as in combat, his M4A1 carbine is close by, should the need arise. Even in the relative safety of the G Camp, the SF students may come under attack from the OpForce troops at any time.

are the Auxiliary. These are civilian players who for the most part remain anonymous. They offer their homes or barns as "safe houses" for the ODA and Gs; they may provide transportation for a mission, or perhaps bring in some good old home cooking for the freedom fighters of Pineland. Along with the G's supporters, there are those who support the OpForce—e.g., the local sheriff may see the unfamiliar face of an ODA member surveying a target, and lock him up. These local people of the Auxiliary have been assisting in the Robin Sage exercise since the 1960s; indeed, they add a sense of realism to missions.

The exercise ends with a final mission: The ODA has trained the Gs, and they now take on an OpForce target. At this point, Robin Sage is over. The teams will return to Camp MacKall, clean their weapons, gear, and themselves, and await the results of the exercise.

As the evaluations come in, the students are notified whether they have passed or failed the Q-Course. Depending on the recommendation of the evaluators and cadre, a student who does not pass may be recycled for another chance, or he may be dropped. Those who are dropped are sent back to their units.

According the mission brief of the 1st SWTG(A), the soldier who passes will, "Thrive on ambiguity and uncertainty. Think the unconventional and dare the uncommon. Overcome obstacles and persevere when others fail. Adapt to his surroundings and anticipate changes. [He is] physically rugged, morally straight and thoroughly lethal. Triumphs through genius as well as force of arms. [And] immerses himself in the art, science and history of war." Those soldiers who have made it through the course will become members of the U.S. Army Special Forces. They will attend a regimental dinner where they will receive the Special Forces tab, and the coveted green beret. The following day will be the official graduation ceremony from the Q-Course.

Throughout the two weeks of the Robin Sage exercise, the student ODAs will be evaluated on every nuance of their training. Here a Pineland evaluator writes up an "eval" of one of the students following a raid on an OpFor installation.

Every SF Soldier goes through language training. Here members of the 7th Special Forces Group (Airborne) are studying Spanish. Their instructor, who may be from Mexico or South America, is a native speaker. SF soldiers may also learn via computer self-paced training, and from members of the ODA.

The training does not stop here. One of the qualifications of the Special Forces since its inception was that the soldier be conversant in a foreign language. Our newly "tabbed" soldier will now attend language training. Depending on which SF group the soldier will be assigned to, he will be trained in Spanish, French, Portuguese, German, Czech, Polish, Russian, Persian-Farsi, Tagalog, Thai, Vietnamese, Korean, or Modern Standard Arabic.

This training ranges from 17 to 23 weeks, depending on the language. The training stresses basic communications skills with an emphasis on military terminology. Language skills are taught by an instructor indigenous to that country—e.g., the Thai instructor is from Thailand, and the Russian teacher is from Russia, and so on. This assists the SF troops not only in the language, but also with dialects, as well as customs of the country. Each of the Special Forces Groups will also have a language lab for follow-up training.

The next step for the new Green Beret is going to SERE (Survival, Escape, Resistance, and Evasion) School. An SF soldier, or ODA, may be deployed to any location in the world. It may be in the middle of the desert or the side of a mountain; it may range from the extreme heat of the jungle or the frigid cold of subarctic

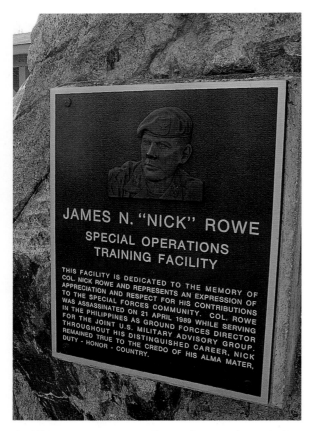

On 8 February 1990, the Rowe Training Facility at Camp MacKall was dedicated in honor of Colonel James N. "Nick" Rowe. Colonel Rowe had survived as a prisoner of war in Vietnam for a period of five years, until he managed to escape from his captors. Colonel Rowe was killed in the Philippines during his tour as senior adviser to that country.

lines; and it is not outside the realm of possibility that he will be captured. The SERE School was developed for these reasons and is mandatory training for all SF soldiers. The school is located at the Colonel Nick Rowe Training Facility, at Camp MacKall. Here, members of Company A, 1st SWTG(A), will impart their survival skills to the students.

The key word for the course is S-U-R-V-I-V-A-L. The students will learn that each of these letters represents a technique. By learning all eight of the skills, they will afford themselves a greater chance of staying alive and returning to base. The eight skills are as follows: S: Size up the situation (the surroundings, your physical condition, equipment); U: Undue haste makes waste; R: Remember where you are; V: Vanquish fear and panic; I: Improvise; V: Value living; A: Act like the natives; and L: Live by your wits (or for the new students, L: Learn basic skills). Put them all together and they spell SURVIVAL, the difference between life and death.

The objective of the course is "to provide students with an understanding of what to expect if captured; explain the Code of Conduct and provide a clear understanding of what is expected of them should they become a prisoner of war (POW); prepare the student to survive in unique and adverse conditions, and to evade the enemy; teach resistance to exploitation by the enemy if captured, and to escape captivity and return home with honor." The SERE course lasts 19 days, ending in an evasion exercise that will expose the SF soldier to increased levels of physical and mental pressure, testing their endurance as well as their resolve. During this course, students will also receive instruction in hand-to-hand combat and sentry take-down techniques. Upon successful completion of the course, the students go through a critique and graduation. At this point the SF soldier will head off to his appropriate group as a new member of an ODA.

regions. Most of the time the team will be working together, and will draw on each other's strengths. There may be times, however, when an SF member could find himself alone, with little or no personal equipment. Due to the very nature of the Special Forces missions, it is very likely he will find himself behind enemy

Warrant Officer Technical Certification Course

The 1st SWTG(A) also teaches the Special Operation Warrant Officer Technical Certification course. The training provides for growth within the SF organization, as it draws from senior Special Forces NCOs. The experienced sergeants, who will have already taken the Army's basic warrant officer program, will receive additional training in special operation command structure, missions, mission preparations, doctrine, SERE, UW classes, isolation, and briefbacks. The training duration is 19 weeks, and culminates with a field training exercise (FTX), Mystic Watchman. Those soldiers graduating from this program are commissioned as warrant officers and go on to serve as the executive officer on an SF ODA.

Advanced Special Forces Skills

Training for the Special Forces soldier never ends. While he continues to hone the skills learned during the Q-course, he will also receive additional training in a variety of techniques to assist him in executing his mission with the greatest probability of success.

Military Free Fall (MFF)

Further airborne infiltration training is available to SF soldiers through the U.S. Army Military Freefall Parachutist School at Ft. Bragg, North Carolina. The mission of the school is to train personnel in the science of HALO (High Altitude Low Opening) military free-fall parachuting, using the Ram-Air Parachute System (RAPS). MFF parachuting enables the theater commander to infiltrate an SF team into an area that would prohibit the use of static-line parachute operations. Special operations missions require rapid and covert infiltration into operational areas.

During week one of this course, the future SF troopers will go through the normal in-processing

High Altitude Low Opening (HALO) and High Altitude High Opening (HAHO) techniques are taught to those SF members who are assigned to a HALO team. Here a member of the 7th Special Forces Group (Airborne) floats down to earth on the Ram-Air Parachute System (RAPS). This jumper is prepared to drop his rucksack, which is suspended by webbing straps. Note the M4A1 carbine tucked along his left side.

and be issued their equipment. At this time they will be assigned to a HALO instructor who will remain with them throughout the four-week training cycle. It is also during week one that they will be matched up with a "jump buddy." Their "buddy" will be approximately the same weight and height, so they will fall at the same rate.

In ground school they will learn about the ram air parachutes, substantially different from the usual T-10B or MCI-1B that they jumped with at Basic Airborne School. The MC-5 ram air parachutes are rectangular shaped as opposed to circular, and are extremely maneuverable. Course students learn about equipment, rigging, and repacking the parachutes. They also learn special jump commands, as well as use of the oxygen systems employed in high altitude jumping.

In case of trouble, the course also teaches emergency procedures involving parachute malfunctions, cutaways, entanglements, and how to recover. These exercises are run over and over until they become second nature to the jumpers. Falling at a rate of over 180 feet per second, you do not have the luxury of thinking about the problem—you must react.

During week one, the candidate spends time in the Military Free Fall Simulator Facility. Completed at Ft. Bragg in 1992 at a cost of $5 million, this 11,000-square-foot facility contains an enclosed vertical wind tunnel, 32 student classrooms, an operator control room, and communications and equipment rooms. "This facility is a marked improvement," says Carol Darby of the Special Warfare School. "Prior to having the facility, the students had to practice [body stabilization] by lying on table tops."

The simulator is approximately 18 feet high and 14 feet in diameter, and it can support two jumpers with equipment up to 375 pounds each. The simulator's fan generates winds up to 132 miles per hour. Suspended in a column of air, the students will learn and practice body-stabilization techniques. The wind tunnel will simulate the effects of free-falling at a speed of approximately 200 feet per second.

After they complete ground week, the students will travel to Yuma Proving Grounds, Arizona. Weeks two through five will find our candidates jumping, jumping, and jumping again, beginning at 10,000 feet with no equipment, and working up to 25,000 feet with full equipment load and oxygen system. The course provides in-the-air instruction, where the student will concentrate on stability, aerial maneuvers and parachute-deployment procedures. Each student will receive a minimum of 16 free fall jumps, which include two day and two night jumps with oxygen and full field equipment.

SCUBA Training

U.S. Army Combat Divers School is in Key West, Florida. At this location, our man will learn to use SCUBA gear to stealthily infiltrate his target area. This training is essential to the SF teams, since they may be asked to infiltrate into denied territory via underwater methods. Unlike U.S. Navy SEALs operations, for the most part Special Forces missions do not take place in the water. The water is merely a means of infiltration and/or transportation to their deployment or objective.

Training will include waterborne operations both day and night. Students will be taught ocean subsurface navigation, deep diving techniques, marine hazards, how to read tides, waves, and currents. They will also be instructed in the proper procedures of submarine lock-in and lock-out, the method of entering and exiting a submerged sub. Training in both open-circuit and closed-circuit equipment will be taught. This is no recreation diving, as depths in training go down to 120 feet under diverse operating conditions.

This training phase will last four weeks. Week one begins with PT, and further physical conditioning to get the trainee prepared for the balance of the class. Week two will find the trooper in the water receiving training to build up his confidence and strengthen his swimming. In week three, students will dive, dive, and then dive some more.

In the final week each student will perform an underwater compass swim. It is not sufficient

Some SF soldiers are trained on SCUBA (Self-contained underwater breathing apparatus) techniques. When necessary for an over-the-horizon insertion, the SF may use LAR-V rebreathers or open circuit systems. This combat swimmer has come ashore to perform a beach recon prior to bringing the balance of the team onto the shore.

to just know how to SCUBA dive; he must be able to execute his mission via underwater ingress. Equipped with a compass board, SCUBA tank, weapon, and rucksack, he will carry out an infiltration to a point on the beach. Final week brings more night dives, a Field Training Exercise, and graduation.

Special Operation Target Interdiction Course (SOTIC)

The SOTIC, as explained by Major Kimm Rowe, commander Company D, 2nd Battalion 1st SWTG(A), "trains SF personnel in the technical skills and operational procedures necessary to deliver precision rifle fire from concealed positions to selected targets in support of special operations forces missions." This is also known as sniper training. SOTIC students all volunteer for this training. They must have a rating of expert with their weapon, pass a number of psychological evaluations, and have Secret clearance. SOTIC is a Level 1 category course for Special Forces and Rangers. This means those who graduate from the course are qualified to instruct U.S. troops, train soldiers from foreign nations, and shoot at close proximity to U.S. troops and noncombatants. What that means in simple terms is that a SOTIC sniper can drop an enemy if he is standing right next to you.

The class has a ratio of one SOTIC instructor for every four students, and the students learn the ins and outs of the M24 Sniper Weapon System (SWS), a bolt-action, single-shot rifle chambered in 7.52mm x 51mm; the Leuopold Mark IV M3A 10 power rifle scope; XM144 15x-45x spotting scope; and M19/22 binoculars. They will familiarize themselves with the Soviet SVD 7.62mm x 39mm, the Barrett M82A1, 50 caliber, the Stoner SR25, 7.62mm x 51mm and various other U.S. and foreign sniper weapons. They will also receive training in the use of night vision devices, and in the technique and creation of the ghillie suit.

The ghillie suit is a camouflage suit that is used to break up the outline of the sniper. There are a number of options and it often boils down simply to personal preference. The two most common versions, however, are the one-piece, made from a flight suit, and the two-piece BDU version with separate shirt and trousers. The student sews netting onto the clothing, attaches various lengths

SF soldiers may also attend the Special Operations Target Interdiction Course (SOTIC) at Ft. Bragg, North Carolina. SOTIC, better known as sniper training, is the best the U.S. military has to offer. SOTIC is a Level 1 category course for Special Forces and Rangers. Level 1 means, in simple terms, that an SOTIC sniper can drop an enemy if he is standing right next to you.

of burlap to the netting, and then strip by strip shreds the burlap until the outline of the uniform has vanished. A "boonie hat" is often given the same treatment to break up the silhouette of the sniper's head, and then is used for concealment once in position. Vegetation is often added to the burlap for further camouflage. The instructors at the SOTIC favor a mix of 30 percent burlap strips and 70 percent vegetation, which is stuffed into the netting and held in place by rubber bands. One of the SOTIC instructors explains, "By using the local vegetation, the sniper will blend into his surroundings." Students also learn to adjust the foliage in the suit as they move from one position to the next to remain invisible.

During one of the stalking phases, the student-sniper must get to within 200 meters of the spotters. These spotters are SOTIC instructors with ranger finders and binoculars who scan the woodline for the students as they stealthily approach. When the student has reached his position and is confident he has not been sighted, he will fire a blank round. The instructor will call in one of the "walkers" who are out in the brush. They are there to tag the student out if he is spotted. SOTIC instructor, SFC George Simmons, radios to the walker, "Move three feet to your left . . . sniper there." The walker, who knows where the snipers are but does not tell the spotters, responds that he is not within three feet of the sniper who has just fired. Sergeant Simmons then holds up a white card with a number on it. Radio contact is again established with the walker, "Have the student ID the card." The walker responds that the student correctly identifies the number "7." Having moved into position without being sighted, the student is allowed to take a second shot. This time the instructors are looking for telltale signs of a sniper—things like the muzzle blast of the weapon, or the movement of the foliage as the shot is taken. If it's a nada, zip, zero, this student has done well and gets a passing score for the stalk.

During this six-week course, 24 students will be taught the skills of advanced rifle marksmanship, sniper marksmanship, field shooting, field craft, judging distance, observation techniques, camouflage, stalking, counter stalking, and airborne insertion. In the final exercise, the students jump in, move over land, and take a final shot. In a third of the scenarios, they must make a first round hit, or else they don't graduate. Those who do graduate will return to their ODA where they will take up their position as one of two snipers on the team.

Special Operation Training (SOT)

The SOT course was formed back in the late 1970s. SOT trains SOF solders in the tactics, techniques, and procedures required to conduct direct action and unilateral special operations that are of limited scope and duration. SOT also develops the precision marksmanship needed in the MOUT (Military Operations in Urban Terrain) environment. According to Major Rowe, "The real intent for SOT is to train somewhat organic teams together, thus strengthening team cohesion."

Training emphasis is on advanced marksmanship, ballistic and mechanical breaching, limited explosive breaching, building climbing and rappelling, and Close Quarters Battle (CQB)

in various building environments, culminating in a 24-hour FTX.

SFARTAETC

This is the third course carried out by the instructors of Company D, 2nd battalion, 1st SWTG(A).

This rather long abbreviation stands for Special Forces Advance Reconnaissance, Target Analysis, and Exploitation Techniques Course. Although the course is highly classified, the unclassified description states that "SFARTAETC provides the basic entry level training in the tactics, techniques, and procedures needed by personnel being assigned to a theater CinCs in extremis force (CIF).

Special Forces Advance Reconnaissance, Target Analysis, and Exploitation Techniques Course (SFARTAETC). SFARTAETC provides the basic entry-level training in the tactics, techniques, and procedures needed by personnel being assigned to a theater. These skills include precision marksmanship, integrated CQB, and interpretability with other specifically designated forces.

These skills include: precision marksmanship, integrated CQB, and interpretability with other specifically designated forces."

This eight-week course is a counterterrorism (CT) type of CQB usually involving a hostage, POW, or similar situation. Training will also encompass engaging linear targets. Training emphasizes advanced marksmanship, close proximity shooting; ballistic mechanical and explosive breaching techniques for doors, windows, and walls; building-climbing and -rappelling procedures; fast rope techniques; CQB in multi-team and multi-breach points along with multi-story and multi-building environments; and interoperability techniques. Weapons training includes the M4A1 carbine with Aimpoint and tactical light systems, M9 pistol with tactical light, HK MP5, Remington 870 breaching shotgun, ballistic protection, breaching devices, night vision devices, M155 & MK141 flash bangs, fast rope, and climbing equipment.

SFAUC

Special Forces Advanced Urban Combat (SFAUC) was developed by the U.S. Army Special Forces Command in response to the ever-increasing number of urban operations confronting the SF soldier. The driving force behind the program is Major General William Boykin, who had been in charge of the SF Command until March of 2000, when he assumed command of the Special Warfare Center and School.

The general is very familiar with the cost of urban combat on special operations forces, as he was the commander of 1st Special Operations Detachment - Delta in October 1993. It was during this time that Task Force Ranger, the 160th SOAR(A), and Delta Force were engaged in a firefight for their lives in the streets of Mogadishu, Somalia.

General Boykin initiated the SFAUC program in May 1999 with a plan to have every SF soldier

trained in the three-week session. Each of the SF groups are responsible to disseminate these techniques and procedures to their ODAs. Major Richard Steiner, Operations Officer, 2nd Battalion, 3rd Special Forces Group (Airborne) explains, "The intent of Special Forces Advanced Urban Combat is to improve Special Forces soldiers' already formidable skills in CQB, especially as it concerns direct action missions, raids and ambushes—and especially as they apply to conducting direct action missions in an urban environment." The world is urbanizing, the population is becoming more and more dense, and SF must be able to operate in that environment. According to Major Steiner, "National Command Authority assumes when they commit Special Operations Forces in general and Special Forces in particular they're getting soldiers that can apply lethal force with a high degree of precision. SFAUC is not necessarily for hostage rescue, rather to pick an enemy out and engage that enemy without a number of unwanted casualties or unwanted collateral damage. SFAUC may be applied in the force protection arena. Where zero U.S. casualties in peacetime or in combat is the goal, then SF must be dominant in CQB tactics. This would include during a DA or even in a SR mission, anywhere in the world. He will have the capability of doing that in a dominating way while still maintaining the precision of U.S. SOF."

SFAUC is operations in urban terrain, involving engaging only hostile or theater enemy forces, sophisticated shooting techniques, identifying the target and engaging, breaching and entering buildings. The SF soldier is trained for every contingency, from bamboo huts to reinforced steel doors—get in and leave the building standing. This is contrary to the Russians' approach: One only has to look at Chechnya to see how they define urban combat—lots of rubble, not very precise.

SFAUC is taught in three phases. Phase I is Combat Marksmanship, advanced shooting skills

As the world urbanizes and the population becomes more dense, the SF soldiers must be able to operate in that environment. SFAUC—Special Forces Advanced Urban Combat—is operations in urban terrain. The skills taught involve engaging only hostile or theater enemy forces, sophisticated shooting techniques, identifying the target and engaging, breaching, and entering buildings. The U.S. Army Special Forces continually hone these skills to ensure they remain the premier special operations fighting force.

with the M4A1 carbine and the M-9 pistol. Targets are engaged from 0 to 50 meters—single targets, multiple targets, from the prone, kneeling, and standing positions. Targets are engaged head-on and laterally and in depth. During this time the soldier will undergo stress firing, 2-1/2 minutes to ID and engage 20–25 targets in various scenarios. He will also face pop-up targets, reactive, and non-reactive targets, from 3–25 meters. He will fire and reload using his primary weapon (M4A1) and secondary weapon (M-9).

Phase II covers Breaching/CQB. Mechanical breaching involves the use of sledge hammers, battering rams, crowbars, and glass and bolt cutters.

Ballistic breaching is using a shotgun with a variety of ammunition, such as #9 bird shot and "shock locks" and other specialty ammo to defeat a door, primarily the locking mechanism. Explosive breaching covers a diverse selection of explosives and techniques—flex linear charge, det-cord, C-4. A favorite is the silhouette charge—a cardboard silhouette with one to three wraps of det-cord around the perimeter, with a charge to the center does a good job of cutting through a door. Replace the det-cord with the proper amount of C-4 and the silhouette will now blow out a substantial passageway through a cinder block wall. Assorted initiators are also taught for instant detonation.

Phase III is CQB. During this phase the SF will be trained in and practice single-man, two-man, and four-man entry into a room, engaging targets, and collapsing on their sector. They will learn how to "stack," which is lining up for dynamic entry into a room or building. The SF soldiers will conduct a breach, enter the building, clear the room, secure the structure; if on a DA mission, they will recover personnel or equipment, or destroy the target, and clear the structure.

While each mission will vary, the standard deployment for SF CQB is the four-man entry team. From the time the team members initiate the breach, enter the room, collapse and secure their sector, finally clearing the room, it will take an average of four seconds.

The SF primary weapon for SFAUC training is the M-4 carbine. Choice of scopes range from standard iron sight, ACOG 4x scope, Aimpoint with red dot, or ACOG Reflex sight—the latter two are used with both eyes open. Additionally the M-4 carbine may be fitted with a white light that has a pressure on/off switch. It may be used for securing an individual, or searching a room once secure. The SFAUC troops may choose a more stealthy approach and go in with weapons suppressed. Major Steiner says, "Since the 5.56mm round is supersonic, you will hear the bang. What the suppressor does for you is buy you some time while the bad guys are trying to figure out, 'what was that?' 'Where did it come from?' By the time they figure out what is going on, you should be in dominance of the situation." Suppressors will also keep the muzzle blast to a minimum, assisting the entry team in situation awareness.

Weapons are not the only edge the SFAUC Green Beret has in his kit. Currently the SF ODAs are looking at a new headgear for CQB, a combination Kevlar and communications helmet. In the meantime, they will continue to train with the current Kevlars. During the three-week session, with an average of 36 students, the SFAUC course will expend more than 75,000 rounds of 5.56mm ball, 75,000 rounds of 9mm ball, 15,000 rounds of simmunitions (simulated munitions, using a plastic bullet), and hundreds of 12 gauge assorted loads.

There is a reason for the amount of ammunition used. Some would call it "muscle-memory," in which the body automatically brings the weapon up to the ready. Others called it automatic response. Whatever term you choose, SFAUC trains the SF soldier in the fundamentals of sight alignment and trigger control. Once you can reflexively apply those two skills, you will get hits, whether you are standing on the corner, sitting in a HUMMV, or jogging down the street. The SF soldier is taught to neutralize the hostile until he is no longer a threat.

SFAUC is about engaging hostiles in a DA or SR mission. This is not intended to replace the training for hostage rescue. The techniques and procedures taught in this course will aid the SF soldier as he takes down a radar installation or command post, recovers equipment, or deals with guards. SF takes weapons skills so seriously that there are four "shooting houses" on Ft. Bragg alone. Major Tom McCollum, SF Command, relates, "These guys are just about artists at their profession. The training is repetitive, and you build on those skills. Then you begin to use your imagination, to think outside of the box: What if . . . ? Suppose we do this . . . ? Then you build in the contingencies for the what-ifs."

All of the training, and the acclimation of that training, is the reason the SF soldiers are in constant demand around the globe. Their advanced training is what makes them the Quiet Professionals within the U.S. military, and provides the expertise that makes the Special Forces soldiers the most lethal warriors on earth.

Equipment and Techniques

Special Forces soldiers are schooled in unconventional techniques and procedures that will prove beneficial to their missions. The communications sergeant is capable of rigging up a radio antenna with some branches, 550 cord and Meal Ready to Eat (MRE) spoons. The engineer sergeant, with items from under the kitchen sink, can construct an explosive devise to take out a target, while the weapons sergeant is able to assemble an assortment of lethal weapons, from slingshots to shotguns. SF soldiers are trained to be effective with whatever is at hand. But in real-world situations, where they are almost always vastly outnumbered, these men are equipped with the best weapons and technology available to fulfill their missions.

Weapons

Special Forces soldiers are familiar with and expert in numerous types of weapons systems, U.S. and foreign, new and old, allied and enemy. They must know how to operate a World War II German MG34 machine gun being used in a Third World country, or the latest Mark 19, 40mm Grenade Machine Gun, in use with Coalition Forces. They are masters of small arms, such as revolvers, semi-automatic pistols, rifles, and submachine guns. Use of crew-served weapons, like the 60mm and 81mm mortar, and recoilless rifles is a common task for the SF troopers. Where is the best place to position a .30 caliber or .50 caliber machine gun? The SF will instruct in the placement, fire lanes, and interlocking fields of fire to maximize these lethal instruments. Engaging an enemy tank or bunker? The Operational

Detachment-Alpha (ODA) will survey which system will best do the job—e.g., the AT-4, Carl Gustov, or M-72 LAW. Whether engaging personnel, tanks, helicopters, buildings, or aircraft, the Special Forces soldiers are the best trained fighters in the world to accomplish this mission.

To cover all of the weapons systems in use by the Special Forces Groups would require volumes.

The M9 9mm Berretta pistol was adopted by the Department of Defense to standardize the 9mm round for U.S. and NATO forces. The M9 is the standard issue pistol for all U.S. military troops including the Special Forces. While it is an acceptable weapon, there are many within the special operations community who still favor the .45 caliber round.

Consequently, we will address those weapons organic to the ODA, the primary firearms intrinsic to the team.

SOPMOD M4A1

All Special Forces soldiers are currently issued the Special Operations Peculiar Modification (SOPMOD) M4A1 Carbine. The M4A1 from Colt Arms of Connecticut is a smaller, compact version of the full-sized M16A2 rifle. This weapon was designed specifically for the U.S. Special Operations Forces. The M4A1 is designed for speed of action and light weight. The barrel has been redesigned to a shortened 14.5 inches, which reduces the weight while maintaining the gun's effectiveness for quick-handling field operations. The retractable butt stock has intermediate stops allowing versatility in Close Quarters Battle (CQB) without compromising shooting capabilities.

The M4A1 has a rifling twist of 1 in 7 inches, making it compatible with the full range of 5.56mm ammunitions. Its sighting system contains dual apertures, one for 0–200 meters and a smaller opening for targets at 500–600 meters. Selective fire controls for the M4A1 have eliminated the three-round burst, replacing it with safe semi-automatic and full automatic fire.

The SOPMOD Accessory Kit allows the SF soldier to modify the weapon per mission parameters. Using the Rail Interface System (RIS), numerous components may be secured to the weapon. The kit includes a 4x32mm Trijicon Day Optical Scope, allowing the soldiers to judge range and deliver more accurate fire out to 300 meters; Trijicon Reflex sight, designed for close-in engagement; and Infrared Target Pointer/Illuminator/Aiming Laser AN/PEQ-2 (for use with night vision devices), which places a red aiming dot on the target—very useful in building and CQB. Additionally, the kit includes Visible Light, a high-intensity flashlight mounted on the rail system; backup iron sight (since the carrying handle of the M4A1 can be removed, this backup sight can be employed in the absence of the handle); and a forward hand grip, which helps in stabilization of the weapon and keeps the user's hands away from the hand guards and barrel, which tend to heat up in combat. Finally, the kit includes a sound suppressor, which significantly reduces the noise and muzzle blast.

The primary weapon for the Special Forces soldier is the Colt M4A1 Carbine. This shortened version of the M16A2 rifle features a collapsible stock, a flat top upper receiver with an accessory rail, and a detachable handle and aperture sight assembly. The M4A1 fire selector has three settings: safe, full automatic, or single shot. The M4A1 shown here has been modified with the Special Operations Peculiar Modification (SOPMOD) accessory kit. A special Rail Interface System (RIS) allows the attachment of numerous aiming devices and accessories depending on the mission. This M4A1 has been modified with a Trijicon ACOG (Advanced Combat Optical Gun-sight) 4x32 scope; on the handgrip is a AN/PEQ-2 Infrared Target Pointer/Illuminator/Aiming Device. The PEQ-2 emits a laser beam for precise aiming of the weapon. It may also be used for lasing targets for the delivery of smart bombs. Finally, attached to the barrel is a Quick Attach/Detach Sound Suppressor. With the suppressor attached the muzzle, blast, flash, and sound are significantly reduced.

The M203 grenade launcher is a lightweight, single-shot breech loaded 40mm weapon specifically designed for placement beneath the barrel of the M4A1 Carbine. With a quick- release mechanism, the addition of the M203 to M4A1 carbine creates the versatility of a weapon system capable of firing both 5.56mm ammunition as well as an expansive range of 40mm high explosive and special purpose munitions.

Colt M203

The M203 grenade launcher is a lightweight (three-pound), single-shot, breech-loaded 40mm weapon specifically designed for placement beneath the barrel of the M16A1 and M16A2 rifles and M4A1/M16A2 carbines. Attached with a quick-release mechanism, the M203 creates the versatility of a weapon system capable of firing both 5.56mm ammunition as well as an expansive range of 40mm high explosive and special purpose munitions.

The most commonly utilized M203 ammunition is the M406 antipersonnel round. This grenade has a deadly radius of five meters. Another option is the M433 multi-purpose grenade, which in addition to the fragmentation effects is capable of penetrating steel armor plate up to two inches thick. Other types of ordnance available are buckshot, tear gas, and various signal rounds.

The receiver of the M203 is manufactured of high-strength forged aluminum alloy. This provides extreme ruggedness, while keeping weight to a minimum. A complete self-cocking firing mechanism, including striker, trigger, and positive safety lever, is included in the receiver. This will allow the M203 to be operated as an independent weapon, even though attached to the M16A1 or M16A2 rifle or M4A1/M16A2 carbine. The barrel is also made of high-strength aluminum alloy, which has been shortened from 12 to 9 inches, allowing improved balance and handling. It slides forward in the receiver to accept a round of ammunition, then slides backward to automatically lock in the closed position, ready to fire.

Special Operations Forces depend on rapid deployment, mobility, and increased firepower. Where the emphasis of a small unit, such as the SF, is placed on "get in and get out" fast, the M203 lends added firepower to the already-proven and outstanding family of M16 weapons.

M9 Beretta

Since 1985, the M9 has seen service as the standard issue side arm for U.S. troops, both conventional and special, in Operation Urgent Fury in Grenada, Operation Desert Shield/Storm in Kuwait, Operation Restore Hope in Somalia, and with IFOR in Bosnia and KFOR in Kosovo. Along with the standardization of the 9mm round, the M9 brought the armed forces a larger-capacity magazine. The M9 holds 15 rounds, compared to the Colt 1911's seven or eight rounds. Although the 9mm ammunition was lighter and smaller, it was viewed as ade-

The M240B replaces the M-60 machine gun in the ODAs (Operational Detachment-Alpha). The highly reliable 7.62mm machine gun delivers more energy to the target than the smaller caliber M249 Squad Assault Weapon (SAW) in use with the Rangers and other Army troops.

quate for line troops. This trade-off also allowed the troops to engage more rounds in a fire fight before having to reload. The original M9 was viewed with some apprehension among operators in the Special Operations community because +P ammunition reportedly caused stress fractures of the weapon's slides. Beretta addressed this problem and today's M9 has an average life of 72,250 rounds.

The slide is open for nearly the entire length of the barrel. This facilitates the ejection of spent shells and virtually eliminates stoppages. The open slide configuration also provide a means for the pistol to be loaded manually. As with all weapons in use with Special Operation Forces, the operators are always trying to get that extra "edge." One of the most likely features to be added to the M9 was a sound suppressor. For such a device the military turned to Knight Arma-

ment Company. The smooth cylindrical suppresser is manufactured of anodized aluminum with a steel attachment system. Weighing a scant 6 ounces, it can be replaced or removed in three seconds. Carrying over the Vietnam-era name, the suppressor was dubbed the "Hush-Puppy."

M-240 Medium Machine Gun

After extensive operational testing, the U.S. Army selected the M240B medium machine gun as a replacement for the M60 family of machine guns. Manufactured by Fabrique Nationale, the 24.2 pound M240B medium machine gun is a gas-operated, air-cooled, linked-belt-fed weapon that fires the 7.62 x 51 mm round. The weapon fires from an open bolt position with a maximum effective range of 1,100 meters. The rate of fire is adjustable from 750 to 1400 rounds per minute through an adjustable gas regulator. It features a folding bipod that attaches to the receiver, a quick-change barrel assembly, a feed cover and bolt assembly enabling closure of the cover regardless of bolt position, a plastic butt stock and an integral optical sight rail. While it possesses many of the same characteristics as the older M60, the durability of the M240 system results in superior reliability and maintainability.

M249 Squad Automatic Weapon (SAW)

Fielded in the mid-1980s, the M249 SAW is an individually portable, air-cooled, belt-fed, gas-operated light machine gun. A unique feature of the SAW is the number of alternate ammunition feeds. The standard ammunition load is 200 rounds of 5.56mm ammunitions in disintegrating belts. These rounds are fed from a 200-round plastic ammunition box through the side of the weapon. The normal link ammunition for the SAW is four rounds of M855 ball ammunitions followed by one round of M85 tracer. Additionally, it can use standard 20- and 30-round M16 magazines, which

M249 SAW is an individually portable, air-cooled, belt-fed, gas-operated light machine gun. The standard load is 200 rounds of 5.56mm ammunitions in disintegrating belts. These rounds are fed from a 200-round plastic ammunition box through the side of the weapon. Additionally, the SAW can utilize standard 20- and 30-round M4A1/M16 magazines, which are inserted in a magazine well in the bottom of the SAW. Using the same 5.56mm ammunition as the M4A1, it allows the ODA to carry common ammunition loads. The M249 is capable of engaging targets out to 800 meters.

The weapon of choice for the Special Forces sniper is the M24 SWS, or Sniper Weapon System. Based on a Remington 700 action, it is equipped with a Leupold Mark IV 10 power fixed scope referred to as the "Ma-3 Alpha." The M24 SWS is a bolt-action rifle capable of engaging a target at well over 500 meters.

are inserted in a magazine well in the bottom of the SAW. Since the SAW uses the same 5.56mm ammunition as the M4A1, it allows the ODA to carry common ammunition loads. The M249 is capable of engaging targets out to 800 meters.

M24 Sniper Weapon System (SWS)

The current issue sniper rifle for the Special Forces is the M24 SWS, two per ODA. The M24 is based on the Remington 700 series long action. This action accommodates chambering for either the 7.62x51mm or .300 Winchester Magnum round. The rifle is a bolt-action six-shot repeating rifle (one round in the chamber and five additional rounds in the magazine). It is issued with the Leupold Mark IV 10 power M3A scope, commonly referred to as the "Ma-3-Alpha." The sniper

may also make use of the weapon's iron sights. Attached to the scope is the M24/EMA ARD (Anti-Reflection Device). Less than three inches long, this honeycomb of tubes cuts down the glare of the scope. The M24 SWS does come with a Harris bipod; however, most of the time the bipod remains in the deployment case. The rifle weighs 12.1 pounds without the scope and has an overall length of 43 inches, with a free-floating barrel of 24 inches. The stock is composite Kevlar, graphite, and fiberglass with an aluminum-bedding block. The stock has an adjustable butt plate to accommodate the length of pull.

Heavy Sniper Rifle

When the mission calls for a Hard Target Interdiction (HTI) at very long range, e.g., over 1,000 meters, the SF will turn to the big guns. HTI would be taking out such targets as an airplane, helicopter, or vehicle. Currently, the SF has the M82A1 in their inventories. It is a one-man portable, semi-automatic rifle with a magazine

When hard targets must be engaged over 1,000 meters away, the SF will turn to the Barrett M82A1 semi-automatic .50 caliber rifle. Here a member of the 5th Special Forces Group (Airborne) is inundated with the desert sand as he sends rounds down range. The M82A1 currently in the SF armory will soon be augmented with the M107 bolt-action, magazine-feed .50 caliber rifle.

Mark 19, 40mm Grenade Machine Gun is a self-powered, air-cooled, belt-fed, blow-back operated weapon. The MK19 is designed to deliver accurate, intense, and decisive firepower against enemy personnel and lightly armored vehicles.

holding up to 10 rounds of .50 caliber Browning machine gun (BMG) ammunition. These are group weapons and are drawn out per mission requirements. Now that the SF soldiers are in the new millennium, USASOC will add a new .50 caliber weapon to their Table of Organization and Equipment (T.O.& E.). Each ODA will now be issued one Barrett M107 .50 caliber rifle. The M107 weighs 23 pounds, with a length of 45 inches. It can be reduced in size by further takedown of the weapon, allowing for more covert transport. Using a bullpup design, it is a bolt-action system with a removable five-round magazine, and is chambered for all NATO .50 caliber BMG cartridges. Other features include a quick-detachable bipod with spiked feet, iron sights, and an M1913 (Picatinny) optical rail to accommodate various sighting and aiming devices. The

addition of the M107 to the T.O.&E. will give the Special Forces more punch, readily accessible to the A-teams.

Vehicles

GMV (Ground Mobility Vehicle)

The GMV has its origins in Desert Storm. During the Gulf War, the Special Forces modified HUMMVs for extended desert missions, dubbing them DUMMV (pronounced "Dum-Vee." The modifications included a heavier suspension, more powerful engine, and an open bed and back for storage of water and fuel and other mission-essential item. The GMV has a cupola on top, similar to that used for mounting a tow system. It is used for mounting various weapons systems, e.g., M2, .50 caliber

The Ground Mobility Vehicle, or GMV, had its origins in Desert Storm. During the Gulf War, the Special Forces modified HUMMVs for extended desert missions, dubbing them DUMMVs, pronounced "Dum-Vee." The modifications included a heavier suspension, more powerful engine, and an open bed and back for storage of water and fuel and other mission-essential items. The GMV has a cupola on top, similar to that used for mounting a TOW missile system. It is used for mounting various weapons systems, e.g., the M2 .50 caliber machine gun and the Mark 19, 40mm Grenade Machine Gun.

The F470 Zodiac Inflatable Boat is the mainstay of water-borne operations with Special Forces. Extremely versatile, it can be launched from submarines and other boats. It can be air dropped via parachute or other deployment methods from an assortment of fixed- and rotary-wing aircraft. When using the outboard motor, the Zodiac is fast and quiet.

machine gun and the Mark 19, 40mm grenade machine gun.

Used by the SF Mounted Teams, the basic make-up is four GMV per team, with a crew of three men per vehicle. The GMV greatly enhances the capability of the mounted ODAs, extending their mission endurance and flexibility.

According the Colonel Gary Jones, Commander 3rd SFG(a), Mounted Team soldiers attend special schools, such as the Rod Hall Advanced Military Off-Road driver training in the desert of Nevada. Here they are taught how to drive the GMV safely and effectively in on-road and off-road environments. The Special Forces soldiers learn techniques such as brake modulation, which allows them to work the ups and downs of the harsh environment and navigate over rocky, uneven terrain. The soldiers also learn how to maintain the vehicle and make necessary repairs in the field.

Zodiac Rafts

The F470 Zodiac Inflatable Boat is the mainstay of water-borne operations with Special Forces. Extremely versatile, it can be launched from submarines and other boats. It can be air dropped via parachute or other deployable methods from an assortment of fixed- and rotary-wing aircraft. When using the outboard

Wearing PVS7 Night Vision Goggles and carrying M4A1s, two members of the 3rd Special Forces Group (Airborne) infiltrate under the cover of darkness. The Klepper Arius 2 Military Canoe, more commonly referred to as a sea kayak, features speed and stealth. The canoe gives the lowest signature of all the surface vessels in use by U.S. Special Operations Forces.

motor, the Zodiac is fast and quiet. Each fuel bladder will allow the craft approximately one hour of operation with an average load of six men and equipment. The low profile and the fabric provide little or no radar signature to be detected by hostile forces. An interesting cache method that can be deployed in a team insertion is to totally submerge the Zodiac, caching the boat, outboard, and other equipment. Upon mission completion, the team will return to position, locate the boat and, using special compressed air tanks, reinflate it, power up the outboard, and exfil the area.

Klepper Arius 2 Military Canoe

The Klepper is more commonly referred to as a sea kayak. It possesses many of the Zodiac's advantages, except for air droppability and motor operations. The sea kayak features speed and stealth. Using the paddles, a crew of two can travel extended distances in a relatively short time. The canoe gives the lowest signature of all the surface vessels in use by U.S. Special Operations Forces. The two SF soldiers sit just below sea level with only their upper torsos elevated above the clandestine craft. Their Load Bearing Equipment and mission-essential equipment are placed in storage positions within the craft.

Snow Terrain Vehicle

For operations in snow-covered mountains, the Special Forces teams employ a snow terrain vehicle, "mil-speak" for snowmobiles. Currently in the inventory of the 10th SFG(A) are Polaris Model 600, wide track, 500cc machines. Each man on the ODA will have his own snowmobile, allowing the team to run split-team operations and provide backup transportation of team members should one of the snowmobiles break down or become disabled in combat. The SF soldiers load up the snowmobiles with kit gear, snowshoes, snow shovel, tent, and food. The M4A1 weapons are placed in an M1950 rifle case mounted on the side of the unit. Additionally, each member will carry a minimum of three five-gallon cans of fuel. One of the techniques employed by the 18Ds is placing IV bags in an ammo can under the cowling next to the engine. In the event one must be used, it is not only not frozen, but warm so as not to lower the patient's body temperature when administered. Team members have also found this procedure useful for warming their Meals Ready to Eat (MREs). In addition to the snowmobiles, the teams also employ sleds called "Pulks" to carry their rucksacks and other mission-essential equipment.

The Army calls it a Snow Terrain Vehicle, more commonly known as a snowmobile. This Polaris Model 600 is currently in use with the 10th SFG(A). Each man on the ODA has his own snowmobile, which he will load up with his kit gear, snowshoes, snow shovel, tent, and food. The M4A1 weapons are placed in an M1950 rifle case mounted on the side of the unit.

Global Positioning System (GPS)

While all Special Forces soldiers are trained in land navigation using the standard issue Lensetic Compass, sometimes the A-team must have pinpoint accuracy, as when conducting an SR mission through the desert, or across the frozen tundra, in enemy territory, in the middle of the night. They will need to know the position of an enemy division, a radar station, or perhaps a SCUD when reporting in to headquarters. For such instances they will use a device known as a Global Positioning System or GPS.

The GPS is a collection of satellites that orbit the earth twice a day. During this orbiting they transmit precise time, latitude, longitude, and altitude information. Using a GPS receiver, special operations forces can ascertain their exact location anywhere on the earth. It is the same technology used by certain civilian automobile navigation services.

GPS was developed by the U.S. Department of Defense (DOD) in the early 1970s to provide a continuous, worldwide positioning and navigational system for U.S. military forces around the globe. The complete constellation, as it is called, consists of 24 satellites orbiting approximately 12,000 miles above the earth. These 22 active and two reserve or backup satellites provide data 24 hours a day for 2D and 3D positioning anywhere on the planet. Each satellite constantly broadcasts precise time and location data. Troops using a GPS receiver receive these signals.

Members of the 5th Special Forces Group (Airborne) call in the position of their Mission Support Site. Using the Rockwell "Plugger" GPS unit, they can convey their exact position to higher headquarters.

By measuring the time interval between the transmission and the receiving of the satellite signal, the GPS receiver calculates the distance between the users and each satellite. Using the distance measurements of at least three satellites in an algorithm computation, the GPS receiver provides the precise location. A special encryption signal is used in the military's Precise Positioning Service. A second signal called Standard Positioning Service is available for civilian and commercial use.

The Special Forces ODAs are issued the Rockwell "Plugger" or PSN-11. The precise name for the unit is PLGR+96 (Precise Lightweight GPS Receiver). The PLGR96 is the most advanced version of the U.S. DOD hand-held GPS unit. It serves the increasingly demanding requirements of the SF soldiers, as well as all the U.S. Special Operations Forces.

Secure (Y-code) Differential GPS allows the user to accept differential correction without zeroing the unit. Differential accuracy can be less than one meter. Other features of the "Plugger" include Wide Area GPS Enhancement for autonomous positioning accuracy to 4 meters CEP, jammer direction finding, targeting interface with laser range-finder, remote display terminal capability, and advanced user interface features.

Weighing in at a mere 2.7 pounds (with batteries installed) the GPS unit is easily stowed in the cavernous rucksack carried by the ODAs. In addition to hand-held operation, the PLGR+96 unit can be installed in various vehicles and airborne platforms.

For missions requiring underwater infiltration, there is the MUGR, Miniature Underwater Global Positioning System Receiver. This small device weighs 1.2 pounds and provides the team with position and navigational information needed for infil/exfil, fire support, Special Reconnaissance, and target location. Once the unit acquires the satellite fix, the waterproof MUGR can be taken to a depth of 33 feet. Alternately, the unit may work underwater employing the optional floating antenna.

SOFLAM

Special Operations Forces - Laser Acquisition Marker (SOFLAM). Special Forces soldiers would use this equipment in a direct action mission for the direction of terminal guided ordnance. This technique is referred to as "lasing the target." When it absolutely, positively has to be destroyed, you put an SF team on the ground and a fast mover with a smart bomb in the air; results—one smoking bomb crater. This newly issued laser marking

Communications is the lifeline of the SF team. Here a member of the 10th Special Forces Group (Airborne) uses the AN/PSC-5 (V) "Shadowfire" by Raytheon.

device is lighter and more compact than the current laser marker in service with the U.S. military. It can be used in daylight, or with the attached night vision optics it can be employed at night.

Radios

Communications is the lifeline of the SF team. For long-range communications, the Special Forces use the AN/PSC-5 (V) "Shadowfire" by Raytheon, issued two per ODA. The PSC-5 is a multi-band, multi-mission communication terminal with capability for UHF/VHF (Ultra High Frequency/Very High Frequency) Manpack LOS

Another useful communication device is the PRC-137. This ultra-lightweight HF radio is unique to Special Operations Forces. Using a small keyboard, the SF soldier will type in the message to be sent; it is then down-loaded into the radio. He then may continue on his mission. When the base station comes online, an automatic link will be established with the PRC-137 and the message will be up-loaded.

(Line-Of-Sight) and satellite communications (SATCOM). For satellite use, the set provides both TDMA (Time Division Multiple Access) and DAMA (Demand Assigned Multiple Access). This device supports the DOD requirement for a light-weight, secure, network-capable, multi-band, multi-mission, anti-jam, voice/imagery/data communication capability in a single package. The Shadowfire weighs 11.7 pounds without the battery, 8 pounds heavier with it.

For tactical intra-team communications, Multi-band Inter/Intra Team radios provide the SF teams with the ability to communicate on user-selected frequencies from 30 to 512 MHz using a single hand-held unit. The radios have power up to 5 watts in VHF/FM, VHF/AM, UHF/AM, UHF/FM(LOS) for ground-to-ground and air-to-ground connectivity. Weighing only 31 ounces, the radios come in two versions, immersible to six feet and 66 feet. The units have embedded COMSEC (Communications Security) for full digital voice and data operations. The MI/IT radio will replace the current AN/PRC-126, AN/PRC-68, Saber I/II/III, and MX-300 Series.

Rappelling

This old mountaineering technique has served SF troops since the first Special Forces soldiers operated in the mountains of Bavaria, near Bad Tolz, Germany. Whether working in a mountainous terrain, or in an urban environment, rappelling is a valuable skill. Often, traversing a steep hill carrying an 80- to 100-pound rucksack, it is the best way down the contour.

SF teams will train in this procedure with full combat gear, as well as rappelling with a casualty. Attaching to a regular military assault line through carabiners, or a specially designed rappelling device (known as a "Figure 8"), the team will negotiate down the side of a mountain like a mountain goat, or the side of a building as rapidly as Spiderman.

This member of the 7th Special Forces Group (Airborne) is suited up for a High Altitude Low Opening (HALO) parachute jump. HALO is one of the means by which SF teams can be inserted into denied or hostile territory. The jumpers are capable of exiting an aircraft at 25,000 feet using oxygen. They will then free fall to a designated altitude where they will open their RAPS and then form up together. This jumper has his rucksack strapped in front and his M4A1 attached to his left side, ready to go.

FRIES

The Fast Rope Insertion/Extraction System is the way to insert your assault force on the ground in seconds. This system begins with small woven ropes made of wool, which are then braided into a larger rope. The rope is rolled into a deployment bag and the end secured to a helicopter. Depending on the model of chopper, it can be just outside on the hoist mechanism of the side door or attached to a bracket off the back ramp. Once over the insertion point the rope is deployed and even as it is hitting the ground the ODA members are jumping onto the woolen line and sliding down, as easily as a fireman goes down a pole. Once the team is safely on the ground the flight engineer or gunner, depending on the type of helicopter, will pull the safety pin and the rope will fall to the ground. Such a system is extremely useful in the rapid deployment of Special Forces personnel. An entire ODA can be inserted within 12–15 seconds. FRIES is the most accepted way of getting a force onto the ground expeditiously. Unlike rappelling, once the trooper hits the ground, he is "free" of the rope and can begin his mission.

The second part of FRIES is the extraction method. Although both insertion and extraction systems were originally referred to as SPIES, or Special Procedure, Insertion & Extraction System, the Army has combined both methods into one term. While fast-roping gets you down quickly, there are times when you have to extract just as fast. The problem is, there is no Landing Zone for the Blackhawk of the 160th SOAR to land, and the "bad guys" are closing in on your position. This technique is similar to the McGuire and STABO rigs developed during the Vietnam War. Both used multiple ropes, which often resulted in the troops colliding with one another; the latter at least let the user fire his weapon while on the ride up. The techniques that served the Special Forces troops of the 1960s have been refined to the new FRIES method.

Fast Rope Insertion/Extraction System or FRIES is the fastest method of inserting Special Forces soldiers. An entire ODA can be inserted within 12–15 seconds. Once over the insertion point the rope is deployed and even as it is hitting the ground the ODA members are jumping onto the woolen line and sliding down, as easily as a fireman goes down a pole. Extremely useful in the rapid deployment of Special Forces personnel, FRIES is the most accepted way of getting a force onto the ground expeditiously. Unlike rappelling, once the trooper hits the ground, he is free of the rope and can begin his mission.

The second part of FRIES is the extraction method. Originally referred to as SPIES, or Special Procedure, Insertion & Extraction System, the system was changed by the Army to combine both methods. While fast-roping gets you down quickly, there are times when you have to extract just as fast. A single rope is lowered from the hovering helicopter. Wearing a special harness, the SF member or team attaches to the rope via snap links. Once the men are secure to the line, the helicopter will whisk the team out of harm's way. *Defense Visual Information Center Photo*

To extract with FRIES, a single rope is lowered from the hovering helicopter. Attached to this rope are rings, woven and secured into the rope at approximately five-foot intervals. There can be as many as eight rings on the rope. The SF soldiers, wearing special harnesses similar to a parachute harness, attach themselves to the rope via the rings. This is accomplished by clipping in a snap link that at the top of the harness. Once all team members are secured, a signal is given and the soldiers are extracted out of harm's way. This method allows the team members to maintain covering fire from their weapons as they extract. Once the SF soldiers have been whisked out of enemy range, and an LZ can be located, the helicopter pilot will bring the troops to ground again.

At this time they will disconnect from the rope and board the chopper to leave the area.

Rubber Duck

A "rubber duck" is the term SOF troops use to describe a mission involving deployment of a Zodiac raft. In a Soft Duck, a fully inflated Zodiac raft is deployed from the rear cargo ramp of a "NightStalker" MH-47 Chinook, or an AFSOC MH-53 Pave Low. The raft is slid out the back of the helicopter and the ODA follows right behind. Once in the water, the team jumps in, fires up the outboard engine, and heads out on its mission. An alternate to this is the Hard Duck, which involves a craft with a metal bottom delivered in the same manner as the Soft Duck. The Zodiac may also be

Members of the 3rd Special Forces Group (Airborne) perform a Rubber Duck operation from an MH-47E. Immediately after the Zodiac raft has cleared the ramp, the SF team will follow it out. Swimming to the raft, they will then load in and continue their insertion to their target area.

deployed via parachute, as would be the case when delivered via AFSOC assets such as a Combat Talon or Combat Shadow. Moments after the loadmaster releases the package, the SF troops will shuffle to the end of the ramp and parachute in after it. An additional method is the Double Duck, where two Zodiacs, fully inflated, are stacked and deployed via parachute together, again via the Hercules aircraft.

Delta Queen

While the Rubber Duck is used for inserting a SF team, the Delta Queen is a method for retrieval and extraction of the team. Upon mission completion the team will return to the Zodiac, and go "feet wet" into the water, whether an ocean, a lake, or river. The team will meet up with an MH-47E Chinook of the 160th Special Operation Air Regiment (Airborne). The pilot will bring his aircraft to a hover, then bring the heli-

copter down, closer and closer to the water's surface. He will continue his descent until the rotary-wing craft actually rests on the water.

With the rear cargo ramp lowered, the MH-47E will begin to take on water. Wave after wave begins to cascade over the ramp and soon the flight engineers are standing in water over the tops of their boots. As the Zodiac begins to line up with the rear of the chopper, the crew member holds a red-filtered light to signal the team. The exfiltrating team guns the engine, ducks their heads, and aims for the ramp and the now-flooded fuselage. With a splash and a thud, the team is aboard and already the ramp begins to raise slightly. The pilot raises the behemoth aircraft from the surface, creating what looks like a small version of Niagara Falls as the water pours from the rear of the helicopter. The extraction complete, the NightStalkers and the Special Forces team or return to base.

"Mission complete. Request Exfil." Called a Delta Queen, the Night Stalker pilot of this MH-47E Chinook will set the large helicopter down so the aircraft is literally taking on water. Guided by members of the flight crew signaling with a flashlight, the SF ODA will then pilot the Zodiac up the ramp and into the fuselage. Once secure, the pilot will lift off and return to base.

Special Forces in the 21st Century

When the Special Forces was formed in 1952, the biggest threat to world peace and democracy was from the Soviet Union. The A-teams of the 1950s practiced for Unconventional Warfare (UW) against the Russ-ian "Bear" and made preparations to conduct guerrilla activities in World War III. With the collapse of the Soviet Union, there is a new perspective on warfare. The predication of World War III with masses of Soviet T-80 tanks rolling

Around the world, around the clock. Members of the U.S. Army Special Forces stand poised to defend freedom on a moment's notice. From the frigid Arctic winds to the humid, insect- and snake-infested jungles, the men of the Green Beret carry on in the tradition of their predecessors to defend liberty at all costs.

As the U.S. Army Special Operations Command advances further into the 21st century, the dynamic world of today will find the Special Forces soldier in the position of warrior, diplomat, and commando. Once shunned by conventional troops and commanders, the Special Forces today are in constant demand by U.S. ambassadors and theater CinCs.

Whether preparing for all-out war or OOTW due to the regional instability around the world, they stand poised, mission capable to deploy, on a moment's notice, a threat-adaptive force. During the Cold War the U.S. deterrent to a nuclear holocaust was the Strategic Triad: Inter-Continental Ballistic Missiles in silos, Strategic Air Command bombers flying around the globe, and submarines on patrol. The Special Forces of the 21st Century comprise a new "Triad" for democracy: the Operational Detachment-Alphas (ODAs), the regional orientation of the teams, and the latest specialized equipment.

The Special Forces soldier of the 1950s and 1960s has evolved from a guerrilla/counter-guerrilla fighter to the consummate paragon of special operations. In today's dynamic world the Special Forces soldier is warrior, diplomat, and commando. Once shunned by conventional troops and commanders, the Special Forces today are in constant demand by U.S. Ambassadors and theater CinCs. The ODAs of this century possess strategic agility, ubiquitous presence, state-of-the-art equipment, and the latest intelligence for information dominance.

Strategic agility is the Special Forces' capability to meet the contingency needs of the regionally engaged CinC and Special Operations Command with forces based Outside of Continental United States (OCONUS) and forward-based forces.

Ubiquitous presence is evident in the forward deployed teams, e.g., Europe, Korea, and the Caribbean. In addition to these teams, there are regionally assigned SF Groups to support various engagement plans of the theater CinCs. This regional deployment creates a cultural exchange, establishes credibility, and builds trust and relationships between the SF soldiers and host nation forces. These Foreign Internal Defense (FID) missions can have long-term benefits. A sergeant that a SF team trains in patrolling today may be a

across Europe has been replaced with discussions of Operations Other Than War (OOTW) and Small Scale Contingencies.

As the years have gone by the Special Forces have adapted to the geopolitical nature of warfare.

Special Forces ODAs are heavily engaged throughout the world. They are a highly relevant force of choice when circumstances require the use of small specialized teams. Capable of easy transition from peacetime to conflict, the SF teams are known as the "Quiet Professionals." These low-key forces are earning trust, building relationships, and establishing credibility around the world.

future colonel. That captain with whom they share a Meal Ready to Eat may someday be the leader of the country. By teaching these countries how to defend themselves, it may mean the United States does not have deploy multiple divisions of troops to an area. Establishing a warrior bond with these host nation soldiers may very likely create a strong ally for the United States in the future.

In addition to mastering the established conventional skills and military occupational specialties, SF soldiers are taught many special skills to develop the unique proficiencies that give them a wide variety of capabilities. They stand ready to execute their missions in any environment by any means of infiltration, air, land, or sea. This sergeant from the 7th Special Forces Groups (Airborne) in HALO equipment is ready to jump in to perform an FID, UW, SR, DA, or any other mission he is tasked.

119

The M2 Selectable Lightweight Attack Munition, or SLAM. Weighing a mere 2.2 pounds and small enough to fit in a BDU pocket, it is a low-volume, multipurpose munition. The M2 is self-contained, can be easily emplaced, and is compatible with other munitions for anti-material, anti-vehicular, and anti-personnel uses. It has four detonation modes, passive IR, magnetic influence, time delay, and command detonation.

Part of the Special Operation Forces Demolition Kit. This kit provides the SF soldier the capability to custom build, attach, and waterproof demolitions charges for specific target and operational scenarios. Seen here is the Explosive Form Penetration device or EFP. The device is packed with C4, thus creating a shaped explosive charge. For stability and deployment, it is placed upon a tripod. The EFP has a picatinny rail on the top; this allows an aiming device, such as an Aimpoint, in this case, to be attached. Once the target has been sighted in, the optical sight is removed and the EFP is set for detonation. This explosive device will penetrate concrete walls or rolled hardened armor.

I am an American Special Forces soldier. A professional! I will do all that my nation requires of me.

I am a volunteer, knowing well the hazards of my profession.

I serve with the memory of those who have gone before me: Rogers' Rangers, Francis Marion, Mosby's Rangers, the First Special Service Forces and Ranger Battalions of World War II, the Airborne Ranger Companies of Korea. I pledge to uphold the honor and integrity of all I am—in all I do.

I am a professional soldier. I will teach and fight wherever my nation requires. I will strive always to excel in every art and artifice of war.

I know that I will be called upon to perform tasks in isolation, far from familiar faces and voices, with the help and guidance of my God.

I will keep my mind and body clean, alert, and strong, for this is my debt to those with whom I serve. I will not bring shame upon myself or the forces.

I will maintain myself, my arms, and my equipment in an immaculate state as befits a Special Forces soldier.

I will never surrender though I be the last. If I am taken, I pray that I may have the strength to spit upon my enemy.

My goal is to succeed in any mission—and live to succeed again.

I am a member of my nation's chosen soldiery. God grant that I may not be found wanting, that I will not fail this sacred trust.

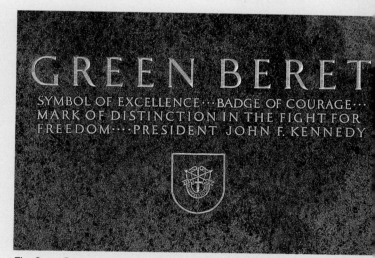

The Green Beret is more than a headgear issued to graduates of the Q-Course. Today, as when it was adopted, it stands for liberty, freedom, and professionalism. The SF soldier who dons a beret colored forest green is a diplomat, a soldier, and a warrior. Ask a collection of SF soldiers, and they will tell you, "the beret is hot in the summer, and cold in the winter; but don't even think of taking it away. It's like the flag."

The RQ-1A Predator is a medium-altitude, long-endurance Unmanned Aerial Vehicle or UAV. This aerial craft is considered a joint forces air component, and is deployed for reconnaissance, surveillance, and target acquisition in support of the Joint Force Commander. More than a mere aircraft, the Predator is a system, equipped with color camera in the nose, a day variable aperture television camera, a variable aperture infrared camera (for low light/night). It is also equipped with a synthetic aperture radar for looking through smoke, clouds, and haze. The Predator UAV system can provide real-time imaging that will assist in the often unique missions tasked to Special Forces ODAs. *Photograph provided by General Atomics Aeronautical Systems, Inc.*

Good intelligence can mean the difference between success or failure, life or death, on the battlefield. Information Dominance is a focus of new technology to keep the Special Forces at the leading edge. Referred to as "Ground Truth," officially it is called "IT-21" for Information Technology for the 21st Century. It is designed to enhance Command and Control, Communication, Computers and Intelligence (C4I), and to ensure connectivity with joint, combined, and coalition forces, while maintaining situational awareness.

Today's SF team will deploy with the latest state-of-the-art equipment, yet it is constantly looking at ways to improve its edge in combat. For this purpose, U.S. Army Special Operations Command (USASOC) has Lieutenant Colonel Daniel Moore, the G-7, Force Integration. The job of the G-7 is strategic planning, force structure, and equipment for the next decade to ensure the ODAs are appropriately equipped to meet future contingencies. From thermal underwater to body armor, from remote reconnaissance camera systems to complex combat simulations, if it will enhance the ODA, you'll find a file covering it on the G-7s PC.

New explosive devices are finding their way into the rucksacks of current SF ODAs—items like the M2 SLAM, or Selectable Lightweight Attack Munitions. The SLAM weighs a mere 2.2 pounds and is small enough to fit in the pocket of a battle dress uniform (BDU). The explosively formed penetrating warhead can pierce targets of 40mm rolled homogeneous armor out to 25 feet. It has four operating modes: Bottom attack (magnetic influence fuse)—as a vehicle passes over the M2, it will sense the magnetic signature and will detonate upward; Side attack (passive IR)—detonation occurs when sensing a passing vehicle's infrared signature; Time demolition of a target in four settings—15, 30, 45, and 60 minutes; and finally, Operator-initiated command detonation, using the standard Army blasting caps with the new time delay firing device (TDFD).

Another useful explosive device is the M150 Penetration Augmented Munition (PAM). The PAM is a lightweight man portable demolition device developed for special operations forces. It is compact at 33 inches, weighs 35 pounds, and can be emplaced by a single SF soldier. The primary use of the munition is against reinforced concrete bridge supports, piers, walls, and abutments. The munition can easily be carried in the rucksack or affixed to the soldier's Load Bearing Equipment without restricting his ability to walk, climb, rappel, or fast rope. It can be ignited by any standard military detonation device.

The PAM is hung against the target. The warhead consists of a forward charge, which cuts any rebar; a hole-drilling charge, which forms a hole in the target; and a follow-through charge, which is propelled to the bottom of the hole where it detonates. The explosion fractures the structure and results in a loss of at least 75 percent of the load-bearing capacity. The PAM's efficiency at destabilizing a structure allows two SF soldiers with two PAM units (70 pounds) to set up the devices and be ready to exfil in two minutes.

In the realm of information dominance, the G-7 shop is looking at the use of Unmanned Aerial Vehicles, or UAVs, to provide up-to-the-minute

Currently under consideration for possible addition to the SOPMOD kit is the Lightweight Shotgun System or LSS. Similar to the M-203, 40mm Grenade launcher, the LSS would be mounted under the barrel of the M4A1 Carbine. The LSS is a 12-gauge weapon that would most likely be carried by the point man, giving him an extra punch. It would also prove useful in the Special Forces Advanced Urban Combat role and Close Quarters Battle operations. *USASOC*

With the demise of the Soviet Union, the world is seeing numerous wannabe dictators and terrorist threats to U.S. and allied interests alike. The U.S. Army Special Forces are prepared for such contingency operations. By training its soldiers in the Special Forces Advance Reconnaissance, Target Analysis, and Exploitation Techniques Course, USASOC is mission capable of handling any threat. Pictured here is a terrorist's worst nightmare, a SFARTAETC trained stack ready to perform a dynamic entry.

aerial reconnaissance of the battlefield. A prime example of such a craft is the RQ-1A Predator UAV, manufactured by General Atomics Aeronautical Systems Inc. The Predator is a medium-altitude, long-endurance UAV. It is a Joint Forces Air Component Commander–owned theater asset for reconnaissance, surveillance, and target acquisition in support of the Joint Force command. The Predator UAV is equipped with a color nose camera, a day variable aperture TV camera, a variable aperture infrared camera for low light/night, and a synthetic aperture radar, for looking through smoke, clouds, or haze. The camera produces full-motion video and SAR still-frame radar images. The three sensors are carried on the same air frame but cannot be operated simultaneously. With a speed of 80 miles per hour and a range of 400 nautical miles, the Predator can loiter up to 25,000 feet for a period of 24 hours. With a gross weight of 2,250 pounds, this is definitely a support aircraft. However, USASOC is looking at the feasibility of small UAVs that could be carried into enemy territory in a rucksack. The small hand-held versions of the UAV could provide the team with immediate imaging of their AO.

Along with the UAV and numerous satellites with Multi-speed Transient Imaging (MTI), Multi-Hyper Spectral Imaging (HSI), and Synthetic Aperture Radar (SAR), NASA's shuttle missions have been used to map the world to within a meter. When you combine all of this input and run it through a simulator, you have an extremely accurate view of your target area. Throw in some blueprints and 3-D modeling software and you now have a full mission profile from insertion to exfil, all inside the computer. Teams can use such a simulation to actually plan their missions: What is the best route in? There, from the Northwest. Where is the best vantage point for the sniper? There, just beyond that outcropping of rocks. The team can even enter the building and recon, all from the safety of the simulator in the Isolation Facility. It is called "Virtual Recon." The unclassified look was amazing—one can only imagine what the classified version looks like.

Communications devices will also get a revamping as the technology improves. Eventually, we'll see the iridium phone and radio technology becoming so prevalent that instead of an ODA carrying a large PSC-5 and MBIIT radios, each SF soldier will have his own personal communication device small enough to fit into the pocket of the rucksack, or in an M16 magazine pouch. The device will have all the current features, including SATCOM communications with the Mission Support Site, CinC, group, or even National Command Authority, if necessary, all on a secure uplink.

One last item from the G-7 shop is fused imaging. This technology will combine thermal imaging with image intensifiers, day/night vision, integrated HUD (Heads Up Display) with a laser target reticle of the weapon, and a Global Positioning System microchip, all in one set of glasses. All of this technology is here today; it is just a matter of time before it is incorporated into a working unit.

Without a doubt USSOCOM and USASOC provide the best weapons and equipment for the men of the Special Forces Groups. Their efforts are paramount in providing the SF soldier with what is necessary not only for mission success, but also personnel survival. However, it is still the man on the ground that makes the difference— the sergeant who hoists a 150-pound rucksack on his back; the SFC who serves as the only U.S. military presence in a foreign country; the ODA that HALOs out of an MC-130 and lives in the bush for weeks, months, or longer. You only have to spend a short amount of time with the men who wear that woolen headgear and have that tab on their shoulder to understand that the Green Berets are warriors par excellence. Whether equipped with the SOPMOD M4A1, a SLAM and a UAV overhead, or a K-Bar, a block of C4, and a map, the SF soldier will execute his mission.

A command brief from the 7th SFG(A) lists the following SOF Truths: Humans are more important than hardware. Quality is better than quantity. Special Operations Forces cannot be mass produced. And, competent Special Operations Forces cannot be created after emergencies occur. With the experience gained over the years through sweat and blood, continuing in the heritage of those who have gone before, the Special Forces soldiers are trained, prepared, and equipped to operate in any environment, anywhere on the globe, anytime they are needed.

The Special Forces are a lethal, intelligent, decisive, and high-risk force for combat. Whenever needed, they will be ready to answer the call. The green beret remains "the symbol of excellence, a badge of courage" for the "Quiet Professionals" of the U.S. Army Special Forces.

Steeped in the heritage of the last five decades . . . armed with the lessons of those who gave the ultimate sacrifice . . . trained to master the art and science of unconventional warfare . . . ever vigilant to their creed and the motto, "De Opresso Liber," To Free The Oppressed: The men of the U.S. Army Special Forces remain the tip of the spear.

Glossary of Terms

AT: Antiterrorism. Defensive measures used to reduce the vulnerability of individuals and property to terrorism.

C4I: Command, Control, Communications, Computers, and Intelligence.

CinC: Commander in Chief.

Civil Affairs: The activities of a commander that establish, maintain, influence, or exploit relations between military forces and civil authorities, both governmental and nongovernmental, and the civilian population in a friendly, neutral, or hostile area of operations in order to facilitate military operations and consolidate operational objectives. Civil Affairs may include performance by military forces of activities and functions normally the responsibility of the local government. These activities may occur prior to, during, or subsequent to military action. They may also occur, if directed, in the absence of other military operations.

Clandestine Operation: Activities sponsored or conducted by governmental departments or agencies in such a way as to ensure secrecy or concealment. (It differs from covert operations in that emphasis is placed on concealment of the operation rather than on concealment of identity of sponsor.) In Special Operations, an activity may be both covert and clandestine and may focus equally on operational considerations and intelligence-related activities.

Close Air Support (CAS): Air action against hostile targets that are in close proximity to friendly forces. Each action requires detailed integration with the fire and movement of those forces.

Collateral special operations activities: Collateral activities in which Special Operations forces, by virtue of their inherent capabilities, may be selectively tasked to participate. The activities may include security assistance, humanitarian assistance, antiterrorism and other security activities, counter-drug operations, personnel recovery, and special activities.

Counterproliferation: Activities taken to counter the spread of dangerous military capabilities, allied technologies and/or know-how, especially weapons of mass destruction and ballistic missile delivery systems.

Counterterrorism: Offensive measures taken to prevent, deter, and respond to terrorism.

Covert Operations: Operations that are planned and executed so as to conceal the identity of, or permit plausible denial by, the sponsor.

Crisis: An incident or situation involving a threat to the United States, its territories, citizens, military forces and possessions or vital interests that develops rapidly and creates a condition of such diplomatic, economic, political, or military importance that commitment of U.S. military forces and resources is contemplated to achieve national objectives.

Direct action mission: In special operations, a specific act involving operations of an overt, covert, clandestine, or low-visibility nature conducted primarily by a sponsoring power's special operations forces in hostile or denied areas.

Ducks - Types of Zodiac deployments.
> **Double:** Twin Zodiacs
> **Hard:** Zodiac with hard metal bottom
> **Soft:** Zodiac raft

Exfiltration (Exfil): The removal of personnel or units from areas under enemy control.

First Line Belt: Specially designed webbing with shock cord inside, used when traveling on aircraft. One end has a standard carabiner, and the other end a quick-release carabiner.

Foreign Internal Defense (FID): Participation by civilian and military agencies of a government in any action programs taken by another government to free and protect its society from subversion, lawlessness, and insurgency.

Guerrilla Warfare: Military and paramilitary operations conducted in enemy-held or hostile territory by irregular, predominantly indigenous forces.

Host Nation: A nation that receives the forces and/or supplies of allied nations and/or NATO organizations to be located on, operate in, or transit through its territory.

Humanitarian assistance: Assistance provided by Department of Defense forces, as directed by appropriate authority, in the aftermath of natural or manmade disasters to help reduce conditions that present a serious threat to life and property. Assistance provided by U.S. forces is limited in scope and duration and is designed to supplement efforts of civilian authorities that have primary responsibility for providing such assistance.

Infiltration (Infil): The movement through or into an area or territory occupied by either friendly or enemy troops or organizations. The movement is made either by small groups or by individuals at extended or irregular intervals. When used in connection with the enemy, it implies that contact is avoided.

Insurgency: An organized movement aimed at the overthrow of a constituted government through the use of subversion and armed conflict.

Internal defense: The full range of measures taken by a government to free and protect its society from subversion, lawlessness, and insurgency.

Inter-operability: The ability of systems, units, or forces to provide services to and to accept services from other systems, units, or forces and use the services so exchanged to enable them to operate effectively together.

Low-intensity conflict: Political-military confrontation between contending states or groups below conventional war and above routine, peaceful competition among states. It frequently involves protracted struggles of competing principles and ideologies. Low-intensity conflict ranges from subversion to the use of armed force. It is waged by a combination of means employing political, economic, informational, and military instruments. Low-intensity conflicts are often localized, generally in the Third World, but contain regional and global security implications.

Maquis: Active guerrilla groups, World War II.

Military Civic Action: The use of indigenous military forces on projects useful to the local population at all levels in such fields as education, training, public works, agriculture, transportation, communications, health, sanitation and others contributing to economic and social development.

Mission: A statement of an entity's reason for being and what it wishes to accomplish as an organization.

Nation Assistance: Civil and/or military assistance rendered to a nation's territory during peacetime, crises, or emergencies, or war, based on agreements mutually concluded between nations. Nation Assistance programs include, but are not limited to, security assistance, FID, other DOD Title 10 programs, and activities performed on a reimbursable basis by federal agencies or international organizations.

NCA: National Command Authority. The President and the Secretary of Defense together, or their duly deputized alternates or successors. The term signifies constitutional authority to direct the Armed Forces in their execution of military action.

Objectives: Specific actions to be achieved in a specified time period. Accomplishment will indicate progress toward achieving the goals.

Operator: See "Shooter."

Psychological operations: Planned operations to convey selected information and indicators to foreign audiences to influence their emotions, motives, and objective reasoning, and ultimately the behavior of foreign government, organizations, groups, and individuals. The purpose of psychological operations is to induce or reinforce foreign attitudes and behavior favorable to the originator's objectives.

Ranger Assist Cord: 550 parachute line, used to attach anything and everything to an operator.

Shooter: Special Operations Forces trooper, e.g., U.S. Army Special Forces, U.S. Navy SEAL, U.S. Army Ranger, SAS (British or Australian), etc.

Special Reconnaissance: Reconnaissance and surveillance actions conducted by special operations forces to obtain or verify, by visual observation or other collection methods, information concerning the capabilities, intentions, and activities of an actual or potential enemy or to secure data concerning the meteorological, hydrographic, or geographic characteristics of a particular area. It includes target acquisition, area assessment, and post-strike reconnaissance.

Strategy: Methods, approaches, or specific moves taken to implement and attain an objective.

Unconventional Warfare (UW): A broad spectrum of military and paramilitary operations conducted in enemy-held, enemy-controlled, or politically sensitive territory. Unconventional warfare includes, but is not limited to, the interrelated fields of guerrilla warfare, evasion and escape, subversion, sabotage, and other operations of a low visibility, covert, or clandestine nature. These interrelated aspects of UW may be prosecuted singularly or collectively by predominantly indigenous personnel, usually supported and directed in varying degrees by (an) external source(s) during all conditions of war or peace.

Abbreviations

ARSOC	Army Special Operations Command
AT-4	Anti-Tank Weapon
CAS	Close Air Support
CIA	Central Intelligence Agency
COIN	Counterinsurgency
COMINT	Communications Intelligence
CSAR	Combat Search And Rescue
CT	Counterterrorism
CQB	Close Quarters Battle
DA	Direct Action
DAM/T	Direct Action Mission/Team
DIA	Defense Intelligence Agency
DOD	Department of Defense
DZ	Drop Zone
E&E	Evasion and Escape
ELINT	Electronic Intelligence
FID	Foreign Internal Defense
FOB	Forward Operation Base
FOI	Forward Operating Location
FRIES	Fast Rope Insertion/Extraction System
GPS	Global Positioning System
HAHO	High Altitude High Opening
HALO	High Altitude Low Opening
HE	High Explosive
HUD	Heads Up Display
HUMINT	Human Intelligence
INTREP	Intelligence Report
JCS	Joint Chiefs of Staff
JSOC	Joint Special Operations Command
JSOF	Joint Special Operations Forces
JSOTF	Joint Special Operations Task Force
JUWTF	Joint Unconventional Warfare Task Force
LBE	Load Bearing Equipment
LZ	Landing Zone
MFP	Major Force Program
MGF	Mobile Guerrilla Force
MPU	Message Pickup
MRE	Meal Ready to Eat
MTT	Mobile Training Team
NOD	Night Optical Device
NVG	Night Vision Goggles
OPCON/M	Operational Control/Command
OPSEC	Operational Security
PSYWAR	Psychological Warfare
SEAL	Sea Air Land (U.S. Navy Special Operations Forces)
SAR	Search and Rescue
SAS	Special Air Service
SBS	Special Boat Squadron
SF	Special Forces (U.S. Army)
SFAUC	Special Forces Advanced Urban Combat
SFARTAETC	Special Forces Advanced Reconnaissance, Target Analysis & Exploitation Techniques Course
SFOB	Special Forces Operating Base
SOCOM	Special Operations Command
SOF	Special Operations Forces
SOFLAM	Special Operations Forces Laser Acquisition Marker
SR	Special Reconnaissance
SWS	Sniper Weapon System
USASOC	U.S. Army Special Operations Command
USASFC	U.S. Army Special Forces Command
UW	Unconventional Warfare
WM	Weapons of Mass Destruction

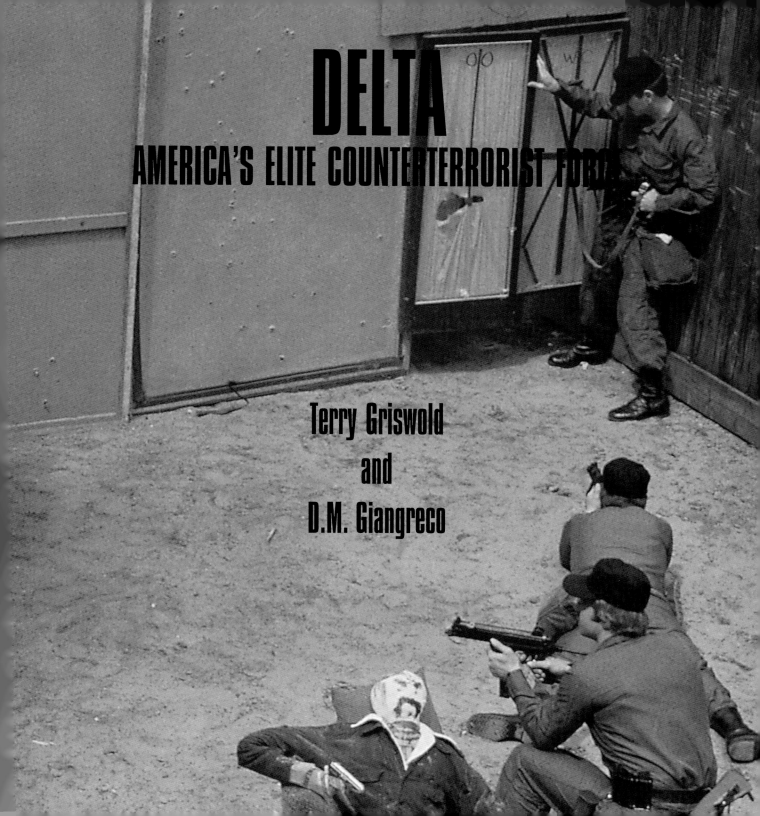

DELTA
AMERICA'S ELITE COUNTERTERRORIST FORCE

Terry Griswold

and

D.M. Giangreco

Preface

*This is another type of war, new in its intensity, ancient in its origins—
war by guerrillas, subversives, insurgents, assassins . . . seeking victory
by eroding and exhausting the enemy instead of engaging him.*

President John F. Kennedy, 1962

The success of Fidel Castro's Cuban revolution in 1959 and rising tide of insurgencies around the globe made it clear to newly elected President of the United States John F. Kennedy that the focus of communist expansionism had shifted to the Third World. Kennedy firmly believed that the communist's ominous Cuban foothold in the Western Hemisphere could be countered by a program aimed at stimulating peaceful evolution instead of violent revolution. His response to the communists' challenge was the Alliance for Progress.

The Alliance for Progress was a serious effort to promote stability in Latin America through political reform, as well as economic and social development, and it served as a model for similar US commitments in other less–developed regions. Embryonic communist insurgencies threatened this evolutionary process, and Kennedy moved quickly to blunt their threat by devising and implementing a doctrine of counterrevolutionary warfare. More than thirty years later, the descendants of his elite, unconventional warriors continue to assist dozens of potential or fledgling democracies while specifically tasked, direct–action arms of the Army, Navy, and Air Force stand ready to fight an insidious by–product of Third World instability and the recent Cold War: terrorism.

In the years following the Iran hostage crisis and disaster at *Desert I*, a great deal has been written on the 1st Special Forces Operational Detachment–DELTA. Most of the focus has been on the origins of the failed rescue attempt, the major players, technical problems, and in some cases, the strategic and tactical leadership of the units involved. However, the guts and backbone of DELTA and similar units is the individual trooper. For the most part, he is typical of those in the special operations community.

But there is more to the soldiers who make up DELTA. Each man is a self–starter who not only displays personal initiative but can work well when part of a team. They are mature individuals, confident in themselves and their unit, who are unquestioned experts in their craft. These qualities are more than just factors in what makes a good DELTA trooper, they are the essence of DELTA. And while most of the unit's officers stay around long enough to learn the art of counterterrorist (CT) operations, it is still the old hands, the highly professional noncommissioned and warrant officers, that keep DELTA on the straight and narrow. This story examines CT training and operations from their viewpoint: the elite special operations team members who must wade into the dirty business of counterterrorism to protect US lives and interests.

In a free—and financially strapped—society, there is immense pressure on units costing the taxpayer millions of dollars to produce and show results. Because of the clandestine nature of DELTA's mission, however, the full story of this extraordinary and sophisticated unit cannot be told no matter how important its unique capabilities are to the ongoing war against international terrorism. This relative anonymity makes DELTA an easy target for congressional budget cutters searching for a "quick fix" and the unit may well find itself as an expensive toy up for funding cuts in the austere future. Such actions would be disasterous.

The information in this book is based upon the research and experience of the authors and does not represent the positions or policies of any official, agency, or department of the United States government, British government, or any other government. The information was derived from unclassified publications and sources and is intended to neither confirm or deny, officially or unofficially, the views of those governments.

Uncredited photos in this book were taken by US armed forces personnel and are in the public domain. The names of current DELTA troopers are classified and, unless otherwise noted, all names given for soldiers below the rank of colonel are pseudonyms.

Chapter 1
Out of the Desert

The takeoff had to go right the first time. There would be no second chance. As the last item on the pre–flight list was checked off, the pilot revved up the EC-130E's Allison turboprops to gain maximum power. Releasing the already–straining brakes and pushing the throttles to the firewall, the pilot nursed his aircraft slowly forward out of the jumbled mass of wheel ruts furrowed deeply into the Iranian desert. The straining engines created a mini sandstorm that all but obliterated the ghastly funeral pyre they were leaving behind. Resembling some prehistoric bird of prey, the dark Hercules sluggishly lifted away from the makeshift desert runway and the disaster that Operation *Eagle Claw* had become.

This aircraft was one of the last special operations birds leaving Iran after the aborted rescue attempt to free American hostages in Teheran. The Ayatol-

RH-53D Sea Stallions from the USS *Nimitz* practicing low–level formation flying before the attempted rescue of American hostages in Iran.

lah Khomeini's Revolutionary Guards had held their fifty–three prisoners in the captured US Embassy compound for nearly six months and the half–dozen Hercules had been slated to play a key role in rescuing them. Now, as five heavily loaded aircraft flew into the early morning darkness, an EC-130E tanker and RH-53D Sea Stallion helicopter lay blazing in the desert. Through the swirling sand, passengers with portholes could clearly see what each had never believed possible: failure. Despite well–laid plans, the team's efforts had ended in an inferno of exploding ammunition and twisted, burning aircraft.

What happened at the refuel site code–named *Desert I* has been argued about and even embellished in a Hollywood adventure film, but the basic facts remain the same. The six special operations aircraft that penetrated Iran on the night of April 24–25, 1980 were configured either as tankers to refuel the Sea Stallion helicopters or as transports to bring in the assault teams and their ground support. After reaching the site, the mission was scrubbed

137

and the force had to prepare for exfiltration.

The decision to abort was made after three of the eight Sea Stallions either failed to reach *Desert I* or could not proceed because of mechanical difficulties. Not enough helicopters were available to carry out the mission, so there was nothing for the rotary and fixed–wing aircraft to do but return to their separate starting points. In preparation for the exfiltration, one of the RH-53Ds had to be repositioned. During that maneuver, the helicopter's main rotor smashed into the cockpit of a parked EC-130; both aircraft erupted into flame, and the explosions turned the stark desert night into a ghastly beacon. During the hasty evacuation of the site, the remaining Sea Stallions were left behind.

On board the EC-130E were members of America's newly formed counterterrorist unit known simply as DELTA. The unit had been activated in November 1977 but was untested or, as military professionals would say, "unblooded," and this was to be their first operational mission. But while the troopers anticipated that their baptism of fire would soon come in Teheran, they instead found themselves trapped in a terrifying inferno fed by thousands of gallons of aircraft fuel. As one of the survivors would later report, the DELTA Blue Team troopers and air crew from the stricken EC-130 struggled to "unass the muther" as best they could, bearing their injured with them.

Caught in the tanker's burning, smoke–filled cargo bay, Master Sergeant Leonard M. Harris was quickly overcome by smoke as he attempted to rescue an Air Force crewman. Luckily for both men, they were pulled from the burning plane by other

(**Top**) RH-53D Sea Stallions on the aft hangar bay of the USS *Nimitz* before launch and (**left**) a burned–out hulk at *Desert I*. Note the .50cal machine guns mounted in the cabin doors at the extreme left and right of the top photo. *Wide World Photos*.

members of DELTA.

Harris and the other survivors were loaded into various aircraft for the trip out. Now, as the last Hercules flew in a rough trail formation through the inky darkness toward the Indian Ocean and safety, Harris began to regain consciousness. Watery eyes fixed on a light on the cabin roof and then wandered down to scan the confusion around him in the crowded cargo bay. DELTA troopers, dressed in Levis, boots, and black field jackets, were interspersed with air crews, combat control team members, and other support personnel. Some sat in stunned silence, still wearing their woolen naval watch caps, while others were stripping off layers of body armor, web gear, and sweat–stained clothing. Checking his own physical condition, Harris was surprised that, despite his brush with death, the only damage that he was able to perceive, other than a raw throat from smoke inhalation, was a good singeing of his field jacket and a relatively minor burn across the back of his left hand.

Looking down at his recently black–dyed field jacket, he absently picked at the melted tape that covered the only insignia on the assault teams' tactical uniforms: a small American flag sewn on the right jacket sleeve. The troopers were to have displayed the flags after entering the Embassy grounds so that the hostages would readily follow them out during the exfiltration. After all, in their uniforms, the rescue team looked more like muggers in a New York subway than members of an elite counterterrorist unit.

Peering across the red–lighted cargo compartment, Harris realized that he and the rest of the passengers were sitting, lying, or in some other way trying to get comfortable while riding on the bouncing fuel bladder covering the length of the plane. While team medical personnel provided aid, others appeared to be sorting out what had happened to them. Regaining a sense of stability, Harris was

helped into a sitting position by another trooper. He noticed that his palms were wet with sweat, and not really knowing if it was from fear or just shock, he wiped them on his faded Levis. Leaning his head back against the cold metal skin of the Hercules, he muttered, "Good ol' Herky Bird." The vibration and steady hum of its engines made him think of his airborne instructors at Fort Benning, Georgia. "Damn if they weren't right," he thought. "The 130 *is* a living creature."

In the absence of the fear and pain that fatigue brings, he began to reflect on the events that brought him to this godforsaken situation. "How in the hell did I get in this mess?"

The Reception Committee

As the last of the special operations aircraft lifted off from the chaos of *Desert I*, another intense drama was taking place in the Iranian capital. From a clandestine communications site well outside Teheran, Dick Meadows, a highly decorated and skilled former Green Beret, received word of *Desert I*'s disaster. His vulnerable advance party of Special Forces soldiers had infiltrated the city only a few days earlier under various cover stories designed to hide all traces of their true identity and mission. Now, however, events beyond their control had forced them to immediately execute their own escape and evasion plans.

Nearly six months before *Eagle Claw*, on November 4, 1979, "subject matter experts" from all relevant military and civilian agencies were drawn to-

Revolutionary Guard checkpoints in Teheran surreptitiously photographed by Army personnel. They are armed with a variety of 7.62mm Heckler & Koch G3 rifles manufactured in Iran under a license obtained from the West German firm. (**Top**) A Revolutionary Guard is carrying several weapons to comrades up the street while, (**left**) the mountains ringing Teheran are clearly visible.

gether to form an ad hoc joint task force (JTF) charged with both the planning and execution of the hostage rescue. Like so often in the military, the "old boy" network was initially used to fill the JTF. This approach brought in many talented people whose broad range of expertise at first quickened the planning phase of the operation. Unfortunately, though, interservice and interdepartmental bickering soon created coordination problems. Despite later denials, virtually everyone either wanted a piece of the action or seemed intent on distancing themselves from the operation. The resulting problems—demonstrated by the initial lack of cooperation from the Central Intelligence Agency (CIA) and State Department officials—tended to frustrate rather than facilitate planning by the JTF's staff officers under the stewardship of Major General James B. Vought, a highly respected paratrooper who had much experience working with Rangers.

Ideally, CIA operatives would have already been in the "area of interest" providing current intelligence and would have been responsible for obtaining critical items such as "safe houses" and locally procured trucks in Teheran. However, at this time in its history, the agency was undergoing a number of reorganizations prompted by highly publicized criticism of its role in major incidents going back as far as the Bay of Pigs invasion of Cuba. Sensational reports of alleged assassination attempts on foreign leaders, Vietnam's numerous "black" or covert operations (including the unjustly maligned *Phoenix* program), and the increasing number of former CIA employees who turned into authors of "tell–all" books added to the growing public perception of a bumbling group of spies running amuck.

After Jimmy Carter assumed the presidency in 1977, he installed a fellow Annapolis graduate, Admiral Stansfield Turner, to oversee the restructuring of the CIA and the institution of his administration's "Georgia approach" to governmental man-

agement. Under Turner, hundreds of experienced personnel were laid off (referred to in the government's bureaucratic language as a reduction in force or RIF). The agency soon became heavily dependent on mechanical and technical means as the primary method of intelligence gathering instead of using them in conjunction with, or as a complement to, human intelligence collection, or HUMINT. By the time the Embassy in Teheran was seized, Middle Eastern operations were in a major decline; in fact, the last full–time operative in Iran had already slipped into the warm embrace of retirement.

Despite the CIA's reinfiltration of one of its agents into Teheran, DELTA's thirst for intelligence on a broad range of matters was not satisfied. The "black boxes" were clearly failing to produce the information required to carry out this delicate operation, and the *Eagle Claw* planners in DELTA began to look within the special operations community for HUMINT collection means to make up the shortfall. The search led them to Dick Meadows.

This was not the first time that Meadows had participated in an effort to free US prisoners. Ten years before, he had been in charge of the compound assault team during Operation *Ivory Coast* (more commonly known as the Son Tay Raid), an airborne assault on a prisoner of war camp only twenty miles from Hanoi in North Vietnam.* Other exploits in Southeast Asia included the capture of North Vietnamese artillery pieces in Laos and the recapture of a major CIA outpost in that same country. He was an expert in what are referred to as "low–visibility insertions" and "takedowns."

Meadows had become a civilian advisor to DELTA after retiring from the Army, and his extensive background in clandestine cross–border operations, as well as his completion of the British Special Air Service (SAS) selection course, carried a great deal of weight in choosing him to enter Teheran ahead of the rescue force. Above all, the JTF planners knew he could be trusted to do his best to accomplish the mission——and, besides, he knew DELTA inside and out. This knowledge, however, could prove to be a rather negative aspect of his qualifications if he were caught.

Meadows' orders were to infiltrate the chaos of Teheran, establish a safe house, locally procure covered trucks to transport the rescue force, and guide the rescuers from the landing zone to their assault positions near the Embassy. In military terms, he was the reception committee and, on paper at least, this part of the operation was one of the less–complicated portions of the entire plan. One critical concern of Meadows was his cover and its associated background information and the story

---

(**Top**) A mass demonstration at "Freedom Square" on Eisenhower Avenue about a half–dozen miles west of the US Embassy. In the unlikely event that Iranian mobs would react quickly enough to threaten the rescue mission, an orbiting AC-130H Specter gunship would perform "crowd control" around the embassy and prevent the armored vehicles based at an army ordnance depot to the north and the police headquarters near the Ministry of Foreign Affairs to the south from intervening. If the Specter found itself hard–pressed to keep the threats at bay, a second gunship covering Mehrabad International Airport to the west, would destroy Iranian F-4 Phantom jets, capable of chasing down the rescue aircraft, and assist at the embassy. (**Left**) A Revolutionary Guard bunker in central Teheran. The broad avenues which criss–crossed the capital, such as Roosevelt, which ran between the embassy and the soccer stadium and north to the army depot, were fed by an intricate—but well–mapped—maze of narrow streets fully or partially blocked by these randomly placed defensive positions.

*The over four dozen US prisoners were held at the camp but were moved shortly before the raid and remained in captivity until after the 1973 signing of the Paris Peace Accords. One side benefit of the operation, however, was an accidental attack on a nearby compound that apparently killed as many as 200 East Block or Soviet specialists involved in upgrading North Vietnam's air defenses.

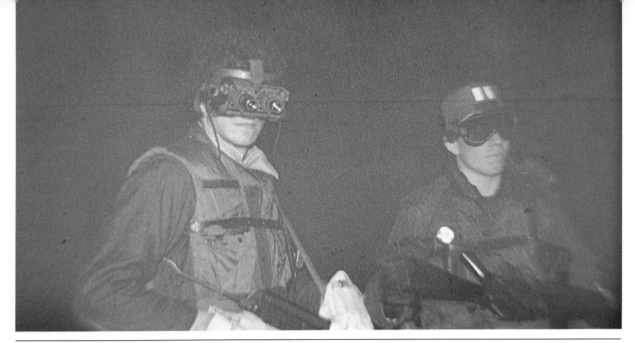

A force of a dozen US Army Rangers and DELTA members made up two teams to secure the road running through the *Desert I* refuel sight. (**Above**) Troopers armed with a Colt M16 assault rifle and Walther MP-L submachine gun peer intently through the night. The relatively heavy PVS-5 night vision goggles, used during the operation, could only be worn for about thirty minutes at a time before a pilot or trooper would have to hand it off to a designated partner to wear. Within minutes after they rode their Yamaha motorcycles out of the belly of the first MC-130 to land, the team captured a bus with forty–four Iranian civilians, blew up a gasoline tanker truck with a light antitank weapon, and ran off another truck.

Although *Eagle Claw* planners were later criticized for establishing the refuel site in a moderately traveled area, mission parameters left them little choice, and DELTA planned to fly any Iranians taken into custody back to Misirah Island on the returning MC-130s. The Iranians would then be flown back to Iranian territory and released at Manzariyeh Air Base the following night. There were never any plans to hold any detained Iranians in exchange for the US hostages (such a move would have had disasterous political repercussions), and if the mission were aborted after they had been flown from *Desert I*, the Iranians would be speedily turned over to the International Red Cross for repatriation.

fabricated to explain what brought a Westerner to this hostile land. CIA liaison officers supplied him with an Irish background, including all the necessary documentation and accessories, while the JTF provided additional backups and an enhanced language capability in the form of three sergeants recruited in Germany, two from a covert Special Forces unit and one from the Air Force.

Unlike Meadows, these men already had covers and were conducting their daily lives under that blanket of anonymity. All were foreign–born na-

tionals who had joined America's armed forces and were now US citizens. One of the men was a native of Germany and was intimately acquainted with the murky world of working with and supporting intelligence requirements levied on the Army by other agencies such as the CIA. Another of the operatives was born in the British Isles and was easily cloaked with the mantle of a Scottish background. The third (who had undergone no previous Special Forces training) was a native of the Middle East and was fluent in Farsi, the primary language of Iran. These men would provide Meadows with the additional skills required of the advance party.

When it was discovered, rather late in the planning, that three high–ranking hostages were being held in the Ministry of Foreign Affairs building six miles from the Embassy, an additional thirteen soldiers were recruited from a clandestine unit in Germany. Not enough time was available to change the basic plan as well as shift existing personnel to other targets, so it fell upon these men to fill the operational void created by the last–minute intelligence. Special Forces detachments like theirs had been preparing to fight potential Soviet invaders in the extensively built–up areas of western Germany since the late 1950s and were composed of experts in urban warfare.

Eagle Claw's mission profile called for the advance team to rendezvous with the DELTA rescue force staging out of a little–used airfield near Qena, 300 miles south of Cairo in central Egypt. Upon receipt of the execution message, the 132 men of the rescue force and additional support personnel flew on two C-141s from Egypt to an air base operated by British and Omani personnel on the large Arabian Sea island of Misirah. At the same time, the helicopter element located on the aircraft carrier USS *Nimitz* "patrolling" nearby in the Gulf of Oman prepared to launch its RH-53D helicopters to an isolated spot, code–named *Desert I*, in Iran's Dasht–e Karir (Salt Desert). While all this was taking place, a contingent of four AC-130E and H Specter gunships were readied for their launch the following night. They would fly directly from Qena to Teheran where they would support the rescue. The Specters would be refueled by KC-135 tankers as they passed over Saudi Arabia.

The next phase of the operation called for DELTA's surgical assault force, along with its security and support element, to take off from Misirah in EC- and MC-130Es of the 8th Special Operations Squadron.

Their destination, *Desert I*, had already been surveyed by an Air Force Combat Control Team member who placed remotely operated infrared beacons along the "hasty" landing strip. After the force successfully rendezvoused at *Desert I* near Garmsar, 265 nautical miles southeast of Teheran, the assault element was to load onto the helicopters and fly on to *Desert II* in the rugged, mountainous region just southeast of the capital. Once there, the choppers would be hidden nearby, at a site codenamed *Figbar*, while the assault force linked up with the reception committee before dawn.

The assault force would settle in for the day while the DELTA commander, Colonel Charlie A. Beckwith would infiltrate Teheran along with a select group of twelve troopers who would receive the trucks gathered by Meadows' team near the city at a secure warehouse called the "Mushroom." It was their job to drive the small convoy out of the city on the second night of the operation and collect the rest of the rescue force from the hide site. After transferring to the six large, tarpaulin–covered Mercedes trucks and a Volkswagen van, 106 DELTA and Special Forces troopers would journey to the capital where final preparations for the impending rescue would be made. The plan called for the rescue force to depart from *Desert II* at 2030 hours and be in their designated assault positions by 2300 hours. Meadows would take Colonel Beckwith on a personal reconnaissance of the target before the attack at approximately the same time that the AC-130s were lifting off in Egypt.

The main assault group's three teams (code–named *Red*, *White*, and *Blue*) and Foreign Ministry assault group would use the principles of surprise, shock, and coordinated movement to take out the Ayatollah's Revolutionary Guards. As soon as the short, violent rescue operation erupted at the walled Embassy compound, the hidden RH-53D helicop-

(Top) An M151 roars over a a sand dune in Egypt. The soldiers given the mission of guarding the dirt road running through *Desert I* were not picked until after the main body of Rangers, slated to seize Manzariyeh Air Base, had arrived at Qena, Egypt. Intensive training was immediately begun for both the road–watch and airfield–seizure teams. (Above) Before operations could begin, Air Force ground personnel had to be flown into both Qena and the British–Omani air base on Misirah Island to set up communications and logistics for the thirty–four special operations tankers, transports, and gunships involved in *Eagle Claw*.

ters would emerge from their camouflaged position near *Desert II*. One would head for the large park surrounding the Foreign Ministry, while the rest would fly to sites at the rear of the Embassy compound and the Amjedeih soccer stadium across the

street, where both hostages and rescuers would be picked up. If the compound site couldn't be cleared of obstructions in time, all extractions would be conducted from the stadium.

Throughout the ground phase of the operation, one AC-130 gunship would orbit over the target area providing fire support, and another would cover the two Iranian F-4 Phantom jets on strip alert at Teheran's nearby Mehrabad International Airport. Two additional Specters would orbit close by in reserve. All parties concerned were fully confident that the massive firepower the Specters could bring to bear on the surrounding area would be more than enough to suppress any Revolutionary Guards attempting to reinforce their Embassy security force and prevent the infamous Iranian mobs from interfering with the rescue. As one of the gunship pilots was later to explain, the Specters' awesome firepower was the "best crowd–control measure" available.

While the AC-130s dominated the area, the helicopters would leave the chaos of Teheran for nearby Manzariyeh Air Base only thirty–five minutes away. Manzariyeh was to have already been secured by a seventy–five–man Ranger contingent and support personnel flying directly from Qena on four MC-130s. This elite light infantry unit was composed of experts in airfield seizure. Using M151s (commonly, if erroneously, referred to as jeeps) and commercial off-road motorcycles, they were capable of gobbling up the sprawling but lightly defended facility in a matter of minutes.

Throughout the exfiltration, F-14A Tomcat fighters and KA-6D Intruder tankers from the USS *Nimitz* would orbit over Persian Gulf waters— on call to knock down any hostile aircraft coming after the vulnerable transports, and gunships leaving Manzariyeh. If all went well, the entire force— Rangers, Special Forces, Meadows' team, support personnel, DELTA, and their newly rescued char-

Sea Stallions receiving preflight preparations on the deck of the USS *Nimitz*. The RH-53Ds had been freshly painted to mimic the look of Iranian helicopters and also carried green, white, and red Iranian identification roundels that could be added to further confuse prying eyes.

ges—would be quickly loaded aboard a pair of C-141s, which had made a quick dash from Dhahran, Saudi Arabia, and exfiltrate to Qena before the Iranians could take any effective countermeasures. There was no way to fly the helicopters out of Iran, and they were to be destroyed before the last Rangers left the airfield.

The catastrophe at *Desert I* changed all that. After Meadows received word over a clandestine radio to abort the mission, he notified the team, which dispersed from the safe house, and all made their individual ways to the passenger terminal at Teheran's Mehrabad International Airport. Security within the terminal was visibly increased. Unshaven and clad in an irregular mix of civilian and military clothing, the pride of Iran's Revolutionary Guard nervously paced back and forth near entrances, fingering their newly acquired Heckler & Koch G3 rifles. The menacing looks—as well as a healthy respect for the weapons' stopping power—caused Meadows to give each of the guards a grudging deference. Swallowing hard, Meadows entered the terminal entrance and walked directly to the Swiss Air ticket counter. Very deliberately, and somewhat slowly, he reached into the inner pocket of his corduroy jacket for the cash necessary to open the

first of many doors to the waiting jet and freedom.

While being processed, he noticed that his "Scottish" comrade was in another part of the terminal area, being heavily questioned by a combination of Revolutionary Guards, customs officials, and men in soldiers' uniforms. Meadows later learned that the large amounts of US currency that had initially brought this unwanted attention to the Scotsman stayed in Iran with that "interested" group of officials. The newfound hatred of the "Great Satan" obviously did not extend into financial matters, and well-placed bribes of American greenbacks continued to do the trick.

Reaching down to retrieve his carryall, Meadows realized that despite the fact that word had been received about an "invasion" to the south, the security efforts within the airport remained disjointed and uncoordinated. Walking at a casual but determined gait toward the Swiss Air jet, he wondered what things were like at the Embassy.

Chapter 2
A New Game in Town

Kill one and terrorize a thousand.

Sun Tzu, 500 BC

estering Arab resentment of America's direct and substantial support of Israel grew steadily after the United States became the Jewish state's chief sponsor in the wake of the 1967 Six Day War. By 1973, when massive American arms shipments played a critical role in blocking an Egyptian–Syrian victory in the Yom Kippur War, the United States was firmly planted on a collision course with the rising tide of pan–Arab nationalism. From now on, Americans would no longer be incidental victims of terrorist attacks. They would be the targets.

During the Six Day War, the sweeping successes of the Israeli military machine made it clear to the Arab world that change could not be guaranteed by conventional forces alone. One of the key audiences watching from the sidelines with a great deal of interest were the millions of Palestinians living in forced exile not only in the Middle Eastern countries, but also in Europe. Across the Atlantic, the United States was focused on the problems of the war in Vietnam, internal strife centered on the civil

rights movement, and there was growing unrest on college campuses. Against this background, the United States hoped that every effort would be made to solve the numerous long–standing issues in the Middle East peacefully. Failing that, preventing disagreements from boiling up into open warfare was the least that could be strived for. But as world affairs would have it, the Palestinian issue exploded to the surface, amid smoke and gunfire, in the Hashemite kingdom of Jordan.

When shoved into a corner by Soviet–sponsored, Syrian–armed Palestinian forces intent on using his country as a staging area for raids on Israel, King Hussein ibn–Talal used his army to drive the Palestinians into Syria and reasserted his authority. The king and his Hashemite followers had never enjoyed an easy relationship with the various *fedayeen* groups making up Yasir Arafat's Palestine Liberation Organization (PLO), and its military arm, the *Fatah*, which was openly encroaching on the country's control of the Jordan River Valley. One faction, George Habbash's Popular Front for the Liberation of Palestine (PFLP)—the largest and most anti–Hashemite of the *fedayeen*—had worked feverishly to undermine Hussein's throne

One of the terrorists holding Israeli athletes at the Munich Olympics relays demands to German negotiators in front of millions of television viewers.

Television crews and reporters line the balcony of the Beirut International Airport terminal during the nine–day hijacking of a TWA jet, June 22, 1985. The media was—and continues to be—one of international terrorism's most important weapons. *Wide World Photos*

long before the bloody confrontation.

The intense fighting for the capital of Amman and across northern Jordan in September 1970 caused a great deal of worry in the Western world, and supplies were sent in from a number of countries. Military forces were also alerted to move in and provide help, but the Jordanian Army succeeded without them. This stunning defeat of the *Fatah*–led Palestinians, however, laid the groundwork for the emergence of full–fledged terrorist organizations such as Black September, a radical group that operated as an arm of the "moderate" PLO until it split off on its own. The name itself commemorates the *fedayeen's* expulsion from Jor-

dan, and they took their revenge on the man who directed King Hussein's forces, Premier Wafsi Tal, by assassinating him the following year in Cairo.

While terrorists have never hesitated at murdering any Arab leader who was not in strict agreement with the dogma of their particular group, it is generally not considered socially acceptable to blame other "brother" Arabs for their numerous defeats to Israel. The fledgling terrorists saw the Western world as the cause of virtually all Arab problems—whether perceived or real—and several factors combined to make Western Europe an excellent target for their activities. Initially, these countries made particularly juicy targets because of their close proximity to the Middle East and the fact that their open societies allowed the terrorists a remarkable degree of freedom to carry out their activities.

These new terrorists were also a particularly media–savvy bunch who fully understood the rami-

The grand finale of the Palestine Liberation Organization's September 1970 hijacking of three civilian airliners. Their 300 passengers were held for a week and, after their release, the aircraft were blown up at an abandoned airfield near Amman, Jordan.

fications of the still–evolving revolution in global telecommunications. Recent advances in television technology allowed the terrorist networks to increase their range beyond the printed word of newspapers, and much of the world's population now lived with their acts as a daily fact of life. Ratings–conscious news agencies and the viewers themselves had enabled the television camera to become one of the terrorists' chief weapons.

The use or threat of violence against individuals to affect a much larger, related group is not a new phenomenon; what is call "terrorism" today is a tactic of warfare that has been employed throughout history. Bombing, hijacking, assassination, and kidnapping are simply facets of this type of warfare magnified a thousand–fold by the electronic media. In the early 1970s, the world was introduced to such new television stars as Black September* and the Baader–Meinhoff Gang. Their activities were caught on television in 1970 when several commer-

cial airliners were hijacked and taken with their 300 passengers and crew to Dawson Field, a desert airfield 40 miles from Amman that had formerly been used by Britain's Royal Air Force. After a week, the hostages were removed from the aircraft which were then blown up in full view of the world. But the event having the deepest and most far–reaching impact was the drama which unfolded at the 1972 Olympic Games in Munich, West Germany.

*One of the many organization names used by Sabri Khalil al–Banna (alias Abu Nidal) in an effort to sow confusion in the West as well as make the "armed struggle" against Israel appear larger than it is. In addition to Black September, other names used by the Abu Nidal Organization include: Fatah Revolutionary Council, Black June Organization, the Arab Revolutionary Brigades and Revolutionary Organization of Socialist Muslims.

Viewers were stunned by image after image of the wanton murder of innocents flashing across the screen, and governments in the West soon felt their power to control events slipping from their hands. Terrorist actions—or even the threat of such actions—were increasingly shaping policy decisions on major questions.

One ramification of these terrorist attacks not observed by the public was the new requirements

As an instructer looks on, a member of SAS takes position and returns fire against mock terrorists during a training exercise. He is positioned behind the engine block, which can provide adequate protection against most conventional pistol and rifle ammunition.

placed on international law enforcement and military forces. After the failure to negotiate or rescue successfully for the release of the Israeli athletes, West Germany's security needs were scrutinized from every possible angle with Teutonic efficiency. The findings were many, but the realists who would have to face the next round of fighting concluded that virtually every Western nation was now in the battle with this ancient form of warfare. The emergence of a new combatant—the counterterrorist—marked Western Europe's response.

Each country dealt with the new problem based on its own perception of how various political, economic, social, and, in some cases, religious factors af-

fected security considerations. The Germans established a special unit within its border police—later presented to the world as GSG-9, short for *Grenzschutzgruppe 9*—and the French formed the *Groupe d'Intervention de la Grendarmerie National* (GIGN). The British turned to their old standby, the SAS, while the Americans took the approach of wait and see, or more typically, "This will not happen to us." Yet, as the world continued to spin through the early 1970s, it was painfully obvious that the terrorists were moving a step or two ahead of the various national security forces and could attack whenever or wherever it was to their advantage. The organizations established to blunt terrorist attacks would, however, soon prove that they were forces to be reckoned with.

In October 1977 at Mogadishu Airport in Somalia, the German GSG-9 took revenge for their country's embarrassment at Munich by accomplishing a difficult aircraft "takedown" in response to a hijacking. Unknown to the terrorists, the Germans had learned much from the tragedy of Munich, and, with the help of two SAS commandos who blew open the aircraft's doors, a thirty–man GSG-9 force stormed the plane during the early morning hours. Later, in May 1980, the SAS gained international fame by conducting one of the most daring and highly publicized hostage rescues, when Pagoda Troop of B Squadron, 22nd SAS Regiment, launched their spectacular assault on the Iranian Embassy in Princess Gate, London, as television cameras broadcast the action around the world.

Preceding these events was the most famous rescue operation of the period: the raid on Entebbe Airport in Uganda, conducted by the Israeli special forces. Launched from bases within their own borders, more than 2,500 miles to the north, the commandos of Unit 269 flew directly into the site where 103 hostages were held. In the early morning darkness of July 4, 1976, Operation *Thunderbolt* was

Great Britain's 22nd SAS and US Special Forces have enjoyed a long, close relationship which began in earnest during the late 1950s. (**Above**) Lieutenant General Sir Charles Richardson, Britain's Director General of Military Training, inspects an SAS unit during an exercise with 5th and 7th Special Forces Groups at Camp Troy, North Carolina, September 28, 1962. General Richardson's visit turned out to be a pivotal event for the SAS. While the conservative British military establishment had grudgingly conceded the regiment's value in certain situations, the unit was generally thought of as little more than a "private army" of ill–disciplined mavericks that skimmed some of Britain's best soldiers from the top of traditional regiments. A tour with the SAS could kill a young officer's career.

At Camp Troy and Fort Bragg, Richardson witnessed SAS troopers studying advanced demolition and field medicine techniques plus engaging in specialized training in foreign languages, as well as a worldwide assortment of weapons. He left North Carolina greatly impressed with what he saw, and the almost immediate improvement in the attitude of the British military establishment toward the SAS was credited to the general's glowing report.

The same month that General Richardson visited SAS elements training in the United States, the US Special Forces soldier who would later found DELTA, Charlie Beckwith, was leading a troop from A Squadron, SAS, in a combined exercise with the French "paras" of the *1st Bataillon de Parachutistes de Choc* in Corsica. Beckwith had been attached to the regiment as part of an ongoing exchange program and, in 1963, would ship out to Malaya with the SAS to take part in deep–jungle penetration missions against guerrillas along the Thai border. The tour nearly cost him his life but, upon his return to Fort Bragg, he pushed hard (very hard) to have SAS training and organizational techniques adopted by Special Forces.

Israeli commandos, circa 1960, are representative of the high degree of individuality commonly found in elite special operations units. Informally dressed in a variety of military jackets, coats, scarves, and sweaters, they are a diverse lot with members who might easily pass themselves off as Britons, Arabs, Frenchmen, or Americans. Indeed, they may have once been Britons, Arabs, Frenchmen or Americans before emigrating to Israel. Such elite troopers from Unit 269 were responsible for the successful hostage rescue at Entebbe. Note the use of personal weapons of different types and calibers attuned to the taste of the individual soldier. The soldier in the center is armed with the standard Soviet assault rifle of the day, the 7.62mm Kalashnikov AK-47, while the others carry 9mm Uzi submachine guns, which were based on earlier Czechoslovakian weapons but designed and produced in Israel.

carried out with clockwork precision. Keeping it simple, the rescue force landed in four C-130s (why jump your men in when they can be landed in a nice neat package?). The lead Hercules casually taxied to within 200 yards of the terminal building holding the hostages, and a black Mercedes sedan— the standard mode of transportation of all Ugandan officers from company commander on up—rolled serenely down the ramp. The sedan cruised up to the brightly lit building, followed by a pair of non-descript Land Rovers, and suddenly disgorged nine Unit 269 commandos.

Within minutes, the Israeli strike force had secured the terminal area and airfield perimeter, removing a potential problem by blowing up the Ugandan MIG fighter aircraft and then loaded up the rescued hostages. The rescue force commander, Colonel Jonathan Netanyahu, was killed, as well as the entire terrorist gang and an undetermined number of Ugandan soldiers protecting the hostage takèrs. All but one of the hostages, an elderly woman who had been taken to a hospital and was later murdered, were quickly freed and flown to Nairobi, Kenya, where casualties were transfered to a waiting jet airliner equipped for medical emergencies. The GSG-9 chief, Colonel Ulrich Wegener, had also accompanied the Israelis, probably because two West German terrorists were involved in the hijacking.

Americans Become Targets

The United States entered the CT arena as a very unwilling participant. The primary reasons were America's deeply engrained tradition of keeping military and police powers well separated and the resultant conservative approach of the US military leadership when dealing with what they felt was inherently a police problem. Neither the political nor military hierarchies originally supported the view, held by many in the lower echelons, of the increasing danger to the United States and its interests by media–savvy terrorists.

US intelligence agencies gained their first direct lessons from the *nouveau* terrorists during the September 1970 uprising in Jordan. It was feared that *Fatah* insurgents would seize the US Embassy in Amman, and US paratroopers were alerted to, if necessary, seize the International Airport, allow an armored force to land, race into Amman and retake the Embassy.

As with Operation *Eagle Claw* some ten years later, the Jordanian rescue plan was complicated, unwieldy, and fraught with unnecessary risks. For example, the 509th Airborne Infantry, which was selected to seize the airport, would have had to fly to Jordan via an extremely lengthy, circuitous route from their staging area in West Germany. Instead of taking the normal route over continental Europe to reach the eastern Mediterranean, their operational plan called for a flight out into the North Sea and Atlantic Ocean around Spain to the Gibraltar slot, and then travel the length of the Mediterranean. The force would have to take this roundabout route because the "allies" of NATO would not grant overflight rights—a situation unpleasantly similar to what F-111 pilots would find sixteen years later during a retaliatory raid on Libya for sponsoring a terrorist bombing.

American planners were faced with a number of similar situations over the next two years, and missions were not approved for execution. Either White House or State Department jitters prevented the launching of airborne or Special Forces units to counter terrorist assaults. Terrorist networks in the Middle East, however, could easily strike soft targets and continued to target Israeli citizens. Americans stationed in Germany, as well as West Germans, found themselves the targets of former antiwar students now turned terrorists. In May 1972, the Baader–Meinhoff Gang, also known as the Red Army Faction, finally forced the issue on the United States by conducting six separate bombings.

Their targets were such sacred areas as the officers' club in Frankfurt and the headquarters building of US Army, Europe, located in the sleepy university town of Heidelberg. The news media provided some coverage of these strikes but, understandably, only a fraction of the blow–by–blow reporting which characterized the debacle of that year's Olympic Games.

While the taking of American hostages was not yet a problem, perceptive military leaders realized that the United States needed to be ready and able to respond to terrorism, and units within the Army's Special Forces community were tasked to conduct rescues using what is commonly referred to as the "hasty option response." In lay terms, this means that if the hostage takers begin to harm their prisoners, the team attempts a rescue as quickly and efficiently as possible. The lives of the hostages are of utmost concern, but the hasty response does not allow for the meticulous planning, coordination, and rehearsals that are required to carry out the surgical strikes so often associated with the highly skilled CT units. The hasty response is the operation that all counterterrorists hope they never have to conduct. It is the option that makes a commander wake up at night in a cold sweat.

Due to command relationship conflicts and the numerous constraints on personnel and funds, which prevent in–depth training, the hasty option mission is still found in a number of Army Special Forces groups around the world. This approach, however, leaves little for the in–depth training required to perfect even the most fundamental aspects of aircraft or room entry techniques.

Soon after Munich, a number of American military and civilian advisors recommended that a suitable force be established to fight terrorism. But it was not until the increased threat was brought home to President Jimmy Carter and the feasibility of creating a unit like those who struck at Entebbe

The aftermath of a Red Army Faction car bomb explosion at Rhein–Main Air Base outside Frankfurt, West Germany, August 8, 1985. Over twenty people were injured and the blast killed one US airman and the wife of another. The explosives were packed into a car with forged US license plates and driven to the parking lot outside the headquarters of the 435th Tactical Air Wing. It is believed that the terrorist who drove the vehicle gained access to the base by using the identification card of a US serviceman murdered the previous night.

and Mogadishu that the United States acknowledged the need to establish its own full–time, state–of–the–art counterterrorist response unit. The success of Operation *Thunderbolt* further confirmed the idea that many US planners had been fostering. The United States needed to have a small, surgical force capable of carrying out such operations. It was their contention that, despite the claims of the airborne community, Ranger companies and battalions were neither trained nor equipped for hostage rescues.

From the smoke of military infighting and political intrigue, 1st Special Forces Operational Detachment–DELTA was formed in 1977. Its name is derived from standard Special Forces terminology. Six ALPHA detachments (A teams), commanded by captains, make up a company–sized BRAVO detachment (B team), commanded by a major. A CHARLIE detachment (C team) is a battalion–sized organization commanded by a lieutenant colonel. Since the 1st Special Forces Operational Detachment was commanded by a full colonel and structured along completely separate lines, following the squadron–troop structure of Britain's famed SAS, it became a DELTA detachment. Using the concept of the troop and the squadron as the building block or base, it initially trained to conduct counterterrorist operations. Recent activities in Iraq and Kuwait, however, reveal that DELTA's one–dimensional media image of a super–secret counterterrorist team falls well short of reality. The 1st Special Forces Operational Detachment is a multifaceted unit much like its counterpart, the SAS.

DELTA and *Blue Light*

Both DELTA's sponsors and opponents within the military held firm––and diametrically opposed—ideas on who should respond to the terrorist challenge. The majority of DELTA's sponsors were typical of America's military leadership. They were extremely conservative officers who were slow to respond to the terrorist threat, but once convinced that it was very real indeed, they were bulldogs in their support of the unit. And, like its sponsors, those who had worked hard to undermine or side-track DELTA (primarily because they didn't understand the nature of the threat) eventually gave it their full support when ordered.

At the top was Army Chief of Staff General Bernard Rogers. This astute Kansan and Rhodes scholar watched as the armies of Great Britain and West Germany rapidly took on what most American policymakers refer to as "police powers" normally kept out of the military's hands. After the Carter White House made it clear that they wanted a unit with specialized capabilities, Rogers gave his blessing for DELTA's formation. He told the relevant senior planners that he wanted the unit operational—and wanted it now!

The individual most instrumental in DELTA's birthing process was Lieutenant General Edward C. "Shy" Meyer. As the Deputy Chief of Staff for Operations, he was one of the most influential senior officers on the Army staff. It was from his office, that plans and policy for how the US Army would operate were issued. General Meyer took a direct, personal interest in DELTA. From the time that the need for a counterterrorist force was identified through its birth and Operation *Eagle Claw*, Meyer was always present in some form, providing guidance and support. The rest of the Army may have called him "Shy," but to DELTA he was "Moses" because he always seemed to be able to part the waters for them.

Next in the line of supporters came General William DePuy, commander of the Training and Doctrine Command. General DePuy was *the* expert in training; even though he was as conventional a soldier as any, he clearly recognized that a force was needed "like the SAS," as he was often quoted as saying during major policy meetings. He had to be won over before General Rogers and others could be addressed, but that proved to be easy after his inquiries about similar organizations in Europe demonstrated that an effective CT unit could be formed within the US Army. He would provide the training support.

The remainder of the cast were found at Fort Bragg, North Carolina. Fort Bragg has often been referred to as "home of the airborne" because of the vast numbers of parachute and related units based there. Bragg was also the home turf of the members of the US Army's Special Forces. The individuals making up these organizations possess unique skills, and it was from this elite body that DELTA's supporters and opponents would come.

The architect of DELTA was the commandant of the Special Forces School: a gruff veteran of the guerilla wars in Southeast Asia named Colonel Charlie Beckwith. Not only did "Chargin' Charlie" have a wealth of experience in the realm of unconventional operations, but he also knew who the power brokers were and how to use them. For example, in 1975, when General "Iron Mike" Healy was reassigned from his command at the John F. Kennedy Special Warfare Center at Fort Bragg, his replacement was Major General Robert "Barbed Wire Bob" Kingston. Kingston's association with Beckwith could be traced back to the days when Beckwith was an exchange officer with the SAS and Kingston was with the British Parachute Regiment. The two had also just served together at the Joint Casualty Resolution Center in Nakhon Phanom, Thailand, in 1973–1974. Kingston would work closely with General Meyer to establish an SAS–type unit.

It was during Colonel Beckwith's tour as commandant that the special operations community watched Europe's response to the outrages of various extremist groups. Located in an area known as "Smoke Bomb Hill," members of the Special Forces refined their traditional skills and added the hasty response to their repertoire. Special Forces, however, were responsible for carrying out a wide range of missions and could not dedicate much of their training efforts toward hostage situations.

Other soldiers who lent their guidance and support during this critical period were the commander of the 10th Special Forces Group, Colonel Othan "Shali" Shalikashville; General Frederick J. "Fritz" Kroesen, of Forces Command, who controlled all units stationed in the United States; and the XVIII Airborne Corps's chief of staff, Brigadier General James Lindsay. At one point during DELTA's shaky beginning, Shalikashville lined up all his senior commissioned and noncommissioned officers and told them flatly, "The job that Colonel Beckwith has to do is more important than the job we have to do. I would encourage anyone who has the desire to try out for this unit." As for Lindsay, when General Kingston's successor refused Beckwith's request to move DELTA into Bragg's underutilized post stockade, he saw to it that the unit would get it, reasoning, "Here we've got a nice stockade facility where we're keeping eleven bad guys. . . . Why don't we take the eleven and put them downtown in the Fayetteville jail? Your use of the stockade is better than the use it's being put to now. Colonel, you've got it!" Beckwith was obviously pleased that his problem had been solved so quickly but believed that the general would never see another promotion because he was just too practical. Ten years later, however, Lindsay would wear a total of eight stars on his shoulders and become the commander of the newly created Special Operations Command responsible for providing combat–ready special operations forces for rapid deployment to other unified commands around the world.

Still, support of the special operations community was not very strong at this point. Meticulously trained Special Forces units had conducted numerous missions during the Vietnam War, but now there was not a need for such specialists—or so the conventional leadership thought. And the conventional leadership controlled the Army and downsizing in forces that was taking place. Providentially, control of Special Forces fell to the commander of the JFK Special Warfare Center, and since General Kingston, his boss, was in control, Beckwith had the degree of freedom required to bring DELTA on line.

Charlie A. Beckwith of DELTA, circa 1979.

Complaints by the Rangers that DELTA would deepen their current manpower problems (partially true) and that the unit duplicated some of their functions (untrue) were brushed aside early on. Beckwith's only real opposition came from the commander of the 5th Special Forces Group at Bragg, Colonel Robert "Black Gloves" Montell, who believed that the shoot–from–the–hip hasty response was perfectly adequate. Montell was one of the Army's most professional and experienced officers. Always impeccably dressed, he wore what was commonly referred to as the "Bad Tolz" uniform. With pistol belt stripped and worn over olive drab jungle fatigues, spit–shined jungle boots, and an ever–present pair of black gloves topped off by the coveted green beret, he provided even the most hard–eyed professional with a source of pride in those days after Vietnam.

About the time that the DELTA program seemed to be a sure thing, Kingston was transferred to Korea, and Major General Jack "Bobo" Mackmull assumed command. No doubt Mackmull had received his marching orders from Washington to keep the program on track, but as a West Pointer and aviator, he was not very familiar with the missions and capabilities of this strange little unit under his command and, unfortunately, made little effort to learn. Once DELTA was approved for activation, Mackmull was told to come up with a backfill unit until DELTA was certified for operations some two years in the future. Montell's 5th Special Forces Group received the nod.

To meet this requirement, Montell selected forty Special Forces troopers from within the community and trained them in hasty response techniques. This unit was code–named *Blue Light*. Operating under the principle that a bird in the hand is worth two in the bush, Mackmull threw his weight *Blue Light's* way regarding both funding and personnel. Despite reassurances from insiders, it appears that Beckwith feared that Montell's stalwart professionals would derail DELTA before it had a chance to prove its concept. If Beckwith lost his support in Washington, he would lose his unit. And DELTA was truly his.

As with most endeavors, it is not necessarily who is the best qualified, but who has the most support. Initially, that is what kept DELTA and its concept of a full–time, low–visibility CT organization alive. When General Rogers discovered that expected resources were being routed away from DELTA, he, as they say, "went ballistic." From that point on, through the support from the chief of staff on down the line, DELTA was allowed to gain the necessary breathing room to grow from nothing to a full–fledged force.

After 1st Special Forces Operational Detachment–DELTA was activated in October 1977, Beckwith had to select and train his new unit. DELTA troopers would have to be able to blend perfectly into the civilian world, when required, and possess unique skills that included everything from the relevant military arts to climbing the sides of buildings and hot–wiring cars. As luck would have it, DELTA had just completed their certification exercises. The date was November 4, 1979.

159

Weapons and Equipment

Pistols

In the special operations community, an oft–repeated comment on the controversy over which round is better, the .45cal ACP (automatic Colt pistol) or the 9mm parabellum, goes like this: "Opinions are like assholes, everyone has one." Stopping power, mass versus velocity, number of rounds versus weight—the argument seems neverending but, over time, weapons firing the 9mm (.38cal) round have become respected additions to DELTA's arsenal.

Modern conventional warfare generally calls for relatively light–weight, high–velocity rounds such as the Colt M16's .223cal/5.56mm or NATO's standard .308cal/7.62mm, that are effective out to ranges of several hundred yards. For the takedown of a hostage holding site, however, 100 feet is considered an extreme range. What the counterterrorist needs is a heavy slug that will knock a man down with as few shots as possible, and rounds smaller than .45cal have often proven themselves to be inadequate against a determined enemy. As early as the beginning of this century, Moro warriors battling US soldiers in the Philippines were not stopped by government issue .38cal pistols and, most recently, in the GSG-9 operation against aircraft hijackers at Mogadishu, Somalia, the German commander was forced to empty his snub–nosed .38cal into a psyched–up terrorist who continued fight even as six bullets ripped into his body. For this reason, many operatives prefer to have a bigger weapon.

A big (*very* big) round like that from the Smith & Wesson .44cal Magnum will drop a hijacker in his tracks but, unfortunately, the high–powered bullet is likely to go through its intended target as well as several seats and passengers before it stops. Moreover, the .44 Magnum's substantial kick when firing can delay reacquisition of the same or other targets—possibly with disastrous results. The .45 ACP round fired by the Colt or Springfield Armory M1911A1 and other automatic pistols has a great advantage over its famous friend during takedowns. An old joke among shooters is that the .45's bullet travels so slowly that, for an instant, you can actually see it speeding towards the target. With such a low muzzle velocity—at roughly 830 feet per second, it's almost half that of the .44 Magnum—hostage safety is greatly increased since there is more likelihood that the captors' bodies will stop the bullets.

But while this would seem to make the .45 the obvious weapon of choice for takedowns, many shooters have gravitated to the 9mm Beretta Model

(**A**) The basic Colt 5.56mm M16A2 assault rifle, (**B**) Colt 9mm submachine gun, and (**C**) Colt 5.56mm Model 733 Commando assault rifle. (**D**) The Mossberg 12–gauge Cruiser 500 shotgun; (**E**) the Remington 7.62mm M40A1 sniping rifle mounting a ten–power US Marine Corps telescope instead of the Redfield twelve–power telescope commonly used by DELTA; and (**F**) the Springfield Armory 7.65mm M21 sniping system based on the M14 rifle. (**G**) The Beretta 9mm Model 92F pistol, called the M9 by the US Army and (**H**) the Colt .45cal M1911A1 automatic pistol. (**I**) The General Motors Guide Lamp Division .45cal M3 submachine gun often described as "a pleasant gun to shoot"; (**J**) the Walther 9mm MP-K submachine gun, which served as a useful bridge between the M3 and (**K**) the Heckler & Koch 9mm MP5 submachine gun. (**L**) The Heckler & Koch 9mm MP5 SD3 submachine gun with integral silencer.

When DELTA was formed, its armorers developed special lighting equipment that could be attached to weapons for night operations. Today, such devices can be obtained off–the–shelf from manufacturers or are integral to the weapons. (**Top**) A Hensoldt aiming point projector fitted to a Heckler & Koch MP5 A2 submachine gun and (**bottom, lower left**) a laser pointer built into the forearm of a Mossberg 12–gauge shotgun. Also note the Stabo rings attached to the soldier's tactical vest and the flash/bang grenade (an SAS invention) ready for use in his left hand.

92 pistol. The high velocity of its 9mm parabellum slug is easily brought below 1,000 feet per second by reducing the round's charge, and, depending on which variant of the Model 92 is carried into a fight, the counterterrorist can count on making almost twice as many shots before reloading than he would if he carried a conventional .45cal automatic.

The automatic pistol made by Colt and the higher–quality product manufactured by the Springfield Armory, normally fire from eight– and seven–bullet magazines respectively, and can each carry an additional round in the chamber, while the Model 92 and its variants have thirteen– and fifteen–round magazines. The tradeoff is that while 9mm bullets are indeed smaller, their size is *adequate* and the Model 92 has more of them. Moreover, the ammunition a DELTA trooper carries on his body and in his weapon is all that he can count on having available

to him during a takedown. If everything goes as planned, there will be very little shooting. If the operation "goes sour," its just DELTA and the terrorists in a high–intensity shootout of unknown duration. A situation can easily develop where the first side to run out of bullets loses and, with a weight nearly half that of a .45cal bullet, 9mm rounds can be carried in great quantity without encumbering a trooper.

Submachine Guns

The same holds true, of course, for submachine guns. Although pistols are preferred in most hostage situations, submachine guns become a necessity when large target areas or many terrorists (four and up) are involved. DELTA initially settled on the domestically produced .45cal M3A1 "grease gun," a World War II vintage weapon that went out of production in the early 1950s and was generally shunned by the US Army. Interestingly enough, though, the very features that made it unpopular with most soldiers, enabled it be an extraordinarily effective tool for room–clearing: a low muzzle velocity which allowed its heavy slugs to slam into—not through—a terrorist and a rate of fire slow enough to enable single shots to be squeezed off

The Heckler & Koch MP5 SD3 fires 9mm ammo and, with its collapsing stock and integral silencer, it is an outstanding weapon for the closein fight. The sound supressor is a two–stage external silencer. The first stage of the system will absorb gasses while the second absorbs the muzzel blast and flame. The bolt noise is absorbed by buffers made of rubber. If you use subsonic ammo, the report cannot be heard more than fifteen to twenty feet away.

without disturbing the shooter's aim.

Acquiring adequate replacement parts for the weapon was an armorer's nightmare, however, and the old friend soon made way for a variety of submachine guns. Selection of weapons is a personal choice that often revolves around such factors as weight, reliability, how often must you clean it between firings, amount of ammo per magazine, and accuracy after it has been beat up in a parachute jump. The Heckler & Koch MP5 and the less expensive, easily concealable Walther MP-K are both German arms that fire 9mm rounds, as does the Colt submachine gun that has many parts common to the M16 rifle. The compact Colt Model 733 Commando assault rifle also benefits from this commonality and can be used on missions requiring its higher velocity 5.56mm round.

163

Trooper in southeastern Iraq armed with a Colt Model 727 carbine. Note the troopers sterile uniform (no identification or other markings) and longish hair. A three–power telescopic site is mounted on the carbine.

Shotguns

Shotguns are also useful in a variety of situations but are most commonly associated with forced entry techniques. Heavy rifled slugs can be depended on to supply the pure smashing power needed to quickly and efficiently blow the hinges off most doors. Sabot rounds, on the other hand, allow deeper penetration of the target and are best employed against vehicle or aircraft engines and door–locking mechanisms. After initial entry has been gained at a hostage holding site, shotguns can be used to force additional doors or, if necessary, against the hostage takers.

A 12–gauge rifled slug (**left**) and 12–gauge sabot slug (**right**).

Ammunition

Terrorists cannot be reasoned with and will attempt to kill their captives if a rescue is attempted, so when choosing ammunition, CT specialists want a man stopper that will knock a terrorist down and keep him down. While the heavy .45cal remains an ideal round for hostage situations, the lethality of smaller slugs, like the 9mm, can be greatly enhanced by using "soft–point" bullets with hollow or flat tips. The unusual point causes the soft, lead slug to expand into a broad, mushroom–shaped projectile upon entering the body, often doubling in diameter and increasing its shock effect dramatically. In a war where the armed forces of one nation are openly pit-

(**Left** to **right**) Flat–point, hollow–point and conventional bullets.

ted against those of another, the rules of land warfare prohibit the use of such ammunition. DELTA troopers participating in a hostage rescue, however, are not subject to the restrictions of the Geneva Convention. Like their police counterparts, they can legally use hollow–point ammunition (or exploding rounds that shatter on impact) to subdue captors and save the lives of the hostages.

The actual weapons and ammunition used on a mission are determined by the nature of the target.

A takedown of an oil platform, for example, is a very different affair from that of an airliner cabin crowded with hostages sitting upright. Only the team members assaulting areas likely to contain the platform's captive crew need to worry about carrying weapons with limited velocity.

Advances in technology have also complicated matters for DELTA and other CT specialists by adding dangerous factors to the equation such as handguns and bombs with almost no metal parts. Initially, only law enforcement agencies and the military had access to the lightweight body armor made from Kevlar fabric (which, incidentally, does *not* set off metal detectors). Over the passage of time, however, this type of highly effective armor has greatly proliferated and, if not already in terrorist hands, can be easily obtained by third parties or simply stolen. When worn in thin, easily concealable layers, Kevlar will stop the low–velocity slugs normally required for passenger safety. Technology and tactics have provided solutions to these and other problems but the decades–old argument over the most appropriate weapons to use is something that will die harder than any flesh–and–blood fanatic.

Sniper Rifles

Nearly all DELTA weapons—whether old or new—have been "accurized" to some degree by the unit's own gunsmiths. Loose–fitting parts typically found even in quality mass–produced weapons are replaced by custom–built pieces with closer tolerances, specialized trigger mechanisms, and better sights. For example, before it was superseded by the heavy–barrelled 40XB sniper rifle (which was specially manufactured for DELTA by Remington Arms), modifications were made to the trusty old M14A1 to upgrade its already formidable performance as a sniper rifle.

Modifications typically included polishing and hand fitting of the gas cylinder and piston to im-

prove operation and reduce carbon buildup. Barrels were always carefully selected to ensure correct specification tolerances and are bedded into the forearms with a fiberglass compounds. Trigger housing groups were carefully fitted and polished to provide a crisp hammer release and suppressors fitted to eliminate sound and flash which could give the sniper's position away. Receivers could also be individually fitted to stocks using a fiberglass compound. The US Army now purchases an off–the–shelf versions of this weapon from the Springfield Armory called the M21 sniping rifle. DELTA troopers often use this weapon during training and it also receives considerable reworking such as having plastic spacers added to customize the length of the stock. The M40A1 and M24 sniping systems,

---

Flash/bang grenades with no–snag caps in an Eagle Industries hip pouch. Center pockets hold thirty–round clips for 9mm Heckeler & Koch submachine guns.

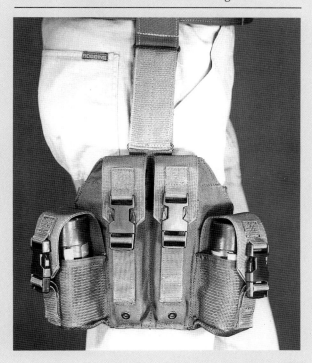

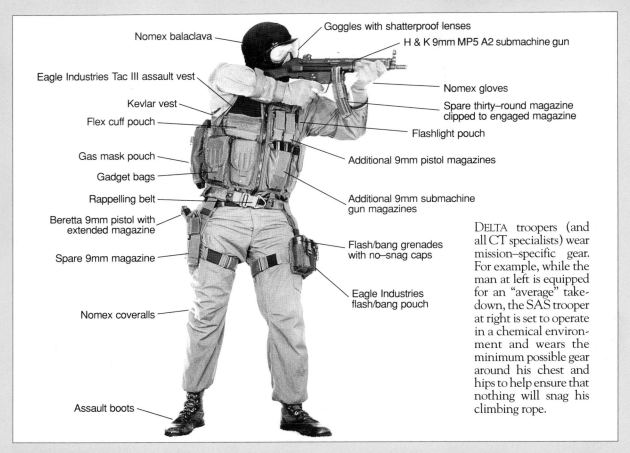

Nomex balaclava

Goggles with shatterproof lenses

H & K 9mm MP5 A2 submachine gun

Eagle Industries Tac III assault vest

Kevlar vest

Flex cuff pouch

Nomex gloves

Spare thirty–round magazine clipped to engaged magazine

Gas mask pouch

Flashlight pouch

Gadget bags

Additional 9mm pistol magazines

Rappelling belt

Beretta 9mm pistol with extended magazine

Additional 9mm submachine gun magazines

Spare 9mm magazine

Flash/bang grenades with no–snag caps

Nomex coveralls

Eagle Industries flash/bang pouch

Assault boots

DELTA troopers (and all CT specialists) wear mission–specific gear. For example, while the man at left is equipped for an "average" take-down, the SAS trooper at right is set to operate in a chemical environment and wears the minimum possible gear around his chest and hips to help ensure that nothing will snag his climbing rope.

standardized versions of the 40XB, are also being acquired by the Army and Marine Corps.

Grenades

The famous "pineapple," more properly known as the Mk II fragmentation hand grenade, is what most people think of when this type of weapon is mentioned, but the long–obsolete pineapple was pulled from front–line service with the US Army over a decade before DELTA was formed. A cylindrical canister, about the size of a shaving cream can, is used for concussion grenades, chemical grenades (such as tear gas), and the flash/bang grenade (a description of the grenade's employment is on page

57). This design allows the grenade's user to gently role it a predictable direction and distance into a room, unlike the Mk II and its similarly shaped or round descendants which are designed for throwing and, if rolled, could wobble almost anywhere— including back up against the very wall that a trooper is using for shelter! Before the recent fielding of the flat–sided M560 series fragmentation grenades, if a mission profile called for use of an antipersonnel grenade with a predictable roll, an M57 or M61 would have to be soldered into an appropriately sized tin can to achieve the desired effect. Once the pin was pulled and the safety lever fell away, a nearly perfect roll could be achieved every time.

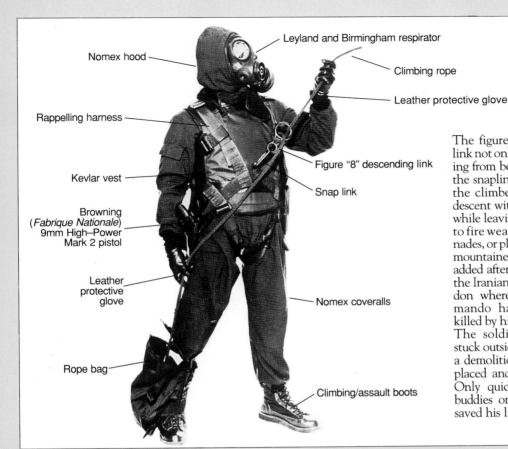

Nomex hood

Leyland and Birmingham respirator

Climbing rope

Leather protective glove

Rappelling harness

Kevlar vest

Figure "8" descending link

Snap link

Browning (*Fabrique Nationale*) 9mm High–Power Mark 2 pistol

Leather protective glove

Nomex coveralls

Rope bag

Climbing/assault boots

The figure "8" descending link not only prevents clothing from being dragged into the snaplink but also allows the climber to control his descent with only one hand while leaving the other free to fire weapons, throw grenades, or place charges. This mountaineering device was added after the operation at the Iranian Embassy in London where an SAS commando had almost been killed by his own explosives. The soldier had become stuck outside a window after a demolition had been emplaced and its fuse ignited. Only quick action by his buddies on the roof above saved his life.

Clothing

From the early days of hasty option operations, counterterrorist equipment has steadily evolved. Lightweight, highly rigid specialized clothing and equipment has now become a standard for CT teams. Several European units such as the SAS and Germany's GSG-9 found out through practical experiences at the Iranian Embassy in London and at the Mogadishu airport that general issue equipment is great for conventional forces but suffers from dangerous shortfalls when used during specialized operations. Much of the evolution in equipment has focused on the tactical assault vest and modular pouches attached to the upper torso and hips.

They incorporate such items as extra ammo, radio, and first aid pouches along with rappelling rings. Counterterrorist operations are very personal affairs. Despite the fact that the soldiers belong to teams, each man puts a great deal of faith in his individual gear. The equipment *must* be capable of accommodating number of modifications to handle, for example either flash/bang or gas grenades; MP5 magazines or Colt 733 Commando magazines. The problem was solved by creating a basic vest capable of handling interchangeable sets of pouches and holders for the problems specific to a given mission.

Chapter 3

The Making of a DELTA Trooper

In the 82d Airborne, I was better than any guy in my company. Over here I gotta hustle just to keep up.

a DELTA trooper

Joining a counterterrorist unit is very similar to breaking into the big leagues of pro sports. There are a few differences, however. Major league ball clubs have quite a few rookies on the squad, whereas the CT arena requires that units be composed exclusively of veterans with basic special operations skills already refined to a razor edge. And an error in the major leagues won't cost you your life or the lives of your team members.

CT units are composed of senior noncommissioned officers (NCOs) and several rather well–qualified officers. Continuous assignments in such units have not always been career enhancing, and despite the Army's recent elevation of Special Forces to full branch status, few officers stay around for more than one or two tours with the Special Forces groups. Those who do are usually *extremely* dedicated to their units, its troops, and the basic

US and German counterterrorists conducting a joint exercise involving rappelling, door–busting, and room–clearing techniques.

idea that the worldwide terrorist threat and its network of supporters should be met head–on and eliminated. They usually hold the respect of their fellow team members, who are not as concerned with an officer's rank as they are with his ability to shoot straight and back up his team.

Counterterrorism is only one of the missions assigned by law to the special operations community. The men who are charged with carrying out these low–visibility operations are chosen from a wide range of backgrounds and spheres of our society. Each is selected based on his talents and the unit's need to fill particular slots within its ranks. The question, "How does the whole process start?" begins with this fundamental requirement to fill open positions.

Selection and Training

Special operations units, and especially the close–knit counterterrorist outfits, recruit in several different ways. Special attention is given to the "old' boy network." As with any other business or

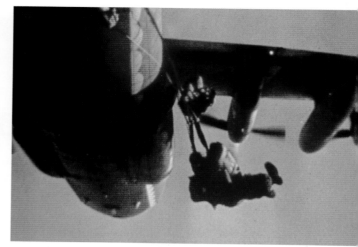

All DELTA trainees are jump qualified, and previously acquired skills, such as scuba diving are further refined during training. Troopers are assigned to specialized teams containing soldiers with the same skills. Many teams and elements are multidisciplined.

occupation, word of mouth and vouching for someone are key ingredients in the selection process. A second method is to simply advertise the need for people. DELTA recruitment teams make the rounds of training centers, troop posts, and such facilities as the Command and General Staff College or NCO advance schools. These recruitment drives preceed DELTA's fall and spring selection and assessment courses. Recruitment letters are also routinely mailed from Army personnel centers and, more recently, as the unit has edged out of the black into a rather dark grey, volunteers have been openly solicited in Army journals.

DELTA's rigid entrance requirements are clearly spelled out for career officers and NCOs who may be enticed to leave behind the warm comforts of their current postings for a new adventure. The pitch is always straightforward and unambiguous:

"ASSIGNMENT OPPORTUNITIES are available in the 1st Special Forces Operational Detach-

ment–DELTA. DELTA is the Army's special operations unit that has been organized to conduct missions that combine rapid response with the surgical application of a wide variety of unique skills and the flexibility to maintain the lowest possible profile of US involvement. . . . DELTA gives commissioned and noncommissioned officers unique opportunities for professional development. . . ."

A fourth and less–known method is for soldiers to be individually sought out by recruiters, based on a screening of their official records. This method may also be used with word–of–mouth recommendations. Recruiters are usually looking for specific assets, such as language skills, key past assignments, military qualifications, or schools attended. From the compiled list of likely candidates, individuals are contacted and asked to volunteer.

Drawn from the Active Army, Army Reserve, and Army National Guard, all DELTA members must pass a background security investigation, be at least twenty–two years old, male, and a US citizen. Each soldier's records are screened for psychological abnormalities or recurring discipline problems, and those accepting the challenge receive very thorough physical and eye examinations. Commonly referred to as the Scuba/HALO physical, it is akin to the in–depth exams pilots receive.

After getting the thumbs up from the doctors, or "chancre mechanics," the prospective counterterrorist is subjected to a battery of tests to determine if he is psychologically sound. The last thing a unit in the midst of a mission needs is to find itself saddled with a would–be Rambo or a real–life psycho. The cost of not conducting extensive psychological tests was graphically displayed as early as the Munich incident in 1972. At one point, the terrorists moved into the sights of the German sharpshooters who then froze. The results were quite unsatisfactory from the Israelis' standpoint.

Approximately 100 prospective counterterrorists receive intensive physical testing every session and high scores are an absolute requirement. In DELTA's formative stage, its selection process closely followed the British SAS model. This was due to the fact that many of the individuals who had a hand in setting up the unit were the products of SAS–Special Forces exchange programs and the close working relations these units have always had. This aspect of the month–long selection process has not changed.

The candidate's ordeal begins with six grueling events which must be completed within a designated period and earning a minimum of sixty points each. The candidates are, of course, expected to do better than the minimum. Periodically, small modifications are made to the test; examples of what is expected of the volunteers include: forty–yard inverted crawl in twenty–five seconds; thirty–seven situps in one minute; thirty–three pushups in one minute; run, dodge and jump course in twenty–four seconds; two–mile run in sixteen minutes, thirty seconds; and 100–meter swim while fully clothed and wearing boots.

Following the test, the candidate has the opportunity to show how well he can accomplish a speed march. The route covers eighteen miles, and the

Soldiers using the Stabo technique to land on a Fort Bragg rooftop. Hanging free from the helo during their approach, the men land simultaneously instead of one at a time. The target area is framed with a two–by–four barrier in case any of the soldiers loses his footing.

individuals must traverse it as rapidly as possible. Since this is one of the psychological problems to overcome, the passing times are never published. However, most of those who have passed it seem to agree that ten–minute miles are almost too slow!

Those who have made it this far into the selection process now receive a real treat. Just like in the SAS course, the candidates now are asked to really show what they are made of and are taken to one of several sites for a combination speed march, compass course, and survival exercise. Tests were originally conducted near Troy, North Carolina, in the Uwharrie National Forest, but are now done on the even more rugged terrain of Camp Dawson, West Virginia; recently, a test site has been added in the secured areas of Nellis Air Force Base, Nevada.

The Freedom to Fail or Succeed

If you were one of the few candidates to reach the forty–mile land navigation exercise, you'd find that the basic scenario goes like this: With all the ceremony of going off to a maximum–security prison, you and the other candidates are trucked out to the test site, where each is dropped at separate starting points. As dawn begins to break, you are given a set of instructions that amount to little more than a compass heading and a point on the map marking the final destination perhaps a half–dozen miles away. You are to pick out your route, keeping in mind that the object is to get there as quickly as possible.

Off you go. As soon as you leave the gentleman who gave you the instructions, your thoughts run the gamut of, "What the hell am I doing here?" to "I hope I can pull this off." Even though you made some rough calculations at the starting point, you drop off to the side of the trail to double check the situation and ensure your initial calculations are correct. (Besides, you didn't want to look indeci-

sive in front of the guy at the drop–off point.) Squinting more closely at the map, you find that the contour lines are so close together that they look like some gigantic drunk worm. In other words, it is all up and down, with a few nice cold creeks in between. Off again, you settle into the comfortable trot the old hands taught you back at Bragg's Smoke Bomb Hill or Fort Benning. As usual, it starts to rain a little, but for the average Airborne, Ranger, or Special Forces type, rain is not a stranger. Checking your compass to keep oriented, you now settle into the routine. In most cases, the trial would be more enjoyable if you didn't remember that this was much more than just an exercise. You are here to show someone that you can hack whatever it takes to be part of that group called DELTA.

As you navigate along the trail, the shoulder straps of your fifty–five–pound rucksack begin to make themselves known to you—especially as the ruck gets wetter. Sweat trickles down your armpits, gets in your eyes, and seems to find refuge in your already chaffed crotch. After about the first hour and a half, the experience factors of Ranger School and the Special Forces qualification course, along with the numerous Special Forces Group exercises, take over. So it's time to stop, take stock of the situation, and drink some water. Pausing along the trail, you look around the dense hardwoods that make up much of the terrain along the mountains. Sensing something in the underbrush near your left jungle boot, you slowly retreat a few steps as "Jake no shoulders" decides to rattle a friendly greeting. Your mind comprehends the danger, but in some ways you really do not want to think about what could have happened, especially if he got upset as you were sitting down to check your feet.

Moving down the trail, you find a better place to get out of the drizzle and change your socks and apply some Vaseline to your sensitive areas. You get your bearings one more time and are off. Whether you are running the selection course in the mountains of Appalachia, with its forests and numerous streams, or driving on in the Sierra Nevada wastelands, the expected results are the same. Just like General Forest, get there "firstest with the mostest." In .your case, get there fastest—period.

You've been at this all day, the sun dipped below the wooded hills uncounted hours ago, and at each rendezvous, you hope that it will be the one site where you will be told to throw your ruck into the truck and get aboard. But for some bizarre reason, the only words you hear at each brief stop are the location of your next rendezvous. After about a dozen hours of this, many volunteers begin to rest too long or slow down so much that they are unable to make the twenty–hour time limit. Even good soldiers begin to look for excuses to quit, and many inevitably find them. But not you. Cold, wet, and numb with exhaustion, you move off again, continuing in search of whatever you are out here for until well after midnight, when you are unceremoniously informed that the exercise is over. The survivors rarely remember exactly where they've been and, as with the speed march, even know how far they went or how long it took.

By now, the steady attrition of volunteers has weeded the field down to perhaps a dozen or so survivors. Many of those returning to their home units have been cut because they were unable to

An exhausted instructor from the John F. Kennedy Special Warfare Center training group, after negotiating a demanding confidence course like DELTA's. He is indicative of the highly motivated, professional soldiers in the US special operations community.

meet the tough physical and navigational challenges, while others were sidetracked for other legitimate reasons, such as knee, ankle, or back injuries. Some, however, drop out because they simply were not mentally prepared to follow the course through to the end without the accustomed "you can do it!" prodding that had been an integral part of all previous training. The NCOs overseeing the selection course steadfastly refuse to provide this encouragement. In any event, DELTA makes a great effort to ensure that those not selected know that they are

A trainee negotiates stairsteps to a room mock–up during entry technique training at the SOT. The object is to engage the pop–up silhouette targets from uncomfortable angles while in motion.

not failures. Each candidate receives a certificate of training and is simply told he was not selected.

Looking back at the physical side of the selection process, a key aspect becomes crystal clear: It is structured to put the maximum psychological pressure on those being tested. The individual is provided the freedom to succeed or fail on his own. A candidate not only must know his physical, mental, and emotional makeup, but must be able to use it to his advantage. In the CT arena, there are many occasions where individual actions are required, and in those life–and–death situations, you get only one chance to succeed. As Sun Tzu pointed out

so long ago, you have to know yourself as well as your enemy. If you are not ready to run in seemingly aimless directions for hours through the dark, wet, torturous terrain of overgrown, forested mountains, the cross–country land navigation exercise is not for you. If you are not ready to know what real fear is, to meet it head on and beat it, DELTA is not for you.

The trip back to Fort Bragg takes on an unreal atmosphere after what has occurred. Every selection course will have a variable number of thoroughly exhausted candidates who will go on to face the final and, according to some, hardest part of the selection process: the interview. A board of DELTA veterans grills the survivors and determines who goes on for training.

"So you're infiltrating an unfriendly area prior to taking down a terrorist hideout. Say you come across two little girls. You can't leave them. Do you take them along, tie them up, or do you kill them?"

"Tell us a little about Machiavelli."

"What were the arguments for and against our acquiring the Virgin Islands during World War I?"

"Was President Truman right or wrong to fire MacArthur?"

By this point in the four–hour grilling, some volunteers have taken on the look of frightened animals. The questions are asked seriously, and the DELTA veterans expect serious answers.

"Well, Sergeant, you've given a fine performance so far. Now tell us what you tend to blow it on."

"Why should we take you? What can you offer DELTA?"

"You're a good soldier!? So what!? Sergeant, we're up to our ears in good soldiers. Tell us about your unique skills, what you're really good at that's not military related."

In this tension–charged atmosphere, there are few right or wrong answers. The board is looking at the individual as a whole: his values and how he is able to handle himself in this situation.

The objective of the selection course is to find individuals who can both work with the team and yet operate independently without orders. In the end, only about ten percent or fewer of the initial candidates actually make it into DELTA; and a rumor circulating through the special operations community contends that one group moving throughout the selection process lost virtually every man before the assessment was finished. While such an occurrence could certainly wreak havoc with the manning levels of a small, highly specialized organization, such problems can be ironed out if they are not persistent. Moreover, the nature of DELTA necessitates that its emphasis must remain focused on the quality, not quantity, of personnel entering the unit.

The SOT

As the new DELTA trainee drives along Gruber Road past MacKeller's Lodge, he thinks back to the recent events of the selection course. Now the staff sergeant is at Fort Bragg, reporting in for some of the finest—and toughest—training in the world. To his right, he sees a high cyclone fence and dirt road used by the security force who patrols it. Beyond the fence and nestled within the rough horseshoe formed by Gruber, Lambert, and Manchester Roads is the secure training facility constructed for the training of America's elite CT units and the home of DELTA. Called the Special Operations Training Facility (SOT), the multimillion–dollar complex became a reality through the increased support from congress and the president for the war on terrorism in the early 1980s.

Almost as if the world has opened up its secrets, the SOT unfolds in the form of large two– and three–story buildings and training areas for heliborne insertions. The staff sergeant is immediately struck by how easy it is for virtually anyone to get a look at this surprisingly well–publicized facility. With counterterrorism such a security–conscious business, this visual access seems odd, but he writes it off as the price DELTA must pay for being on an "open post" like Fort Bragg and chuckles to himself when he remembers what started the whole process that led him to Gruber Road today: a public announcement in his branch journal, *Infantry*, that "assignment opportunities" were available in DELTA.

The newcomer passes the SOT's entrance and continues to drive north toward Manchester Road. He is rewarded with a clear view of numerous open–aired and enclosed ranges he'll be seeing a lot of over the next two years. A thrill rushes through him. This is going to be the ultimate adventure! Coming back to the reality of the moment, he makes an unauthorized U turn and pulls up to the brick guardhouse at the gate. His identification is scrutinized

A trainee practices pistol shooting at multiple targets at one of the SOT facility's numerous ranges. Note the semi–crouch stance and two–handed pistol grip.

against the incoming roster for the day, and he is directed to park and await his escort. The games, as they said in ancient Rome, are about to begin.

So far, everything the trainee has seen speaks well of the command emphasis placed on the Army's counterterrorist mission, from the White House down through the major subordinate headquarters, the Joint Special Operations Command (JSOC). In military terminology, it is a "high–speed" operation. As DELTA's newest recruit waits for his escort, he is startled to see an MH-6, bristling with darkened human figures instead of gun pods, zoom overhead. Along each side is a trio of soldiers buckled into special side platforms for rapid egress. Unseen by the trainee, the six commandos slip wearily from their "Little Bird" just a moment later at a helicopter pad near Lambert Road.

This specially modified Hughes chopper belongs to another important part of the team, the 160th Special Operations Aviation Regiment (Airborne), or SOAR. This unit is a result of the many problems experienced during *Desert I* and objectively outlined in its after–action review. Commonly referred to as the Holloway Report, it pointed out that a major area to restructure, if future missions were to stand a chance, was helicopter operations, and the covert aviation unit was duly formed at Fort Campbell, Kentucky. Originally named Task Force 160, it soon became the major US Army aviation support element for DELTA.

The commandos clearing the aircraft have darkened faces and wear a patrol, or "Ranger," cap. Clad in sturdy, olive drab jungle fatigues plus a wide assortment of specially made vests and other web gear, they also carry rappelling gloves, snaplinks and nonstandard Heckler & Koch MP5 submachine guns. As the SOAR 160 bird rises back into the sky, its stubby, rounded frame gives it the appear-

American counterterrorist team practicing pistol shooting from several different positions. Ranges such as this one provide enclosed areas to practice room–clearing methods out of sight of prying eyes.

ance of an overweight bumblebee or lethargic beetle attempting to gain flight.

Most CT operations require lightning fast entrances into the target area, along with shock effect and disorientation of the hostage takers. Carrying out such complicated maneuvers requires a great deal of training, teamwork, and the building of mutual respect for each member's abilities. That is what the new recruits are to learn during DELTA's five–month operators course at the SOT.

The facility's mission is to teach new methods and refine old skills in the art of counterterrorism. Many writers and observers have referred to the skills of eliminating a terrorist situation as antiterrorism. This, however, is incorrect. Antiterrorism is a term that refers to skills and techniques used by people or organizations which will help *prevent* them from becoming the victim of a terrorist attack. There are schools and courses where basic antiterrorist methods and tactics are taught, but the SOT addresses the final options of dealing with a terrorist incident that has *already occurred*. This is where DELTA comes into play: the counterterrorist arena.

Whenever the complex subject of counterterrorism is raised for discussion or debate, the argument that a specialized unit for CT operations is too expensive in terms of manpower and money usually comes to the fore. Regardless of whether this view is correct, it is undeniable that the political impact of a successful terrorist attack is often immense; the economic costs alone can run into the tens of millions of dollars, and priceless, innocent lives are put at risk or even lost. That is why dedicated units tasked to conduct CT operations are a must. How such units are configured is the decision of each country that fields them. Yet, one piece of the equation remains firm: Counterterrorist skills are highly perishable and must be kept at razor's edge if the team hopes to succeed. Appropriate training and constant studying of the enemy's methods, personnel, and organizational structure are an absolute necessity. The required skills and support apparatus are manpower– and resource–consuming, but countries employing counterterrorist units must be prepared to accept the costs. In the long run, it is a low–budget affair when compared to the economic and human costs of a successful terrorist strike.

A CT operation is composed of several distinct phases. First, the unit must get to the area of operations— possibly many hundreds or even thousands of miles away— by reliable, secure transportation. Simultaneously, immense amounts of intelligence must be collected, analyzed, and disseminated by a number of supporting agencies. A critical issue at this phase is who is in charge. The Army's Special Operations Command (SOCOM) supports the DELTA's training and related operational requirements but, in time of crisis, JSOC bypasses the SOCOM link and directs the unit and the nation's other CT assets. Once deployed, the State Department is the key desision–making element for foreign operations, while the Justice Department deals with problems within the United States. This clean, simple chain of command allows a "stovepipe" of direction and support to the unit and cuts out a number of middlemen who would unintentionally hinder the execution of a mission.

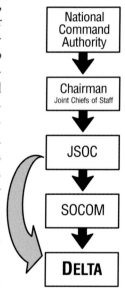

After arriving at the site of the "incident," the next phase deals with preparation. In its simplest form, this means that target surveillance is begun;

outer and inner security rings are checked; command, control and liaison functions are established; and incoming intelligence is analyzed. After all the players are satisfied (or the situation forces the issue), the next phase is the assault, or "takedown," of the objective. Closely on its heels is the swift withdrawal of the force back to their homebase.

With this as background, where does the new trooper fit in? He is likely to fill a number of roles or positions, and his titles may be many. As he progresses within the organization, he will use his past skills and experiences to benefit the team he is assigned to. For example, he may be a sniper because he went to sniper school while assigned to a Ranger battalion. If his demolitions background is good, he may find himself dealing with some very exotic toys designed to blow off the smallest locks or take down the entire wall of a room with minimal disturbance to the occupants of the next room. As a "door kicker" or "shooter," his skills will be fine–tuned in the art of lockpicking, room entry, and target identification. Common phrases often associated with the skills or strengths of these unique professionals include the "double tap," "happiness is a head shot," and "reach out and touch someone."

The SOT provides troopers with various methods of entry, seizure, and exit of terrorist situations. They learn to rappel into second– and third–story windows to get at the terrorists and their victims, as well as how to most effectively kick open a door, use specially manufactured stun grenades to disorient the terrorists and then closely follow the blast into the room. Each member of a four–man team must know not only where he is going, but also precisely where his teammates will be and in which direction their fields of fire are directed.

In this closely orchestrated ballet of death known as close–quarters battle, the troopers learn to pick their targets quickly and then instantly place a minimum of two shots in an eye socket–sized kill zone from as far as fifty feet away. This technique is known as the double tap. Moving quickly through the area, the team learns to secure everyone (regardless of who they are) with plastic flex cuffs and leave the sorting out and medical treatment to the follow–on police forces. These strong, yet pliable, restraining bands not only are easy to use, but a large number can be carried by one man.

It is this type of assault that most people associate with counterterrorist forces. During a takedown, terrorists and hostages alike see only dark apparitions, akin to *Star Wars'* Darth Vader, entering behind the stun or flash/bang grenades. From the top down, every trooper is clad in a modern array of sophisticated armor. Heads are protected by a dark gray or black Kevlar helmet identical to current military issue. Under his "Fritz" helmet is fitted a flame–resistant Nomex balaclava. An earphone and/or microphone provides him instant tactical communication with the rest of the unit. The principle is that everyone involved in the decision–making process and execution must be provided with real–time information in order to control the unfolding operation.

Depending on the situation, a trooper is wearing eye protection in the form of either shatterproof goggles or a protective chemical mask which also provides a degree of eye safety. His upper torso is encased by a Kevlar vest, for gunshot and blast fragmentation protection, over a dark Nomex coverall or a tactical battledress. Over this, a variety of general equipment is worn, along with items that will support his specific tasks. Some troopers will have ammunition and myriad survival aids, such as powerful miniature flashlights and radio receivers. Others will have a variety of grenades, different types of ammo and first–aid equipment or knives. When medical assistance is not likely to be immedi-

ately available, CT teams carry a medical pouch containing assorted dressings, IV tubing, saline solutions, and tourniquets.

As with everything else, individual weapons are dictated by the situation. Of course, everyone has a particular favorite, but training on all available CT weapons is a must. Most room entries begin with the lead man using a submachine gun or a semiautomatic pistol. To expedite door–kicking procedures, shotguns firing a sabot or lead slug will be used to blow off the barrier's hinges. Many team members will insist that a submachine gun or shotgun, which can be carried in one hand, is the ideal weapon, and some even mount laser pointers or mini flashlights on their weapons for operations in buildings or dimly lit areas. Plenty of ammo is always strategically placed around his uniform.

Regardless of how much equipment the team member has, each man is aware that one lucky shot or a well–placed booby trap can ruin the best–laid plans. From the soles of his Gore–Tex assault boots to the crown of his Kevlar helmet, a team member's equipment is constantly reviewed and updated. A takedown is an affair that one must come properly dressed for.

Training generally falls into two categories. First the FNG (f——ing new guy) will go through individual skills training designed to break old habits that come from the conventional side of the Army, such as not shooting outside of the prescribed safety limits, and much emphasis is placed on individual action and initiative. New habits, like the double tap, are instilled in the FNG. These come from lessons learned through both successful missions and failures. In the case of the double tap, a pumped–up terrorist in the midst of a takedown cannot be reasoned with or talked into surrendering.

Once this basic training is completed, the FNG enters the team training phase where he is taught how to handle himself in any close–quarters battle,

(**Above**) A CT operative demonstrates how to use a shotgun during a window entry. (**Above right**) A close–up of a "best–case" anchoring system, with abundant safety features. In the heat of a fast–paced takedown, such fine points often have to be bypassed. (**Right and below right**) An assault team conducting a forced entry and room–clearing demonstration of a "hotel conference room." Lock picking is conducted with a charge of C4 plastic explosives. Also note the 360–degree protection and the Walther 9mm P5 pistol and MP-K submachine gun, protective masks, and ballistic (bulletproof) helmets. Expertise with personal weapons while wearing a variety of different equipment combinations is a requirement. (**Below**) If you can't go through the door or a window, go through the wall! Like high tech termites, two US operatives prepare to follow the blast into the next room.

or CQB, whether it is conducted in a building, train, or aircraft. For example, the trooper will be given his first taste of an aircraft takedown at a large mockup of a generic civilian passenger liner at the SOT before training on a great variety of actual aircraft happily supplied by the major carriers at various sites around the country.

Additional CT training is also conducted to teach numerous infiltration methods for moving into isolated target areas. These include parachuting into the area using high–altitude, low–opening (HALO) or high–altitude, high–opening (HAHO), underwater rescue operations using Scuba techniques and miniature submersible vehicles for long–distance travel, and rappelling and fast–roping from helicopters. Teams may also have to learn techniques for driving various types of all–terrain vehicles. Lockpicking is also taught.

Upon completion, the FNG is assigned to a team, and maintenance of his new skills is begun within his troop. Regular cross–training will now occur with related foreign and domestic CT units, such as Britain's SAS or our own Navy SEAL (Sea–Air–Land) teams. Some DELTA troopers will also find themselves temporarily assigned "personal protection duty," providing security to key US personnel, such as ambassadors in Central America and the Middle East.

The Killing House

Take a break you heroes."

The team sergeant chuckles to himself every time he uses that line. If everything is going as it should, his jibe would either cause a rush of sarcastic curses and catcalls or receive a deep–throated moan from the assembled trainees. This time, the muted response indicates that the humid North Carolina weather is having an impact on the strength of the team. More importantly, it was a good indicator of the amount and type of training that should be con-

ducted for the remainder of the day. Based on his observations, the team sergeant decides to deviate from the published training schedule and walk through a room–clearing exercise without the required live ammunition. Training accidents are acceptable in this business but are not sought after.

Fifty meters to the west of this training area, a second and much more experienced team is also working its way through the day's training. Having just finished with their own room–clearing exercise, the men are given one of the most beloved commands in the lexicon of military language: "Take a break."

The break is planned for thirty minutes, but to the team members, it should be longer. Sprawled in various positions underneath the pines, each trooper brushes pine cones out of the way and tries to find a comfortable position while attempting to keep equipment from becoming too dirty with grit and sand. Small rivets of sweat trickle down grimy faces as nomex gloves are removed and calloused hands reach up to brush the sweat away from bloodshot eyes. Each team member wears an assault suit of black Nomex, and some of the team had already removed their black Kevlar helmets and flashproof balaclavas. Goggles, used to provide protection from flying debris, lay in the crown of the helmet, along with sweat–soaked gloves and face masks. Sensitive individual communications earpieces and microphones are inspected to ensure they were switched off.

Each trooper wears body armor, designed to protect throat and chest areas, and "armored shorts" to protect vulnerable groin areas. Some troopers have also added knee and elbow pads under their assault suits, while shin protectors are pulled on by some of the veterans who have grown tired of the bruises and cut shins received in the furniture–cluttered "killing house." Individuals are equipped with either a special–purpose Mossberg automatic shotgun

"Walk–throughs" of room–clearing operations are run with troopers wearing progressively more equipment so the men will gain a clear idea of how different protective sets restrict vision and movement. They must attain extreme levels of proficiency while wearing all combinations of gear. (**Above**) Troopers in coveralls prepare to enter a SOT "killing house" and (**opposite**) perform their ballet of death. Note the mannequin terrorists and hostage in closet.

or a 9mm Heckler & Koch MP5 submachine gun. Most of the free world's CT forces swear by this weapon, and some even argue that it is the best export the Germans have had since *Fräuleins*, Mercedes and beer. In addition to the MP5s, the sniper teams on this exercise are equipped with M24 sniper rifles. Though there are more advanced systems, the accurized Remington 700 bolt–action rifle with five–round fluted, detachable magazine is still the favored standby. Its stainless–steel barrel, and hefty .300 Winchester Magnum round provide this team with the power required to "reach out and touch

someone." All members of the sweeper team carry 9mm Beretta Model 92F pistols: the standard sidearm of the US Army.

While some troopers "smoke and joke," others inhale nourishing liquids from canteens and jugs. Like the fondness each man has for his individual weapons, team members also have a distinct enjoyment of anything liquid. Gatorade, bottled spring water, juices, or just plain H_2O is found in the individual backpacks. Unlike what Hollywood would have one believe, hard–drinking troopers are not the norm. The shakes are not conducive to good teamwork. And to the experienced eye, the soldiers are an organized and tightly knit group of professionals, men who can easily operate as either individuals or a team, making decisions that could have far–reaching impacts at world levels.

"Saddle up, you assholes."

Staff Sergeant Dawkins hated it when the sergeant major tried out his hard, John Wayne voice, and comments sarcastically, "I really wonder if John Wayne ever called anyone an asshole." A number of other uncomplimentary thoughts are voiced as the troopers slowly rise to their feet and adjust their equipment. Gathering around the team leader, Sergeant Major Greg Tusconey, the men fall in to form a loose formation facing their boss.

Looking up from his notebook, Sergeant Major Tusconey begins with an in–depth critique of the morning's past exercise. He cites their strengths as well as their weaknesses. When finished, he faces his soldiers and says in a matter–of–fact tone, "OK, girls, let's get our shit together and try it again." The resounding reply to the implication that there is a collective lack of masculinity within the unit is indicative of a team who can give as much as it can take.

Sauntering back to their briefing area, the team members arrange themselves on wooden benches placed in front of a graphic representation of the

rooms within the killing house. A key factor in these exercises, as well as an actual assault, is the need for critical, accurate, and up–to–date information about the physical layout of the passenger aircraft or building, as well as the locations of the hostages and their terrorist keepers. Stepping up in front of the diagram, the sergeant major begins to describe the mission for the team in clear, concise, and pointed terms:

"At 1730 hours last night, terrorists assaulted the US Embassy, and took sixteen State Department employees as hostages. Two US Marines were killed during the initial assault. We are to prepare for a deliberate takedown of the building on order from higher." Stopping to scan the team for questions, he continues. "Outer security has been established by the local police, and inner security has been established by the hasty response team from the 10th Special Forces Group until after we arrive and take over responsibility for the mission. Recon of the building has been conducted, along with a debrief of our people and the locals who have solid, current intel."

Tusconey proceeds to outline the rehearsal schedules and timetables, who is responsible for what, and how he envisions the takedown will be accomplished. After the thorough briefing is completed, individual troopers are quizzed and then individual and team rehearsals are begun. As the last rays of the fading sun are engulfed by the approach of a cool, wet front, the last preparations are wound up. For this exercise, the chopper support for the takedown will come from "the Task Force" as the 160th SOAR is usually referred to.

The team is divided into sniper and assault elements, which coordinate the operation's precise timing, and move out. The two sniper teams each consist of a spotter and a shooter. They are linked together with the assault team, sweeper team, and command center by radio. Each sniper team moves along individual routes previously reconned and takes positions offering vantage points overlooking the target area. The assault element, meanwhile, is moving toward their pickup zone, or PZ, to rendezvous with an inbound chopper. The word circulates that the order has been received. The mission is on.

Because the operation will take place at night, infrared reflective tape is added to each member's equipment. Strips are applied around the chest, wrists, ankles and helmet. Using AN/PVS-7 night vision goggles (NVGs), all assault members will be easily seen in the heat of night combat. The sun has long ago set, and a steady drizzle falls through the tall pines as the team divides evenly and prepares to board the chopper. Right on schedule, the air is disturbed by the pounding of rotor blades beating the heavy night mist. Like a giant dragonfly, the MH-60 Black Hawk glides into the PZ, where the team immediately loads through the side doors. The pilot's eyes are unaided but his copilot wears aviator's AN/AVS-6 NVGs. Immediately, the team leader places the spare set of headphones over his ears and communicates with the pilot.

"Evening," says the pilot in a slow, Southern drawl.

"How's it going?" replies the sergeant major.

Formalities exhausted, Tusconey quickly briefs the aircrew on how the team will carry out the infil as the aircraft nears the target. Due to the lousy weather, the landing zone, or LZ, will be the building's sloping rooftop, and the team will drop onto a very small area at its peak, where a flat space had been located during photo recon analysis. Normally, the team would rappel or fast–rope in, but the wet weather and reduced visibility give them an added advantage and they'll be able to get closer to the target. With clockwork precision, the Black Hawk angles into the rooftop LZ and flares out level and steady. Looking through his NVGs, Tusconey sees that everyone is ready and in a low, distinct voice says, "Stand by, stand by." Prompted by his warning, the sniper teams report in: "Sniper One, ready. Target sighted." "Sniper Two ready. No target." At his hand signal, the lead team members prepare to exit. Taking a deep breath, he gives the command, "Go!"

The soldiers leap onto the mist–shrouded roof and fan out across its tricky incline in a predetermined (and well–rehearsed) pattern. Almost as quickly as the bird arrived at the LZ, it disappears into the gloom. Two team members attach green nylon climbing ropes to anchor points, drop them over the sides of the building along predetermined entry sites, and kneel in anticipation after attaching their snaplinks. Six other men move to a rooftop door and, after determining that it is locked, move into a tight file along the outside wall. The door hinges will have to be shot off.

The Number One man, armed with a Mossberg 12–gauge shotgun, prepares to blast the offending hinges off the wooden door. Despite the fact that every soldier is in communication with the rest of the team, discipline is absolute and the only sound breaking the silence is the constant hiss over each man's earpiece.

It has been ten seconds since the team landed. At the command, "Go!" the hinges disintegrate in a shower of sparks and splinters as the shotgun's solid lead slug crashes into each hinge, starting with the top and working down. Yanking the door to the side, the Number Two trooper rapidly steps into the doorway, where he immediately places his back to the dimly lit stairwell wall. Sweeping the staircase with his NVG, he breathlessly alerts follow–on troopers to the situation he is observing. Number Three now bursts through the doorway and in calculated steps moves down the stairs and secures the top floor stairwell. Peering down the hallway, he speaks in clear, crisp, and rapid tones into his microphone: "Number Three, hallway clear." Trooper Number Four is immediately at his side, having followed his partner down the stairs. As Number Three moves to the right, Number Four moves left and blends into the darkened hallway. Both troopers' H&Ks move in measured arcs: ceiling to floor, left to right. Whenever a trooper's eyes move under their NVG, the stubby barrel of his MP5 follows, ready to spit out a lethal three–round burst along that same visual arc.

The second assault element of four men moves along the right side of the hallway toward a door on the right. The lead man (Number Three) senses motion in the room. Reaching down along his left thigh, he extracts a pop can–sized flash/bang grenade from his leg pouch. Bringing it up to his right hand, which still clutches an MP5, he slides the grenade's pullring over his right hand's gloved thumb. While holding the safety spoon, he pulls the ring. Gently rolling the grenade into the room, he flattens himself against the wall as he warns his teammates. "Grenade" reverberates through the soldier's earphones and, almost immediately, "Go!" is commanded before the nonlethal grenade has expended its package.

Number Five slides into the left side of the doorway as the room erupts in multiple flashes and explosions designed to disrupt, disorientate and illuminate. As he moves through the door, Number Six follows and slides into the black, smoke–filled room along the doorway's right wall. He is followed by Numbers Seven and Eight who had entered the floor through windows on the other side of the building. Number Seven backs Number Five by taking on any targets from his twelve– through three–o'clock (the right hand wall). Number Five already has acquired a target through his NVG in his twelve–through nine–o'clock area along the left wall.

A masked terrorist is wildly trying to bring his Polish–made AK-47 assault rifle to bear on a young

(**Above**) A team wearing ballistic helmets takes up position along the wall, to avoid being silhouetted against an open door, as their shooter takes aim at a European–style door latch with a pump shotgun. (**Opposite**) After entry, the team fans out along the walls before picking targets.

woman strapped to a chair near the center of the office. Number Five squeezes a three–round burst into the throat of the terrorist, who goes down in a spasmatic heap.

As Number Seven checks the terrorist for other weapons and vital signs, Number 5 maintains a steady aim on the lifeless corpse. Flipping the terrorist over on his stomach, Number Seven expertly

pins his wrists together with flex cuffs. After a quick check of the room, Numbers Six and Eight now check the bound female for booby traps. More than one rescue has ended in disaster when the rescuers failed to check for explosives secreted somewhere on a hostage. A grenade or stick of dynamite can turn a rescue into a sticky affair. After the check is completed, the team exits the room. Eight seconds have passed. As the leader leaves, he announces "Number Two, one terrorist down, one hostage secured, main room, top floor" to the command post and the other team members. Now it is up to the sweepers and backup police forces to take charge of the room.

This ballet of death will continue until the "embassy" is cleared of terrorists and all the hostages are accounted for. After the team exits the building, they move to an assembly area and are whisked away for an in–depth debriefing. If this had been a real takedown, actual terrorists and hostages would be considerably more unpredictable than the mannequins and pop–up targets the team had to deal with. Local police and medical personnel, as well as the sweepers, would have also been moving simultaneously through the building to deal with the carnage left behind and make a complete record of what happened. It may have to be used later as evidence.

This is a typical exercise.

During such exercises, the trooper is trained not to fall into the Rambo approach to CT operations: Never fire from the hip and always extend your folding stock. Fire at close range and don't waste ammo. You learn how to move: dropping to a crouch, firing, dropping and firing again, and moving to the next position. You learn to move quickly through doorways and get in position and maintain proper trigger control.

Chapter 4
Decade of Frustration

General [Bernard] Rogers told me of a note from the President. It had surfaced in the tank earlier in the day [October 18, 1977] and asked, "Do we have the same capability as the West Germans?" Much discussion ensued before it was decided that we did not. One of the generals present had said, "Well I'm not going over to the White House and tell him we don't."

Colonel Charlie A. Beckwith, US Army (Retired)

Throughout the 1980s, DELTA was beset by a number of events that might have caused lesser organizations to collapse. The troopers trained hard but were seldom deployed. They watched helplessly as Americans were whisked from streets and university offices in Beirut and seized in large groups in hijacked airliners and ships. Worse yet, the men found themselves gearing up for rescue operations that were cancelled time and again for a variety of reasons. During this same period, the unit also found themselves on the receiving end of a disturbing amount of unwanted publicity. In addition to a highly publicized financial scandal involving DELTA members, the easy visual access to the Special Operations Training Facility (SOT) may have been a factor in the media's knowledge of deployments during several hostage crises.

A US flag burns on the Rhein–Main Air Base perimeter fence during a period of mass left–wing demonstrations and terrorist strikes against American targets in Germany.

Although it's shocking to think that a unit on the cutting edge of America's war on terrorism was—and still is—in appearance at least, so vulnerable, it was only the tip of the weak links plaguing counterterrorism. In addition to the expected security problems associated with CT operations, numerous interdepartmental squabbles and convoluted command and control issues abounded. An excellent example concerned justification for CT operations within the continental United States. The Justice Department's Federal Bureau of Investigation is responsible for tackling terrorist incidents at home, yet DELTA had to provide badly needed assistance during both the 1986 Statue of Liberty centennial in New York City and the 1984 Olympics in Los Angeles in spite of numerous jurisdictional and legal problems.

When CT operations are planned for overseas, numerous diplomatic issues become critical elements in the military/political equation, and the State Department steps to the forefront. Probably

189

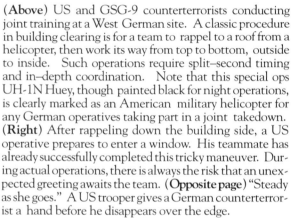

(**Above**) US and GSG-9 counterterrorists conducting joint training at a West German site. A classic procedure in building clearing is for a team to rappel to a roof from a helicopter, then work its way from top to bottom, outside to inside. Such operations require split–second timing and in–depth coordination. Note that this special ops UH-1N Huey, though painted black for night operations, is clearly marked as an American military helicopter for any German operatives taking part in a joint takedown. (**Right**) After rappeling down the building side, a US operative prepares to enter a window. His teammate has already successfully completed this tricky maneuver. During actual operations, there is always the risk that an unexpected greeting awaits the team. (**Opposite page**) "Steady as she goes." A US trooper gives a German counterterrorist a hand before he disappears over the edge.

the most basic question that must be asked before contemplating operations on foreign turf is: What sovereign nation wants to relinquish command and control to United States military forces conducting such highly visible operations on their soil? It has to be remembered that no matter how discreetly DELTA may conduct itself in the run–up to an operation, every hostage rescue is undeniably a high–visibility operation *after* its well–publicized conclusion. The implication for the nation hosting DELTA is, of course, that it does not have the re-

sources to take care of its own internal problems. The domestic, as well as international, political ramifications for a government can be enormous. Add to this mess the fact that the Joint Special Operations Command, the direct link between DELTA and the president (known as the National Command Authority) and the Joint Chiefs of Staff (JCS), can receive marching orders from both. The JCS is better qualified to oversee any operations involving DELTA, but common sense remained a missing ingredient in this war, as can be seen by the less–than–desirable results in Grenada.

Aftermath

The fallout from the inferno of *Desert I* was complicated and far reaching. Not only did President Jimmy Carter lose his bid for re–election, but Egypt's supportive president, Anwar Sadat (who was already on a number of hit lists for his part in the Camp David Accords), was now a principal target of Iranian–sponsored fanatics for allowing the "Great Satan" to launch Operation *Eagle Claw* from his country. He would soon die at the hands of Muslim fundamentalists.

JCS planners continued their work, and soon a new mission to rescue the hostages in Iran, code–named *Honey Badger,* was put together under the direction of the renowned and much–respected General Richard Secord. Armed with the proper special operations support—and the hard–learned lessons gleaned from *Eagle Claw*— he assembled a powerful force of special operations aviators, Special Forces and DELTA troopers, intelligence collectors, and agents who were prepared to go it again. But it was not meant to be. Some two minutes after Ronald Reagan was sworn in as President of the United States, the hostages were released.

To help dampen the firestorm of criticism that erupted after *Desert I*, a six–officer review group was appointed by the chairman of the JCS, General David C. Jones. It was chaired by Admiral James L. Holloway, and the balance of its membership consisted of generals from the Army, Air Force, and Marines who had experience in either special or clandestine operations.

These investigators came to the conclusion that *Eagle Claw* was plagued by untested operational methods, poor communications procedures, and a dangerously informal command structure lacking unity of command. Training for the mission, moreover, had been conducted by its various compo-

nents at different sites without a full dress rehearsal using all the assigned elements—something that would have highlighted the most glaring operational and equipment shortfalls. The commission recommended that "a permanent field agency" of the JCS be established with "assigned staff personnel and certain assigned forces" and that a "murder board" of military experts be formed to independently examine mission plans before execution.

As for Colonel Beckwith, he was asked by General Meyer to formalize an earlier proposal for a permanently operating joint task force that would fall directly under the JCS and combine dedicated Army, Navy, and Air Force elements during its training and planning. Beckwith and others had long voiced the opinion that this type of organization was needed, and Major General John Singlaub put it best when he stated *Eagle Claw* didn't work because "we tried to bring disparate units from all over the Armed Forces—from all over the world— and then put them into an ad hoc arrangement to

A key ingredient in CT operations is covert intelligence collection. Here, an intel specialist supports a DELTA training mission by conducting surveillance operations from a concealed site.

do a very complicated plan."

Beckwith's proposal to establish a Joint Special Operations Command (JSOC) was approved by Meyer in May 1980, and he was soon transferred from DELTA to the newly formed, independent organization he helped create. He badly missed the excitement of leading a combat team, though, and remarked that his staff billet "ain't as good a job [as DELTA]." He retired to the Lone Star State in 1981 and opened a security service. Harkening back to his days with Britain's Special Air Service, he gave his company the name SAS of Texas.

The establishment of the JSOC was one of many honest attempts to put teeth in America's counterterrorist effort in the wake of *Desert I*. As expected, the new government programs became battlegrounds for interdepartmental squabbles. The major catalyst for this fighting was, of course, money since counterterrorism was now in vogue and took funding away from other programs.

DELTA's friends in high places went to even higher places, and the post–Beckwith organization thrived during this period. The unit's strength before *Eagle Claw* of just over 100 men, making up two small A and B squadrons plus support, grew to a relatively stable force of 300 during the early 1980s— enough for three full-sized squadrons— with its selection and training as brutally efficient as ever. The unit also benefited greatly from production of *Task, Conditions and Standards for DELTA*, or, as it is more commonly known, "the Black Book." This document was produced only because General Meyer essentially grabbed Beckwith by the shoulders, pushed him down into a chair, and forced him to compose it.

Meyer, now the Army's chief of staff, was anxious that DELTA not reinvent the wheel with each new commander and wanted to ensure that it would retain its SAS–type structure, one that is unique within the US Army. Four troops of approximately sixteen men make up a squadron, with each troop able to reconfigure itself into eight–, six–, four–, three–, or two–soldier teams or elements. This degree of flexibility is one of the key ingredients in DELTA's ability to handle virtually any terrorist scenario.

DELTA also moved its headquarters from the old post stockade to the new, state–of–the–art SOT, appropriately nicknamed "Wally World" after a lavish theme park in the *National Lampoon's Vacation* movie. But, in a sense, it wasn't just DELTA that came up a big winner from the increased awareness of the terrorist threat. The whole military benefitted because it was identified as the obvious candidate to receive the now readily available funds. And the funds did flow: to Air Force special operations, Navy SEALs, Army aviation, Rangers, and Special Forces, as well as a large supporting cast in the various services, such as the Army's Intelligence Support Activity (ISA).

The State Department, however, was soon to emerge as the biggest winner. Being in the best position to judge the political ramifications of US actions on a host nation's territory, it received the responsibility for overseeing all overseas counter-terrorist operations. But despite the fact that the United States now had its CT apparatus well–organized and in place, the future proved to be not so rosy as the optimists hoped.

Operation *Urgent Fury*

After Ronald Reagan assumed the presidency in 1981, he "let it be known to friend and foe alike" that he had learned from the hard lessons of his predecessors. Surrounded by capable and, in some cases, hawkish advisors, President Reagan was determined that, like the sheriffs of the Old West, he would clean up the world and make it safe for women and children. All he needed was a place to start and the force to sweep up the mess. He didn't have long to wait. At the southern end of the Antilles chain lies the beautiful Caribbean island of Grenada. A former ward of the British Empire, this idyllic eight– by fifteen–mile island was to be the testing ground for the new president and the changes that had been made in the special operations community since *Desert I*.

On October 19, 1983, Grenada's Marxist prime minister, Maurice Bishop, and several cabinet members were lined up along the walls of old Fort Rupert and executed by former associates who formed an even more radical "Revolutionary Military Counsel." Bishop had aligned himself with the Soviets and their Cuban surrogates, who had, among other things, constructed a large military communications facility, a 10,000–foot runway capable of handling long–range transports, and extensive airfield support facilities, ostensibly to support its meager tourist industry. While a single air base would not allow a hostile force to control the entrance into the southern Caribbean during a war, it would provide an excellent stopover for aircraft bringing in material and personnel support for "peoples' revolutions" in Central and South America.

MH-6 Little Birds of the 160th SOAR operating in the Persian Gulf. Among other operations they took part in was the September 1987 capture of an Iranian mine–laying vessel that threatened oil tanker traffic.

With the execution of the genuinely popular leader, widespread protests broke out on the island, and when the military opened fire on the demonstrators, the die was cast. The threat to the region caused an uproar among the neighboring Caribbean nations, and the Reagan administration believed that a radical, Marxist government (that thought nothing of shooting its own citizens) would, sooner or later, get around to using the roughly 600 American students at the island's medical school as pawns in a dangerous game to keep the US military from closing down the airfield. The young students were a hostage situation waiting to happen, so the United States moved quickly to launch Operation *Urgent Fury*.

Leading the assaults were several of the US military's elite as well as (until then) classified units. UH-60 Black Hawks of Task Force (TF) 160 flew directly from the United States to a nearby island launch site, with the help of additional internal fuel tanks, while MH-6s were brought in by Air Force cargo planes. During the early morning hours of

Counterterrorist specialists must be able to use any ruse or disguise to get close to hostage holding sites, such as an aircraft or buildings. Here, US Army CT operatives display equipment and various disguises during a briefing for General Bernard Rogers, Supreme Allied Commander, Europe, in the early 1980s. (**Left**) One of the typical "European businessmen" holsters his 9mm Beretta pistol and (**right**) a "street cleaner," standing beside a "municipal worker," shows off his protective vest and ammunition belt. Note the equipment on display.

October 25, the expert aviators of TF 160 ferried their ground counterparts, DELTA, to targets near the airfield at Point Salines, where they were to carry out a direct action mission ahead of two Ranger battalions parachuting in at dawn. Their target was the airfield control facilities which, it turned out, were heavily ringed by misplaced, but marginally effective, automatic weapons. A second mission entailed the takedown of Richmond Hill Prison, where one Black Hawk was lost to Soviet-made

ZSU-23-2 (twin 23mm) antiaircraft guns. In both cases, men and aircraft were lost (some figures are still classified). The lack of timely, on–the–spot, intelligence had again raised its ugly head.

Several members of the elite Navy SEAL Team 6 have privately related that they had an especially rough time as DELTA and the TF 160 units were running into their own problems in the south. One deadly incident occurred when four of their members parachuted into rough seas to conduct a linkup with a surface vessel that was to take them in close for a water infiltration. The drowning of these four men did not stop the mission, but it did tragically demonstrate that even the best of the best are sometimes incapable of overcoming the odds.

A major concern during *Urgent Fury* was the safety of the British government's representative. Tasked to keep the gentleman from falling into the hands of the Grenadan "Peoples' Revolutionary

(**Above**) Unlike situations depicted in movies, actual aircraft takedowns must be accomplished quickly, violently, and with surgical precision. Here, a suspected hijacker in a mock airliner cabin is controlled the best way: with a pistol to the head. (**Right**) "Tickets please!" A terrorist's view of a US operative taken during a train–clearing exercise in Europe.

Armed Forces," twenty–two other members of SEAL Team 6 flew in by chopper, fast–roped onto the rooftop and grounds of the governor's residence, and took control. A stunned Grenadan defense unit located nearby summoned help from two Soviet supplied BTR-60 armored personnel carriers mounting multiple machine guns. The sudden appearance of substantial hostile elements forced the planned evacuation of Government House to be hastily cancelled. They were, as one SEAL member later described, "in a world 'a shit" and had to fight in place. With neither antiarmor weapons nor good communications, the team held out as best they could until a Specter gunship came to their rescue and eliminated the problem. But even with the help of the AC-130's massive firepower, up to half of the rescue party is reported to have been wounded by the time Marines reached them on the second day of *Urgent Fury*.

Months later, a veteran SEAL discussing the operation sighed after draining his beer and said, "Thank God it was just the Grenadans." When pressed, he continued, "Every time some nonqualified son of a bitch plans or directs our operations, we get our asses handed to us on a silver platter. It just ain't right." Right or wrong, the end result from the problems of *Urgent Fury* was that closer control over the planning of special operations would, at least for a while, be handled by people who "had been there," which means thoroughly qualified in special operations planning.

An interesting wrinkle on special operations on Grenada came from the media's coverage of *Urgent Fury*. Although the Army had refused to either confirm or deny the use of special operations forces for nearly eight years, ABC News was able to extract a concession that one TF 160 captain was killed and eleven DELTA troopers injured after

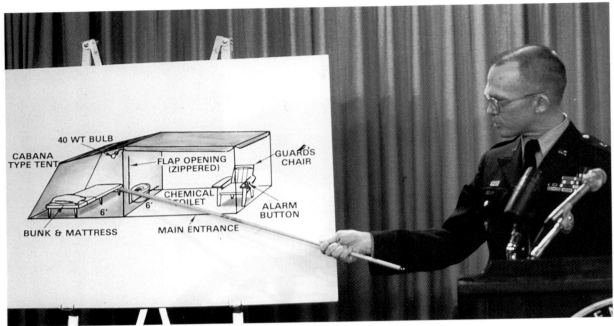

broadcasting footage of the downing of his Black Hawk— an event previously unaccounted for in the Pentagon recap of the operation. An American resident of Grenada had shot the film; other footage showed MH-6s, aircraft for which no procurement information had been publicly released. They were identified by ABC News as Hughes 500 helicopters, its civilian designation.

After the operation, increasingly bitter complaints over the "veil of secrecy" surrounding special operations were heard from some quarters of the media. Also being made was the highly dubious claim that only the American public was being denied access to information since the Soviets supposedly already knew all about such activities. While this is a subject that will certainly never be concluded to everyone's satisfaction, it is an undeniable fact that even relatively low losses can have a severe impact on the capabilities of a small unit. And if the small unit performs a mission of vital strategic importance, that loss may be magnified a hundred-fold. Not only do Western intelligence agencies monitor terrorist networks, but the terrorists themselves monitor CT organizations, with the assistance of various friendly governments that track Western units and capabilities largely through press reports and, occasionally, espionage. It is not in the best interests of the United States to reveal losses in key covert units within days—or even months—after they were suffered. In this case, freedom of information must take a back seat to security

Trouble in the Mediterranean

Almost immediately on the heels of *Urgent Fury*, members of Italy's own homespun terrorist organization, the Red Brigade, abducted an American one–star general named James L. Dozier from his apartment on December 17, 1982. Authorities were later to learn that Dozier was not the intended victim, but, instead, a Navy admiral had been the group's actual target. Regardless of who was snatched, the impact all over Europe was the same: NATO military

facilities soon became prison camps for the Allies. Virtually every senior officer seemed to see himself or his family as a prime target for the terrorists.

Against this background of confusion, the experts from various special operations units converged on Italy. Much to their credit, the Italians told everyone to kindly go home since this was their turf. But while all door kickers were sent packing, they did keep some special operators who could assist with such exotic needs as radio and telephone intercept.

When the alarm was sounded, one of the units offered was the European Command's own hasty response detachment. Its commander found himself on the first plane into the area. He was also on the first plane out. The Italians recognized incompetence when they saw it, and had enough problems of their own without having to wet–nurse a rookie counterterrorist in addition to the US State Department. With the help of the US signal intercept folks, the Italians found and rescued the kidnapped general, and American CT "experts" learned one

General Dozier's kidnappers erected a tent inside a safehouse room to hold their prisoner. (**Opposite**) Dozier displays a diagram of the tent and nearest guard position after Italian counterterrorists forcibly freed him from the Red Brigade. (**Above**) Lebanese rescue workers and US Marines gather outside the flattened Marine barracks in the aftermath of a terrorist truck bombing. The suicide driver had driven directly past Marine guards, who had been ordered not to carry loaded weapons. There were lessons to be learned: Listen to the warnings of counterterrorist specialists, plus shoot first and worry about CNN later.

more lesson in dealing with the real world.

In 1982, Iran had sent roughly 2,000 of their fanatical Revolutionary Guards to the Lebanese free–for–all civil war as "volunteers." While a good number of them would go to paradise after falling in regular combat against Christian militiamen (and leftist Shiites and Druz militiamen and renegade Palestinians and US Marine snipers, as well as Israeli, Lebanese, and Syrian soldiers), a select few were destined to meet Allah in a less conventional man-

The television image of a TWA pilot being prevented from talking with reporters by an armed hijacker at Beirut airport in June 1985.

ner. These "martyrs" drove explosives–laden trucks into barracks, embassies, or other high–priority targets. On the night of April 18, 1983, forty French paratroopers and 241 US Marines were killed by a pair of these truck bombers after failing to heed the lessons of a similar attack earlier that year on a US Embassy building.

Another incident in late October of that year concerned members of the 10th Special Forces Group who were billeted in a downtown hotel while training and advising the Lebanese Army. The group's commander, Colonel Richard Potter, was warned by associates with connections to the Shiite fundamentalists that the group's quarters were targeted for yet another suicide bombing. Potter, DELTA's former deputy commander and a veteran of *Desert I*, was not about to let such warnings go unheeded and immediately moved his force to a Lebanese Army base north of the city. In this case, the training of one man, along with past friendships nurtured over years of frustration, spared the wives of the 10th Special Forces a visit from a chaplain and the ever present survivor assistance officer.

On December 4, 1984, DELTA was sent to assault a Kuwaiti airliner hijacked on its way to Pakistan. Two American passengers were killed during the incident, and the aircraft was forced to fly to Iran, where both the terrorists and hostages were released before the unit could intervene. Six months later, on June 14, the unit was sent back to the region in preparation for an assault on TWA Flight 847, but the affair ended before they could be employed; one off–duty Navy serviceman on board was singled out and murdered. DELTA failed to come to grips

Throughout the 1970s and 1980s, terrorists in Germany were like fish swimming in a great sea of militant leftist/Marxist/ecologist/misfit/nationalist extremists and sympathizers. (**Right**) A masked demonstrator protesting outside the US air base at Rhein–Main and (**below**), an arms cache believed to have been hidden by Germany's Red Army Faction. Terrorist groups rely heavily on hidden caches of arms and other supplies.

with terrorists again in October, during the *Achille Lauro* affair, and the resulting fiasco at Sigonella Naval Air Station, Sicily, pointed out that the Italians were not about to change their position on whether they or the Americans have jurisdiction on Italian turf. Members of SEAL Team 6 attempted to take the hijackers into custody and were re-

minded that they were not the ones in charge.

The Palestinian extremists who commandeered the Italian vessel had been persuaded to leave it at Alexandria, Egypt, in return for safe conduct to friendly Tunisia, where the PLO maintained its headquarters. They boarded a commercial passenger jet and left Egypt immediately ahead of DELTA's arrival but was quickly intercepted by US F-14 Tomcat fighters, which diverted it to the US–Italian air base. Once the airliner was forced to land, it was quickly surrounded by the SEALs, who were, in turn, surrounded by Italian *carabonari*, who also blocked their C-141 with security vehicles. Since both groups were attempting to carry out their orders and

(**Above**) The unmarked limousine of General Frederick Krossen, commander of US Army forces in Europe, after a failed assassination attempt by Germany's Red Army Faction in September 1981. Only a month before, the general had finally heeded the advice of West German counterterrorists and obtained the special armored Mercedes that deflected the blast of the Soviet–made rocket–propelled grenade away from the car's interior. In the car was the general, his wife, an aid, and a German driver/bodyguard. (**Right**) A West German wanted poster for known terrorists. As various fugitives were apprehended or killed, they were crossed off the poster by the US CT team that mounted it on their headquarters' wall.

apprehend the hijackers, a tense situation developed between the senior US officer present and Italian officers. The situation quickly degenerated and the *carabonari* loaded and locked their trusty Berettas and drew down on the equally well–armed SEALs. It was an Italian standoff until the diplomats intervened and determined that it was in ev-

eryone's best interest to let the Italians take charge.

Yet another incident occurred the following month, when a commercial airliner was hijacked to Malta by Palestinian extremists. This time, DELTA was on hand but not used. In fact, they were initially not even allowed to land. Since the hijacked aircraft was Egyptian, that country's commandos, trained by US special operations personnel, were allowed to conduct the takedown. It turned sour, and fifty–seven hostages lost their lives.

Troubles at Home

From 1970 through the mid–1980s, more than 1,000 Americans had been killed, taken hostage, or otherwise injured by foreign terrorists. Virtually all of these incidents had occurred overseas, but CT planners believed that America's luck might not hold out much longer: The upcoming 1984 Summer Olympics to be held in Los Angeles was an awfully tempting target. As part of the $1 billion effort to provide security from possible attacks, DELTA deployed to a nearby naval facility and stood ready to counter any terrorist situation. Along with DELTA was a massive CT force incorporating city and state SWAT (special weapons and tactics) teams and the Federal Bureau of Investigation's Hasty Response Team, commonly referred to as HURT. All were given varying degrees of responsibility to counter threats, depending on their level of expertise and available manpower.

One interesting sidenote to DELTA's deployment at the Olympics was their use of a mobile command post disguised as a Budweiser beer truck for surreptitiously transporting a response team to the site of an incident. While mention of such a vehicle almost invariably brings snickers to the mouths of listeners accustomed to seeing similar tricks on scores of television cop shows and films as diverse as *Good Neighbor Sam* and *Stripes*, the fact remains that a vehicle camouflaged in this unconventional manner looks like it "belongs" and can move virtually unnoticed if that is what is required. Thankfully, the truck was not needed, but it had to be a comforting sight to those in the know.

Unlike the funds spent on producing the Budweiser truck, not all monies funneled through Army covert accounts were spent wisely or even legitimately. Army auditors discovered a number of irregularities in a covert account between 1981 and 1983. A disturbing amount of double–dipping had taken place and such items as a hot–air balloon and Rolls–Royce sedan had been purchased supposedly to support clandestine operations.

In a climate that one DELTA member described as "sheer hysteria," standard cost–accounting techniques were applied to ongoing covert operations

and training. The result was dozens of reprimands and perhaps a score or more transfers resulting from nonjudicial punishments in lieu of court–martials. Some soldiers, however, were not so lucky. Nor did they deserve to be. In one case, an ISA lieutenant colonel, who supported DELTA set up a firm named Business Security International as a conduit for covert funds and misappropriated more than $50,000 in just six months. In a series of discreet courts martial and a civil criminal trial running through 1986, at least two officers were "assigned to the long course" and are still serving prison terms at Leavenworth Penitentiary.

For most DELTA troopers, though, life remained at its grueling, hurry–up–and–wait pace. Troopers continued their meticulous training and provided advice and support to CT units around the world as they did during the Los Angeles Olympics, when a team was quickly dispatched to Willemstad, Curacao, in the Dutch Antilles, to assist in the takedown of a hijacked Venezuelan DC-9. Both fanatics were killed and seventy–nine passengers were freed. Meanwhile, in Lebanon, kidnappings continued unabated and two of the hostages were murdered, CIA station chief William Buckley in 1985 and Marine Colonel William Higgins in 1989. Frequent changes in hostage holding sites and lack of solid US intelligence sources within the terrorists' camp prevented rescues from being undertaken, and at least one major operation involving DELTA and the SEALs was scrubbed. The professionals at DELTA were, in effect, all dressed up with no place to go. Sometimes, though, this was distinctly good news— as was the case when New York City's vulnerable Statue of Liberty centennial celebration passed without a hitch in July 1986.

On other occasions, events took care of themselves— as in San Salvador and Manila. On November 21, 1989, DELTA was dispatched to the Salvadoran capital of San Salvador to rescue Green

West Berlin police sifting through the rubble of the La Belle discotheque, a bar popular with American servicemen, where a soldier and Turkish woman were killed by a bomb. Intelligence analysts soon discovered that the explosives were planted by Libyan agents based out of their embassy in communist East Berlin.

Beret trainers trapped in the Sheraton Hotel during a guerrilla offensive. The trainers escaped unharmed, however, before the detachment could be put into action. Almost two weeks later, DELTA received another alert for a possible rescue attempt, this time in the Philippines. American citizens were again trapped, this time by an Army coup d'état, but emerged unscathed when the revolt fizzled.

Berlin presented a more interesting—and long-lasting—problem for US, as well as British and French, CT units stationed in the city's Western sectors. Along the seven crossing points through the Wall between East and West, Communist East German border guards, called *Vopos,* checked passports to prevent East Germans from passing into the West, while the British, French, and American guards allowed people to pass unimpeded both ways since they didn't, for political reasons, view East Berlin as a "foreign" territory. A situation was thus created where potential terrorists, finding some access restrictions from Western nations, could simply cross into the city from East Berlin, where the Syrians, Lybians, Iranians, and even the PLO, maintained diplomatic missions. A US hasty response team was always on a high state of alert and an active exchange program was conducted with DELTA. They operated in close conjunction with Berlin's other Western security organizations, but could not prevent terrorist attacks like the April 5, 1986, bombing of the La Belle discotheque, a club fre-

quented by many American servicemen, in which two people were killed and 230 others were injured. The twilight world of terrorism and counterterrorism, espionage and counterespionage, did not end until the East German communist system finally collapsed of its own weight, bringing the Berlin Wall down with it.

Throughout it all, the frustrations and false starts, DELTA troopers maintained their high degree of professionalism and managed to keep their sometimes–irreverent sense of humor. All knew that the beeper clipped to their belts could sound its annoying electronic bleep at any time to signal a recall and they'd casually drop whatever they were doing with an offhand, "Looks like it's time to head on back to the Ranch,"* and disappear out the door for who knows how long.

*The affection of some shaggy–haired troopers for Levis, chewing tobacco, and cowboy boots led their original headquarters at Fort Bragg's old stockade to be called "the Ranch," and even after the unit moved to its new digs at Wally World, the name persisted.

(**Top**) The US Army's hasty response team in Berlin and several DELTA troopers pose for a group photo during a break in a training exercise. (**Above**) During antiterrorist training in West Berlin, an American serviceman is "snatched" by a group of mock terrorists.

Operation *Just Cause*

A public affairs release from Operation *Just Cause* stated simply that all units from the "special operations command participated" in the operation. DELTA's most publicized mission was the rescue of an American businessman and Rotary Club member held in Panama's notorious Modelo Prison. Kurt Muse was a resident of Panama and, in concert with fellow Panamanian Rotarians (dubbed the "Rotarians from Hell" by *Soldier of Fortune* magazine), had been causing Panama's strongman, Manuel Noriega, trouble by operating a clandestine radio station, filling the air waves with propaganda and, in some instances, reporting misleading or confusing instructions to the Panamanian Defense Forces (PDF) on military radio frequencies. Muse was eventually turned in by the wife of a former co-conspirator and was jailed at Modelo, located a stone's throw from Noriega's command post/headquarters turned fortress called the *Comandancia*.

In the early morning hours of December 19, 1989, Muse was rescued by members of DELTA in a classic CT operation. Transported to the rooftop of the prison by an MH-6, the assault team, backed up by a man on the inside who disabled the facility's emergency generator, cleared the upper floors from the top down and fought their way to the cell holding area where Muse was imprisoned. White beams of light from the troopers' weapon-mounted pointers pierced the smoke-filled cell, after its door was blown, and Muse was whisked to the roof up a darkened stairwell as Specter gunships pummeled the *Comandancia* across the street.

Armed with MP5s of various configurations, the troopers took out the armed guards with lethal shock and firepower and used just enough explosives to open the door without harming Muse. The waiting MH-6 was piloted by a lone soldier from the 160th SOAR. Two troopers fought their way to Muse's cell, two more provided security on the stairwell, and four more were on the roof, exchanging fire with prison guards in the barracks beyond a small courtyard. The operation, so far, had unfolded with the clockwork precision of a Wally World exercise. As the security and rescue teams loaded into the helo and along its outside–mounted seats, the heavily laden Little Bird lifted into the night sky.

What Muse saw was as close to a living hell as Wagnerian opera. AC-130s were tearing great chunks out of the *Comandancia's* defenses, while tracers streamed upward at buzzing Black Hawk helicopters and, in the streets below, conventional mechanized infantry forces brought maximum pressure to bear on the PDF. In this deadly concert, the overloaded chopper, unlike a *Valkyrie* of lore, did not bear the men off to *Valhalla*, but was hit by ground fire and landed with an unceremonial thud on the street below. The iron–nerved aviator maneuvered it down the street like a taxi and pulled into a parking lot. Using several tall apartment buildings as a shield, the pilot again tried to make his getaway but the Little Bird was knocked down again, this time for good, and the men formed a defensive perimeter nearby. Seconds after one DELTA trooper held up an infrared strobe light, they were spotted by a Black Hawk, and the cavalry came to the rescue in the form of three 6th Infantry Regiment M-113 armored personnel carriers. Four DELTA troopers were hurt, one seriously, but unlike the events some nine years earlier in Iran, this plan was carried out and with the intended results.

(**Top**) The MH-6J Little Bird that lifted Kurt Muse to freedom is moved out of the street by US mechanized forces after they secured the area around General Manuel Noriega's headquarters. Note the three–man troop seats along each side and the large crane–like appendage for fast–rope operations. It folds forward against the side of the bird when not in use and inadvertently prevents troopers from easily exiting the interior from the right side. (**Right**) The battered *Comandancia*, located just across the street from Muse's prison cell. *Soldier of Fortune*

Air Support

Rotary– and Fixed–Wing Assets

The Holloway Report on Operation *Eagle Claw* laid bare the grevious deficiencies in special operations aviation that contributed to the disaster at *Desert I*; chief among them was the lack of interoperability between the armed services. The conglomeration of hardware fielded by special operations aviation was the most visible manifestation of this shortcoming.

Throughout the early 1980s, special operations aviation soldiered on with an unwieldy mix of helicopters. Depending on the mission (and what was available), a DELTA trooper might easily find himself working with CH-3 Jolly Green Giants, CH-53C Sea Stallions, UH1-1N Twin Hueys, CH-47D Chinooks, some newer (and extensively modified) UH-60A Black Hawks, HH-53B and C Pave Low IIIs, and substantially upgraded versions of the OH-6A Cayuse called AH and MH-6 "Little Birds." One highly capable helicopter that DELTA

could *not* count on using, except, perhaps, in the most extreme emergency, was the RH-53Ds of *Eagle Claw*. The Navy's entire fleet of this counter–mine version of the Sea Stallion amounted to only twenty–four aircraft before a half–dozen were lost in the Dasht–e Kavir, severely degrading the fleet's mine–sweeping capability. They had been tapped for the mission because the stretched HH-53s, specifically designed for special ops, were literally too long to fit in the elevators of most aircraft carriers without time–consuming removal of their rotor blades, a problem that persists today, even though many of the vessels with smaller elevators have been retired.

Members of all armed services found themselves in general agreement with the Holloway Report's findings, and some organizational, equipment, and training improvements were made. But the most basic problem remained: the lack of "jointness" be-

A Pave Low jockey wearing AN/PVS-5A night vision goggles. Even relatively lightweight goggles require that a counterweight be attached to the back of a pilot's helmet, and after a year of night flying an airman's collar size often increases a size or two from the increased exercise of his neck muscles.

tween the Army, Navy, Marines, and Air Force. Under pressure from congress, the Department of Defense attempted, unsuccessfully, to put an end to the interservice rivalries by advocating that the Army become the sole operator of rotary–wing special operations assets, while the Air Force continued to develop its long–range, fixed–wing capability.

Although this particular proposal went nowhere fast because of both congressional backpedaling and continued resistance within the Air Force to anything that would cut into its turf, the future security of the nation was immeasurably enhanced by passage of the 1987 Defense Authorization Act,

which established a unified command incorporating the special operations forces from all services. The new Special Operations Command (SOCOM) could train and deploy forces throughout the world and was given the authority to develop and acquire equipment, services, and supplies peculiar to special ops. Of particular interest to DELTA, was the funding and authorization to modify existing aircraft and develop new helicopter variants.

Under the act, the UH-60 Black Hawk would be reconfigured into three basic models to support all services. The Army's 160th Special Operations Aviation Regiment, Airborns (SOAR) would use the MH-60K Pave Hawk to replace its less–capable MH-60As* in the assault role; the HH-60H "Rescue

*The L variant Black Hawks, with their more–powerful engines, uprated transmissions, and HIRSS (Hover Infrared Supression Subsystem) would not enter service till the following year, 1988. All MH-60As and many UH-60As have since been retrofitted with the HIRSS.

207

(**Above**) The aftermath of an unscheduled Pave Low landing in Korea. No one was injured in the accident which occurred during a night training exercise. (**Opposite**) HC-130 Combat Shadow tankers and MH-53 Pave Low helicopters.

Hawk" would enhance the Navy's search and rescue as well as special warfare capability; and the Air Force MH-60G Pave Hawk would both replace its aging search and rescue aircraft as well as act as an armed escort for the new MH-53J Pave Low IIIs just entering service. All aircraft would be provided with tiedowns to allow shipboard operations.

The newest Pave Low III variant of the CH-53, called the MH-53J, was tasked to perform the heavy–lift, rotary–wing effort for the near future. A superb special ops aircraft, it is, unfortunately, rather short–legged, and even with the addition of a 600gal fuel bladder, it requires frequent air refuel-

ing during long missions. Congressional sponsors of the 1987 legislation—as well as the Air Force hierarchy—envisioned that it would be phased out of special operations and into search and rescue as MH-47Es came on line.

The special operations variant of the venerable, heavy–lift CH-47D Chinook would complement the MH-60K's mission. Unlike the Pave Low IIIs, MH-47Es can easily fit into the elevators of all aircraft carriers and, thus, offers planners more deployment options. The MH-47E would also have an interoperable avionics system with its smaller cousin and could engage in full and open competition with the CV-22A Osprey for the long–range strategic special ops mission. Unfortunately, the extremely versatile tilt–rotor Osprey, which incorporated the lift, range and speed of a fixed–wing transport with the vertical–lift capability of

a helicopter, was canceled by the Defense Department during the post–Cold War budget cuts.

Unlike other special ops helicopters, the AH and MH-6 Little Birds are not dealt with in the published versions of congressional defense appropriations. These descendants of the trusty old Cayuse were developd and fielded through the use of covert funds in much the same way as the F-117 stealth attack aircraft and, interestingly, started to edge out of the "black" at approximately the same time as the the F-117, primarily because of their high visibility during the 1987–1988 retaliatory attacks on Iranian targets in the Persian Gulf and the 1989 overthrow of Panamanian dictator Manuel Noriega.

The 160th SOAR, which carried out these operations, is known as the Night Stalkers, because of their effective use of darkness during missions, and many of its pilots have logged 2,000 or more flight hours wearing night vision goggles. The regiment, headquartered at Fort Campbell, Kentucky, is composed of four battalions: the 1st with eighteen AH-6s, eighteen MH-6s and thirty MH-60 (incorporating the forward–deployed 617th Special Operations Aviation Detachment (Airborne) in Panama); the 2d with twenty–four MH-47s; the 3d with ten MH-60s and eight MH-47s, based at Hunter Army Airfield, Savannah, Georgia, to support the 1st Ranger Battalion, as it did during the Grenada operation; and an Oklahoma National Guard battalion, the 1/245, based at Tulsa, Oklahoma, with more than three dozen aircraft including fifteen UH-60Ls which will eventually be replaced by MH-60s.

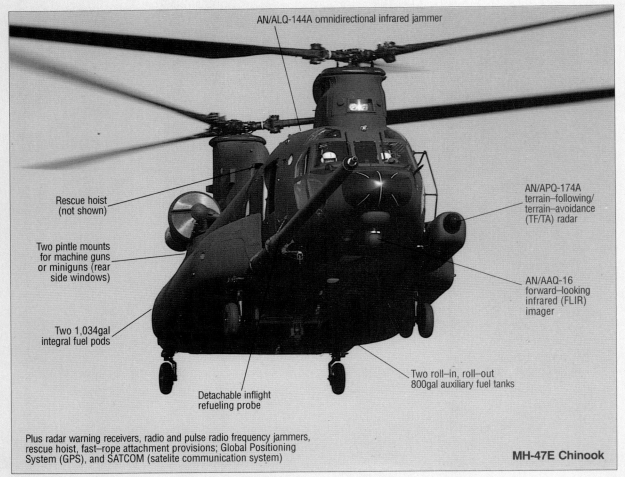

AN/ALQ-144A omnidirectional infrared jammer

Rescue hoist
(not shown)

Two pintle mounts
for machine guns
or miniguns (rear
side windows)

Two 1,034gal
integral fuel pods

Detachable inflight
refueling probe

AN/APQ-174A
terrain–following/
terrain–avoidance
(TF/TA) radar

AN/AAQ-16
forward–looking
infrared (FLIR)
imager

Two roll–in, roll–out
800gal auxiliary fuel tanks

Plus radar warning receivers, radio and pulse radio frequency jammers,
rescue hoist, fast–rope attachment provisions; Global Positioning
System (GPS), and SATCOM (satelite communication system)

MH-47E Chinook

MH-47E Chinook and MH-60 Black Hawk Variants

(**Above**) The MH-47E's highly advanced, integrated avionics system and extended range allow it to complete clandestine, deep–penetration missions. The aircraft can easily use nap–of–the–earth tactics at night and in any weather conditions while placing a minimum workload on the pilot. Special operations enhanced UH-60 Black Hawks have performed spectacularly in long–range combat operations from Grenada to Iraq. (**Opposite top**) An MH-60 Enhanced Black Hawk (sometimes referred to as a Pave Hawk) of the Army's 160th SOAR named *Executioner*, upgraded from either an UH-60A or L. (**Opposite center**) A newly built MH-60G Pave Hawk undergoing flight testing. (**Opposite bottom**) An Air Force MH-60K Pave Hawk upgraded from a UH-60A. All of these helicopters wear infrared–suppressing paint.

MH-60 Enhanced Black Hawk

Two pintle mounts for machine guns or miniguns (forward side windows)

AN/ALQ-144 omnidirectional infrared jammer

Hover infrared suppression subsystem (HIRSS)

AN/AAQ-16 FLIR imager

Two 7.62mm miniguns

Two nineteen–round 70mm rockets launchers

M–130 flare/chaff dispenser tied to missile detector

Plus radar warning receiver, rescue hoist, fast–rope attachment provisions, GPS, and SATCOM

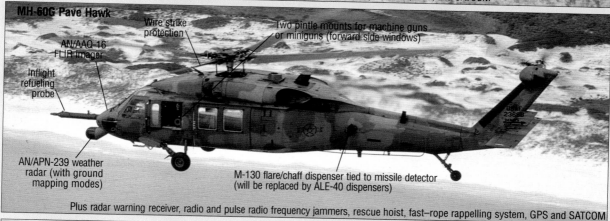

MH-60G Pave Hawk

Wire strike protection

AN/AAQ-16 FLIR imager

Two pintle mounts for machine guns or miniguns (forward side windows)

Inflight refueling probe

AN/APN-239 weather radar (with ground mapping modes)

M-130 flare/chaff dispenser tied to missile detector (will be replaced by ALE-40 dispensers)

Plus radar warning receiver, radio and pulse radio frequency jammers, rescue hoist, fast–rope rappelling system, GPS and SATCOM

MH-60K Pave Hawk

AN/ALQ-144A omnidirectional infrared jammer

Wire strike protection

HIRSS

M–130 flare/chaff dispensertied to missile detector

Two crash–worthy 230gal external auxiliary fuel tanks

AN/APQ-174A TF/TA radar

Inflight refueling probe

AN/AAQ-16 FLIR imager

Two pintle mounts for machine guns or miniguns

Mounts for air–to–air or air–to–ground rockets

Plus radar warning receivers, radio and pulse radio frequency jammers, rescue hoist, fast rope rappelling system, GPS, SATCOM, and laser detector

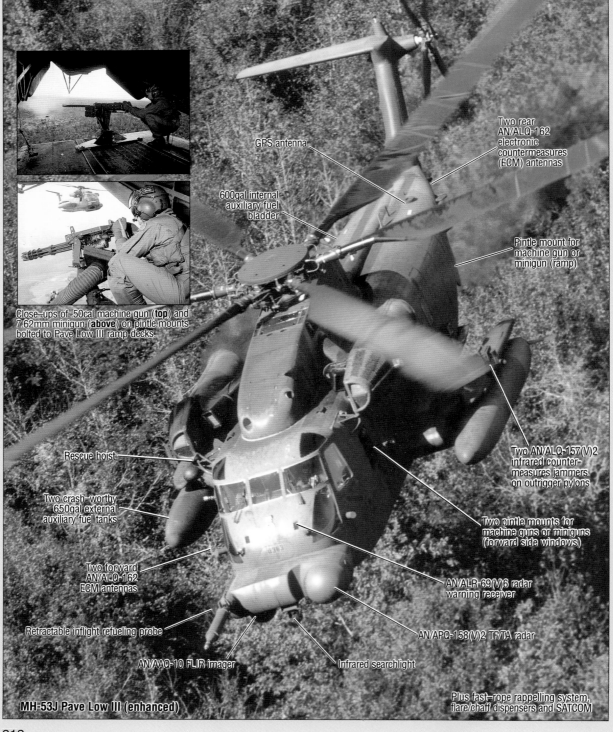

Two rear
AN/ALQ-162
electronic
countermeasures
(ECM) antennas

GPS antenna

600gal internal
auxiliary fuel
bladder

Pintle mount for
machine gun or
minigun (ramp)

Close-ups of .50cal machine gun (**top**) and
7.62mm minigun (**above**) on pintle mounts
bolted to Pave Low III ramp decks.

Rescue hoist

Two crash-worthy
650gal external
auxiliary fuel tanks

Two AN/ALQ-157(V)2
infrared counter-
measures jammers
on outrigger pylons

Two pintle mounts for
machine guns or miniguns
(forward side windows)

Two forward
AN/ALQ-162
ECM antennas

AN/ALR-69(V)6 radar
warning receiver

Retractable inflight refueling probe

AN/APQ-158(V)2 TF/TA radar

AN/AAQ-10 FLIR imager

Infrared searchlight

MH-53J Pave Low III (enhanced)

Plus fast-rope rappelling system,
flare/chaff dispensers and SATCOM

212

MH-53
Pave Low III

The MH-53H and J Pave Low IIIs are descended from a long line of Sikorsky helicopters that have performed rescue and special operations from the Korean War through Vietnam and the aborted 1980 raid to free American hostages in Iran. Of a family that is second only to the Soviet–built Mi-26 Halo in size and heavy–lift capability, the Pave Low III is capable of operating with pin–point accuracy in all weather conditions and at night. It also shares many components with other Air Force assets, such as the FLIR on the AC-130 Specter gunships

and MC-130 Combat Talons transports. (**Top**) Special operations forces exit the rear of a Pave Low III via a flexable ladder and (**above**) by fast–rope. (**Opposite**) An MH-53J skimming the trees. One recent night training exercise included seven Pave Lows receiving four inflight refuelings each during a nearly eight–hour flight. The exercise concluded with the helicopters arriving within two seconds of their target time and unloading thirty men each in five seconds.

213

MD 530MG

Little Bird Variants

Based on an extremely popular airframe that can be found in extensive use by both civilian and government entities in every corner of the globe, the Little Bird offers great agility, adaptability, and its own version of visual stealth if such is warranted by a mission. The aircraft is manufactured by McDonnell Douglas and carries a basic civilian designation of either MD 500 or MD 530. The 500, 500C, and 500D aircraft were produced with a round, bubble–like nose through 1982 when all subsequent helicopters of these types were manufactured with the more pointed nose of the MD 500E, 500F, and 500MG, as well as the slightly larger and more powerful MD 520 and 530 series aircraft. The US Army's orders for these helicopters after 1982, however, have generally called for the retention of the bubble nose to maintain the option of installing a TOW antitank missile aiming sight and keep visual commonality with the large number of pre–1982, nonmilitary aircraft of this type.

The high civilian and foreign–military demand for a small, reliable, inexpensive helicopter was coupled with the manufacturer's effort to fill that demand by incorporating a large variety of powerplant, transmission, rotor, and other changes on what is essentially the same airframe. This proliferation of different aircraft types found its way into the 160th SOAR's inventory since there was never a specific production line opened for the US Army, all purchases being made in bits and pieces over a decade of off–the–shelf buying to supplement its original OH-6A Cayuse helicopters. This proliferation has led to a mind–boggling alphabet soup of aircraft types in the 160th's 1st Battalion, the unit that most directly supports DELTA. Jane's *All the World's Aircraft* states that the MH-6B and AH-6C are derived from the OH-6A; the AH-6F and MH-6E from MD 500MG; and the AH-6G, MH-6F and MH-6J from the MD 530MG. "A" designations are given to the heavily armed attack versions of the Little Bird, which can be armed with a variety of miniguns, machine guns, rockets, and missiles. Nearly all Little Birds are equipped with a swinging, crane–like arm for fast–rope rappeling and Stabo operations, and the AH-6G, MH-6E, MH-6F, and possibly the AH-6F, have multifunction displays and forward–looking infrared (FLIR) imagers to be used in association with night vision goggles.

(**Opposite**) MD 530MG unleashing a salvo of 70mm rockets during weapons testing at the US Army's Yuma Proving Grounds, Arizona and closeups of seven–tube 70mm rocket launcher and TOW antitank missile pod. (**Top to bottom**) 160th SOAR AH-6G Little Bird bereft of any identifying markings or "sterile"; an MD 530N equipped with NOTAR (no tail rotor) system, including close–up of steering louvres on underside of tail; and MD 530N configured for transportation with louver cone and tail fins folded upward and main rotor blades stowed along tail boom. Note that the MD 530 models in the lower photos have both the pointed nose, for streamlining, and the pre–1982 bubble nose of the MD 500 series aircraft still used on most military variants.

Of great benefit to DELTA in urban counterterrorist situations is the 160th SOAR's conversion to the NOTAR system on its Little Birds. The NOTAR uses a variable–pitch fan and direct jet thruster to push cool air through longitudinal steering louvres on a circulation control tailboom. Although early tests by the 160th showed "higher than desired pilot workload" due to a tendency for the nose to wander at low speeds, yaw–only stability augmentation corrected the problem. With the NOTAR system, AH/MH-6 aircraft display a greatly reduced acoustic signature, increased hover stability, and roughly double the lateral and rearward speeds of conventional helicopters. The absence of a tail rotor also eliminates the danger of tail strikes on ground crew and allows DELTA troopers more freedom of movement around the aircraft during operations.

AN/ALQ-144A omnidirectional infrared jammer

Two seven–tube 70mm rocket launchers

AN/AAQ-16 FLIR imager

AH-6G

MD 530N

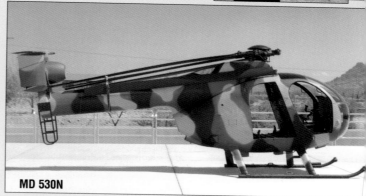

MD 530N

AC-130 Specter Gunship

The AC-130 Specter gunship is a basic C-130 modified with side–mounted weapons and various sensors that make it highly adaptable to a variety of special missions. When fielded against targets with few antiaircraft defenses and a minimal air threat, the Specter is able to provide close air support much more efficiently than a large force of fighter aircraft and is a particularly effective platform for interdiction and armed reconnaissance missions. The Specter has the ability to aid in perimeter defense, escort, surveillance, search and rescue, infiltration/ exfiltration, illumination, and landing zone support operations, as well as to conduct limited airborne command and control functions for other strike aircraft.

The AC-130H is armed with two 20mm Gatling–type guns, a rapid–firing 40mm cannon and 105mm howitzer supported by a laser rangefinder (which can also be used for marking targets for laser–guided bombs), an infrared sensor to identify heat sources such as people and vehicles, a beacon–tracking radar, a fire control computer, two–kilowatt searchlight and a low–light–level television capable of amplifying even faint traces of starlight to monitor both targets and friendly forces. The newer AC-130U models have retained the 40 and 105mm weapons but use a single 25mm Gatling–type gun fed by a two–canister, automated loading system instead of the H models' 20mm guns which required their linked ammunition to be hand–loaded. Other new features have also been added such as the F-15's fire control radar, lightweight Kevlar armor, inflight refueling capability, and a highly efficient, soundproof battle management center.

Depending on the type of target, threat environment, weather, and desired level of destruction, weapons can be accurately employed at altitudes from 3,000 to 20,000 feet above ground level. The Specter fires from a constant angle of bank and, at a typical slant range of 10,000 feet, the remarkably stable gun platform can deliver ordnance within ten feet of its target even under conditions of low cloud ceilings or poor visibility. Unlike fighter aircraft, which must make separate runs on hostile forces, targets are continually visible throughout the gunship's entire orbit and can be fired on at will. But even though the run–in headings required by fighter aircraft are not needed, no–fire headings may be imposed from the ground or automatically computed by the aircrew if there is a risk of short rounds hitting friendly forces from a particular angle.

The Specter's two–kilowatt searchlight can be used to illuminate targets and landing zones, aid in search and rescue, and supply light for the television sensor if its illuminator is inoperative. In combat, the searchlight is normally used in a covert infrared mode, to provide illumination for night vision devices, since its overt white light mode would easily pinpoint the gunship's position for hostile forces. Its effectiveness is reduced with altitude and weather.

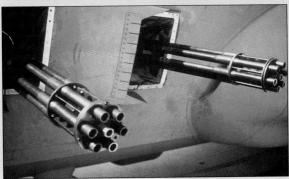

DELTA troopers in a tight spot can mark their ground position with a wide variety of items. First, Mk-6 and Mk-25 ground markers can be dropped by hand from the rear of the Specter, itself, and will burn for forty–five and thirty minutes, respectively. Next, transponders, including the handheld SST-101 miniponder, can be picked up by the aircraft's beacon tracking radar at up to ten nautical miles and the powerful AN/UPN-25 and SST-181x transponders can be received by the ship's navigation radar at up to sixty nautical miles. A standard survival vest strobe light with a removeable infrared filter can also be used either visually or with the filter installed. The infrared filter provides the same information to the aircrew as the unmasked strobe but prevents visible light from revealing the friendly ground position to the enemy forces. Positive identification is provided by turning one or more strobes off and on in response to radio instructions for the aircrew. The old standby, lightweight three–by–five–foot cloth reflective panels, can clearly mark ground reference points when illuminated by the Specter, either overtly or covertly. Other methods of marking positions include flashlights, vehicle lights, pen gun flares, tracer rounds, fires, fire arrows, signal mirrors, and simply running a vehicle engine with the ignition unshielded.

(**Opposite**) An AC-130H Specter fires its 105mm gun during a night exercise; (**top**) airmen loading a Specter's 40mm gun; (**left**) twin 20mm Gatling–type guns aft of the cockpit; and (**right**) 40mm and 105mm guns forward of the aircraft's loading ramp.

MC-130 Combat Talon and HC-130 Combat Shadow

The mission of the MC-130E and H Combat Talons is to conduct day and night infiltration, exfiltration, resupply, psychological operations, and aerial reconnaissance into hostile or enemy controlled territory using air landings, air drops or surface–to–air recoveries. The use of FLIR imagers enables aircrews to visually identify targets and checkpoints at night while terrain–following/terrain–avoidance(TF/TA) radar and an inertial navigation system allow extreme accuracy while navigating to unmarked drop zones. Missions are normally flown at night using a high–low–high altitude profile. The high portion is flown prior to penetrating and after exiting the target area at an altitude that minimizes fuel consumption and enemy detection. The aircraft then descends to the lowest possible altitude consistent with flying safety and uses its TF/TA radar to penetrate and operate in hostile territory.

The Talon's range depends on several factors, including configuration, payload, en route winds and weather, and the length of time spent at fuel–guzzling, low–level flight. For planning purposes, its range (without refueling and factoring in two hours at low level) is 2,800 nautical miles. With inflight refueling, the Talon's range is limited only by the availability of tanker support and the effect

that crew fatigue may have on the mission. The Talon is not a rapid response aircraft. Operating deep in heavily defended enemy territory requires extensive preflight planning, and units normally receive notification at least forty–eight hours out with a final briefing on threats and positions of friendly forces before takeoff.

Aircrews are capable of successfully operating at unmarked drop zones (DZs) but usually have something they can hang their headphones on. When ground and air component commanders agree to use a specific DZ, reception committee personnel coordinate with the aircrew on the type of markings to be used, configuration of the DZ, method of authentication and release point determination. The most frequent cause for mission aborts is a lack of coordination or confusion over marking procedures; it is important to note that terrain–following is made difficult during moderate showers and even further degraded during heavy thunderstorms.

Depending on mission, an aircrew makes either a static–line, low–altitude air drop; a high–altitude, low–opening (HALO) air drop; a surface–to–air recovery (STAR) using a Fulton extraction system; or may simply land the aircraft. For static–line drops during combat operations, a Talon is flown as low as 750 feet while a HALO drop, which requires a free fall before parachute opening, is never conducted from lower than 1,500 feet. For static–line drops combining both men and equipment (such as rubber rafts), troops exit immediately after ejection of equipment. A STAR can be used for the extractions dur-

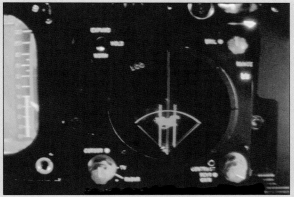

ing either day or night but requires fairly good weather to accomplish the mission safely. Either two people or 500 pounds of equipment can be picked up over land or water per pass. During air landings, the minimum length necessary is the takeoff/landing roll plus 500 feet for a total of approximately 3,000 feet. The Talon's minimum required runway width is sixty feet and, while the capability exists to set down at a landing zone that has no lights or is lit with infrared lights, use of the Special Forces seven–light panel marking system (which includes a 250–foot/ten percent safety zone at each end out) is preferred.

The HC-130P Combat Shadow tankers have essentially the same extensive radar and navigational aids as the Combat Talon, as well as the ability to refuel two helicopters simultaneously in flight. After the tanker unreels its fuel line and slows to approximately 120mph, the Shadow's customer slowly edges its refuel probe closer to the drogue–tipped hose while making certain that it stays beneath or to the outside of the tankers turbulent slipstream. It generally takes an MH-53 less than ten minutes to top off and an MH-47, with its huge fuel blisters, can get its fill in about fifteen minutes.

(**Opposite**) The retracted nose prongs, which, when extended forward and out, snag the line of a target balloon during surface–to–air recoveries, can be clearly seen in this shot of a MC-130 receiving fuel from a KC-135 tanker. See page 120 for a complete recovery sequence. (**Top left**) A Vietnam–era MC-130 rigged for a pick–up with guard cables running from the top of its bulbous nose to its wingtips and (**top right**) a similarly configured MC-130E or H variant. Note the difference in radar bulge configuration on the newer aircraft, to accommodate its expanded TF/TA, FLIR, and other systems, as well as its lengthened prongs. (**Above left**) TF/TA radar screen, displaying an obstruction in the aircraft's path as a blob below the upwardly bowed line, and a portion of the FLIR display off to the left. These systems and all other internal controls can be made to glow in a subdued mode so that they do not interfere with the pilot's night vision goggles. (**Above right**) An MH-60 carefully maneuvering its refuel probe up to an HC-130's extended fuel line and drogue.

Chapter 5
Back to the Desert

The deep sleep of the early morning hours was interrupted by the familiar obnoxious sound of a pager going off. Reaching for his clothing, the young Sergeant kissed his wife's head and ambled down the hall to check on his son. Allowing the hall light to play over the boy's sandy hair, the trooper bent down to kiss him goodbye as he had so often in the past. Waiting until he had left the house, he sat on the front steps to pull on his well worn cowboy boots. He climbed into his pickup truck and drove to the post. In less than two hours, the young sergeant's troop was winging away from Pope Air Force Base near Fort Bragg. As the wheels of the lumbering C-141 Starlifter retracted into their wells, his troop commander was already scanning the initial intelligence reports from the agencies supporting the unit. Things were not so good in the land of oil and sand.

At 0400 on the morning of Thursday, August 2, 1990, mechanized elements of Saddam Hussein's elite Republican Guards stabbed across the desert frontier separating Iraq and Kuwait east of the disputed Rumalia oilfield. Iraqi forces had been massing steadily across the border for almost two weeks before the invasion, but both Western and Arabian governments believed this to be nothing more than a show of force to bolster Saddam's financial claims against the oil-rich kingdom. By midday, all meaningful resistance by Kuwait's tiny army had been crushed and its royal family had fled to a sumptuous exile in Saudi Arabia.

The Baathist government in Baghdad rejoiced

A thirsty trooper inhales bottled water in the shade of a C-141 StarLifter in Saudi Arabia.

over its quick victory and believed that it had been accomplished with such speed that the world was presented with a *fait accompli*. Saddam expected a toothless condemnation from the United Nations and perhaps even a half-hearted economic embargo that would soon fade away. But his analysis was fatally flawed. US and British leaders meeting in the United States immediately resolved that the rest of the Middle East's oil resources must be kept out of Saddam's bloodied hands, at all costs. Even before his generals gathered their forces for the next morning's move to the Saudi border, numerous elements of America's special operations forces were either already deployed or were going "wheels up" from bases in the United States and Europe.

From the first moment President George Bush was notified that Iraqi forces were plunging across

Kuwait's border, one of the prime challenges to face him as the National Command Authority was the possibility—indeed probability—that large numbers of Americans would become prisoners in a dangerous diplomatic game. The specter of a second major Middle East hostage crisis loomed over the Pentagon and the White House. Although public speculation was kept to a minimum, no one needed to be reminded that the Carter administration fell because of the prolonged hostage crisis in Iran. The extreme vulnerability of the US Embassy staff and numerous Americans associated with Kuwait's petroleum industry was evident. When coupled with the Baathist regime's close ties with terrorist groups, history of wanton aggression against its neighbors, and deadly abuse of its own people, the president had no choice but to act. Although special operations forces assets already in the Gulf were capable of performing the hasty option response, the National Command Authority launched the first DELTA assets into the Middle East.

Crisis action teams were dispatched to Saudi Arabia and other friendly nations to establish C^3 (command, control, and communications) sites for future operations and to provide a terminal for information to and from Washington. Launch sites for missions were identified and staging areas hastily opened. Meanwhile, back at Fort Bragg, the Joint Special Operations Command (JSOC) worked hard to avoid being caught flatfooted and began building a massive workup of target folders for the "long war" that was sure to come.

Other important assets moving into the area were elements of the Intelligence Support Activity (ISA). Like so many other parts of the special operations force, ISA was an offshoot of the *Desert I* after-action review. A critical failing during the hostage crisis in Iran was the lack of information from human intelligence sources or HUMINT. In Iran, DELTA did not have an "eyeball" on its target. In Iraq and

Kuwait, ISA would provide the needed eyes.

Various elements of the myriad special operations units in Europe and the United States continued to trickle in, and most of the burden of working with the resistance inside Kuwait was assumed by the Special Forces units that already had that mission in accordance with theater war plans. As predicted, US and other foreign nationals did indeed become "guests" at selected Iraqi strategic military and nuclear sites but were eventually allowed to leave as a "gesture of goodwill" when their continued captivity threatened to precipitate, not prevent, an assault on Iraq. DELTA remained.

Commencement of the coalition air campaign raised fears that hostages might be taken in retaliation at widely scattered locations around the globe, and additional target folders of possible hostage-holding centers began to take shape. While significant terrorist operations never emerged, the public display of Allied prisoners of war did cause concern at the highest levels, and plans were formulated to rescue those individuals. Small teams were also selected to carry out a number of sensitive, direct-action missions against targets in Iraq's command and control nets.

Initially, special operations units were faced with the same problem they have always had to deal with: How to get the conventional force commanders to use their capabilities properly or even at all. For example, the 75th Ranger Regiment's assessment team left the Gulf after finding out that there was very little they could do in the theater, and the elite light infantry of the 82d Airborne Division was severely handicapped on the billiard table–terrain without an immense amount of support.

Colonel Jessie Johnson, commander of Central Command's (CENTCOM's) Special Operations Command (SOC), drafted his campaign plans for the upcoming desert war from his headquarters at King Fahd International Airport near Dhahran. A

(Right) All–terrain Fast Attack Vehicles (FAVs) and motorcycles **(above)** saw extensive use by special operations forces, including DELTA, during operations in Iraq and Kuwait and operated from forward bases in Saudi Arabia or base camps established far behind Iraqi lines. Motorcycles with heavily muffled engines offered troopers individualized, high–speed movement coupled with the ability to approach a target from several axes simultaneously and, on some types of missions, would be used in combination with FAVs.

Capable of being armed with a wide assortment of goodies—machine guns, antitank weapons, grenade launchers and almost anything else one might think of—FAVs offered substantial hitting power and the ability to travel extended distances across the desert at speeds up to 80– plus mph. The vehicles pictured here both mount AT4 antitank missile launchers on the outsides of their frame roofs and M60E3 machine guns forward of the passenger seats. An additional gunner sits in the elevated, rear seat, which can swivel around for firing at targets behind the vehicle. In the top photo, this position mounts a .50cal machine gun while the vehicle above sports a 40mm grenade launcher. Note the dart board taped to the nose of the FAV at lower left, a not–so–subtle comment by its crew on their vulnerability. *Soldier of Fortune.*

veteran of *Desert I*, where he commanded the joint Ranger–DELTA road–watch teams, Johnson knew what difficulties awaited his forces. Luckily for him, his boss at CENTCOM, General H. Norman Schwarzkopf, had the utmost confidence in his special ops commander. Despite attempts by elements within the Joint Chiefs of Staff, to replace him with a two–star officer, Schwarzkopf kept his faith in Johnson, who in return, became the architect for several brilliantly executed operations.

Saddam's Vengence Weapon

As the war progressed, another in history's long line of terror weapons was unleashed in the Middle East: the Scud B medium–range ballistic missile, successor to Hitler's infamous V-1 and V-2 rockets

223

DELTA operated out of secure, remote bases dotting the desert wastes south of the Saudi–Iraqi border. (**Above**) A C-130, of unidentified type, sits baking under "big red" across from a special operations Black Hawk with external, add–on fuel tanks. (**Left**) Air base security armed for bear with a combination M16 assault rifle/M203 grenade launcher. His vest is packed with twenty 40mm grenades for the M203, and he is using night vision goggles, which turn even the blackest nights into a green day, to scan the perimeter.

of World War II. On those earlier weapons, The "V" designation was, itself, part of Hitler's psychological warfare campaign aimed at terrorizing the British people. Nazi English–language propaganda broadcasts gleefully warned Britons of the immense destruction that would be wreaked on their cities by the "vengeance" weapons. Since their target was an English–speaking public, the Nazis named their rockets the V-1 and V-2, instead of giving them an "R" designation for the equivalent German word, *rache*.

The Scud retained many of the V-2's basic characteristics, along with many deadly improvements. Highly mobile, it nevertheless required more than an hour to fuel and its involved targeting procedures took excruciatingly long to complete, even when performed by experienced crews at preplotted sites. To make matters even more interesting, homemade

(**Right**) A Scud B medium–range ballistic missile on its MAZ-543 transporter–erector–launcher and (**above**) a rare photograph of a Scud impact. Even before certain changes were made to the weapon that degraded its accuracy, it was not known for its ability to make pinpoint strikes. The weapon in the above photo was fired by Soviet forces at Afghan guerrillas who had surrounded Loyalist troops at an isolated garrison. It missed the guerrillas and instead landed within the government troops' defensive perimeter. Above: *Soldier of Fortune*.

versions of the missile, like the *al Hussein*, incorporated range enhancements that both reduced its warhead capacity and severely degraded its ability to strike near its target.

The Soviets designed the Scud to deliver small nuclear warheads, or as an area saturation system when fired in conventional battery salvos; the Iraqis instead used it as simply a fire–in–the–general–direction–of–your–adversary–and–then–wait–for–the–results weapon. Fixed launch sites containing both real and dummy missiles existed at airfields in western Iraq, targeting Israel, and in eastern

Iraq, aimed at Iran and Saudi Arabia. These sites were well known to US and Israeli planners and could be easily removed from the picture. It was Saddam's surprisingly large number of wheeled

launchers for the Scud and shorter–range Frog missiles that proved to be exceedingly difficult targets for air reconnaissance assets to locate. This difficulty in targeting the mobile launchers in the wide expanses of Iraq set the stage for one role the troopers of DELTA never dreamed of or trained for: Scud hunting.

The scenario thrust upon DELTA was a far cry from the world of takedowns and hostage rescues each man became immersed in the moment he entered Wally World. Many, if not all, the troops deployed to the Gulf had extensive training in their initial Special Forces specialties and were already experts in carrying out such standard missions as unconventional warfare, special reconnaissance, foreign internal defense, plus search and rescue operations, to name just a few, but it was the introduction of Saddam's terror weapons that forced the counterterrorists to revert to these basic war-fighting specialties and become what the press dubbed "super commandos." Curiously enough, though, since Scud missiles served no real military purpose —when used as they were by the Iraqis— DELTA troopers could still be said to be involved in a new, unanticipated form of counterterrorism.

The war was going poorly for the Iraqi warlord, and he knew that his best bet to overcome the military setbacks around was to drive a wedge between the Arab and Western elements in the coalition arrayed against him. If attacks on Jewish population centers could push Israel into a knee–jerk military response, Saddam believed that indignant Arab masses would finally heed his call for a *jihad*, or holy war, and either overthrow unfriendly governments like President Hosni Mubarak's in Egypt or, at the very least, force their governments to withdraw from the coalition. Western elements isolated at the end of a very long logistics line would be forced into an ignominious withdrawal.

Saddam's strategy was not difficult to anticipate,

and the White House made it crystal clear through strong public statements (coupled with a rapid, showy deployment of a Patriot surface–to–air missile battery to Tel Aviv) that the drawing of Israel into the war would be prevented at all costs. CENTCOM had no choice but to commit its Air Force component to a resource–consuming search for mobile launchers with little to show for its efforts.* This same mission was also handed to the Army's Special Forces, who, if necessary, would actually target individual vehicles for air strikes— an extremely risky business for the troops involved but a mission that was, in light of the strategic situation, of immense importance. CENTCOM quickly discovered, however, that a critical shortage of trained special recon teams existed in the Kuwaiti Theater of Operations (KTO).

Every available Green Beret was committed to serving as liaison with the Saudi Army, training Kuwaiti resistance forces, or conducting intelligence–gathering missions for General Schwarzkopf's headquarters. When it became necessary to scrape together additional assets to help locate Scuds, the only force in the KTO was the counterterrorists of DELTA, as well as some British SAS personnel. Reports by the European and American news media later referred to this use of DELTA as if the unit were some sort of key reserve, when, in reality, it was all Schwarzkopf had at the moment.

Special operations assets made available by the coalition forces, primarily DELTA and the desert–wise SAS, were formed into teams and prepared for the upcoming operations.* At first, though, Colonel

---

*The continued success of the Iraqis at hitting Israeli and Saudi population centers necessitated that a full squadron of F-15Es be essentially pulled from the air campaign and assigned the task of eliminating mobile Scuds. Other air assets were soon added as the equivalent of three squadrons became tied up by the effort, and the number of sorties by Scud–hunting intelligence, refueling and strike aircraft sometimes climbed to more than 300 per twenty–four hour period. Although a severe drain on US resources, this heavy and prolonged commitment was instrumental in convincing the Israelis to call off two planned raids into western Iraq that could have had a disasterous effect on the war effort.

Johnson's professionals from Smoke Bomb Hill and the Ranch were understandably missing from the almost–continuous Gulf news coverage, while other forces from Fort Bragg, the XVIIIth Airborne Corps, 1st Corps Support Command, and the renowned 82d Airborne Division received their share of the limelight. But it wasn't long before reporters were hearing strange tales of parachutes gliding silently through the Arabian night to deposit their human cargo on the desert floor. The stories are many, but all have the same theme and similar scenarios. The following is just one of them. Maybe it's just a good piece of propaganda; then again, maybe it's true.

Prepping the Battlefield

An in-depth mission analysis was conducted on the upcoming Scud hunt by the intelligence agencies supporting the theater's special operations forces. The intel experts looked at such subjects as the terrain and infiltration/exfiltration routes

*The SAS not only retains a great deal of institutional knowledge on desert warfare but also makes frequent use of a training area in the Gulf state of Oman.

US special operations forces did not truly "own the night" as the often–repeated slogan claimed, but did operate extremely effectively in that environment, due to a combination of superb training and equipment. (**Above** and **above right**) Troopers viewed through a NVG move out under cover of darkness and rappel from a Black Hawk.

through Iraqi antiaircraft belts and known locations of enemy units were plotted on the situation maps. As this information was analyzed, a clear picture emerged indicating that the majority of the target areas could be easily reached by Army MH-60 Pave Hawks of the 160th Special Operations Aviation Regiment (Airborne) or Air Force MH-53 Pave Low IIIs of the 1st Special Operations Wing.

Unfortunately, the extremely heavy demand for the specialized helicopters in the KTO, as well as various other considerations, meant that they could not be used in every situation. For tactical reasons, it was decided that the target area around which this story centers necessitated that DELTA conduct a HAHO infiltration. HAHO (pronounced *hey–ho*)

is the acronym for high–altitude, high–opening and essentially means that the drop is conducted at about 30,000 feet or higher, with the jumper opening his parachute almost immediately after clearing the plane. The trooper then glides his maneuverable, double–canopy parachute through the sky and lands with pinpoint accuracy at a predetermined site. The distance from the point that the jumper pulls his rip cord and where he lands can be as much as fifty miles.

The team participating in this unique Scud–hunting mission is required to prepare a "briefback" on how each trooper will carry out his duties. The briefback is standard operating procedure within the special. operations community and covers the friendly versus enemy situation, the mission, its execution, support requirements, command structures, and a short, concise, yet detailed narrative of how the trooper will help accomplish the mission. The briefback is normally given to the leadership of the unit and not only demonstrates to the commander that his men are ready, but also assures the team that everyone is playing off the same sheet of music.

After a few carefully considered questions, the team is given the go–ahead and conducts final rehearsals, equipment checks, and other preparations. On this mission, they are more concerned with the "sneak and peek" than direct–action aspects of the operation. If they can find the missile's elusive transporter–erector–launchers (TELs), they will call

in an air strike and, if circumstances require it, use a portable laser to target the weapon for destruction by the fast–movers of the Air Force.

The basic plan is simple. The team will move undetected from their drop zone to a hidden observation point overlooking a likely area for Scud activity. When confirmed targets enter the area, SOC will be notified, and an E-2C Sentry's airborne warning and control system (AWACS) will vector strike aircraft into the target area. During their approach, the jets follow voice or signal beacon wavelengths to their prey. Air attacks will be conducted visually but any TELs obscured by darkness, camouflage, or poor weather will be lased, or "painted," by the recon team. Rolling in on their bomb runs, the fast–movers' sensors will lock on a laser guided bomb or rocket and release the "smart" munitions to glide along the laser's invisible path like a road map to the target. The jets will then maneuver away from the area, having only teased the outer perimeters of the lethal antiaircraft systems' kill zones, and the DELTA troopers, if necessary, will continue to lase targets for incoming aircraft from their concealed hideout. As many Iraqi units found out, the laser's invisible beam brought very visible destruction.

Reaching the austere departure airfield, the team is ushered into a secured hangar cordoned off from the rest of the facility. It is here that all of the specialized gear needed for the mission is stored. The departure airfield will also be the mission support site (MSS) for the operation, and a mobile communications van, mated to the main SOC communications bunker at King Khalid Military City,* has been moved into the hangar. The mobile van constitutes part of a duplex communications network

An Air Force Special Operations combat control team member exits from the open ramp of a MC-130 Combat Talon. Control teams are often inserted before the arrival of special operations or conventional forces to mark landing or drop zones that must be used at night by pilots using NVGs and aircraft fitted with infrared imagers. For example, a control team member had already arrived at and marked the *Desert I* refuel site in Iran before the arrival of the aircraft bearing DELTA. The lack of weapon and rucksack indicates that this was taken during a practice exercise.

*Designed and constructed by the US Army Corps of Engineers during the Iran–Iraq War, King Khalid Military City is one of three huge base complexes around which the outer defenses of the kingdom are formed. The "Emerald City" (as it was called by many US soldiers, who were surprised at the sight of it rising out of the desert wastes) is located roughly 110 miles southwest of Kuwait's westernmost point almost halfway to the major Saudi Arabian city of Buraydah.

(**Above**) The control and reporting center outside King Khalid Military City which linked US and Saudi mobile and airborne communications. (**Left**) An internal view.

that ensured reception of the team's vital intelligence even if one part of the network went down from either systems failure or enemy action. Except for the team's communications specialist, who is coordinating preselected frequencies and transmission times, the troopers take little notice of the signals experts moving to and from the van and stay focused on checking and rechecking their weapons and field gear. All weapons had been test–fired before leaving the isolation site, and at the hangar, a ritual of sorts takes place, which will wed the jumper to his air items and other essential

equipment. This union ends only when the mission is completed—or worse.

The six troopers wear sterile desert camouflage fatigues with the required face scarves and flop hats. Struggling mightily, they pull on cumbersome, insulated jumpsuits to help fight off the cold which sometimes exceeds –50 degrees at 35,000 feet, even in the Middle East. In addition to its insulation properties, the jumpsuits have radar–absorbing capabilities that will impede the enemy's ability to pick up the soldiers as they glide across the sky. Fortunately, the February night—cold even in the desert—engulfs the airfield, providing a small amount of relief as they don their main and reserve parachutes and oxygen masks. Before high–altitude drops like this one, both the jumpers and the crew of the unpressurized aircraft have to start breathing oxygen one hour before takeoff or "launch time." The team receives final jumpmaster inspections, and the troop commander arrives for that one last visit a leader makes. He is more of a fellow member than a

commander, and everyone in the hangar knows the way the boss feels. He'd trade in his major's oak leaves to be going with them into Iraq.

Following the safety NCO out into the desert darkness, each man finds his own release to the inevitable tension. A flick of a "bird" finger to the top sergeant with a muffled, "Up yours, Top," or "See ya at the NCO club," mark the beginning of another mission. Their transportation, a huge C-141B, rests majestically next to the hangar, its gaping clamshell doors exposing the broad tail. The team struggles up the StarLifter's ramp into the cavernous cargo bay, while the crew chief and loadmaster guide the men around the small patches of hydraulic fluid habitually dotting its deck. An oxygen console rests securely in the center of the compartment, and each jumper

A C-141 prepares for a night takeoff from an airstrip in the Saudi desert.

plugs into it after disconnecting the oxygen mask from his individual bailout bottle.

As the StarLifter slowly pivots and then begins to taxi, the crew chief switches the internal lighting to the red lights required for the team to gain their night vision. The pilot reaches the main runway, and as he revs up the four powerful Pratt & Whitney turbofans for takeoff, each team member is caught in the thoughts of the moment: the myriad details that must be covered so that the mission succeeds, his wife, family, or the girl back home—the same thoughts soldiers have had to deal with since the second–oldest profession began.

231

The Jump

The C-141B flies on an easterly heading to its rendezvous point with two B-52s flying in from the tiny island base of Diego Garcia deep in the Indian Ocean. Snuggling into the number three slot, the formation portrays just another inbound bomber formation for any Iraqi radar still operating.

As the unlikely trio nears Iraqi airspace, the jumpmaster receives updates from the navigator. At prescribed checkpoints, he notifies the team of their exact coordinates so that all know where they are in the event that they are forced to bail out early. Thirty minutes from jump time, the team prepares for the "infil." The men assist each other in making sure that their rucksacks ride snugly against the bottom of the main parachute. Checking their padded–leather jump helmets, goggles, and oxygen masks one last time, they prepare to change over from the oxygen consoles to the bailout bottle strapped to their left sides. On command from the jumpmaster, the jumpers switch to their bailout bottles and waddle toward the open troop doors on each side of the fuselage.

Staff Sergeant Len Rodgers and the rest of the recon team work their way to positions along the walls of the StarLifter as their communications man, serving as jumpmaster, completes his visual checks and gives the hand signal for "Stand by." The cabin's eerie red lights, green jump light, and the howling winds whipping in the open troop doors could easily meet the needs of a good nightmare, and Staff Sergeant Rodgers is nearly deafened by the roaring wind and mournful banshee whine of the engines. He marvels that some people actually think this is fun! Moving closer to the door, he receives the "Go!" signal, as the jumpmaster disappears out the open troop door.

Pivoting on the ball of his right foot, Rodgers swings out behind him and falls into the position commonly referred to as the "frog." He's immediately followed in quick succession by the rest of the team. Plummeting through the moonless night, arms and legs extended, Rodgers begins to feel the penetrating cold. Behind him, each man monitors the altimeter securely strapped to his left wrist and assumes the glide position as they prepare to deploy their parachutes. At 30,000 feet, the aerial ballet continues as the team members pull their silver ripcords.

To the casual observer, this particular maneuver looks like a giant hand shaking each jumper loose from his very life. In reality, the men feel very little, and each checks the double–layer canopy above to see if his is fully inflated. Fortunately for this team, all now resemble airfoil–shaped wings, and the jumpers line up in a rough, follow–the–leader formation, taking the planned westerly heading as Staff Sergeant Rodgers navigates through the frozen night air. Settling into the parachute harness, he scans the panorama unfolding before him. Far to the north, flashes appear from the bombing mission the team's C-141 had joined. Craning his neck around to the southeast, he can barely make out green* tracers darting skyward in a futile search for the destroyers of a known Scud site's command and control bunker and wonders if it was done in by one of the F-117 stealth attack aircraft. He turns back and looks toward the unseen drop zone and toys with the idea that the display is for their benefit. He knows,

*Munitions manufactured by former Warsaw Pact countries such as the Soviet Union and Czechoslovakia give off green tracers, but the spectrum of hues sometimes runs to a yellow–green. US and many Western munitions give off a red trace.

however, that the distant explosions mean that real, flesh–and–blood men are dying.

As the team continues on its noiseless flight, each jumper lines up on the dull luminescent strip on the helmet below. Altimeter checks show that the gradual warming they feel is due to the descent. At 12,000 feet, they remove their individual masks and inhale the night air. With each passing minute, the team gets closer to the drop zone. This is when the paratroopers are most vulnerable. All are sure that the entire Iraqi Army is waiting to pounce on them, but the only living things awaiting the DELTA troopers are some stray goats from a Bedouin camp that run bleating into the night when they strike the earth. The men are relieved

Special Forces trooper on a practice jump, taking up the "frog" position. Note that the soldier wears an altimeter on his left wrist. Rucksacks are always strapped below the main parachutes and, in the second photo, a rucksack can be seen dangling fifteen feet below the jumper so that it will be out of his way when he lands.

that no reception committee is on hand to greet them, but there will be plenty of time for surprises. One of the greatest shocks of this desert war for the special operations soldiers was the fact that whenever you thought you were in the middle of nowhere, someone was always showing up—usually at the most inopportune time.

Chapter 6

The Scud Busters

The Lord said to Moses, "Send men to spy out the land of Canaan, . . . from each tribe of their fathers shall you send a man, everyone a leader among them."

Numbers 13

The team quickly assembles after landing. The troopers move to a nearby depression, and while half take up defensive positions, the others strip off their heavy jump suits and then roll them up with their 'chutes and jump helmets to make compact, easily buried bundles. The gear is quickly buried and the now–unencumbered troopers silently take their turn guarding the perimeter. Preparing to move out, each man goes through his mental checklist to ensure that every piece of equipment is in place. Faint vehicle noise drifts through the black night and the telltale signs of light are seen to the south.

Staff Sergeant Christopher Gleason, the point man for this operation, silently moves to his right, where the team leader is making last–minute com-

Troopers in the desert viewed through an image–intensification device.

pass checks and using his handheld satellite navigation system to pinpoint the team's exact location. Chief Warrant Officer Gary Van Hee intently studies the tiny screen's luminous, digital readout, which arrived as coded signals from a Global Positioning System (GPS) satellite drifting in orbit above the desert. Only one–third of the complete twenty–four–satelite constellation needed to blanket the earth had yet been sent aloft, so the lack of full–time, three–dimensional coverage sometimes made reception problematic. Tonight, though, Van Hee is having no trouble and he smiles broadly as the staff sergeant moves within whisper distance.

Gleason points out the rather obvious activity to the southwest, "The whole place is crawling with ragheads, Chief!" Van Hee's camouflaged face breaks into a devious grin and he retorts with his typical, "No shit, Sherlock." The team leader's time–honored response reassures the edgy point man, who steps gingerly back to his position and prepares to move out.

Each man's personal equipment is designed for specific tasks. Black balaclavas have been replaced with desert flop hats and face paint of pale yellow and brown. "No sweat" bandanas and camouflage scarves are wrapped tightly around necks and tucked into the now–familiar "chocolate chip"–patterned camouflage jackets. The men carry ammunition in pouches hung from their vests, and distributed about their bodies are canteens, first–aid equipment, a powerful miniature flashlight, and a Beretta pistol. Two of the six–man team also carry silencers so that their Barettas can be used to noiselessly kill an enemy guard or nosey point man. The unique silencers are so efficient that, using subsonic rounds, only the sound of the hammer striking the firing pin and the gun's action cycling can be heard—a small sound in this noisy environment.

The threat of "getting slimed" by Iraqi poison gas is far more than rhetorical in this war, so each trooper also carries a gas mask, securely strapped within easy reach on his left leg, and a complete protective suit in his rucksack. Rucks for this mission are configured with extra ammunition and smoke grenades. Additional water, medical supplies, a small quantity of food, and limited decontamination gear, complete the major items. Personal weapons are based on the defensive requirements of the mission, and the team carries either Colt M16A2 assault rifles or Heckler & Koch MP5 submachine guns.

While these final checks are being made, the communications expert, Sergeant First Class Michael Cranson, sends the team's initial entry report, a codeword transmission advising the MSS that they have arrived safely at the drop zone. For this signal, Cranson uses his radio's burst–transmission capability, and with the touch of a finger, the pre-

coded message is instantaneously sent. The split–second broadcast provides no time for hostile direction finders to get a fix on the team's position.

Armed with an integrally silenced MP5 SD3, Staff Sergeant Gleason slowly leads the way out of the depression and toward a large, rocky outcropping. The team members swing into their allotted positions behind him, forming a loose file. This and every action these soldiers will complete during the mission has been practiced over and over. Gleason and his fellow troopers use AN/PVS-7 night vision goggles to guide them through the rocky terrain. Popularly known as NODs, for night observation devices, the 1.5 pound goggles fit against a trooper's forehead and literally turn the desert darkness into a greenish, but very visible, day.

A Global Positioning System receiver.

By amplifying existing light, they enable man–sized targets to be recognized at almost 100 yards on all but the very darkest nights, with good moonlight extending their range by fifty percent or more. Operating under a last quarter moon, the men can see extremely well, but spotty cloud cover creates sudden, unexpected drops in visibility, in addition to the device's limited peripheral field of vision.

The point man's stubby, silenced MP5, his night vision goggles, and modified tactical vest give him an unearthly appearance. The bleak terrain, coupled with the patrol's appearance, could easily be mistaken for a Hollywood supernatural thriller. Walking behind the point man, the compass man, Staff Sergeant Rodgers, not only navigates for the patrol with his compass (for direction) and altimeter (for elevation), but also by watching his distance count (by how far he walks). The team leader occupies the number three position, and his communications, or "commo" man, Sergeant First Class Cranson, holds down number four. Positions five and six are rounded out by the team medic, Master Sergeant Frank Rodrigues, and the demolitions expert, another staff sergeant, who doubles as the patrol's tail gunner. His primary responsibility is to ensure that no one surprises the team from the rear and, like the point man, the tail gunner also resembles an alien stalking through a moonscape.

While approaching the low ridge where they will set up their observation post, it becomes painfully clear that they have, indeed, dropped into an area full of Iraqi units. Reaching their destination, the team immediately sets up security, sends out a two–man recon of the area, and digs in (one of the veterans later likened the experience to hacking into an asphalt parking lot). Flexible prefabricated covers are stretched over their holes to make the hide site complete, and the men will use disposable plastic bags to contain their bodily wastes so that no wild or stray animals will be attracted to their position—

a potentially disastrous occurrence that could attract curious Iraqi eyes and expose their position.

The troopers are prepared to lie low for days, watching for the elusive Scuds, but the arrival of dawn quickly reveals that part of Saddam's missile inventory is already operating in this area.

At first, only normal military, and civilian, traffic can be seen speeding along the east–west highway stretched out before them. It isn't long, though, before Van Hee recognizes some very familiar friends. Tailing along behind a westbound string of large civilian Mercedes tractor–trailers is a Ural-375 truck, mounting a mobile crane, and a pair of Type ZIL-157V tractors hauling elongated cargoes covered by tarps. The vehicles continue down the road for almost two miles and then pull off to the right about a hundred yards into the desert. Excitement is running high in the team and reaches a peak a half hour later when an eight–wheeled MAZ-543 transporter–erector–launcher (a TEL vehicle known to carry Scud missiles) and a ZIL-157V tanker towing a trailer appear to the east. They zoom by and continue on to the other waiting vehicles which, by now, include numerous supply trucks, C^3 vans, and a mix of towed quad 23mm and dual 30mm antiaircraft guns in the process of deploying on both sides of the highway. The top of the TEL is still well–covered by sand–colored tarps, but Van Hee is willing to bet his life and the lives of his men that it mounts a Scud missile.

The suspicious TEL remains with the other vehicles for only about ten minutes before all but the antiaircraft element suddenly begin to move off in column across the desert. After only a few hundred yards, the lead truck turns abruptly to the left into a deep wadi that arches back toward the road passing under it at a long, thin bridge a quarter mile past their original turnoff. As far as the team leader's concerned, this confirms it. There is no reason for an Iraqi unit this far afield of the main weight of coalition air attacks to go to this kind of trouble to hide itself unless it's a missile unit. At night, the TEL and select support vehicles will emerge back onto the flat, tabletop terrain to fire its terror weapon at Israel.

Sighting through his 7x40 Steiner binoculars, Van Hee begins to list what he sees as the vehicles disappear one by one down the now–apparent path bulldozed to the dry streambed. His time as an exchange member with one of West Germany's famed long–range reconnaissance companies is now paying off. As he reels off the NATO names, the team's radio operator writes them on his notepad. After one more sweep of the target area, Van Hee tells Cranson to inform headquarters that the "mother of all targets" is in front of them. He then slides back into the two–man foxhole, closes his eyes, and wearily tries to relax.

Opening his rucksack flap, Cranson closely examines the Satellite Communications System (SATCOM). From the ruck's outside pocket he pulls a miniature black satellite antenna folded in such a way that it looks like little more than a small, closed umbrella. Unfolding its legs and arms, Cranson places the device just beyond the lip of the hide hole and checks its frame to ensure that each prong is extended to its maximum position. With a diameter of only 17in, the antenna's profile will provide an observer with little clue as to what it is, even if the device could be seen from the highway. Cranson plugs the antenna's black, coaxial cable into the SATCOM and turns it on.

While the system hums and ticks through its self–checks and calibrations, the commo man listens through his headsets and consults the *Equatorial Satelite Antenna Pointing Guide* for the necessary elevation and azimuth angles required to orient the SATCOM's antenna for sending and receiving signals. Cranson moves the frame dish back and forth until he hears the unmistakable peep of the orbiting satel-

lite and then settles in to start his transmission. He speaks in slow, distinct tones into his microphone, sending the entire intelligence picture of what the recon team is viewing to a receiving station in the SOC communications bunker at King Khalid. Immediately, this vital information is passed through the US Air Force liaison officer to CENTCOM's air component tucked away in a basement corner of the Royal Saudi Air Force building in Riyadh.

Within minutes of the initial report being sent, coalition jets, pulled from the air campaign to hunt for Scuds, are vectored from their stations as others scramble from Saudi fields far to the southeast. Twenty–two minutes after the initial report, the first aircraft arrive over the highway. The jets briefly circle well out of range of the frustrated Iraqi anti-aircraft gunners while coordinating their attack, and then make straight for the well–camouflaged vehicles parked along the dry streambed.

Tipped off to the Iraqis' exact location, the ungainly looking A-10 Thunderbolt IIs (affectionately

A man–portable satelite communications system.

238

Mission accomplished. (**Left**) A missile and its mobile launching platform caught out in the open and destroyed. (**Above**) A missile rearm vehicle burned to the ground by Air Force jets.

called "Warthogs" or simply "Hogs") turn the wadi into a death trap. Resembling sharks during a feeding frenzy, the jets continuously roll in and pound the missile unit, and then begin to work on targets of opportunity up and down the highway. Their method of attack, however, seems strange to the hidden team members watching the show with intense interest. All had at one time or another seen live–fire exercises where the hog drivers swooped in and plastered targets from treetop heights, but now their hogs seemed to rarely venture below 8,000 or 10,000 feet because of the antiair assets.

Throughout the rest of the day, air strikes continue to hit what can only be described as "a target–rich environment." Periodic, huge explosions rend the wadi, and Cranson, who is monitoring the Warthogs' communications net, informs Van Hee that the hog drivers claim "two Scuds TANGO UNIFORM" (Tits Up—slang for "destroyed"). Later strikes are conducted almost exclusively by F-16s, with some help from Tornado attack aircraft of unknown origin. The team hadn't been briefed that

Tornadoes would be in on the show, and although Cranson picks up their cryptic transmissions, he can only state that they are *not* speaking *American* English. He can't make out if they are piloted by Brits, Saudis, or Italians (all of whom field the multirole jet), and is the butt of several rude jokes from his friends until they, too, fail just as badly at deciphering the jet jockeys' nationalities.

These aircraft, and all others working the many targets, fly no lower than the Warthogs and, consequently, there are a lot of misses. But even through the smoke and dust kicked up by the strikes, Van Hee can clearly see that the cumulative weight of the air attacks has destroyed nearly every vehicle in the area by using a combination of rockets, iron bombs, and cluster munitions. The medium–altitude attacks have, moreover, rendered the defenders' antiaircraft guns nearly useless by striking from beyond their *effective* range. No one in the team sees any coalition aircraft go down.

As evening draws near, the team leader fears that their position is becoming increasingly vulnerable.

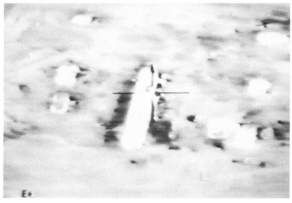

(**Opposite**) A night–stalking F-15 taking on fuel during *Desert Storm*. (**Above**) A disabled fuel truck in Iraq, and (**left**) an actual Scud TEL targeted by an F-15E. Target identification was often extremely difficult at night, even with the most sophisticated ground and airborne systems.

Although well–hidden on a barely perceptible ridge, they are, nevertheless, located on the highest terrain feature in the area. It might only be a matter of time before the increasingly active Iraqi patrols unearth them. As soon as it begins to turn dark, the team picks up their gear, quickly sanitizes the area, and heads south across the previously active road, now silent except for the crackling of a few vehicle fires still burning brightly. Moving carefully across undulating ground, the team settles into a steady, cautious march. Upon reaching a small depression dotted with low, thorny bushes, they form a perimeter and rest before continuing on to the exfiltration point that night.

But this is as far as they get. Gleason detects the hot thermal images of several trucks pulling off the highway barely 1,500 yards directly behind them. Both Gleason and Van Hee carry handheld AN/PAS-7 thermal viewers that pick up the heat of the vehicles several hundred yards beyond the system's stated range (the trucks can't be seen at all by the shorter–range NODs except for the occasional glint of reflected moonlight). Almost immediately, they are joined by a larger, semitrailer–sized vehicle.

Could it be another Scud TEL? Through their two thermal viewers, the team watches with nervous excitement—and no small amount of glee—as what appears to be more Scud launchers and support vehicles trickle in. Although the glowing, red, negative images provided by the viewers cannot produce an accurate picture at that distance, Van Hee and crew believe that their new neighbor is a full–blown battery preparing to launch a nasty surprise at the Jewish State.

Under normal circumstances, the lack of clear, sharp images would not prevent the team from determining if this is a Scud battery. With even the little elevation provided by a slight rise, they could look down on the spread of vehicles and make out the telltale signs unique to that type of unit's deployment pattern. Unfortunately, the recon team not only lacks altitude now, but is, in fact, slightly lower than the Iraqis. From their essentially eye–level view, all they can tell is that there are several dozen vehicles—some quite large—arrayed to the north.

Whoever they are, the darkness of night has given them a false sense of security and Van Hee can make out that they are neither properly dispersed nor making any effort at concealment. The team can easily call an air strike in on this unit, but even though the Iraqis are currently not well–dispersed, that could change in an instant. Moreover, if this is a Scud battery, even the fast–movers viewing the target area through their Maverick missiles' powerful infrared sensors will have great difficulty picking out the critical launch vehicles which, it turns out, are almost indistinguishable from fuel trucks and other lengthy vehicles at attack distances. Blanketing the area with cluster bombs will not guarantee the destruction of the mobile launchers either, although it would certainly "attrit" their crews and support personnel.

For obvious reasons, the Air Force was having a terrible time tracking down the nocturnal TELs and, true to the black humor that befriends men in war, the troopers nearly busted a gut a week earlier when they learned that a group of Jordanian tractor–trailer rigs had been rocketed and cluster–bombed when mistaken for one of Saddam's Scud units. It seems that their hapless drivers had pulled off the highway at one of its infrequent rest stops late at night and were inadvertently mistaken for a rearm and refuel site.* A Special Forces team on the ground soon confirmed that the blasted vehicles were civilian and, in any event, the Iraqis had immediately bussed foreign journalists to the scene to record "President Bush's most vile outrage." Word spread quickly from King Khalid "Emerald City" to the intelligence analysts, working out of prefab buildings on a Riyadh soccer field, and the shocked air unit that made the strike.

*If there was a plus side to the mistaken attack, it was the fact that fewer civilian drivers were now willing to brave the highway at night, thus making the job of target identification slightly less complicated.

Now, Van Hee finds the tables completely turned. Although the team leader is considerably closer than any fighter jockey releasing a Maverick missile and has all the time in the world to examine the glowing, shapes, there is no way he can confirm that they are what he believes them to be. Van Hee needs to know exactly what he is looking at before he calls in the fast–movers. Once committed to a strike here, on what is perhaps just some inconsequential heavy–lift unit, there might not be enough time or available air assets to immediately respond if a genuine Scud battery is detected.

Van Hee instructs Rodrigues and the tail gunner to move back toward the highway, to get a closer look, and hands over his thermal viewer. He wishes his team had gotten another of the precious thermal systems but is thankful that they

were able to get any at all. Many Special Forces long–range reconnaissance patrols didn't even have one of the scarce AN/PAS-7s, but the highly critical nature of DELTA's scud–hunting mission allowed Van Hee to get his mitts on two of the lightweight devices.

Gleason watches as their ghostly figures silently disappear into another depression, and settles into what is likely to be a long vigil on the perimeter. Everyone understands that the men may have to move in as close as 200 or 250 yards before their viewer will let them confirm the team's suspicions. If the approach to the Iraqi unit is difficult, the men might be gone for many hours. During their absence, the team checks and rehecks its equipment and notifies SOC of the situation.

The waiting is mercifully short. Helpful terrain features and a surprising lack of security have allowed the scouts to get their job done in barely three hours. Rodrigues reports that at least two of the mystery vehicles are "Spud" TELs, and Van Hee wastes no time setting back out with him to a spot where Rodrigues is confident that each of the confirmed launchers can be painted for incoming aircraft. When Gleason first spotted the gathering Iraqi vehicles at roughly 1,500 yards, they were beyond the effective range of Van Hee's AN/PAQ-3 MULE target designator, and the laser team has to travel almost one–third of the way back toward the road to ensure that their instrument can get a clear fix on the TELs. Newer, experimental handheld designators, that can accurately illuminate targets at roughly three times the distance had recently been sent to the Gulf, but Van Hee's team are not among the lucky few to receive one.

The route back is well known by this time, and the men are able to move with deliberate haste. The midnight hour Iraq often uses for launching its terror weapons is fast approaching, and through

A Scud missile erect on its launcher and ready to fire.

242

AN/AVS-6 Aviator's
night–vision imaging system

Comparative imagery from night vision equipment used by US forces in *Desert Storm*: (**top**) unaided, daylight photograph of an M606 Jeep and the same vehicle shot from a slightly different angle through (**center**) image intensification and (**bottom**) infrared devices.

AN/PVS-7A
Night vision goggles

AN/PAS-7 Thermal viewer

AN/PAQ-3 Modular universal laser
equipment (MULE) target designator

their thermal viewers, both the laser team and Gleason, at the hastily established patrol base, can see the unmistakable pillar of a missile raised on one of the erectors. A brief break in the clouds also allows a faint, grainy image to be seen from the NODs.

At the base, Rodgers peers intently at the shadowy image of assembled Iraqi vehicles and nervously fingers his M16. From his vantage point, he can see only one other trooper, the tail gunner, about twenty yards to his right, who has turned his way, as well, and gives Rodgers a thumbs up. Rodgers knows that he isn't the only man wondering if the fast–movers will make it before the Iraqis launch. He doesn't feel

himself to be particularly expendable and hopes that the Air Force will refrain from using cluster munitions against close–in, ground–lased targets as the team had been briefed before the mission.

Activity suddenly picks up near the road. Several of the smaller Iraqi vehicles start hauling off in all directions and a lone, dual 30mm antiaircraft gun, positioned slightly east of the launch site, begins to pop green tracers into the air. The team watches, mesmerized from their ringside seats as other antiaircraft artillery, or "triple–A," quickly comes to life, sending aloft crisscrossing streams of fire. Cranson, meanwhile, listens in on the approaching jets transmission: "Honey 1, sixty seconds, Maverick. . . . Honey 1, ten seconds. . . . Honey 1, laser on. . . . Spot. . . . Honey 1, lock–launch." *

The men have almost grown accustomed to the awe–inspiring spectacle of light and sound when a huge, double explosion bursts skyward. A Maverick air–to–ground missile has slammed into a TEL and ignited its fueled–up weapon.

Most of the triple–A falls silent for what seems like a long time, but one Iraqi gunner recovers from the shock of the explosion almost immediately and resumes shooting even before the fireball disappears into the air. Long strings of triple–A again arch into the sky as Rodgers and the others watch in fascination, knowing that Van Hee is already painting another Scud: "Honey 2, spot. . . . Lock–launch. . . . Honey 2, terminate." ** A second huge explosion lights the scene and more vehicles can be seen scurrying away from the carnage. As far as the Iraqi grunts are concerned, all Saddam's "little toys" do is attract death from above.

Secondary explosions begin to rock the target area as the laser team moves at a steady trot toward the patrol base. The Air Force is holding back from dropping its deadly packages of cluster bombs, to give them a jump at getting away from the target. Rodrigues and Van Hee's glowing green images can be seen quite clearly during their last 100–meter dash to the base, and some of the troopers can't refrain from greeting them with low–volume (*very* low–volume) whoops and hollers as they clear the perimeter. As if to join in the congratulations, the Air Force begins to hit the site again, and now the whole team moves out at a run. The troopers haven't covered a quarter mile when suddenly,

while cresting a wide ripple in the earth, they smack into an Iraqi squad barely thirty yards away. The Iraqis were apparently on patrol when the air strike erupted and are riding out the fireworks in this shallow depression.

The startled team comes under fire. Dropping to one knee, Gleason pumps two 9mm rounds into the nearest Iraqi's chest. Without pausing, he switches to the next target, who immediately crumples into a heap, his stomach perforated by two slugs from Gleason's H&K. Immediately sizing up the situation, Van Hee yells for the team to break contact. While moving through their leapfrog maneuver, a lucky round from an RPG-7 shoulder–fired rocket launcher lands between Rodgers and the tail gunner. Although most of the explosion is absorbed by the ground, shrapnel rips into Rodgers' right side and the tail gunner is killed instantly by a dime–sized piece of metal piercing his skull just above the right eye.

The four unhurt troopers immediately lay down an intense base of fire, which convinces the Iraqis to fall back to less dangerous surroundings. The firefight has lasted less than two minutes. One American is dead and another's life is leaking into the rocky earth. Hauling Rodgers and the fallen trooper along with them, the team hurriedly resumes their escape south while Air Force jets strike at Iraqi vehicles streaking pell–mell through the area. It is painfully obvious to all that they are in deep trouble, and, if action is not taken quickly, will either be killed or wind up being displayed on the evening news as prisoners of war.

Air–ground communications between the team and SOC is now being maintained by a "fast FAC," or forward air controller, who passes word to Cranson that immediate efforts are being initiated to get them out. They are instructed to keep moving south without delay, but each man knows that they are faced with a decision no soldier wants to make.

---

* "Sixty seconds to laser designator switch–on. . . . Ten seconds to switch–on. . . . Laser spot acquired. . . . Target locked–on and ordnance fired."

** "Laser spot acquired. . . . Target locked–on and ordnance fired. . . . Have visual contact; laser no longer needed."

The venerable A-10 Thunderbolt II "Warthog" and DELTA formed a deadly Scud hunter–killer team in Iraq. A-10s also proved themselves to be an effective search and rescue asset.

The young trooper's body hinders their movement to the extraction point, and they decide to bury him as quickly as possible. In a lonely defile, the team digs a grave for their comrade. It is not very much, as graves go, but it is made with love and respect, and the men dig as deeply as time will permit. Wrapping the staff sergeant up in his poncho liner, they gently lay his body into the desert soil. Van Hee carefully checks, then rechecks, the tight ten–digit grid coordinate he has plotted for the unmarked grave and silently swears to his fallen trooper that he'll be back for him. The team says a quick prayer over their friend, and then, carrying Rodgers, they strike out south again. Rodrigues, the team's medic, recognizes that the multiple shrapnel wounds are worse than previously thought. Rodgers is slipping in and out of consciousness and losing blood. Cranson radios the fast FAC that they have a man who will die if they don't get him out soon.

SOC knows that no special operations helicopters are currently available for a quick recovery, nor are there likely to be any until almost mid–morning. Virtually everything is already committed to the far–flung operations in progress throughout what the Israelis call "Scudinavia" in western Iraq. SOC decides to use a MC-130 Combat Talon equipped with a Fulton Recovery System to conduct a surface–to–air recovery (STAR) of Rodgers. This is not generally a preferred method of extraction because it takes so much time to set up the Fulton and is easily seen, but with helo assets unavailable, Rodgers' condition makes it necessary. Alerting the 1st Special Operations Wing, a hasty plan is worked out to recover the wounded DELTA trooper.

The Extractions

Arar Royal Military Airfield near Banadah is the launch site of some of *Desert Storm's* most inventive operations. It's not an unusual place to find one or two of the 1st Special Operations Wing's MC-130s, and when the call comes down, immediate preparations are made for the STAR. First, a modified delivery canister resembling an old napalm bomb is loaded with all the items needed by the team to set

up the recovery. The canister is then affixed to a waiting A-10's weapons pylon, and the Warthog is immediately launched toward western Iraq. As the "Sandy"* Hog driver and his wingman speed north, the crew of the MC-130 receives their mission brief. Not uncharacteristically, the crew takes the briefing quite professionally; yet, underneath their calm exterior, there is a surge of adrenalin. They are going to execute a mission that they have trained hard for and has not been performed in combat for nearly twenty years. The airmen are confident that the improvements in technique and hardware introduced since the Vietnam War are sound.

Already deep in the desert, the recon team is now told to move beyond their original pickup point into an even more desolate area well away from any known military targets. After several hours, the exhausted team comes upon a group of ruined dwellings and sets up defensive positions as dawn begins to break. Rodrigues has just changed Rodgers' I-V and is connecting a new bag of saline solution when Cranson's radio crackles to life. The Sandy pilot is attempting to contact the team. Hopefully, it will appear to any nearby Iraqis that the hog driver and his wingman are out hunting for targets of opportunity and will avoid any curious overtures.

Van Hee is informed that he should mark their position for a "delivery." Using a mirror, Van Hee

---

*An A-10 pilot specially trained for rescue escort (RESCORT) missions. The rugged A-10's ability to loiter for extended periods of time makes it a perfect aircraft for conducting searches in a high-threat environment, and Sandy's are experts at locating survivors. By marking target locations and supressing enemy fire, they allow more vulnerable rescue aircraft to do their job. The term originated during the Vietnam war as a call sign used by A-1E Skyraider pilots providing gunfire suppression during rescue operations.

signals his location to the Sandys performing their lazy search pattern well away from the team. After receiving an acknowledgment from the pilot, Van Hee moves out about 175 yards from the perimeter, places a single orange panel in the gravel, and immediately moves back to the shelter of the ruins. The pair of Warthogs are continuing their indirect meander toward the ruins when they spot a group of Iraqi trucks moving parallel to the team approximately two miles out. Although they do not appear to be looking for the troopers, the Sandys take no chances and proceed to spoil the Iraqis' morning with fire from their 30mm Gatling nose cannons. As the hogs leave the burning vehicles, they approach the ruins indirectly by flying in a low, wide arc that, hopefully, will not draw attention to the hidden Americans. No extra passes are made over the site and the equipment canister is "pickled off" as the ugly jets roar overhead.

Thirty minutes behind the Sandys, the MC-130 Combat Talon penetrates into "Injun Country." While passing over the berm line, the special opera-

A surface–to–air recovery (STAR) of two troopers using a Fulton extraction system: (**Top row**) A canister containing the system is dropped by an Air Force fast–mover.' Helium bottles, balloon, line and attached suit in a recovered canister. The guard cables and whisker–like probes of an MC-130 yoke, opened to snare the Fulton's line. (**Center row**) Two volunteers with "Are we really going to do this?" looks on their faces. The line being snagged. Up, up, and away! (**Left**) The open rear ramp of the receiving aircraft as the soldiers are hauled aboard.

tions aircraft receives an ominous radio report from the E-3A Sentry orbiting in Saudi airspace behind them. Electronic warfare officers operating the AWACS's highly sophisticated sensors detect a number of hostile radar impulses. Despite the fact that the Air Force owns the sky, being painted over Iraqi territory always causes concern. Most of the Talon's crew had friends on the ill–fated AC-130 Specter gunship that failed to get out of Kuwaiti airspace when "locked on" by a surface–to–air missile. The result was charred debris floating in the Gulf and no survivors.

As the Talon closes on the team's location, Van Hee and Gleason open the canister. Extracting its contents, they find a balloon, nylon line, harness, and suit along with a bottle of helium. Rodrigues checks Rodgers' condition while Van Hee and Gleason prepare to inflate the balloon, and Cranson makes contact with the inbound Talon. Not only is the MC-130 approaching, but the pair of A-10s continue to ply the area in ostensibly random patterns, and a flight of F-16s has already assumed a guardian–angel role well to the east but within easy striking distance if trouble develops. The Warthogs again cruise past the ruins while Van Hee and Gleason affix the helium bottle to the balloon that will stretch Rodgers' lifeline in reach of the specially equipped rescue aircraft. As it inflates, the bulbous cream and silver balloon takes on the shape of a giant fish, its floppy fins growing firmer with each passing second.

While all this is going on, Rodrigues and Cranson gingerly ease Rodgers into the olive green recovery suit sewn firmly to the Fulton's harness. As its furlined hood is placed around Rodger's face, his glazed eyes open slightly to Rodrigues' familiar grin and thick, angular eyebrows. His medic friend has been in DELTA for a long time and has a well–earned reputation as a battlefield doctor. Patting Rodgers' thigh, he says with a chuckle, "You gonna go on a neat ride, my man. It's up, up, and away for you." Rodrigues does his best to put up a brave front for his buddy but fears that Rodgers may have lost too much blood. The furlined face is gray and expressionless, but it seems for a moment that he tries to acknowledge what the medic is saying.

Twenty minutes from the pickup, the balloon is allowed to creep slowly skyward. It reaches its full height and Rodgers sits securely attached to its tether while the team, minus the doc, stands guard in a circle resembling a herd of buffaloes shielding a wounded calf. Rodrigues continues his lively chatter to help keep his patient awake and gently pats and strokes his unhurt left arm. Although he doesn't know it, his determined "woofing" is paying off. Rodgers dimly comprehends that his buddies are doing everything they can for him and takes some comfort from the New Yorker's verbal blizzard.

At 525 feet in the air, the balloon attached to the tethered nylon rope is a beacon for all to see and is the reason that the team had to put so much distance between themselves and the highway. The incoming MC-130's unusual nose now resembles a snout with two large whiskers. These whiskers are actually probes swung outward to form the yoke. Their main function is to guide the line into place at the center of the nose as the plane makes the pickup.

Cautiously lining up on the balloon, the pilot throttles the fat, four–engine airplane down to 112, 105, then only 97 knots for the pickup and aims at the target area on the nylon rope marked by three orange streamers. Striking the target markers, the probes guide the line to the yoke and secure it as the plane flies over the DELTA team. With a minimum of fanfare, Rodgers is literally snatched from the gravity of earth and appears as a small dot hurtling behind the Talon. While the STAR is a nerve-wracking affair for the soldiers to watch, they know that Rodgers actually experiences less of a jolt during the pickup than he did when he opened his parachute.

In the gaping cargo bay, the loadmaster and crew chief now prepare to winch their human cargo on board. The nylon line is pressed firmly against the Talon's belly by the rush of air, and inside the bay, the crew chief and loadmaster move quickly to hook it, much as one snaps a fishing line. Reeling

A special operations helicopter streaking at low level across the night sky.

in the line and attaching it to the Talon's internal, hydraulic winch, the precious cargo is slowly drawn into the cargo bay. Soon, Rodgers is lying in the safety of the aircraft while Air Force Reserve trauma specialists work frantically to stabilize him. The only hitch during the pickup occurs when the balloon fails to release from the line. The Talon's navigator is forced to spear the playfully bouncing object with a harpoon–like device and cut it free with the help of the loadmaster.

As the MC-130 speeds toward friendly airspace, the remainder of the recon team moves out.

A well–timed air operation, centered mainly along the highway to the north, is initiated by the F-16s and a fresh pair of A-10s to mask their movement and the troopers head south by southwest toward a new pickup point several miles away. Although appropriate helo assets will be available in a few hours, SOC has decided to not make the extraction until after dark since Rodgers has been rescued and the recon team is in no immediate danger.

The team had flung their prefabricated hide site covers into their foxholes and buried them when they sanitized their original position, but the rough terrain the men are now moving into offers many opportunities for natural concealment and there is no worry that they no longer have the prefabs. They soon come upon a wadi that offers a reasonable amount of security and decide that it is as good a place as any to go to ground till nightfall. After the midnight firefight, Saddam's forces know that American commandos are in the area, but ongoing airstrikes have given the Iraqis plenty of other things to worry about, and their movement has been heavily restricted for scores of miles in all directions.

The only enemy assaulting the men is a determined legion of sandfleas, which tirelessly press their attack as "big red" moved slowly across the sky. They do, however, also receive periodic visits from various Air Force jets. The pilots make it a point to fly close enough to the DELTA team to scout for hostile forces, yet their seemingly random passes are conducted at varied-enough intervals to give no clue to the whereabouts of the hidden soldiers.

Night comes quickly in this part of the world and the already-cool late January temperature drops like a stone even before the sun disappears from the horizon. As the four men make their final equipment checks before moving out, help is crossing the Saudi-Iraqi border 100 miles to the southeast. Boring through the gathering fog at sixty feet off the ground, a lone MH-60 Black Hawk is finally on its way to retrieve the soldiers.

Almost ten hours has passed since Rodgers was extracted, and Van Hee's team starts to move south again. The welcome night engulfs the dirty, unshaven troopers and their night vision goggles allow them to move with the assurance of prowling nocturnal beasts unencumbered by darkness.

In spite of the sophisticated vision devices and their apparent isolation, the desert holds one more surprise. As they near the pickup point, a young goat herder casually emerges from a depression forty yards to their right. Upon seeing the ghost–like apparitions, he runs screaming through the darkness, scattering livestock in all directions. Fearing a return of Iraqi soldiers, the team moves through the area quickly and sets up a defensive perimeter 600 yards from their encounter. Speaking in hushed tones with the inbound chopper, Van Hee guides the bird in until the troopers can be seen on its infrared imager.

As the Black Hawk's wheels touch the hard–packed dirt, the remaining four troopers scramble aboard and slide across the metal floor plates to hold each other in the embrace only those who have faced the ultimate challenge know. "We made it!" Gleason yells above the pitch of the engines as the helicopter begins to rise above the desert floor.

After looking out of the waist gunner's hatch for any signs of Iraqi forces, Van Hee wearily leans back and says "Christ, I hope so."

Epilogue

Fort Bragg, North Carolina

Along Ardennes Road, framed by a stand of regal North Carolina pines, the John F. Kennedy Special Warfare Center Chapel occupies a place of dignity and serenity. Against the hustle and organized chaos that characterizes this sprawling Airborne post, it provides a safe haven of sanity and peace whether the visitor is a regular church–goer or just passing through.

Framed against the buildup of an incoming spring rain, a memorial service is taking place. It is a closed service designed to avoid the prying eyes of nosy newspaper reporters still trying to write a story connected to *Desert Storm*. Although the service was unannounced, the chapel is crowded. Word has passed quickly around the special operations community that one of their own is being remembered today. Conspicuous in their off–the–rack suits, cowboy boots, and nonregulation mustaches

and haircuts, the members of a DELTA troop have gathered once more. Along with their wives, they are here to help the young widow weather one more storm. It is a unique scene—one that rarely occurred in the past few years but has often been repeated since the operations "over there."

The widow's five–year–old son, sandy blond hair neatly combed and out of character, sits on the edge of his front–row seat. Gently poking an imagined spot on the chapel's maroon carpet with the toe of his Sunday best, he absently wonders, not quite knowing or understanding why he is here. He is aware that his mom's world is in disarray, and her sadness is something he has never seen before. All he knows is that the man whose picture occupies the table in front of the chapel room is not coming home. His father left home late one night "on business." That was not an unusual occurrence in his young life, but now a new twist has occurred. Mom said that his best friend has gone to live with God forever.

A soldier is laid to rest.

His father's friends, gathered around the family in a supportive ring, knew the story all too well. The smiling young soldier, pictured with the coveted green beret had been their friend, and in this close–knit group of professionals, that one word, "friend," was all that required their loyalty.

The emotion of these men was not a complicated show. Each behaved simply but with a degree of maturity in combat that comes only to a veteran. They accepted what was thrown their way in a businesslike manner, hiding their hatred, fear, confusion, and pride behind the mantle of a well–trained special operations soldier. To this group and the many others like them, the specter of death was always an additional member of the team. In this particular case, their friend was no longer able to avoid death's embrace. Thousands of miles away, hidden in an unmarked grave deep in Iraq's rugged western province, their trusted friend and the young boy's father had rested until a subsequent team, under Gary Van Hee, recovered his lifeless form.

As the chaplain exhorts the group not to grieve but to pray for the Great Jumpmaster's protection of their comrade's soul, the thoughts of many of the group drift to other places, other actions, and other services. The veterans of *Desert Storm* looks back over the madness of the past weeks which characterized the operations in the desert.

Hanging back a little from the rest of the mourners, a grizzled old warrior remembers similar services after such operations—code–named *Desert I, Urgent Fury,* or *Just Cause*—and drifts further back in time to days before he left Smoke Bomb Hill to join DELTA at the old stockade. His thoughts go back to the Green Beret Parachute Club, its cold beer, warm friendships and the old jukebox nestled in the corner next to the pool tables. He smiles to himself as he remembers that one song, a song from an unpopular war that saw so many of the special operations community answer the requirements of the ultimate test. Though not all of the DELTA troopers were initially Special Forces–qualified, most ended with that qualification, and an old war song expressed best the thoughts and feelings of this moment: "Her Green Beret has met his fate."

It's not all glory and gunsmoke in the realm of special operations—especially in covert operations. It can be boring for months at a time and then spiked with moments of sheer gut–wrenching, piss–in–your–pants horror. But that is what they signed up for. No yellow ribbons, no victory parades, or grand celebrations would greet these secret warriors. Just a gentle hug, a kind word, or a pat on the back that seemed to say, "Well done." That, plus "Clean up your gear and get ready for the next one!"

And there will certainly be a next one—somewhere, sometime. The odds are that the professionals from DELTA will be used not as they were during Iraq's stinging defeat, but in their traditional counterterrorist role.

For over a quarter of a century, the former Soviet Union and its surrogates in Eastern Europe, Latin America, and the Middle East gave safe haven to the world's most dangerous international terrorists. The collapse of Soviet communism, coupled with the shutting off of the terrorist's revenue by oil–rich Persian Gulf states angered over their backing of Iraq, have left terrorist organizations in disarray. Increasingly isolated politically and cut off from training and supplies from Europe and money from the Gulf, they bicker among themselves over how best to satisfy their grudge against the West and any Middle Eastern government unappreciative of their past deeds. They are, to put it bluntly, out of work and out of cash.

But the breather this has given the West is likely to be short–lived. As the world speeds toward the twenty–first century, it finds itself with more wild cards in its deck of nations. The familiar bipolar dominance of the United States and the former Soviet Union is gone for good, as the "evil empire" disintegrates into numerous successor states of questionable stability. These new countries are, themselves, not homogeneous entities and are likely to be rent by factional fighting in the decade to come. They are also the inheritors of at least 27,000 nuclear weapons. Despite pronouncements of their good intentions, their desperate need for hard currency and sporadic control of their own territory may result in some leakage of nuclear weapons ("loose nukes") or, more likely, nuclear materials and production expertise into the hands of terrorists.

This threat to peace and a new, ghastly form of warfare—environmental terrorism—may also cause elite counterterrorist units like DELTA to re-tool their operational methods. The sight of massive oil slicks released on the Persian Gulf and black clouds boiling up from oil fires to shut off the noonday sun will not be lost on the next gen-eration of would–be terrorists. Moreover, their twisted logic will lead some terrorists to use the re-sults of *Desert Storm* to add fuel to whatever cause is fashionable at the moment.

Literally dozens of captured Palestinian and Shiite terrorists have been dumped into this cauldron of change, let loose by the Iraqis when they invaded Kuwait or released by the Israelis as part of the package deal that freed a handful of Western hostages. Like the wandering free–lance warriors of feudal Japan who traded their violent skills for gold and fame, these modern–day *ronin* are available to any would–be despot or group fanning the flames of ethnic or religious unrest across Eu-rope, Asia, and the Middle East. Key terrorist net-works remain intact, and a number of groups and individuals dropped from sight when the vigilance of America's intelligence assets were directed to combat in the Gulf. Now that the flex of security operations has fallen to its normal lull, the specter of terrorists finding new work in the developing chaos is very real and Americans abroad are, as always, notoriously easy targets for any group desiring big headlines.

The pros of DELTA are ready.

U.S. ELITE
COUNTERTERRORIST FORCE

S.F. Tomajczyk

Acknowledgments

Researching the United States' counterterrorism efforts is by no means a simple task. By its very nature, counterterrorism is a very quiet endeavor that is done behind barbed-wire fences and at remote locations around the nation. Hence I am in great debt to the men and women who allowed me into their special world—a world of shooters and kickers, flashbangs, H&Ks, double taps, live fire drills, personal sacrifice, sweat, and the constant demand for perfection. It is a world where a split-second mistake can cost you your life, the life of your buddy, and/or the life of a hostage. This book is dedicated to everyone involved in U.S. counterterrorism efforts: the men and women who stand at the ready to protect us, as best as they can, from the maniacs in the world.

I am especially grateful to the following individuals and agencies for their kind assistance in making this book a reality: Thomas E. Connor, U.S. Marshals Service; William T. Licatovich, U.S. Marshals Service; George R. Havens, Deputy Director, U.S. Marshals Service; Lou Stagg, Commander, USMS SOG; Walter K. Erni, Task Force Commander, USMS SOG-TF1; Wayne Plylar, Task Force Commander, USMS SOG-TF3; LCDR Steven L. Pagett, Chief, Navy Antiterrorist Alert Center; Louis J. Beyer, Navy Antiterrorist Alert Center; Ronald W. Benefield, Naval Criminal Investigative Service; Mark V. Lonsdale, Specialized Tactical Training Unit; John Collingwood, FBI; Daniel Schofield, FBI Academy; Robin Montgomery, FBI Critical Incident Response Group; Kurt Crawford, FBI Academy; Tase Bailey, FBI (Ret.); Donald Bassett, FBI (Ret.); Oliver "Buck" Revell, FBI (Ret.); John Simeone, Deputy Commander, FBI HRT (Ret.); Richard "Dick" Marcinko, Commander, SEAL Team Six (Ret.) and now CEO of SOS Temps; Norm Carley, Executive Officer, SEAL Team Six (Ret.) and now CEO of Applied Marine Technology Inc.; Tom Dorrety, Central Intelligence Agency; Harold Heilsnis, Department of Defense; Ken Carter, Department of Defense; Col. Johnnie H. Wauchop, ASD (SO/LIC); Sgt. Donna S. Burgess, USAF, NCOIC, Public Affairs Resource Library; Battalion Chief Ray Downey, Special Operations Coordinator, FDNY; Chief Mike Shannon, Oklahoma City Fire Department; Mike McGroarty, City of La Habra Fire Department; Jeff Andrews and John Ventura, Department of Energy; Roxanne Dey, Department of Energy, Nevada Office; Lisa Gordon-Haggerty, Director, Office of Emergency Response, Department of Energy; Steve Wampler, Lawrence Livermore National Laboratory; William Heimbach, Jr., Los Alamos National Laboratory; Kathy Kuhlmann and Ace Ethridge, Sandia National

Laboratory; Sandy Brown, Department of State; Andy Laine, Diplomatic Security Unit, Department of State; Frank Riley and Marina Drancsak, Department of Transportation; First Lt. McKenna, USAF SOC; Major Natalie Perkins, U.S. Army Public Affairs; Lt. Col. Ken McGraw, U.S. Army SOC; Sheila Hein, Dan Jackson, and Joy Bisson, U.S. Army EIGSD; Sgt. Kyle Olson, USMC; Major Roseann Sgrignoli, USMC; Major General "Mike" Myatt, USMC (Ret.); Lt. Gordon, USMC, Quantico Marine Base; Capt. Rick Woolard, Director, U.S. Special Operations Command; LCDR Jim Fallin, NAVSPECWAR; Lt. Eric Goss and Ensign Wendy Snyder, U.S. Navy Public Affairs; C.J. Madden and Russell D. Egnor, Navy Office of Information, News Photo Division; Congressman Charles F. Bass (Rep., NH); Jamie Doyle and Neil Levesque, Congressman Bass' Office; Alfred Testa, Jr., Director, Manchester Airport; Lt. Mark Furlone, SWAT Commander, NH State Police; Donald Gates, NH State Police (Ret.); George L. Iverson, Director, NH Office of Emergency Management; Dick Wesnick, Editor, *Billings Gazette*; Carol Moore, author of *Davidian Massacre*; Ken Good and staff, Combative Concepts Inc.; John Shaw, Mid-South Institute; Caroline Sizer, Glock Inc.; Ginger Ludke and William E. Moles, Defense Technology Corporation of America; Robbie Barrkman, Robar Companies; Mary Scott Smith, Barrett Firearms Manufacturing Inc.; Lise Laberge, Senior Coordinator, International Sales, Simunition; Steve Galloway, Heckler & Koch USA Inc.; Michael Sneen and staff, Thor International; Sgt. Gary Hicks, University of Michigan Police; Col. Jesse L. Johnson, U.S. Army (Ret.); Tom Kukura, U.S. Drug Enforcement Administration; Amanda Gaylor, Rand Corporation; Pat Ravalgi, Federal Emergency Management Agency; Kevin Rowe, SigArms; County of Rockingham Sheriff; Anti-Defamation League; U.S. Secret Service; U.S. Customs Service; U.S. Senate; U.S. House of Representatives; General Accounting Office; and the Gunsite Training Center.

Then, of course, there are dozens of individuals who, by the inherent nature of their jobs, require that their contributions remain anonymous. I salute them one and all for their assistance. Through their efforts and the collective efforts of everyone I met and spoke with over the course of two years, Americans now have a better understanding of the special system that is in place to deal out grief to "Tangos" and "Crows." Having witnessed some of the training firsthand, all I can say is woe to those who foolishly decide to test out America's elite counterterrorist forces.
SF Tomajczyk

PROLOGUE

It's Not Supposed To Happen Here....

"Our sensors are detecting absolutely no sounds of survivors. Our cameras show only death."
Rescue worker, Dan Schroeder

"It was like being forced at gunpoint to eat an elephant...with a plastic knife and fork." That's how Mike Shannon, Special Operations Chief of the Oklahoma City (Oklahoma) Fire Department, compared the task that lay ahead of him as he surveyed the pile of rubble that had once been the nine-story Alfred P. Murrah Federal Building. The elephant was the wrecked building itself; the plastic utensils were the tools available to the rescuers. It was 9:05 A.M. on Wednesday, April 19, 1995, just three minutes after a Ryder rental truck—carrying 4,800 pounds of fuel and ammonium nitrate fertilizer—exploded in front of the building. The bomb had allegedly been placed by Timothy McVeigh and an accomplice. This act of terrorism—the worst in American history—coincided with the April 19 anniversary of the apocalyptic fire at the Davidian Compound in Waco, Texas. Interestingly, the

The bombing of the Murrah building killed 168 people, including several children who were staying at America's Kids, a government-operated day care center located on the second floor. The grief Americans felt caused them to spontaneously place wreaths and toys at the site of the bombing. *Mike McGroarty*

day of the bombing also coincided with the execution of white supremacist Richard Wayne Snell in Arkansas. Either or both events were later believed by law enforcement officials to be the motive behind the annihilation in Oklahoma City.

For Chief Shannon, the morning of April 19 had been routine. He had been reviewing the budget for the fire department's rescue unit with his boss, John Hanson, when they both heard the blast. They exchanged puzzled glances as ceiling dust rained down on them. A former Navy damage controlman, the noise reminded Shannon of an exploding artillery shell. Thinking that a nearby auto body shop may have blown up, he went outside and was confronted with the image of a black mushroom cloud rising into the sky. He knew then that it wasn't the body shop. He and other firefighters scrambled into their vehicles and raced to the scene.

Debris in the road forced Chief Shannon to park a block or so away from the Murrah building. He ran the remaining distance, navigating through concrete rubble and twisted cars, many of them flipped over and burning out of control. An 18-year veteran with the fire department, he had witnessed numerous disasters in his career—tornadoes, fires, floods—but nothing had prepared him for the carnage that greeted him when he finally arrived on scene.

To him, the building looked as if it had been strafed and bombed by enemy fighter aircraft. The explosion had decapitated the face of the Murrah building, causing nine floors of concrete to collapse and pancake on each other, squashing people and office equipment in the process. The air was filled with papers, dust, and smoke, and the ground was littered with desks, file cabinets, chairs, potted plants, and crumbled concrete and twisted steel, not to mention corpses and mutilated body parts. All of this had rained down onto the street, partially filling the 30-foot-wide, 8-foot-deep crater created by the bomb itself.

Chief Shannon took all of this in. He didn't know what had caused the damage—actually that didn't matter—all he knew was that he was dealing with a destroyed, unstable building that still had people in it. So he and another firefighter crawled into the building through a window and began to survey for damage and survivors. They would speculate later about what had caused such devastation.

The Murrah building, which was built in 1974, housed some 15 federal agencies, including the Veterans Administration, HUD, and several defense department offices. The DEA, BATF, and Secret Service also had offices in the building, all located on the ninth floor. There were several hundred workers in the building at the time of the blast, plus an unknown number of visitors. But perhaps the most distressing aspect of the bombing was the fact that the Murrah building also had a government-operated day care center located on the second floor. It took the brunt of the explosion; incredibly small bodies—many of them burned and mutilated beyond recognition—were discovered in the rubble by emergency responders. The photograph of 31-year-old firefighter Chris Fields cradling the limp body of Baylee Almon in his arms became the symbol of the tragedy worldwide. Baylee had turned one year

old the day before. Several toddlers were found wandering around the underground parking lot, searching for their parents. They were scooped up by strangers who were fearful of another disaster happening.

In the first hour, more than 600 injured people were taken from the site to area hospitals. Many were sent by ambulance, but some 400 were transported by what emergency responders refer to as POVs—privately owned vehicles. Volunteers, ranging from nurses to off-duty police officers, offered the use of their cars as ambulances. Specific routes were designated for in-bound and out-bound vehicles, so that traffic jams wouldn't occur. Triage stations, including four surgical units in a nearby warehouse, were set up to assess the severity of injuries and to get help for the most critically wounded. Most of those injured were riddled with lacerations caused by flying glass and debris; one man was pierced in nearly 100 places. Punctured lungs and slashed throats were also commonplace. The blast wave from the explosion was responsible for ruptured eardrums, eyeballs, internal organs, and fractured ribs.

By 10:30 A.M. emergency responders and volunteers had removed all but three known live survivors from the crumpled building. One of them was 20-year-old Daina Bradley, who lay trapped in the basement under a pile of cement girders. She had been at the Murrah building to get a Social Security card for her four-month-old son, Gabreon. Bleeding and laying in about a foot of frigid water, she was lodged in a space so small that the rescuers could barely reach her. Rebar—the steel reinforcing bars used to strengthen concrete—had her tightly pinned. Her left arm was trapped behind her head and her right leg was crushed under a huge slab of concrete. When doctors finally managed to squeeze in, her blood pressure was dropping and she was going into shock. As they deliberated about how to remove her from the rubble, the walls suddenly trembled, threatening to collapse on them. Everyone rushed out, leaving Daina behind begging them not to leave her. They returned 20 minutes later, only to flee once again when word spread that another bomb had been found.

The explosion effectively decapitated the front of the building, and caused the floors to collapse and pancake on each other. Rescuers had to search for victims inch-by-inch through the debris pile. As can be seen by the spray-painted warning in the lower left, it was a dangerous task. *Mike McGroarty*

A rare, inside look at what the rescuers were confronted with: twisted steel, concrete rubble, and debris. Fluorescent paint helped point out structural concerns to rescuers, as well as showed the locations of bodies trapped in the wreckage. An arrow above the plywood sheet points at the location of one such victim. *Mike McGroarty*

In the end, the rescue workers decided that the only way to save Daina's life was to cut off a portion of her right leg that was crushed beneath the concrete slab. An amputation kit was called for. Dr. Andy Sullivan, chief of pediatric orthopedics at Children's Hospital, was the only surgeon small enough to crawl into the space to reach her. Laying on top of Daina, he gave her a shot of anesthesia and then proceeded to cut off her leg below the knee using several scalpels, because the space was too small for surgical saws. The procedure took about 10 minutes. When he was done, firefighters tied a harness around Daina's upper body and pulled her free. Later on, they learned that Daina had lost her mother, her three-year-old daughter, Peachlyn, and her four-month-old son, Gabreon, in the explosion.

Finding people was just the first step. Freeing them from the rubble was the real challenge. As can be seen here, people were often trapped in 18-inch-high voids, which made it difficult to medically treat them, as well as to extricate them. Twenty-year-old Daina Bradley had to have her lower leg amputated to get her out of such a space. *Mike McGroarty*

Using jackhammers, rescuers dug slowly downward through the rubble for 16 days hoping to find survivors. Most debris was hauled out in buckets, as can be seen in the right hand side. The FBI then went through the buckets looking for the tiniest of clues that could help them solve this terrorism case. *Mike McGroarty*

As rescue operations continued into the afternoon and early evening, hope began to fade that any more survivors would be found. The bomb had done its work exceptionally well. Yet firefighters and rescue personnel persisted in probing the rubble, inch-by-inch, for signs of life.

Around 10 o'clock that evening, everyone's spirits soared when a voice was heard calling out from beneath the debris. It was Brandy Liggons, a 15-year-old girl who was trapped in a section of the building known as "The Cave." This dangerous area was directly beneath where the second and third floors of the building had collapsed, creating a small hollow. For rescuers to reach this area, they had to crawl in on hands and bellies, with someone else pushing them in from behind. It was definitely not a good place for claustrophobics. It took them three hours to pry Brandy from this concrete coffin.

As Chief Shannon described it later, every rescue worker was engaged in a "very serious game of pickup sticks." Between the shifting building and live wires, the penalty of a mistake—regardless of how minor—could easily have been death for a rescue worker. As firefighters worked to free Brandy, Dr. Rick Nelson, a surgeon from Muskogee, sat beside her. He held her hand and comforted her—telling her that she would survive—all the while sitting on a corpse of someone who had not.

By the time the Urban Search and Rescue teams (USAR) arrived on site, all the known survivors were

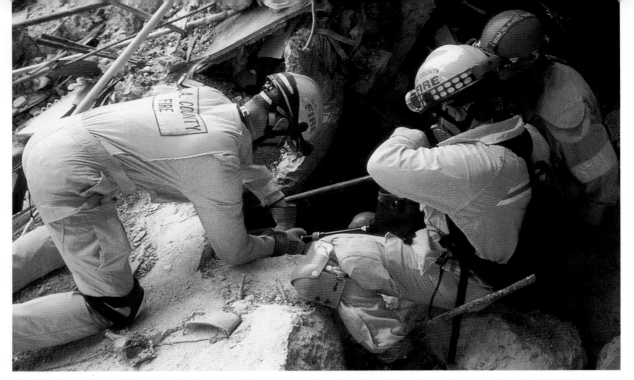

Searching for survivors often meant having to crawl like a cave explorer into tiny voids and crannies created by the rubble. Not a great place for those with claustrophobia. Danger was everywhere: live wires, twisted rebar and shifting debris. More than once rescuers had to flee for their lives as concrete rubble threatened to collapse on them. *Mike McGroarty*

gone. The Oklahoma City Fire Department, with assistance from hundreds of local volunteers, had done an admirable job. Now came the nightmare of finding and recovering any remaining people, which seemed unlikely even though Brandy had been found. Rescuers pawed through the debris with trackhoes, hydraulic lifts, and cranes, hoping to find voids in the rubble that might hold survivors. They even went so far as to use listening devices, ground radar, thermal sensors, fiber-optic cameras and specially trained dogs to detect victims. But all they found were corpses and mutilated body parts. Concerned about the emotional and mental impact that this crisis would have on the firefighters, site supervisors ensured that everyone underwent "defusing"—counseling immediately after they left the scene to help them deal with the stress. Later, group debriefings were held with mental health professionals.

On Friday, April 21, the FBI announced the arrest of bombing suspect Timothy McVeigh. For 48 hours they had followed a trail of obscure clues to a jail house in Perry, Oklahoma—just 60 miles north of Oklahoma City. McVeigh had been picked up two days earlier by police— less than 90 minutes after the explosion—for driving without a license plate and possessing a handgun loaded with Black Talon "cop killer" bullets. Before the FBI finally tracked him down, McVeigh was within a half-hour of being set free after first making a $500 bond hearing. Months later, he and his former-Army buddy, Terry Nichols, would be indicted for murder and conspiracy. The news of McVeigh's arrest by the FBI bolstered the rescuers somewhat, but the horror of the reality they were confronting squelched their enthusiasm.

The search lasted for 16 miserable days. Leather gloves, buckets, and shovels were the tools in high demand. Fatigue set in as rescuers put in 20-hour days. The longer people remained at the scene, the more they began to look at it as if it were a construction site: Loaders plowed debris into piles and cranes hoisted buckets of rubble. The only reminders of the gory task at hand were the orange circles painted around body parts and the letters "DB" (i.e., dead body) spray painted next to corpses. Rescuers dealt with the odor of rotting flesh by wearing masks and placing Vicks Vapor-Rub on their upper lip or sucking on peppermint candy.

The USAR teams began to depart on the 30th day, leaving the Oklahoma City Fire Department behind to wrap up the dirty work. Chief Shannon recalls two firefighters who spent nearly six hours digging for the severed arm of a woman who had died in the explosion. Her husband wanted to bury her whole, as well as to retrieve heirloom rings from her hand. Removing dirt by the spoonful—the concrete rubble was dense—the firefighters labored at their task until they finally recovered the limb. "You would have thought they had found a pot of gold, from the way they beamed," said Shannon. "In the last few days of the rescue effort, we were spending most of our time bringing a sense of peace to those who had lost their loved ones."

On May 4, the search finally came to a halt after 351 gut-wrenching hours. The death toll stood at 168. It was the worst act of terrorism in U. S. history, breaking the hearts of millions and shattering the innocence and sense of security that each American once had. The catastrophe at Oklahoma City was literally buried from sight a few weeks later, when 150 pounds of explosives were strategically placed in the skeleton

Rescuers used everything available to them to find buried survivors, including fiber optic cameras, thermal sensors, ground radar, microphones, and even specially trained dogs. But all they found were corpses. *U.S. Army*

of the Murrah building and detonated. It took eight seconds for the building to collapse onto itself.

The nightmare was finally over.

By disaster standards, the Murrah building bombing was not a major event. Certainly, many people were killed—making it a tragedy—but Oklahoma City did not lose its power, water, or sewage, and residents were not left homeless and without food. In California, earthquakes routinely wreck havoc over 40 square miles. By comparison, the Oklahoma City bombing occupied only 7,000 square feet . . . about a quarter of a block.

As Chief Mike Shannon points out, terrorism is what made the Oklahoma City incident bigger than what it was. And he is convinced that a similar terrorist bombing will happen again in the United States. In fact, Shannon says that FBI agents have thwarted several copy-cat bombings since that horrible April day, including attempts within Oklahoma City itself by wackos who were trying to prove that lightning can strike twice.

"Oklahoma City was the beginning," he warns. "Terrorists are in our midst. The farmer during the day can wear black at night. That's the scary part, but that's why they call it terrorism.

"As much as we're learning about what went right and what went wrong at Oklahoma City, I'll guarantee you that terrorists are learning from it, as well, as to what to do the next time. They'll steal and sanitize the truck—remove all their fingerprints—and then park it there and use a remote bomb on it. They'll wear disguises and won't ask anyone for directions.

"There's lots of things they'll do better."

CHAPTER ONE

A World Under Siege

Terrorism is goal-directed violence. It is also a psychological weapon. Terrorism creates a general climate of fear, so that over time, a specific political, social, or ideological goal can be achieved.

A good example of terrorism as goal-directed violence was the bombing of the World Trade Center on February 26, 1993. Islamic fundamentalists had strategically parked a yellow Ryder rental van and its 1,200-pound explosive cargo in the underground garage beneath the World Trade Center complex. At 12:18 P.M. on that snowy afternoon, the homemade bomb exploded, rocking the 110-story building's foundation and ripping open a 200-foot by 100-foot crater in the basement. The blast and the subsequent smoke and fire killed 6 people and injured more than 1,000. Thousands of people were terrorized as they fled to safety from the building's highest floors. As ugly as this

The car bomb is perhaps the most influential weapon in the modern terrorist's arsenal. It is relatively simple to place an explosive like C-4 or Semtex on a vehicle where it cannot be easily seen. The bomb can be rigged to explode by a timer device or by remote control. *U.S. Army*

The bombing of the World Trade Center in 1993 signaled the arrival of terrorism on U.S. soil. Later on, investigators would learn that this incident was actually the first shot of a war declared on the United States. The dark central area is the crater caused by the explosion. The ladder in the background provides a scale to the enormity of this disaster. *FD NYC*

269

event was, it was not as horrible as the terrorists had hoped for: They had intended for the World Trade Center building to topple over and knock down nearby skyscrapers in a domino-like manner.

They had also planned to poison people trapped inside the building, as evidenced by Judge Duffy's comments during the sentencing of the terrorists: "Death is what you really sought to cause. You had sodium cyanide laying around, and I'm sure it was in the bomb. Thank God the sodium cyanide burned instead of vaporizing. If the sodium cyanide had vaporized, it is clear what would have happened is [that] the cyanide gas would have been sucked into the north tower and everybody in the north tower would have been killed."

What many Americans still do not realize was that this bombing was the opening shot of a Holy War against the United States. It was a plot to frighten the so-called "Great Satan" into changing its Middle East policies. Some 22 Islamic fundamentalists were eventually arrested—after a worldwide manhunt—and brought to trial where they were accused of not only bombing the Trade Center, but also of plotting to kill Egyptian leader Hosni

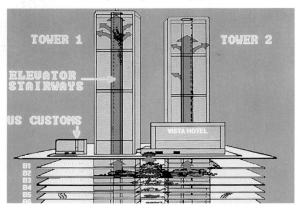

The terrorists who detonated the bomb beneath the World Trade Center had evil aspirations: They wanted one of the 110-story towers to topple over into the other and cause a domino-like disaster. Investigators also found sodium cyanide at the scene. If this deadly chemical had vaporized and been sucked up into the building's ventilation system, thousands of people would have died. *FD NYC*

Mubarak, U.S. Senator Alfonse D'Amato, and U.N. Secretary-General Boutros Boutros-Ghali, and of scheming to blow up the Holland and Lincoln tunnels, as well as other New York City landmarks.

Another example of terrorism as goal-directed violence was the nerve gas attack on a Tokyo subway station on March 20, 1995. Members of the doomsday religious cult Aum Shinrikyo used the tips of their umbrellas to pierce containers of Sarin that had been placed aboard three commuter trains. Within minutes, a deadly cloud of Sarin gas settled over the passengers, causing them to clutch at their throats and collapse to the ground, vomiting. The attack left 12 people dead and more than 5,500 injured, including 2 Americans.

On May 5, cult members tried again. This time they placed a simple binary weapon in the restroom at Shinjuku Station. It consisted of two plastic bags, one filled with powdered sodium cyanide and the other containing diluted sulfuric acid. When discovered by police, the bags were ablaze. Had they broken open, a chemical reaction would have occurred producing enough cyanide gas to kill 10,000 people.

Investigations later disclosed that both of these acts—plus an earlier incident that killed seven and injured 500—were just rehearsals for more evil things. The cult's leader, Shoko Asahara, wanted to initiate a war between Japan and the United States. He planned to assassinate President Bill Clinton and 17 other heads of state with nerve gas when they visited the Japanese parliament in November 1995. Eventually, during the course of the war, Asahara expected to assume control of the Japanese government. In preparation, he had placed cult members within the government and the military to help manipulate the circumstances to his favor.

Had it not been for diligent police work, the world—as you read this—very easily could have been embroiled in war. And it would have been as a direct result of terrorism—goal-directed violence.

Propaganda of the Dead

Although historians say that terrorism has been a problem for ages, today's statistics indicate that terrorism is more widespread and acceptable as a weapon than at any other time. Terror tactics are being used by individuals as a shortcut to shake the public's confidence in their government and to displace the rule of the majority by the edicts of a select few. Terrorism is not only cheap—a few sticks of dynamite are enough to initiate fear—but it is often able to accomplish what modern conventional war cannot.

For instance, the October 23, 1983, terrorist bombing in Beirut, which killed 237 U.S. Marines, was able to immediately undermine the United States' foreign policy in the Middle East. The Marines had been in Lebanon as part of a multinational peacekeeping force that had been deployed to support the central Lebanese government, after hundreds of Palestinians had been massacred by Christian militiamen. The multinational force withdrew from Lebanon in the spring of 1984, just months after the bombing. The message sent by the terrorist's truck bomb had been heard, loud and clear by policy makers. It is doubtful that a war with tanks and jet fighters could have achieved the same outcome. With the advent of the Beirut bombing, the delivery truck was ushered in as perhaps the most influential weapon of the twentieth century.

Profile of a Terrorist

So who are these people who seem to enjoy killing innocent people for their own personal gain? Depending on your viewpoint, the person who terrorizes passengers on a Boeing 707—threatening to blow them to kingdom come—could be labeled as a freedom fighter trying to bring attention to his cause. Others, however, would bluntly call him a terrorist or, in law enforcement parlance, a "tango" or "crow."

A look at past cases reveals that most terrorists are young, usually in their late-teens to late-20s. A logical reason for this is that the terrorist lifestyle of hide-and-seek requires the vigor, daring, and fitness

A martyr-bound terrorist drove a truck bomb frantically past guards into the Marine Barracks compound area in Beirut and detonated the bomb. The huge explosion killed 237 Marines and mangled the building. This incident caused the United States to rethink its involvement in the Middle East, which is exactly what the terrorists wanted. *U.S. Department of Defense*

most often associated with youth. Also, the young tend to be defiant and impressionable and, thus, are more likely to respond to a call-to-arms from activists than are older adults.

One of the Palestinians who hijacked the cruise ship *Achille Lauro* in 1985 was only 17 years old. Oan, the leader of the terrorist group that stormed the Iranian embassy in London in 1980, was 27. Mir Aimal Kansi, who opened fire with his AK-47 assault rifle on people leaving the CIA building in 1993, was 28 at the time. Domestic-terrorist Timothy McVeigh was 27 when the truck bomb exploded in Oklahoma City in 1995. And Ramzi Ahmed Yousef, a militant who was accused of planning to bomb 12 planes in two days, was only 28-years-old when he was arrested. Yousef was also accused of masterminding the 1993 bombing of the World Trade Center.

In addition to being young, terrorists are basically lonely, they feel morally superior to others and believe that violence is justified to support the

Drive-by shootings are a popular way of terrorizing the public and getting rid of VIPs. This tactic, which is often done on motorcycle or by a passing vehicle, is common in the Middle East, Central America, and parts of Europe. *U.S. Army*

Cause. Additionally, a surprising number come from affluent or middle-class families. For instance, Ilich Ramirez Sanches (a.k.a. Carlos The Jackal), the notorious terrorist who began his 25-year reign of terror in his early 20s, is the son of a prosperous Marxist lawyer. This is not to suggest, however, that the tactics of terror are confined to a specific social order. They aren't. Anyone can be a terrorist, regardless of their social standing. That's because it is ideology that is responsible for crafting the mind of a terrorist.

The Training Grounds

Ironically, colleges often unwittingly serve as the mental training grounds for would-be terrorists. Here, in hallowed halls and lecture rooms, students' impressionable minds are exposed to extremist messages from activists and visiting speakers, as well as from some of their professors and peers. In the United States, these teachings are protected by the First Amendment.

When a student decides to support a cause, he has little difficulty making initial contact. Most extremist groups operate public relations arms that disseminate information to gain public support for their movement. These propagandists attract new blood, filtering out those who have difficulty accepting the group's political indoctrination. Because these groups fear the possibility of infiltrators, recruits undergo a probationary period in which they are given tasks that test their commitment.

Over time, as they prove themselves, the recruits learn how to undermine society while remaining within the law. Still later, they may learn about disruptive terrorism and be trained in the use of explosives and weapons. There are numerous training camps around the world, including the United States, that impart combat skills to extremists. A glance through military and gun magazines usually reveals several advertisements for such facilities. The most serious training camps, however, are located in the Middle East. There, professional terrorist training—sponsored by Libya, Syria, and Iran—includes suicide assaults, aircraft hijacking, booby traps, and guerrilla warfare tactics.

The amount of information available to aspiring terrorists is truly astounding. A visit to the library or a flip through the pages of a mail order catalog can result in books and manuals on improvised explosive devices, silent killing techniques, combat tactics, and more. Much of this information is now making its way onto the Internet, where anyone can have access to it 24 hours a day with just a few keystrokes. *SF Tomajczyk*

For non-students and the proverbial loners, who are inspired to action either by the deeds of others or out of personal frustration with the way things are in society, training takes the form of books and manuals. There is an abundance of published information available for the asking. With a telephone and a credit card, a would-be terrorist can acquire detailed manuals on improvised explosive devices, sniping, hand-to-hand combat, and silent killing methods. Still other books on the market teach how to make poisons, effect deadly ambushes, and create a new identity and successfully evade law enforcement.

It is truly mind-boggling that such information is so easily obtainable. Yet, that is just one price of living in an open society.

Agents of Change

As implied earlier, terrorists are agents of change. They use violence and fear to achieve an objective. It is that goal that drives them to threaten, frighten, kill, and destroy—it's at the core of everything they do. Interestingly, terrorists seem to share common goals with each other, whether they are located in Baghdad, Iraq, or Bagdad, Arizona. Examples include

- Seize political power and/or overthrow a regime.
- Win a specific concession through coercive bargaining (e.g., free prisoners).
- Demoralize society by showing a government's inability to protect its citizens.
- Obtain recognition for the group's cause.
- Harass, weaken, or embarrass the government, military, or law enforcement.
- Prevent legislation from being enacted.
- Extract revenge.
- Effect a change in government via civil war, revolution, or war between nations.
- Influence policy decision making.

Such aspirations encourage like-minded individuals to band together. These groups operate either alone or under the control of a government. The Department of State maintains profiles on more than 50 key terrorist groups internationally, many of which are sponsored by various nations. These groups tend to be well-organized, highly trained, and strongly financed. They possess tremendous resources (e.g., weapons, supplies, safe houses), and operate fairly openly, especially in areas of the world where the public supports their efforts.

Correspondingly, within the borders of the United States, the FBI keeps an eye on hundreds of extremist groups and militias. The larger, more established and visible groups (e.g., Posse Comitatus, Christian Patriots Defense League, Aryan Nations) are similar to their international peers, but they possess fewer resources and operate much more clandestinely.

And then there are a multitude of smaller groups monitored by local law enforcement that have very limited resources, are highly mobile, and are nearly invisible to the U.S. public. Examples include the Hillsborough Troop of Dragoons, National Socialist

Seven sticks of TNT with a mercury-switch detonator create a low-tech terrorist weapon that is easy to hide just about anywhere. Yet it can do tremendous damage and influence national policies. *SF Tomajczyk*

Liberation Front, National Strike Force, and New Order Legion.

Regardless of the size of terrorist groups, they nearly always organize themselves into small cells of a dozen or so members for security reasons. Among some organizations, it is common practice to divide a cell into two functional ones when they reach six members. Those with military experience will recognize this tactic from insurgency training.

Regardless of how many people make up a unit, cells are kept in the dark about the locations and activities of other cells. That way if a cell is taken down by law enforcement, the entire organization is not compromised. On a day-to-day basis, the cell members blindly carry out their assignments as ordered, often not understanding how their actions fit into the larger scheme of things. For example, a cell could be ordered to blow up a bridge, not knowing that it will serve as a distraction for a bank heist.

There is another, new way in which terrorists are organizing themselves. Groups now hire guerrillas to commit a specific act of terrorism and then quickly disband. This approach is being used by some Moslem extremists. Often, these terrorists do not claim responsibility for their bloody acts. According to the FBI, it is likely that this type of decentralized organizational model was used in the 1993 World Trade Center bombing. If so, it would explain why so many defendants in the Sheik Abdul Rahman terrorism case had different countries of origin.

It is common for terrorists to help each other out by sharing weapons, money, supplies, expertise, and safe havens. This cooperation is aroused by the simple desire to survive. As a group moves from place to place to evade police and maintain operational security, it loses its ability to be self-sufficient. The group then relies on others for help. Extremist groups in the United States often assist one another in this fashion. For instance, the neo-Nazi group The Order, which wrecked havoc in the western United States during the 1980s, routinely donated money it stole to fellow extremists, including Aryan Nations and the National Alliance.

The United States: Between the Devil and the Deep Blue Sea

The United States is vulnerable to terrorism. Why? First, it is an open, democratic society that preserves its citizens' liberties and allows freedom of movement. Second, it is a large nation. Encompassing some 3.5 million square miles of urban and rural areas, the United States is simply too porous to be adequately policed. Third, Americans don't believe that terrorism can happen to them. Hence, they do not take the precautions they should. And last, there is an abundance of unprotected targets for terrorists to choose from: railway stations, airports, electric power plants, dams, communication facilities, tunnels, government buildings.

Looking at the electric power industry alone, there are 3,500 utility companies, 11,000 power generating facilities, and 365,000 miles of overhead electric lines of 66,000 volts or more. They are all sitting

The United States is vulnerable to terrorism. For example, many of our nation's pipelines are above ground, which facilitates terrorist attacks on them. If the right areas are blown up, it could cause a long-term oil shortage, resulting in outrageous gas prices and gas station lines longer than any of us could imagine. *U.S. Army*

ducks for a terrorist assault. A coordinated attack by terrorists on several substations using homemade bombs could easily knock out power in a large region. A General Accounting Office study confirms this.

A quick look at the U.S. pipeline system reveals a similar vulnerability. Three major pipelines supply more than 4.5 million barrels of petroleum each day for domestic use: Capline, Colonial, and Trans-Alaska. All are easy targets for sabotage by terrorists since the pipes are located above-ground, run through remote areas of the nation, and are largely unprotected. In fact, government investigations reveal that physical security at most key facilities (e.g., pump stations) is inadequate. Should saboteurs destroy one of

these critical locations, it could take six months or longer for repairs to be made.

Don't think it can happen? Think again. In 1977, the Trans-Alaska pipeline was bombed by saboteurs. Fortunately, no oil was lost and no shutdown was required, since the pipeline wall had not been penetrated by the blast. The saboteurs, however, learned from their mistakes. In 1978, they bombed the pipeline again. This time the explosion worked: About 15,000 barrels of oil were spilled, and the line was shut down for 21 hours. That was small potatoes compared to the damage that could have been done by a group of terrorists intent on laying waste.

Lightly defended targets: That's what terrorists look for to ensure their attack is successful. The June 1996 bombing of U.S. military personnel living in Khobar Towers on King Abdul Aziz Air Base in Saudi Arabia exemplifies this. The building was located right next to a main road. The terrorists simply drove up in a fuel truck and ran off before it exploded with the force of 20,000 pounds of TNT. Nineteen airmen died. *U.S. Department of Defense*

Eeenie, Meenie, Miney, Moe

So how do tangos go about selecting a target? Surprisingly, it's more complex than most of us would believe. Terrorists don't make hasty or arbitrary decisions. From the testimony of terrorists, law enforcement officials have learned that target selection is done with care. First, terrorists find politically suitable targets. They select a company, government, organization, or person that they believe is an adversary and, hence, deserves to be punished. Once these "guilty" targets have been identified, the terrorists then determine which one is the most vulnerable—they don't want to fail. Their research efforts may include casing the site, obtaining blueprints, taking photographs, and monitoring security. In some instances, they may even take a job with the targeted company, just to have access to inside information.

In 1978, a domestic extremist group plotted to board and steal the USS *Trepang* and then fire its nuclear missiles against an unnamed city unless they were paid a huge ransom. Fortunately, the FBI thwarted the plot. A humorous aside: The *Trepang* is an attack submarine, not a ballistic-missile submarine. The terrorists obviously weren't too swift. *U.S. Navy*

Of all the factors terrorists consider when selecting a target, one prevails over all others: The target must be lightly defended. This explains the World Trade Center and Murrah Federal Building bombings. Security at both sites was nonexistent. In 1993, the FBI arrested several followers of Sheik Omar Abdel Rahman who were plotting to wage a Holy War against the United States. These individuals had planned to blow up tunnels, bridges, buildings, and landmarks in New York City. All of these targets had one thing in common: They were lightly defended.

When do terrorists strike? Anytime they feel like it, although their attacks tend to coincide with times when security is low and/or when the greatest bloodshed can be attained.

Terrorists also like to do their dirty deeds on important anniversary dates, such as the anniversary of the death of a terror group martyr. In the United States, April 19 has great significance to extremists. On April 19, 1775, the opening salvos of America's Revolutionary War began when Minutemen battled British troops at Lexington and Concord. On April 19, 1985, FBI agents raided the fortified compound of the extremist group known as the CSA. On April 19, 1993, the siege with Branch Davidians at Waco ended with flames and the death of 82 cult members. On April 19, 1995, white supremacist Richard Wayne Snell was executed for murder. And April 19, 1995, was also when the Oklahoma City bombing occurred.

Wading Knee-Deep in Blood

Terrorism has become much bloodier. Terrorists don't seem to think twice about inflicting casualties. A reason for this is that physical security at high-risk targets has improved, thereby forcing terrorists to turn their aggressions against soft targets, namely, people. To today's terrorists, there is no such thing as an innocent bystander. The expression "If you're not part of the solution, you're part of the problem," aptly describes the terrorist mind-set. Thus, if you are not helping them in their cause, you are fair game for their bullets and bombs.

Journalists are another reason why terrorism is bloodier. Reporters routinely cover the horror of mutilated body parts, and terrorists know it. In fact, most terrorist groups orchestrate their attacks to draw the attention of the media. By targeting people instead of buildings or planes, they not only guarantee coverage by the press but also, more importantly, intensify the public's fear. This two-prong approach nearly ensures that terrorists will achieve their goals. As cold as it may sound, the slaughtered victims mean absolutely nothing to them. The message behind their violent actions are directed at the people *watching*, not the targets.

A New Type of Terrorist

When Americans think of terrorists, they picture a menacing-looking foreigner with a bandanna pulled up around his face and carrying a machine gun. Because Americans never see this caricature as they go about their daily lives, they believe that terrorists are not in their midst. Unfortunately, they couldn't be more wrong.

Foreign terrorists *are* operating on U.S. soil. For example, Abu Nidal, which the State Department considers to be the world's most dangerous terrorist group, had three members arrested in Missouri and Wisconsin for plotting to kill Jews and blow up the Israeli Embassy in Washington, D.C. HAMAS, an Islamic extremist organization, supposedly has its political command located in Arlington, Virginia. Two of its activists, both from Illinois, were arrested in Israel for attempting to restructure the organization. And Al-Fuqra, a Black Muslim sect, has been operating in the United States for more than 15 years. The group has been linked to terrorist violence in Arizona, Colorado, Pennsylvania, the Pacific Northwest, and Toronto, Canada.

Supplementing these terrorists is a domestic breed of anarchist. They are citizens who are disgruntled with society, and who have bonded together to commiserate and take action. They are your friendly neighbors by day and covert commandos at night. They are your bankers, store managers, firefighters, police officers, barbers, farmers. They come across as being friendly, committed, and patriotic, not to mention opinionated. All of us would like to make their acquaintance. Yet, this new breed is violently dangerous when cornered.

This movement is known as extremism. For each social, political, and economic concern that exists, there is an organized group of Americans opposed to it and willing to resort to violence to change the system. These groups blame others for the mess that the world is in.

For example, Aryan Nations, the Ku Klux Klan, and the National Socialists blame the United States' problems on blacks (a.k.a. Mud People), Jews, and minorities. If only the whites could reestablish their natural superiority, they argue, everything would be made better again. Some have gone so far as to establish a point system for killing minorities, in an effort to encourage the cleansing of society. During its reign in the 1980s, The Order offered Aryan Warriors a sixth of a point for a dead Jew. Assassinating the President of the United States, however, was worth a full point.

On the other hand, organizations like the African People's Party and the Junta of Militant Organizations, demand that blacks receive self-determination and independent nationhood. They firmly believe that the United States has an unspoken policy to enslave, conquer, and eliminate all non-white people. Some even proclaim that the virus that causes AIDS was created by the United States in an effort to kill blacks.

On the economic ticket, extremists target the Federal Reserve system, the tax system, and welfare. These individuals feel that the government is too regulatory, that they are not required to pay taxes, and that the Federal Reserve is controlled by powerful international financiers who profit at each American's expense. Many of them also believe that two elite groups—the Trilateralists and Bilderbergers—are secretly orchestrating the formation of a world government to which all nations will be subservient by the year 2000. Extremists claim that these two powerful groups—whose members are reported to include Henry Kissinger, David Rockefeller, Bill Clinton, King Carl Gustav of Sweden, Peter Jennings, James Baker, and George Bush—have been responsible for wars and taxes in their effort to establish a New World Order. To thwart this endeavor, extremists have organized into groups devoted to radical decentralization.

One such group, Posse Comitatus, believes that the locus of government should be at the county level and that the county sheriff should be the highest official they have to recognize and respond to. Members of this group have had several conflicts through the years with officials over taxes and weapons.

At the other extreme, the American Militia Organization intends to take over the United States and return the power back to "we the people." This group is training and equipping its members to resist invasion, oppression, and tyranny. William Pierce, a supporter of the militia's beliefs, wrote a book called *The Turner Diaries*, which outlines a scenario for taking over the U.S. government. The book has served as a handbook for numerous extremist groups, including The Order. In fact, there are many similarities between the Oklahoma City bomb-

The Turner Diaries is a popular read among anti-government extremist groups. The book details how small bands of so-called "patriots" wage a war against the federal government, kill minorities, and establish themselves as the nation's governing body. *SF Tomajczyk*

For 18 years, the Unabomber wrecked havoc around the United States, killing three and injuring 23 with homemade bombs sent through the mail to people who had ties to airlines, universities, and technology. In April 1996, Theodore Kaczynski was arrested by the FBI in his remote 10-by-12-foot Montana cabin. He was eventually charged in seven of the 16 bombings linked to the Unabomber. *U.S. Federal Bureau of Investigation*

ing and the bombing incident detailed in *The Turner Diaries*. For example, both bombings were of federal buildings, happened just after 9:00 A.M., and involved truck bombs carrying about 4,600 pounds of explosives made from fuel oil and ammonium nitrate fertilizer. Coincidence?

The Compound Dwellers

And then you have the so-called "survivalists," who are convinced that the world is coming to an end and that they will have to fight the forces of evil during Armageddon. (Trust me, you will hear more about them as we approach the year 2000.) In preparation, they have established compounds in remote areas of the country and are hoarding supplies and weapons. They are ready to pull the trigger at a moment's notice against people whom they consider to be evil.

The Covenant, the Sword, and the Arm of the Lord (CSA) was one such group. In 1976, CSA built a fortified compound on 224-acres in Missouri in anticipation of the coming Tribulation. They surrendered to the FBI in a 1985 raid. Upon searching the compound, the FBI made a chilling discovery: a laboratory that manufactured cyanide. CSA had been producing this deadly chemical with the intent of poisoning the water supply of an unnamed city.

Today, dozens of extremist groups have compounds hidden all over the United States. For instance, the Christian Patriots Defense League has a 232-acre compound located near Licking, Missouri, as well as paramilitary training facilities in Illinois and West Virginia. Similarly, the white supremacist group National Alliance has a 346-acre compound in Pocahontas County, West Virginia. And the largest known compound in the United States, the 1,000-acre "Schell City," is located on the Osage River in Missouri. The concept of entrenchment is not lost on foreign terrorists. Al-Fuqra has compounds in Colorado, South Carolina, California, and New York.

As part of my research for this book, I corresponded with several survivalists. I was amazed by their determination to overthrow the so-called "New World Order" and to survive Armageddon. They have concealed themselves throughout the United States and are stockpiling food, water, and supplies to last them for months. Many, in fact, are better armed than our law enforcement agencies. (One correspondent boasted that his group has formed units that would shame Ranger and SEAL teams.) Their arsenals, which are strategically buried inside waterproof containers, include assault rifles, machine guns, automatic pistols and grenades. Additionally, many have night-vision devices, anti-personnel mines and chemical warfare equipment at their disposal. When the time comes, they won't think twice about putting these tools of war to use—no matter who's in their way.

CHAPTER TWO

Monitoring Terrorists

The best defense against terrorism is advance warning, and that's where intelligence comes into play. There are 25 government agencies involved in defeating terrorism in the United States. Many of these agencies play an important role in the intelligence web, quietly monitoring the whereabouts of known or suspected terrorists around the world. Through infiltration and high-tech surveillance methods, they discover what plans terrorist groups have and then work with other agencies to foil them.

During the Reagan Administration, three federal agencies were assigned "lead agency" status in the fight against terrorism. The FBI is responsible for preventing, interdicting, and investigating terrorist activities in the United States. It also has the authority to arrest those whose deadly actions involve Americans, regardless of where the act occurs. Meanwhile, the Department of State is responsible for incidents that take place outside

Plane hijackings are a great way to get the world's attention, and terrorists know it. In November 1996, three terrorists took control of an Ethiopian Airlines 767. The plane crashed in the Indian Ocean off the coast of Grand Comore when it ran out of fuel, killing 125 people aboard, including the three terrorists. In the United States, the Federal Aviation Administration is responsible for handling terrorist incidents that occur aboard aircraft. *SF Tomajczyk*

It's impossible to prevent every act of terrorism from occurring, but there are things that can be done to reduce the risk. One basic method is to keep an eye out for explosives, such as checking the underside of a vehicle with a mirror before it is allowed to pass through a security area. *U.S. Army*

the United States. It orchestrates the use of military units, such as Delta Force and DevGroup, in counterterrorist actions overseas.

The third player is the Federal Aviation Administration (FAA), which handles acts of terrorism aboard aircraft in flight. The FAA also has a Technical Center in Atlantic City, New Jersey, that develops systems and devices to prevent aviation-related hijacking

Key Assets Used in the Fight
Against Terrorists

CRDCOM
TEU

Secret Service
CAT/CST

CIA/CTC
Dept. of State
Navy ATAC
Dept. of Justice
Andrews AFB
NEST

FBI HRT

Technical
Escort
Unit (TEU)

H&K

Lawrence
Livermore
National Lab

Area 51

NEST

Los Alamos
National Lab

166th SOAR

Delta Force
(SOC)

Camp
Pendleton

DoE SRT
Training Facility

TEU

BATF
SRT

32nd OG

Dev Group
USMC FAST
Camp Peary

75th Ranger
Regiment

FLETC

NAVSPECWAR

El Paso Intelligence
Center (EPIC)

USMS SOG

Eglin AFB
Hurlburt Field

US Special
Operations
Command

Nationwide Assets
US Customs Service
FBI Field Offices
US Border Patrol
US Coast Guard
SWAT Teams
US Immigration &
Naturalization Service

predict a terrorist's psychology and decision making process, as well as his modus operandi.

Like the CIA, the Department of State is involved in monitoring terrorists overseas. It operates a database that contains a chronology of important terrorist incidents in each country around the world, as well as personality profiles of terrorists who might be a threat to Americans. The database also features information on terrorist groups and country threat assessments.

As for domestic terrorism, the FBI collects and computerizes information about individuals and groups that pose a potential threat to the United States. One such on-line computer database, the Terrorist Information System (TIS), is used by the FBI's Terrorist Research & Analytical Center to support the Bureau's counterterrorism program. (The center analyzes information collected on terrorists active in the United States and generates forecasts of potential threats.) The TIS has over 200,000 individuals and more than 3,000 organizations on file. TIS allows the FBI to rapidly retrieve information and to make links between persons, groups, or events.

and sabotage. These include such things as explosives detection and airport security.

This three-pronged system works well, although there is absolutely no way every act of terrorism can be thwarted. That's because there is no defense against the spontaneous act of violence say, for example, a distraught person who decides to blow up a federal building in an effort to change the IRS tax code. In situations like that, physical security measures—barriers, closed circuit TVs, ID cards, armed guards—are relied on to obstruct the person as best they can.

Smile! You're on Magnetic Media

Information about terrorists is maintained on computer databases. The largest database in the world is "Kommissar," a German-based computer system that provides backgrounds on more than 10 million suspected terrorists. Information stored in the database includes photographs of the terrorists, their fingerprints, dental records, voiceprints, and a variety of other data. In the United States, the CIA operates a similar computer system, which is known as Desist.

The CIA also maintains FITE, or File of International Terrorist Events. This database is used by analysts to forecast future terrorist behavior on the basis of previous incidents. For example, analysts can

INTERPOL represents a huge international network where member nations can give each other a heads-up about the whereabouts and going-ons of terrorists, as well as an advance warning of impending violence. All terrorist-related alerts and documents are given highest priority so that lives may be saved.
SF Tomajczyk

ANTITERRORIST ALERT CENTER

The Navy's Antiterrorist Alert Center is hidden behind a locked, reinforced door on the fourth floor of a nondescript brick building, overlooking the Anacostia River in Washington, D.C. To enter, you need to have the right security clearance, know the right codes, and possess the right ID card. Once inside, you are confronted by a bustling office of intelligence officers, analysts, and country experts who keep track of terrorist threats around the world.

The Navy's Antiterrorist Alert Center is hidden inside this brick building at the Washington Navy Yard in Washington, D.C. Don't even think about paying an unexpected visit; the numerous armed guards will stop you and politely escort you out. *SF Tomajczyk*

Operated by the Naval Criminal Investigative Service, ATAC is responsible for providing warnings of potential terrorist attacks that threaten Navy personnel or assets worldwide. At any given time, the Navy has hundreds of ships and thousands of personnel dispersed to the far corners of the globe. All make attractive targets to terrorists. The Navy also has conventional and nuclear weapons that some terrorists would love to get their hands on. The center was established in December 1983 in response to a number of terrorist acts directed against the Navy, including the murders of naval officers in Greece and Central America. That year also marked Hizballah's bloody attack on the Marine Barracks in Beirut.

ATAC produces a daily summary of terrorist activity around the world, and periodically conducts in-depth analysis on a country, terrorist group, or trend that may impact Navy personnel. The center collects intelligence from field agents, intercepted signals, photographs, satellite imagery, and so on. "NCIS has special agents at every major naval installation around the world," says LCDR Steven L. Pagett, Chief of the Antiterrorist Alert Center. "Collecting intelligence on terrorist activities is just one aspect of their jobs. They are also involved in counter-intelligence, drug interdiction, criminal activities . . . anything that potentially could be a threat to Department of the Navy assets."

In the event of an impending attack, or if a terrorist act occurs that has consequence, ATAC can send out an alert (a.k.a. Spot Report) to all affected naval commands within 25 minutes.

Commanders of naval amphibious readiness groups and battle groups are briefed by ATAC intelligence officers about potential terrorist threats they may encounter before they set sail. They are then updated as conditions warrant and as the group of warships moves from one theater to another (e.g., sailing from the Pacific Ocean into the Indian Ocean). Terrorist threats change from region to region.

ATAC was the first 24-hour antiterrorism watch in the U.S. intelligence community. The actual watch is stood by Navy and Marine Corps personnel who work 12-hour shifts, around the clock. Today, the CIA, Defense Intelligence Agency, National Security Agency, Coast Guard, State Department, and the U.S. Special Operations Command supplement ATAC's efforts with their own 24-hour command centers. Although they share information with each other, only ATAC is dedicated to protecting naval assets.

One other computer database worth mentioning is the Treasury Enforcement Communications System (TECSII). This system contains descriptions and passport information about people who have aroused suspicions on the part of Customs or INS agents when they presented themselves at a port of entry. TECSII is linked to law enforcement databases in all 50 states.

INTERPOL: The World's Watchman

On a day-to-day basis, there are several agencies that stand quiet vigil in defense against acts of terrorism. Perhaps the largest is the International Criminal Police Organization (INTERPOL), which is headquartered in St. Cloud, France. INTERPOL is an association of 142 countries that share information with each other and provide mutual assistance in deterring international crimes. Each member nation has a National Central Bureau that serves as the liaison between that country's law enforcement agencies and the INTERPOL network. The U.S. bureau is known as the United States National Central Bureau (USNCB). It is a separate agency within the U.S. Department of Justice. The chief of the USNCB reports to the Associate Attorney General.

All requests for information from the USNCB are screened to ensure that the request complies with certain criteria. Only two criteria must be met in order for the USNCB to respond to a request for counterterrorist information: First, the request must be from a legitimate law enforcement agency or INTERPOL member country; and second, the request must relate to an international investigation, even if it does not involve a specific criminal incident or provide details of a crime. By contrast, requests for non-terrorist information must meet six criteria.

Messages come to the USNCB by mail, telephone, FAX, computer link, or the international INTERPOL radio system. As messages are received, each is assigned a priority rating according to its urgency. All terrorist-related messages are assigned a priority level of "urgent" or "critical urgent."

Over the years, the USNCB has provided law enforcement agencies worldwide with counterterror-

The CIA's Counterterrorist Center is located at CIA Headquarters in Langley, Virginia. The center constantly monitors the whereabouts of known and suspected terrorists around the world. Other sections at the CIA are also involved in counterterrorism activities, such as infiltrating foreign terrorist groups to learn of their future plans. *U.S. Central Intelligence Agency*

ism information, including criminal records check, suspect descriptions, license and auto checks, addresses, fingerprints, and passport data. Here are just four examples of the thousands of cases the USNCB has been involved with:

- The Department of Justice requested through the USNCB that foreign authorities hold the PLO terrorists involved in the hijacking of the *Achille Lauro*.
- The FAA sent out an alert advising of information on a planned hijacking. The information was received from airline sources.
- The U.S. Border Patrol requested a criminal history check on a person who was apprehended carrying a bomb.
- An unidentified country requested information about a school located in the United States that offers training in guerrilla warfare and the use of explosives and firearms.

International cooperation also resulted in the discovery of a plot to blow up the U.S. Embassy in Rome in 1984. Swiss police arrested a Lebanese man at the Zurich airport after finding 2 pounds of explosives in his

SF Tomajczyk

AIRPORT SECURITY

Compared to the rest of the world, airline security in the United States is lax. Of the 600 commerical service airports in the United States, most use antiquated X-ray machines, few interrogate passengers about themselves and/or their itinerary, and nearly none have scanners that can detect plastic explosives. In fact, some airports don't even have fences around them to keep people out. This careless atmosphere is often worse in small airports, which worries many aviation experts.

"Once people get through security, they're behind the security network nationwide," says Fred Testa, director of the Manchester Airport. "For this reason, it's more important to beef up security at smaller airports around the United States than larger ones. For example, a small airport may have only one security person and very little equipment. They may not even X-ray your bag. Once you pass through, you're never checked again. You're behind the security network. You're free to fly to Chicago, Los Angeles, or wherever without any further checking. This is where terrorists can easily enter the system."

More maddening than this lackadaisical approach to security is the fact that the government knows the airports aren't safe. In recent security checks, undercover agents from the FAA's Inspector General's office were able to gain entry to secure areas of selected airports 40 to 75 percent of the time. In fact, one agent even managed to slip an unarmed hand grenade through a metal detector.

Another roadblock in security is the fact that even if a terrorist act is imminent and the government knows it, an airport may not be fully aware of it. Why? Because often no one at the airport—including the airport director—has a security clearance to receive the warning. In these cases, the airport may be told that "something's going to happen." Because the specifics are not given, the airport then has to prepare for all possibilities, which stretches security to the limit. Not a very effective way to save lives.

"I'd like to see better information sharing," says Testa. "Perhaps giving key airport personnel a security clearance so they can know what's going on and can respond quickly to it."

In an effort to boost airline safety, President Clinton implemented new security measures in 1996. This included such efforts as inspecting baggage compartments and cabins of all planes flying in and out of the United States, tougher scrutiny of all luggage, more screening of mail, and passengers having to show a photo ID. Efforts are also underway to design a bomb-proof luggage compartment. One design features "blow-out" panels, which direct a bomb's blast away from passengers and the plane's vital systems.

Additionally, the government is trying to get plastic explosive "sniffers" in each airport. Plastic explosives are very difficult to detect. In fact, they can be molded to look like everyday items. It was such a devise—a modified radio—that blew up Pan Am flight 103 over Lockerbie. The highest risk airports—the 19 so-called "Category X" airports like JFK, Dulles, and LAX—are receiving these detectors first. Keep your fingers crossed that the machines are passed out fast enough. By their nature, terrorists are opportunists.

THE DOGS OF WAR

Dogs play a major role in the fight against terrorism. The Secret Service, Customs Service, Park Police, the military, and numerous law enforcement agencies depend on the dog's keen sense of smell to find bombs hidden by terrorists and other wackos.

The U.S. Secret Service (USSS), which protects the President and other dignitaries, has the largest canine bomb detection unit in the nation. Established in 1975, Canine Explosives Detection Teams search structures, vehicles, and individuals for various threats. The unit is comprised of about 30 dog/handler teams, which spend 80 percent of their time doing detection work and 20 percent performing patrol duties. The USSS gets its dogs—German Shepherd Dogs and Belgian Malinois—from a breeder in the Netherlands.

Dogs can detect an odor at concentrations 1,000 to 100,000 times lower than humans. This makes them ideal to sniff out bombs hidden by terrorists. U.S. Army

Training, which lasts 20 to 26 weeks, is done at the Secret Service's Canine Training Facility in Beltsville, Maryland. Here, the dogs learn how to deal with obstacles (e.g., ladders, windows, catwalks) and how to chase down a suspect. They also are taught to find 13 types of explosives, including RDX and Semtex. Unlike drug-detecting dogs, which are trained to bite or scratch a suspect package, USSS dogs are taught to sit when they find a potential explosive. The last thing you want a dog to do is bite and shake a bomb.

At the end of training, the dogs and their handlers join the canine patrol corps. But this does not mean that formal instruction has come to an end. Every dog returns to the Beltsville facility each week for a full day refresher course. This recertification effort is much tougher than that of other agencies. It is justified, however, since the consequences of a Secret Service dog failing in the field are much more dire.

A dog's ability to detect an explosive is determined by temperature, humidity, air currents and eddies, and so on. The handler plays a key role in working the dog in a search pattern that takes advantage of air movements and in reading changes in the dog's behavior that may signal a possible detection. A dog is never punished for a false alert.

Overall, the Secret Service's dogs detect hidden plastic explosives 75 percent of the time or better. Although that figure is not as good as 100 percent, it is still much better than never finding them. It's important to note that the canines are not the sole means used by the Secret Service to find explosives. They are just one tool of an overall bomb detection effort.

possession, as well as a ticket to Rome and an address there. Authorities in Italy were notified, and they arrested seven Lebanese students who had ties to Islamic Jihad. During the arrests, the police found a detailed map of the U.S. Embassy with notes and arrows identifying guard positions, security cameras, and barriers. The entrance to a garage located under the Marine barracks was also labeled, which lead the police to believe that the terrorists intended a suicide truck bombing.

The CIA's Role

INTERPOL and the USNCB aside, the CIA's Counterterrorism Center (CTC) is another noteworthy sentinel. Located on the sixth floor of the CIA building in Langley, Virginia, the CTC monitors the whereabouts of terrorists around the world, 24 hours a day. When a terrorist travels, the center alerts each country on his travel schedule. This permits the countries to either refuse entry to the terrorist or, if he is wanted for a crime, have him arrested when he arrives.

The CTC is staffed by more than 200 CIA employees. In addition, there are a dozen or so people assigned to the center from other federal agencies, including the FBI, Department of Defense and the National Security Agency. The center, which is essentially an aggregate of psychiatrists, explosives experts, intelligence officers, and hostage negotiators, was established in 1986 by CIA Director William Casey. He wanted to bring together each of the CIA's four directorates to address terrorism and coordinate the CIA's efforts with other agencies.

Each directorate provides a unique service to the center's overall counterterrorism effort. For example, the Directorate of Operations, the clandes-

To bring terrorists to justice, the Department of State offers up to $2 million for information leading to the arrest of a wanted militant. This poster is of Mir Aimal Kansi, a Pakistani who murdered two civilians and wounded three others with an AK-47 as they left work at the CIA building on January 25, 1993. He was arrested overseas and brought back to the United States by the FBI's Hostage Rescue Team in June 1997. *SF Tomajczyk*

tine arm of the CIA, uses its trained spies to collect foreign intelligence and conduct covert operations. More often than not, this requires infiltrating a terrorist group overseas. Meanwhile, the Directorate of Science & Technology develops technologies (e.g., video enhancement, laser communications, and satellites) that can be used to collect information about terrorist activities. They are also responsible for processing and analyzing signals intelligence and photographic intelligence to make it usable by other CIA analysts, such as those assigned to the Directorate of Intelligence.

Since the center's creation, it has been involved in numerous terrorism cases. For example, in 1987 it helped the FBI track down Fawaz Younis, a Lebanese terrorist who had hijacked a Royal Jordanian airliner at Beirut International Airport and then blown it up after releasing passengers, two of whom were Americans.

The CTC was also involved in coordinating the United States' investigation of the 1988 midair bombing of Pan Am flight 103 over Lockerbie, Scotland, which killed 259 passengers and crew members. The center was able to determine that Libyan officials ordered the bombing in retaliation for the 1986 air attack of Tripoli by U.S. military forces.

And, during the 1991 Gulf War, the CTC worked with law enforcement agencies around the world to thwart a myriad of terrorist actions that were directed against the Allies. The Center recorded some 120 terrorist acts and more than 100 terrorist threats in the months immediately following the invasion of Kuwait by Iraq. The terrorist group known as 17 November was responsible for 5 of 15 terrorist attacks against Coalition targets in Greece alone, including the assassination of a U.S. Army sergeant.

CHAPTER THREE

The Covert Commandos: Delta Force And DevGroup

> "Terrorists don't operate by any rules."
> Dick Marcinko—Founder, SEAL Team Six

Entire books have been written about Delta Force and SEAL Team Six. Hence, this book only highlights these units so that more information about important-but-little-known domestic counterterrorist teams can be featured.

As mentioned previously, the State Department is the lead agency when an act of terrorism occurs overseas. It orchestrates the military CT forces once they are deployed—in consultation and approval of the President, who is the commander-in-chief of the United States' armed forces. Within the military establishment itself, these elite units are controlled by the Joint Special Operations Command (JSOC) which, in turn, is a component of the U.S. Special Operations Command (USSOCOM). JSOC is headquartered at Pope AFB, in North Carolina.

Delta's 30-day selection process is grueling, with only about a 2- to 3-percent pass rate. Candidates endure painful confidence courses, 18-mile speed marches, and a host of other nasty tasks intended to break them mentally, physically, and emotionally. Those who pass selection undergo five months of intense CT training at "Wally World," Delta's training facility. *U.S. Army*

Assault! SEALs storm the bridge of a ship during a training exercise to hone their maritime assault tactics. When doing such a takedown, SEALs constantly move toward the bridge so that they can take control of the ship. Anyone who gets in the way of a SEAL "train" in a corridor is literally run over. The last two SEALs in the train stop to handcuff and secure the person, and then catch up with the others. *U.S. Navy*

By law, military forces cannot be used in domestic incidents unless the President issues a directive permitting it. However, after the Sarin gas attacks in Japan, in 1995, and with the ever-growing threat of Super Terrorism, pressure has increased to permit the military to respond to chemical and biological terrorist attacks on U.S. soil. Advocates point out that the military already has the proper training and equipment for such missions. Only time will tell if legislation will pass through Congress.

Following is a quick look at the military's elite counterterrorism forces.

U.S. Army 1st Special Forces Operational Detachment-Delta

Popularly known as Delta Force and less often as the Combat Development Branch or Combat Applications Group, this elite unit was the brainchild of Col. Charles Beckwith, a Special Forces officer who had once served with the British SAS in the 1960s. Beckwith was convinced that the United States needed a team to fight terrorists, conduct surgical behind-the-lines operations, gather intelligence, and provide unconventional options to low-intensity conflict situations. Fortunately, the Carter Administration saw a need for this as well; terrorists were having a field day around the world at the time. An elite U.S. force specially trained to defeat terrorists seemed ideal. Delta Force was activated in 1977. Its "coming-out" exercise was conducted at a remote 27-acre site in North Carolina, where the group had to simultaneously assault a building and an aircraft and rescue the hostages. The aircraft takedown, done just before midnight, took Delta only 30 seconds. As for the building, Delta blew the doors off their hinges and cleared each room within seven seconds. The exercise went flawlessly. Delta was operational.

The first Delta operators were selected mainly from Army Special Forces (a.k.a. Green Berets). Only 7 of the 30 who took part in the first selection course were kept. The second selection process—which broadened its search to include other branches of the Army—wasn't much better: only 5 of 60

Becoming a Delta Force operator requires a tremendous amount of training, including helicopter insertion techniques. Here, soldiers practice rappelling from a Black Hawk helicopter. *U.S. Army*

290

made it. By the third course, 14 out of 70 made it. The high attrition rate attests to the strenuous nature of Delta's selection course, which persists to this day.

Today's candidates endure a 30-day selection process that features confidence courses, 18-mile speed marches carrying a 55-pound pack, a 40-mile land navigation exercise through rugged tracts of wilderness at Camp Dawson (West Virginia), Uwharrie National Forest (North Carolina), or Nellis AFB (Nevada) in 20 hours, and a 4-hour-long interrogation by a board of Delta veterans. Only the cream of the crop are invited to stay. Those that are undergo 19 weeks of intense basic training where they learn counterterrorist skills, such as close-quarters battle, infiltration and seizure techniques, rappelling, lockpicking, covert intelligence gathering, HALO/HAHO parachuting, aircraft hostage-rescue assaults, and explosive breaching methods. They are also taught hand-to-hand combat skills, small boat insertion tactics, explosive ordnance disposal, high-speed driving techniques, and high-tech surveillance methods.

Room clearing drills are done using live ammunition in a shooting house (a.k.a. Haunted House, House of Horrors) cluttered with furniture and mannequin terrorists/hostages. The targets often have pictures of real terrorists pasted to them. Each room of the shooting house is designed to present a different hostage situation for the operators to overcome (e.g., aircraft, night fighting). The trainees practice assaults wearing different types of gear so that they become accustomed to vision and movement restrictions. The training is dangerous—accidents do happen.

When George Bush was vice president, he wanted to witness Delta Force do a takedown in the shooting house. He was invited to sit as a hostage, but the Secret Service had serious reservations. One errant bullet—a ricocheting fragment—could kill him. Delta insisted that they were trained to do surgical shooting under stress and pressure. No one would get hurt. The Secret Service still wasn't convinced, but Bush wanted to do it. So they reached a compromise: They dressed the vice president in a bulletproof vest, placed a clear bulletproof shield around him, and positioned two armed Secret Service agents on either side of him. Somewhat amused, Delta operators carried out their assault demonstration without incident.

Delta Force was originally headquartered at the old Ft. Bragg jail. The Stockade, a nine acre site that was later expanded, was affectionately known as "The Ranch," because of the propensity of some operators to wear cowboy boots and chew tobacco. Delta also had a special compound on Mott Lake at Ft. Bragg. The unit later built a multi-million dollar Special Operations Training facility (SOT), which is often referred to as "Wally World" after the theme park mentioned in a Chevy Chase movie. (This facility is also called "Fiesta Cantina" after its stucco siding.) The SOT features numerous indoor and outdoor weapons ranges (including the Range 19 complex of sniping, combat pistol and CQB gunfighting ranges), training areas for heliborne insertions, an Operations & Intelligence Center, and more. It is here that the new operators train.

Once the five-month indoctrination course is completed, the trainees are assigned to a Delta squadron and team. A squadron is comprised of four troops of 16 men each. Each troop is able to configure itself into 8-, 4-, or 2-man teams depending upon the mission. In some instances, the teams are organized by specialty, such as mountaineering or high-altitude parachuting.

Contrary to popular belief, of today's 800 or so Delta Force members, there *are* female operators. Females are assigned to an intelligence detachment known as the "Funny Platoon." They serve as intelligence operatives, infiltrating countries to recon targets for the assault forces. Four women made it through Delta Force training in the early 1980s, but left after their male counterparts hounded them out. An attempt was made again in 1990; five women qualified and are now serving in the Funny Platoon.

Delta's counterterrorism skills are kept sharp by regular cross-training exercises with other CT forces, including SAS, GSG-9, and GIGN.

A rare photo of Delta Force, taken during the December 1989 invasion of Panama to capture General Manuel Noriega. During the operation, Delta rescued American businessman Kurt Muse, who was being held hostage in Panama's notorious Modelo prison. The assault team was inserted by MH-6 mini-helicopters, piloted by the 160th SOAR. *U.S. Army*

Delta Force has also had a long and close relationship with the FBI's Hostage Rescue Team (HRT). It was the FBI that gave Delta its first SWAT training. In return, years later, Delta shared its CT skills and tradescraft secrets with the HRT, after it was established in 1982. Since then, the two units have been like blood brothers helping each other out.

In fact, in 1987, Delta was granted permission by the President to become involved in a domestic crisis in which prisoners were rioting at the federal prison in Atlanta. The HRT was deployed at the time to a similar crisis at the Oakdale prison in Louisiana and was unable to break away to address this new incident. According to Oliver "Buck" Revell, a former assistant director at the FBI, Delta was on the scene within six hours of the FBI's initial request for assistance. It was the first time that JSOC had been used in a civilian capacity. Delta was needed because they had the breaching capability and counter-sniper experience that FBI and local SWAT teams didn't

have. The prisoners, hearing rumors that Delta Force was coming in after them, quickly surrendered. Who says cons don't have brains?

Since Delta's inception, it has been successful in its missions, many of which—understandably—have been kept quiet. For example, in March 1981, an Indonesian airliner was hijacked by five terrorists and forced to land in Bangkok. An American was shot and wounded during the hijacking. The Thai government asked the United States for help in dealing with the terrorists, who were demanding the release of 85 political prisoners. Delta was flown out to resolve the incident. On the morning of March 31, Delta stormed the aircraft and killed four terrorists and captured the fifth. Their assault was approved by President Ronald Reagan just hours before he himself was shot by John Hinkley.

In August 1984, a Venezuelan DC-9 was hijacked by two terrorists on its way to the island of Curacao. The terrorists demanded $5 million for the safe release of the 79 hostages. The government in the Netherlands Antilles requested assistance from the United States, which sent a small team from Delta. Together with a Venezuelan commando unit, Delta Force stormed the aircraft and killed both terrorists, freeing the hostages unharmed.

In December 1984, Delta was again deployed to assist in a hijacking. This time it was a Kuwaiti airliner that had been hijacked by four terrorists who were believed to be affiliated with Islamic Jihad. Two Americans were killed during the hijacking. The aircraft was flown to Tehran where the terrorists demanded the release of comrades-in-arms held in Kuwaiti jails. Delta Force flew to Masirah Island to prepare for an assault. For political reasons, they had to wait for the plane to leave Iran to initiate their takedown. But it never happened: Iranian commandos stormed the plane and captured the terrorists.

Although Delta is essentially a CT unit, it performs a host of other mission profiles. For example, it provided security at the 1984 Los Angeles Olympics, the Statue of Liberty Centennial celebration in 1986, and the 1996 Atlanta Olympics. During the 1991 Gulf War, Delta Force and the SAS went behind Iraqi lines to hunt down SS-1 SCUD missile launchers so they could be destroyed by air strikes. The team also regularly furnishes protective details for high-ranking military officers and diplomats, especially those who serve in the Middle East or Central America, where violence is commonplace.

To respond quickly to incidents in the Middle East, Delta maintains a small forward-deployed unit in Germany. This team provides early intelligence from the crisis scene to the rest of Delta, flying on its way from Ft. Bragg.

On many counterterrorist missions, Delta Force works closely with Navy SEAL Teams (especially DevGroup), the Army's 160th Special Operations Aviation Regiment (a.k.a. Nightstalkers) and "Green Berets," and the Air Force's 16th Special Operations Wing and 720th Special Tactics Group. The Nightstalkers and 16th SOW provide Delta with transportation into harms way via the use of special aircraft (e.g., MH-6 Little Bird, MC-130H Combat Talon, MH-53J Pave Low). Supplementing this is Delta's own mini air force of a dozen or so AH-6 and MH-6 helicopters. These "Little Birds," which are reportedly secreted away in Virginia, are used for undercover transportation; they have fake civilian markings.

Although tire shooting houses are no longer considered to be state-of-the-art, they do come in handy when you need to practice and nothing else is around. During the 1991 Gulf War, special operations forces (e.g., Delta Force, DevGroup, "Green Berets") built this tire house in a remote area of the desert to practice CT and CQB tactics. *U.S. Army*

To become a member of DevGroup, you first have to become a SEAL. And that means having to survive BUD/S, an arduous 26-week basic training course held in Coronado, California. In this photo, candidates perform small boat drills on a raw, stormy day. But as they say, you don't gotta like it, you just gotta do it. All new SEALs receive counterterrorism training following BUD/S, during SEAL Tactical Training (STT). *U.S. Navy*

Prior to deploying on a mission, it is not unusual for Delta Force to build mock-ups of their target at a remote area of Ft. Bragg, the CIA's Camp Peary (Virginia), or the Air Force's Eglin AFB (Florida) to practice their assault choreography. In fact, they built a model of the Tehran embassy compound at Camp Peary in 1980 before heading to Iran on their rescue mission. As mentioned in the next few chapters, this is fairly common practice throughout the counterterrorist arena.

U.S. Navy SEALs and DevGroup

Formerly known as SEAL Team Six, this unit changed its name after SEAL Team Six commander Richard Marcinko published the book *Rogue Warrior*, in 1992, about his military experiences. The Navy felt that the book, an international bestseller that revealed the inner workings of this unit, brought too

much attention to SEAL Team Six. To get out of the spotlight, naval special warfare (NAVSPECWAR) officials gave the team an innocuous sounding title—Development Group, or DevGroup for short—and buried it in the organizational charts. This allowed the Navy's public affairs staff to honestly tell the public that SEAL Team Six did *not* exist.

And yet it does. This so-called "public secret" is known by just about everyone in the military and law enforcement community. DevGroup is the old SEAL Team Six, with essentially the same mission and responsibilities.

SEAL Team Six was established in 1980, just months after the failed attempt to free U.S. hostages in Iran. Dick Marcinko, who was assigned to the Pentagon at the time, working on a follow-up rescue plan, added a nonexistent SEAL element to the joint task force plan. The plan was eventually approved and Marcinko received permission to create SEAL Team Six, his ghost unit. Although the rescue plan was never carried out—the hostages were released as Ronald Reagan took the oath as President—the team became operational in January 1981. Its certification mission involved recovering a stolen nuclear device from terrorists. SEAL Six sent 56 operators in. They performed a high-altitude, high-opening parachute jump from an aircraft at night, and glided 10 miles to the objective: Vieques Island, seven miles east of Puerto Rico. Needless to say, the assault was a tremendous success.

SEAL Team Six (a.k.a. The Mob) established its headquarters and training complex at the Dam Neck Fleet Combat Training Center (Virginia). It's facilities include a $4 million indoor pool complex, and a $3.1 million pistol/rifle range with an attached helicopter landing pad. The unit, which is administratively attached to Naval Special Warfare Group Two, but receives its directives from JSOC, made a commitment to deploy within four hours notice to anywhere in the world. The team's operators come from existing SEAL Teams. They train exclusively for CT missions in the maritime arena, such as ship boardings and oil rig takedowns. The operators are so highly trained, that they are sometimes referred to as "Jedi." Those of you who have seen *Star Wars* know why.

It should be noted that *all* SEAL Teams receive training in counterterrorism. (Some, like SEAL Teams 1 and 5, regularly use paintball guns for close-quarters combat exercises.) This training allows forward-deployed SEAL platoons to respond to a terrorist incident and either resolve it or manage it until DevGroup arrives.

Like all elite CT forces, DevGroup does a tremendous amount of shooting and specialized training. Its operators climb oil rigs in the Gulf of Mexico, parachute in Arizona, chase and board ships all over the world, conduct CQB drills in a remote corner of Eglin AFB in Florida, and do combat shooting at the Mid-South Institute in Mississippi. The team also

The Mark VIII transports SEALs underwater to a target. The 21-foot-long mini-sub holds four combat swimmers in the rear compartment, while being operated by a pilot and navigator in the forward compartment. This SEAL Delivery Vehicle (SDV) is propelled at six knots by an electric motor and features an on-board breathing/intercom system. It can be transported worldwide by surface ships or in Dry Deck Shelters atop modified Sturgeon- and Ethan Allen-class submarines. A plan was developed to use SDVs to do a sneak attack on the passenger liner *Achille Lauro* in 1985. *U.S. Navy*

A Huey rigged for rappelling insertions. Note that both operators are equally balanced outside the helicopter to keep it steady. At a command, they will drop simultaneously to the ground. If one drops before the other, the helicopter can be thrown off station, and potentially cause one or both of the operators to lose control. *U.S. Department of Defense*

A sight no terrorist wants to see: A fire team of four SEALs quietly emerges from the water armed with MP5 submachine guns. SEALs and DevGroup provided maritime security at the Olympic games held in Los Angeles and Atlanta. They ensured that Olympic venue water bodies were safe for competition, and not booby-trapped by terrorists. They provided similar services during the 1996 Republican National Convention in San Diego. *STTU*

The Fast Attack Vehicle is used by Delta and DevGroup for "shoot and scoot" missions. It seats three and is armed with a .50 caliber machine gun and/or a pair of 7.62-mm machine guns. The 2,100-pound FAV is capable of driving cross-country at 80 mph, as well as traversing sand berms more than 6 feet high. Its agility makes it a perfect CT weapon for open environments, like the desert or prairie. *STTU*

cross-trains with the SAS, SBS, GSG-9, and GIGN on a fairly regular basis. And, like Delta Force, DevGroup trains with the FBI's Hostage Rescue Team, sharing its knowledge with them about maritime assaults and underwater reconnaissance techniques.

Actually, the relationship between SEAL Six and the FBI was begun even before the HRT was formed. In the early 1980s, Norwegian cruise lines was concerned about maritime terrorism. It contacted the FBI and invited it to stage a rescue training exercise on one of the Norwegian ships, which was in Jacksonville for a refitting. The FBI and SEAL Team Six could "play" aboard the ship as it sailed to Miami. So a scenario was developed: FBI terrorists would take control of the ship and take the crew hostage and SEAL Team Six would do an assault. John Simeone, who a few years later would become deputy commander of the HRT, was appointed as the lead terrorist. He was in the ship's bridge watching the radar scope when the assault occurred in the middle of the night. Even though he knew both sides of the scenario (he had to, to prevent accidents from happening), he was still shocked by the speed and violence of the takedown.

"Not until the last minute did you really hear them," he said. The helicopters were downwind of the ship, flying low over the water to avoid detection. They flared up at the last second, dropped off the assault teams and were gone. Simultaneously, raiding craft came alongside the ship and operators climbed aboard using caving ladders and extendible painter poles. Within seconds, the entire ship was under attack. SEAL Six hit hard and fast. It was an impressive demonstration, one that Simeone would remember for future operations when he would be with the HRT.

In 1985, the cruise ship *Achille Lauro* was hijacked by four terrorists from the Palestine Liberation Front. SEAL Team Six and Delta Force were deployed to Sicily in case an assault was needed. By coincidence, a SEAL Delivery Vehicle (SDV) team happened to be in the Med on a training exercise, just a few hours away from the ship. SDVs are mini-submarines

SEALs practice doing CQB and room-clearing drills in a makeshift shooting house. Hallways are dangerous since there is limited space for the SEALs to maneuver themselves and their weapons. A determined terrorist can wipe out an entire assault team in a hallway if care is not taken. For this reason, CT forces sometimes resort to blowing holes through the walls (a.k.a. mouseholes) and moving room to room in that manner. *STTU*

that covertly transport SEALs underwater. A plan was drawn up in which this particular SDV team would approach the *Achille Lauro* and either drop off an assault team of four SEALs or foul the ship's screws with chains so that the ship could not get underway. It seemed like a good plan, but the terrorists killed 69-year-old Leon Klinghoffer, an American passenger, and forced the ship to head for Egypt. The underwater assault was dropped.

Another plan took its place: SEAL Team Six would quietly board and assault the *Achille Lauro* at

night, using raiding craft with silenced engines once it arrived at Port Said, Egypt. The Italian elite CT forces—GIS and COMSUBIN—would act as backup, recognizing that Six had the better equipment and training for a maritime assault. Once the assault was over, the Italian units would take over, taking credit while Six left by the proverbial back door. And so, members of SEAL Team Six gathered aboard the amphibious assault ship USS *Iwo Jima* in preparation for the takedown. Unfortunately, the Egyptian government negotiated with the terrorists, offering them

Aerial ballet, the SEAL way. A Seahawk helicopter plucks two SEALs from the water during a training exercise. It is not known if this helicopter is part of the Light Attack Helicopter Squadrons, two elite NAVSPECWAR units (Red Wolves, Firehawks) that support SEALs on missions. Also, note the tubular-shaped Dry Deck Shelter on the rear of the submarine; it holds SDVs. *U.S. Navy*

safe passage out of Egypt if they would release the ship and its passengers. The terrorists accepted the terms, thereby—unwittingly—halting SEAL Team Six's assault plans with just hours to spare.

The terrorists boarded a 737 (which also had four members of Egypt's elite military CT unit Force 777 aboard), and headed for Tunis, which refused the plane permission to land. They then headed for Libya, which also said "no" to the terrorists. As the plane turned and headed for Athens, it was intercepted by four U.S. F-14s and forced to land at the NATO air base in Sigonella, Sicily. SEAL Team Six greeted the plane and terrorists with submachine guns. Six, in turn, was surrounded by Italian military forces, who demanded custody of the terrorists. SEAL Team Six refused. Meanwhile, inside the plane, Force 777 commandos said they would not surrender to anyone, American or Italian. It was a standoff that very nearly ended in a bloodbath had not Secretary of State George Schultz ordered the SEALs to stand down and allow the Italians to have the terrorists. He had received assurances from the Italian government that the terrorists would stand trial for murder.

Unfortunately, Rome allowed the accused mastermind, Abu Abbas, to leave the country since he had an Iraqi diplomatic passport. He and four others (not including another member of the terrorist group who fled Italy while on approved release from jail in 1991) remain at large.

Today, DevGroup has about 300 people and is involved in developing new hostage rescue techniques and counterterrorist assault options. The unit is organized along the lines of a typical SEAL Team: platoons comprised of two officers and 14 enlisted men each. (Note: A platoon is made up of two eight-man squads. The squads themselves, which are color coded, are organized into Fire Teams of four men, with each fire team having two swim pairs. DevGroup likes to organize its assaults around these fire teams.) Like Delta Force, DevGroup has been involved in providing security at the Olympic Games over the years. They typically focus on maritime issues, such as the lakes used for water events like canoeing. At the 1984 Games, they were responsible for securing the port area in Los Angeles. DevGroup performed similar duties at the 1996 Republican Convention in San Diego.

Dick Marcinko, founder and plank owner of the team, is still involved in counterterrorism. He has started his own company, SOS Temps. In late-summer 1995, months before the Olympic games, he was hired to visit Atlanta and play the role of a terrorist. It was not a difficult role for him to assume, since he had spent years anticipating terrorists' moves. His efforts showed law enforcement agencies responsible for security at the Games where to improve their contingency plans.

Operators practice getting into an assault formation commonly known as "the Train," "the Snake," and "the Congo Line." Such a formation allows the team to move quickly through a building (or, in this case a ship) and clear rooms of terrorists. *U.S. Navy*

CHAPTER FOUR

Anywhere, Anytime, Anything: FBI Hostage Rescue Team

"We're not soldiers or commandos. We're first and foremost FBI agents who have been trained and tasked with the specialized mission of saving lives. We aren't used until all other alternatives are exhausted."—Former HRT Member

In the wee hours of one October night, dozing residents of Albuquerque, New Mexico, never realized the danger they were in. Terrorists had placed a nuclear bomb in the city and were threatening to detonate it if their demands were not met; they had taken hostages to prove their point. At the ungodly hour of 2 A.M., armed assault teams were quietly moving into position. Nationwide, officials crossed their fingers, hoping that it could be pulled off. If not, a mushroom cloud would rise over the desert.

After receiving the initial threat from the terrorists, a host of federal and state agencies had leapt into action. Within an hour, an advance team from the FBI's elite counterterrorist unit, the Hostage Rescue Team (HRT), was on its way to Albuquerque. Upon its

arrival, its members quickly established a Tactical Operations Center and began to collect intelligence. The main body of the HRT followed along just hours later in C-130 Hercules aircraft, the cargo bays bulging with vehicles and special equipment.

In the ensuing three days, as negotiations took place, investigators had managed to locate the terrorists' hiding place. Furthermore, the Department of Energy's Nuclear Emergency Search Team (NEST) had found the nuclear device using gamma ray detectors slung from the underside of a helicopter. The bomb was squirreled away in a building in downtown Albuquerque. Now it was time to take down the terrorists and defuse the bomb. Which is why HRT assault teams found themselves—on this warm October night—creeping among cactus and scorpions toward the terrorists' stronghold.

From previous surveillance efforts, the operators knew where all the booby traps were located, as well as who the terrorists were and what they were armed with. They even had a good idea of what the building looked like inside. In fact, they had built a replica of the terrorists' hideaway out in the desert where they practiced the assault choreography that they would perform tonight.

The assault teams got into position, their Heckler & Koch MP5 submachine guns at the ready. Miles away,

Assault! HRT operators, having blown open a door with explosives, enter the tire shooting house to take down "terrorists" during a training exercise. The team uses linear-shaped charges to cut "mouseholes" in the doorway. Notice how quickly the operators have fanned out across the room—covering all points—even before the smoke has settled. It's not unusual for a room to be cleared of tangos in as little as 5 to 7 seconds. *John Simeone* at the site of the nuclear bomb, a local SWAT Team was preparing to do the same thing. Because the terrorists had the ability to remotely detonate the bomb, both targets had to be hit simultaneously. To prevent the terrorists' radio signal from reaching the nuclear bomb's computerized trigger and detonating it, the HRT was ready to flood the terrorists' hideaway with its own electronic signals to "drown" out any emanations.

The assault teams—at both locations—checked their watches, keeping an eye on the second hand as it moved to the appointed hour and minute. When it arrived, all hell broke loose. Using explosive charges, the HRT breached the stronghold in two places simultaneously tossing flash-bang grenades into the rooms as they did so. The light and concussion from the grenades stunned the terrorists. Within seconds, the building was filled with the sound of PFFT! PFFT! PFFT! as suppressed submachine guns spit their hail of lead. Then . . . silence. The assault was over. From start to finish, it had taken only 30 seconds. All the tangos were dead. All the hostages were alive. More importantly, the nuclear bomb had not detonated. Albuquerque and its 380,000 residents were still among the living.

It was an impressive assault—one for the record books—and, more importantly, one that had the heads of Delta Force and senior FBI officials nodding in awe. Too bad it had been just a field exercise. The bomb didn't exist. The terrorists and hostages were volunteers. And the takedown itself took place in a remote area of Kirtland AFB, safely away from curious onlookers. Yet this exercise—which took place in October 1983 under the codename "Equus Red"—was perhaps the most important drill that the HRT would ever do. For it showed skeptics within the FBI's bureaucracy that the skills possessed by the HRT were indeed at a much higher level than a SWAT team, and that the unit was ready to become operational. After Delta Force reviewers signed off on the HRT's performance at Equus Red, the team received FBI Director William Webster's blessings to become operational.

This action was ironic in itself, since Webster had been reluctant about establishing the Hostage Rescue Team. He was concerned that it was too macho an approach to law enforcement and that it had an unpleasant militaristic flavor. It wasn't until he visited Delta Force at its training facility at Ft. Bragg, North Carolina, two years prior to Equus Red that he changed his mind. After witnessing a demonstration by Delta Force, Webster reviewed the equipment used by the team. Noticing that there were no handcuffs, he inquired about it. A Delta operator responded grimly, "We put two rounds in their forehead. The dead don't need handcuffs."

Webster then realized that the United States needed a highly trained unit to bridge the gap between SWAT teams and the military's CT forces. A unit that could execute high-risk operations in law enforcement, such as domestic terrorism, hostage rescue, and the apprehension of dangerous criminals. Delta Force couldn't do that, since it was forbidden under Posse Comitatus from becoming involved in civilian matters unless it received a Presidential directive. And SWAT teams simply didn't have the expertise to handle in-extremis situations. Hence, on this October day in 1983—in the deserts of New Mexico—the HRT was brought into the world.

For Donald Bassett, who had conceived the idea of a "Super SWAT Team" nearly a decade earlier—and for many others at the FBI Training Division and Special Operations and Research Section (SOARS) who had supported that vision—it was a dream come true. But for John Simeone, the HRT's deputy commander, it marked only the beginning of what had to be accomplished in the next several months. The 1984 Summer Olympics and the U.S. Presidential Campaign were quickly approaching. Both events were ideal targets for terrorists.

Creation of HRT

The Hostage Rescue Team is the United States' premiere counterterrorist force—the proverbial 9-1-1 of domestic terrorism. The need for a unit like

The HRT's first leaders: Danny Coulson, commander (right), and John Simeone, deputy commander in front of SAS headquarters during one of their visits to learn more about CT training tactics. The HRT regularly trains with other elite CT teams from around the world, including Britain's SAS, France's GIGN, and Germany's GSG-9. *John Simeone*

the HRT was recognized in the late-1970s as terrorism around the globe increased. Another concern was that crime in the United States was changing: It was becoming more violent, with criminals reaching for automatic weapons instead of .38s.

In 1978, Delta Force invited the FBI to join them in a training exercise. Delta wanted to practice working with the FBI, in case they ever had to handle tan-

gos on U.S. soil. At that time, the FBI only had SWAT teams, which were trained for high-risk arrests, not hostage rescue or counterterrorism. In fact, the FBI had already conceded that if a Level 3 terrorist incident occurred (i.e., an event involving several terrorists and multiple hostages), they would turn it over to Delta Force after getting Presidential authority to do so. Once the tangos were taken care of, the incident would be handed back to the FBI for recovery and post-incident investigation.

The FBI agreed to "play" with Delta Force. So, over Mother's Day weekend in 1978, they visited Jackass Flats, located at the Nevada Test Site. The three-day exercise, code named Joshua Junction, tested all components of the FBI's crisis management machine. The scenario went something like this: A group of Middle East terrorists had taken over an underground nuclear weapons site and had taken several hostages in the process. They were making various demands, including safe passage back to their country. The FBI managed to negotiate some of the hostages free before finally turning the situation over to Delta Force. Delta arranged for two buses to take the terrorists and hostages out to a waiting plane. When the first group boarded the aircraft, Delta did an assault on the plane from prepositioned locations. They then convinced the remaining terrorists, who had stayed behind at the underground bunker until the first group arrived at the plane, to take the second bus to the plane. Along the way, Delta Force did a mobile assault on the bus. The training was so realistic that some of the hostages exhibited the Stockholm Syndrome. In fact, one female hostage grabbed a gun and started shooting at the "good guys" who were trying to rescue her.

Joshua Junction showed those from the FBI's Training Division what the FBI had to do to be a player in the field of counterterrorism. People like Don Bassett, Tase Bailey and John Simeone all realized that the FBI was not equipped to handle a serious terrorist incident. This point was driven home even further two years later, at the 1980 Winter Olympics in Lake Placid, New York.

Prior to the commencement of these Games, the FBI ran a major exercise and discovered, to their consternation, that they were not prepared to handle terrorists. There were three sites that required protection. The FBI was given responsibility for two, the State Police, one. Although the FBI had pulled together some of its SWAT teams to deal with terrorists at the Olympics, the teams did not have the necessary training to respond successfully to such an incident. Furthermore, the leadership was not experienced at managing a terrorism crisis. One witness to all this was Jim McKenzie, who was the deputy assistant director of the FBI's Training Division at the time. When he was eventually promoted to assistant director of that Division, he gave people the impetus to explore creating Don Bassett's "Super SWAT Team." The 1984 Los Angeles Olympics was approaching, and McKenzie wanted the FBI to be better prepared than it had been at Lake Placid.

A group of agents who conducted tactical SWAT training at Quantico was moved over to a new unit: Special Operations and Research Section (SOARS). Negotiators and psychologists were added to this group. Together, they were tasked with finding new ways to enhance the FBI's SWAT capabilities. Each individual was given an area of expertise to research, such as explosives and breaching tactics. Each person also served as a liaison to one of the existing elite counterterrorism teams: Don Bassett worked with GSG-9 and the Israeli teams; Tase Bailey worked with the SAS and Royal Marine Commandos; Bob Taubert worked with SEAL Team Six; and John Simeone worked with GIGN. Nearly everyone was involved with Delta Force; Joshua Junction had established a warm bond between the FBI and Delta.

As part of their liaison duties, the men attended training exercises held by their assigned CT unit. They brought their observations and newfound knowledge back to Quantico, where they shared it with others in SOARS. In addition to doing this, they also evaluated equipment that might be of use to the FBI. It was from SOARS'

efforts that the FBI's SWAT teams switched to using 9-mm handguns and H&K MP5s.

In 1982, the tactical component of SOARS went to Ft. Bragg and attended a week-long training course that was conducted by Delta Force at their stockade facility (a.k.a. The Ranch). There, they performed close-quarters battle (CQB) techniques, room clearing tactics, explosive entries and live-fire hostage rescues. The men from SOARS were learning and doing things that FBI SWAT teams had never done before. They quickly saw how these skills could benefit the FBI in its law enforcement efforts. When they returned to Quantico, they brought along a video of them doing explosive breaches and interior live-fire CQB and showed it to McKenzie. Like them, McKenzie understood the value of having this capability. So he gave them two weeks to put together a presentation that outlined what would eventually become the Hostage Rescue Team. The men quickly got to work. Their plan detailed the team's organizational structure, training requirements, and skill levels to be attained. Their presentation was given to assistant directors, section chiefs and, eventually, to FBI Director William Webster.

"Our initial presentation was received very skeptically by some of the Bureau officials who, quite frankly, thought we were absolutely out of our minds, that we were nuts," says Tase Bailey.

It was indeed a belligerent meeting, with the management constantly interrupting the presenters with negative comments. In fact, one supervisor reportedly slammed his hand down on the table, adamantly declaring that no way in hell would there ever be a blankety-blank Super SWAT Team.

Fortunately, one FBI official did understand the value of having a law enforcement counterterrorist team: John Hotis, in the Office of Legal Council. After reviewing the SOARS video of them training at Delta, he spoke with Webster and convinced him to give the idea serious consideration. Thus, Webster and a host of other FBI officials took a trip to Ft. Bragg, where they watched Delta Force and SEAL Team Six do their stuff.

Oliver "Buck" Revell, a former Marine who was in charge of the FBI's Criminal Investigative Division—under which the counterterrorism section fell—was concerned by what he saw. Delta Force and SEAL Team Six used maximum force and seemed to have no understanding of the criminal process. Revell felt the FBI needed a more restrained version of the military's units. So did Webster; the answer to his handcuff question bothered him.

When Webster returned to headquarters, he asked SOARS to put together a demonstration using the Washington Metro Field Office SWAT Team so that he could see how their approach to a hostage situation would differ from the military's. Inserting by helicopter, they rappelled to the ground, assaulted a building and rescued the hostages. Webster saw the difference immediately. They were using Delta Force's

HRT's logo, which was once known as the "no-go logo," since Webster and other top FBI officials frowned on individual FBI units having their own identity. However, the logo persisted, and is still used. The HRT's slogan To Save Lives—which was borrowed from a comment made by the commander of GIGN—is represented by the Latin words "Servare Vitas." The Eagle stands for hostage rescue personnel, who are known universally as "eagles." Terrorists are known as "crows" and "tangos." *SF Tomajczyk*

tactical expertise, but with the FBI's bridled shooting judgment. It was not a bloodbath: Only those terrorists who brandished weapons with the intent of using them were killed. (Those who didn't, lived and were arrested.) And so he supported the creation of the Hostage Rescue Team.

The First Team

The first commander of the Hostage Rescue Team was Danny Coulson. (Subsequent commanders were David "Woody" Johnson, Richard Rogers, and Roger Nisley.) Coulson was selected because he was a good street agent, possessed a law degree, and had tactical experience as a SWAT Team member in New York. FBI officials knew that he would keep the HRT focused on the law enforcement role (i.e., minimum use of force), which greatly pleased Buck Revell. Coulson's deputy commander was John Simeone.

In March 1982, Coulson and Simeone—with assistance from SOARS—began planning the training regimen that HRT members would undergo. They put together a milestone chart, knowing they wanted to begin training as a team in January 1983 and be operational by the end of that year. They determined when the selection would occur and what types of weapons and equipment would be acquired and by when.

As for the training program itself, they sought input from SAS, GSG-9, and GIGN. (On one of their visits to GIGN, the commander told them that his mission was "to save lives." It was adopted as the HRT's motto.) Of all the teams they visited, it was Delta Force that influenced them the most. Coulson and Simeone spent several weeks at the Ranch. During the day, they trained with Delta operators, and at night, they wrote down critical lesson plans that were modified for law enforcement roles. This became the foundation of the HRT's training program. In one early session, former Delta Force commander Col. Charlie Beckwith sat down with Coulson and Simeone for a four-hour heart-to-heart discussion.

"He gave us valuable insight as to what we needed to do as a team, what we should train for, what our ethos and philosophy should be, and particularly a lot about how you select your men in the selection process," says Simeone.

The very first selection was held in June 1982. Three groups of 30 candidates each spent a week undergoing evaluation. Candidates endured a variety of firearms shooting tests and were seen by a psychologist, who appraised their emotional and mental state. The HRT sought candidates who were in good physical shape, possessed mature judgment, knew how to handle stressful situations, and who had excellent shooting and tactical skills.

"You've got to be careful of the people you get in here," says Tase Bailey, who assisted with the screening process. "You don't want hot dogs that are just looking for an opportunity to get into a shoot-out. You want people who are going to make good, mature decisions and who can handle a lot of stress."

All candidates wore a shirt with a number and alphabet letter on it. This was intended to keep the candidates somewhat anonymous. During the selection process, trainers, instructors, and psychologists wrote down their comments and observations about the candidates on index cards. These cards were placed into the candidates' folders for review by Coulson, Simeone, and a Bureau psychiatrist.

Selection tested people's judgment, physical ability, marksmanship, and ability to work as a team. Candidates ran the Marine Corps' obstacle course next door until they were exhausted, and then were taken to a firing range where they were expected to shoot accurately. The candidates were also tested on law enforcement skills. For instance, they were shown a film of a terrorist incident late at night and then ordered to write a report detailing what they had seen. What were the demands? What were the surroundings? What kind of weapons were present? How many terrorists were there and what did they look like?

The purpose of this training was to put people under stress in a team framework and see how they would work together to accomplish a common goal.

A "shoot/no shoot" drill in the HRT's tire house conducted in the 1980s. HRT operators go from room to room searching for terrorists: armed hostiles are shot; friendlies are freed. Often, live hostages (who are tied up) are placed in a room along with terrorist targets. The operators must enter a room and quickly shoot the terrorists without striking the hostages. This is the closest thing to a real-world operation. *STTU*

The HRT needed people who would not overreact, who would stay cool under stress, who would be resourceful, and who had disciplined patience. They wanted risk takers, not risk seekers.

In the end, 50 of the 90 applicants were selected to be on the Hostage Rescue Team, including one woman, who later voluntarily removed herself from consideration. Of those 50 team members, 35 were tapped to be full-time operators; the remaining 15 were to be alternates who trained with the HRT, but then returned to field offices. This arrangement bothered both Coulson and Simeone, who convinced the Bureau that they needed all 50 to be full-time.

"Why train a bunch of guys and then send them home?" asks Simeone incredulously. "The idea of putting a dedicated group of people together was that they would train together and work together. That's so important. It's like a good football team. You can put 11 all-stars on the field, but unless they've trained together a great deal of time, they won't know instinctively how each other operates."

So the 15 were converted to full-time players. Coulson and Simeone established two assault teams—a Blue Team and a Gold Team. They were supported by two six-man sniper teams.

The Tire House and the Ranch

In the months following the selection process, the HRT busied itself with acquiring equipment so that they could shoot, move and communicate. They also built themselves a tire shooting house so that they could do live fire training, with 360-degree capability. It was built in a field near the HRT's headquarters out at the FBI Academy in Quantico. At that time, the tire shooting house was considered to be ideal for CQB training. Delta Force had one. SEAL Team Six had one.

The HRT's one-story, open-roofed shooting house was comprised of old tires stacked to about 10-feet high and filled with sand. The walls were two-tires wide to trap bullets fired inside the house. The HRT used the tire house to practice explosive entries (they maintained a stockpile of doors for this purpose), room clearing tactics, and live-fire hostage rescues. A viewing stand was built adjacent to the shooting house so that assaults could be videotaped for analysis. The stand also gave instructors and visiting dignitaries a safe place to watch the action.

The shooting house was completed by Thanksgiving 1982, and once the holiday season was over, the HRT finally began its first official training session. During the month of January 1983, everyone's shooting and tactical skills were honed to a certain level. Then they went off to Ft. Bragg for a month of training with Delta Force. According to John Simeone, the kindness extended to HRT by Delta was overwhelming. "They opened their doors to us," he says. "The only thing that they didn't stop was their operator training and any mission training they had to do. All other training stopped so they could

The HRT does more than take down terrorists. It is also trained to provide protection to VIPs in potentially dangerous situations. Here, members from the HRT practice their protective security skills in Washington, D.C., on the mall. The VIP is Buck Revell (gray suit), who was the assistant director of the FBI. The State Department's Bureau of Diplomatic Security provided the HRT with its first training session on how to protect VIPs. *John Simeone*

devote their site, their equipment, their facility to train us during those four weeks." When HRT attempted to thank Delta for its generosity, Delta responded with "Your flag is our flag. Why shouldn't we help you?"

While at the Ranch, the HRT practiced assault options (stronghold, aircraft, mobile), as well as how to do dynamic room entries, how to sweep buildings and search rooms, how to shoot on the move, how to use sniper/observer teams, and how to plan missions. Delta also taught the HRT how to analyze a situation and select the most appropriate assault option, taking into account the pros and cons. The HRT learned how to do this quickly, correctly, and under pressure.

By the time the Hostage Rescue Team returned to Quantico, they were light-years ahead of where they had been just weeks earlier. The team's tradecraft and

CQB skills were honed to a razor's edge. To maintain this level, the HRT members did daily exercises and live-fire hostage rescue drills. The rule of thumb was that if you shot, you also sat. In this case, you sat in a chair next to a target in the shooting house. The assault team entered the room not knowing where you and the target(s) were located. Their mission was to search and shoot without hitting you in the process. This was the closest thing to real life as the HRT could get.

It was obviously dangerous, and the operators accepted that. Spouses, however, were a different story. When Buck Revell's wife, Sharon, found out that he had sat as a hostage, she hit the ceiling. According to Buck, she called Coulson and lectured him. "How could you allow him to do that?" she yelled. "He's a grandpa. Don't you ever do anything like that again."

One of the more impressive presentations HRT did—and still continues to do—was assault a room and rescue live hostages in total darkness while wearing night vision goggles. Visitors who watched this exercise were brought into the room and instructed to stand still and not move around. Then the lights were turned off. Within seconds, the visitors could hear the distinctive PFFT! PFFT! PFFT! sound of suppressed MP5s firing around them. They saw nothing. Then just as quickly as it started, it was over. When the lights came on, the room was empty. The hostages were gone and the terrorist targets were destroyed. The awe the visitors felt was magnified further when they were told to look at each other's back. There they found a small red marker. It had been placed there by HRT operators during the assault to prove that they had been close enough to touch them. The experience left people with goose bumps.

The HRT's sole casualty occurred in 1985, when James K. McAllister fell to his death during a fast-rope training exercise from a helicopter. Notice how the operators intentionally leave the Huey at the same time, so as to keep the helicopter on station. Fast-roping is a vital CT technique because it allows 8 to 12 operators to be on the ground in just a few seconds. Those who have done fast-roping compare it to sliding down a firefighter's pole. *STTU*

Practice Makes Perfect

Once the Hostage Rescue Team became operational in October 1983, it focused on specialized training. For example, a dozen or so operators visited NAVSPECWAR out in Coronado, California—home of the SEALs—to learn underwater procedures that were applicable to HRT's mission (e.g., reconnaissance, underwater navigation). The HRT learned helicopter insertion techniques by training with the Army's 160th Special Operations Aviation Regiment (SOAR), an elite unit that flies Delta Force into harm's way. The unit also did a lot of nighttime training, recognizing that many of their future assaults would take place early in the morning. The Marine Corps taught them small unit tactics and night maneuvering techniques.

The HRT even went down to Camp Peary (a.k.a. The Farm)—a 9,275-acre CIA facility located near Williamsburg, Virginia—for counterterrorism training. There, they took "smash and bang" courses on how to breach barricades and run roadblocks.

Over time, HRT operators went off to learn more about air assault tactics, rappelling, hand-to-hand combat, chemical agents, terrorist psychology, high-tech surveillance methods, sniping/counter-sniping, communications, and more. Whatever tactics and techniques they learned from their training, they brought them back to Quantico where the lessons were shared with others.

As for CQB training, Coulson and Simeone decided to make things more realistic. On advice from SEAL Team Six commander Dick Marcinko, they introduced wax bullets and bursting blood bags. The wax bullets were used in team-versus-team drills in

To make training more realistic, HRT introduced blood bags to its shooting house drills early on. Here, an operator nurses a leg injury while another keeps a close eye on some terrorists. By adding medical issues to the training regimen, HRT operators had to consider triage and medical treatment in addition to their law enforcement duties. In keeping with the HRT's motto, To Save Lives, all operators receive extensive training in emergency medicine. *John Simeone*

The so-called "sniper's tower" represents HRT's earliest beginnings. This building, which is located at Quantico, served as the team's first headquarters. It also afforded operators a place to practice climbing and rappelling techniques. The tower has since been replaced by a larger, more secure headquarters building. A new state-of-the-art, multimillion dollar shooting house and sniper range are being built just behind the tower shown in this photo. The ambulance is for any accidents that occur during training. *U.S. Federal Bureau of Investigation*

the shooting house or in field exercises. The bullets stung like hell, and immediately caused everyone to use cover and concealment like they were supposed to. The days of firing blanks and hearing "I shot you!" and "Did not!" were over. Now there were only howls of pain and tell-tale welts. If you got shot, you knew it. Hell, everyone knew it.

The bursting blood bags were used to simulate injuries during assault exercises. Every HRT member received more than 80 hours of medical training. "If a hostage gets injured and dies from trauma wounds," says Simeone, "you've lost, even if you get all the bad guys."

With these blood bags, a hostage or "good guy" could burst it during an assault, simulating a wound. This meant that assault team members now had to deal with triage and medical treatment, in addition to its primary mission of finding and taking out terrorists.

Day by day, the Hostage Rescue Team metamorphosed into a highly trained and highly capable counterterrorist force. They cross-trained with other teams around the world, including GSG-9, GIGN, and SAS, and modified the tactics they learned to fit the law enforcement arena. They practiced doing assaults on 747s, 727s, DC-9s, etc., in Dallas and Atlanta, as well as at Dulles Airport. They took down cruise ships, trains, buses, and oil platforms all over the United States. They even got permission to practice assaults on the Metro subway system in Washington, D.C., during off hours. In essence, the HRT trained to be deployed anywhere, anytime . . . and to take down anything.

The Triple A's. "Anywhere. Anytime. Anything." It was a daunting task, but they were up to the challenge.

Stronghold Assault

The first major deployment of the Hostage Rescue Team occurred in April 1985, in the Ozark mountains of Arkansas. A neo-Nazi-like group of 200 lived in a fortified compound known as Zarepath-Horeb. This compound occupied 224 acres of land

A meeting in the woods of Zarepath-Horeb. FBI and HRT officials meet with leaders of the extremist group CSA to negotiate a surrender. At this point, the CSA was entrenched in four buildings in the middle of its armed compound, surrounded by about 200 law enforcement officials. The CSA, which was preparing for Armegeddon by manufacturing weapons, eventually gave up peacefully. In its subsequent search of the compound, the FBI discovered gallons of cyanide that were to have been poured by the CSA into the water supply of an unnamed city. *U.S. Federal Bureau of Investigation*

along Bull Shoals Lake. The group was known as the Covenant, the Sword and the Arm of the Lord, or CSA for short. The CSA was a polygamous community that disliked Jews and blacks, and was preparing for Armageddon. To this end, they produced hand grenades and silencers, as well as customized weapons so that they could be fired as fully automatic machine guns. In fact, an Ingram MAC 10 submachine gun they modified was used in the murder of radio personality Alan Berg by the violent neo-Nazi group, The Order.

To prepare for Armageddon and raise some money in the process, the CSA created a boot camp within the compound and solicited people to attend the "End Time Overcomer Survival Training School." These people were taught urban warfare techniques, survival skills, CQB tactics, etc. Perhaps the most popular aspect of this course was Silhouette City, a gunfighting city that featured several mock buildings where cardboard targets jumped up as trainees walked by with their guns held at the ready.

It should come as no surprise that a place like this attracted some of the dregs of society.

On April 15, 22-year-old David Tate was stopped by Missouri State Trooper Jimmie Linegar on a routine traffic check. Tate was a neo-Nazi who was wanted on a federal firearms charge. He also had a history of being involved in Aryan Nations and The Order. Tate was heading for the CSA compound, hoping to find refuge. As Linegar and another state trooper—Allen Hines—approached Tate's van, Tate rolled out and sprayed them with a submachine gun, killing Linegar instantly and wounding Hines. Tate then fled into the woods and disappeared. A massive manhunt was launched.

For six days, Tate eluded the police and FBI. Bloodhounds were called in to help with the search, as were helicopters equipped with infrared sensors that could detect body heat. Eventually, Tate was captured in a city park just north of Branson, Missouri. By then, the FBI knew that Tate had been headed for Zarepath-Horeb. They suspected that several other fugitives were at the compound as well, fugitives that the Marshals Service, BATF, and other agencies had warrants for. Problem was, none of these agencies had the training or equipment to assault the compound.

"That place made Waco look like a picnic," says Buck Revell, who oversaw this operation as the assistant director of the FBI's Criminal Investigative Division. "These people were into real heavy stuff. Recoilless rifles, grenades, mines, .50-caliber machine guns . . . you name it."

The FBI negotiated with the other agencies to be in control of the operation, and then brought in the Hostage Rescue Team, as well as several FBI SWAT teams.

In all, more than 200 law enforcement personnel descended on Zarepath-Horeb. An outer and inner perimeter were quickly established around the com-

Cocky and self-assured, Lebanese terrorist Fawaz Younis reads his demands after hijacking a Royal Jordanian jet in 1985. Two years later, he was arrested by the HRT when he went to a yacht off the coast of Cyprus to discuss a drug deal, which turned out to be a well-conceived ploy. The event marked the first arrest of a terrorist overseas by the FBI. *U.S. Federal Bureau of Investigation*

pound. The outer perimeter kept the press safely out of harm's way; the inner perimeter ensured that no one in the compound got out. An assault was made against the stronghold, with the HRT and SWAT teams quickly occupying the outer buildings. A demand went out for the CSA to surrender. The residents, who were now hiding in four buildings in the center of the compound, refused.

Negotiations between the FBI and the CSA began, with HRT Commander Danny Coulson making the unprecedented effort of talking directly with CSA leaders. The discussions went on for two days, during which time sniper/observer teams from the HRT and SWAT teams maintained surveillance over the compound. Anyone who tried to sneak out from Zarepath-Horeb was turned back. The FBI wanted the CSA to believe that security was tight . . . even though it wasn't. If they felt that escape was impossible, the FBI reasoned, they might become demoralized and give up.

The ploy worked. The CSA surrendered 48 hours after the assault. As the FBI carefully went through the buildings in the compound, they were horrified to discover barrels filled with cyanide. The CSA had been manufacturing cyanide with the intent of poisoning the water supply of an unnamed city. A single drop of cyanide can kill an adult; there were gallons of the poison in the compound. Had the FBI not taken down Zarepath-Horeb, who knows how many thousands of people would have died by taking a shower, brushing their teeth, or drinking a glass of water.

The HRT Goes Abroad

In June 1985, a Lebanese used-car dealer by the name of Fawaz Younis hijacked a Royal Jordanian jet at Beirut International Airport. Younis was part of the Shiite Amal militia. He and his comrades had the plane fly to Tunis, so that he could deliver a message to a meeting of the Arab League. When the plane was refused landing rights, he had the plane return to Beirut, where he blew it up after first releasing the passengers (which included three Americans). Younis managed to escape, but, two years later, an informant for the Drug Enforcement Administration fingered

A close look at the steel door that the HRT blew open during its 1991 nighttime assault on the Alpha Unit at the Federal Correctional Institution in Talladega, Alabama. Explosive breaching charges sliced through the steel, and the blast wave stunned any nearby convicts long enough for the HRT to quickly sweep through the building. Team members were in the room containing the nine hostages within 30 seconds. Note the Nomex gloves and forearm pads worn by the operator on the right. HRT members also wear goggles to protect their eyesight from all the dust that is suspended in the air following an explosion; you don't want to shoot the wrong person. *U.S. Federal Bureau of Investigation*

Younis in Lebanon. The information was relayed to the CIA, FBI, and the Department of State.

These agencies sat down and plotted ways to lure Younis out of Lebanon and into a neutral area where he could be arrested by the FBI, which now had legal authority to go after terrorists anywhere in the world, if an American was involved in the incident. Knowing that Younis had a passion for drug trafficking, they decided to coax him with a drug deal. Through sources, they got word to him about the deal. A meeting was arranged in Cyprus for September 13, 1987. When he arrived, he was told that a change had taken place: The meeting would be held aboard a yacht off the coast, since the dealer was wanted by Cyprus police. Younis bought the story and was taken out to the yacht.

The catch? The yacht had been leased by the HRT and it was now bobbing up-and-down in the Mediterranean Sea exactly 12.1 miles offshore—in *international* waters. When Younis arrived at the yacht, he was greeted by bikini clad women lounging on the deck. (Yes, they were FBI agents.) As he clambered aboard, his festive spirit quickly dissolved as HRT operators placed him under arrest.

Buck Revell, who had been waiting aboard the command ship USS *Butte* 20 miles away, came to the yacht and escorted Younis back to the ship. Younis confessed to his role in the hijacking within the first two hours after his arrest. For the next three days, as the *Butte* steamed to rendezvous with the aircraft carrier USS *Saratoga*, Buck Revell and the HRT debriefed Younis about terrorist groups and activities in the Middle East. They treated him with kid gloves, because they wanted his cooperation. During this time period, the HRT provided security over Younis to ensure that he would not escape and that any rescue efforts attempted by his terrorist comrades would be thwarted.

Ultimately, the USS *Butte* met up with the USS *Saratoga*, and Younis was flown to Andrews AFB just outside of Washington, D.C. At the time, it was the longest nonstop flight from an aircraft carrier in his-

tory. The U.S. Marshals Service's Special Operations Group took custody of Younis upon his arrival. He is currently serving a 30-year sentence at the Leavenworth federal penitentiary.

Breaking *in* to Prison

"I did a dance around the room when I heard what happened on the radio," said John Simeone. "It was the classic thing we trained for. Sneak in, and resolve it without anyone getting injured."

"It" was the HRT's successful assault on Alpha Unit at the Federal Correctional Institution in Talladega, Alabama, in August 1991. By this time, Simeone was no longer with the FBI or HRT, but being a plank owner and former deputy commander of the HRT he had a good idea of what had transpired.

The chaos began on the morning of August 21, when 121 Cuban inmates armed with homemade weapons took over the Alpha Unit, taking 10 hostages in the process. (One hostage, who had been injured during the takeover, was released on the first day.) Many of these inmates were scheduled to be deported back to Cuba the next day and they didn't want to go. The Alpha Unit was an individual prison building—one of five—in the correctional complex. The inmates had control of the entire unit.

In response to this uprising, the Hostage Rescue Team, Bureau of Prison Special Response Teams, and FBI SWAT teams from Birmingham, Atlanta, and Knoxville were dispatched to Talladega. They immediately established perimeters around Alpha Unit and began collecting intelligence so that an emergency assault could be enacted if the inmates started to kill the hostages.

Negotiations were initiated, but the condition that the inmates would not be deported to Cuba was non-negotiable.

On the second day, acting U.S. Attorney General William Barr named the FBI as the lead agency for any tactical resolution to the crisis, and instructed the HRT to conduct any rescue if it became necessary. Given this responsibility, the HRT brought in former

A scene that literally made many HRT operators cry in despair: the cremation of the people they were trying to save. As infrared photos and mini-microphones later proved, the Branch Davidians deliberately set their complex on fire, igniting three separate fires within a 2-minute period. It is not known if the presence of the CS powder contributed to the fire's spread. Regardless, the fires resulted in the deaths of more than 70 people, including women and children. (Autopsies showed that 19 had apparently been shot by their comrades.) Nine people survived the conflagration, including a woman who tried to *enter* the burning building instead of escaping. An alert HRT operator raced in and rescued her. He later received an award of heroism for his selfless efforts. *U.S. Federal Bureau of Investigation*

Waco and the Branch Davidians. Most people truly do not understand what happened there in 1993, and some incorrectly blame the HRT for the Davidians' deaths. In actuality, the ATF bumbled its February 28 raid when it tried to charge the religious sect with possession of illegal weapons. In a surprise firefight, four ATF agents and five Davidians were killed, forcing the FBI to take over the situation. Senior FBI officials and Attorney General Janet Reno made mistakes in handling the crisis, but it was the HRT that ended up as the scapegoat. In this photo, the HRT uses unarmed tracked-recovery vehicles (*not* tanks) on the morning of April 19 to inject CS powder into the buildings and make them uninhabitable. The vehicles repeated this effort off and on for six hours, giving the Davidians plenty of time and opportunity to surrender. In fact, FBI negotiators encouraged surrender by repeating a message over loudspeakers that read in part: "... Exit the compound now and follow instructions ... walk toward the large Red Cross flag ... We do not want anyone hurt ... This is not an assault." Notice the water source in the rear left; by this point it was a cesspool of garbage and human waste, a breeding ground for disease. *U.S. Federal Bureau of Investigation*

team members to assist them with assault and support aspects of the mission. Intelligence gathering was stepped up, the building's internal layout was determined, inmate and hostage profiles were acquired, an entry plan was formulated, and dress rehearsals were performed until everyone knew the assault choreography by heart.

On August 29, it was clear that the hostages were in imminent danger. The inmates refused to negotiate and, being frustrated and angry, had selected the first hostage to be killed. They wanted to send a message to the world that they were serious about

getting their way. Attorney General Barr authorized an assault to rescue the hostages.

At 3:40 A.M. on August 30, the HRT initiated its takedown of the Alpha Unit. Explosive charges were used to breach the prison doors and create entry ways for the assault teams. They began by blowing open the main central door. The force of the blast ripped open the steel-bar door and scattered cement rubble down the length of the hallway. This explosion was immediately followed by a second charge that detonated at the right front portion of the brick building. HRT operators stormed the building through both breaches even as the smoke and debris was still flying. They made their way to pre-assigned objectives, using flash-bang grenades to stun and force aside those inmates who came at them with spears, swords, and clubs. Team members were in the room containing the nine hostages within 30 seconds of entering the building. The hostages were quickly evacuated out of the Alpha Unit to safety.

Meanwhile, the rest of the HRT herded the inmates back into their cells. FBI SWAT teams entered the building and secured the upper tiers of the cell blocks. With all the inmates locked down in the cells, Bureau of Prison Special Response Teams entered Alpha Unit and—going from cell to cell—began restraining and removing the inmates.

According to those who were present, the leader of the Cuban inmates was knocked over backward by the breaching charges. Fear (or the blast wave) caused him to defecate in his pants. When an HRT operator got to him seconds later, all he could say—in a thick Cuban accent—was, "Wha happeeeened?"

Speed. Surprise. Violence of action. The HRT had used all three to their advantage in this takedown, saving the lives of nine hostages and restoring order to the prison complex. To this day, a sharp, handmade sword captured from an Alpha Unit inmate hangs in the HRT commander's office, as a reminder of that early morning assault.

Deserts, Spiders, and Snakes

On May 12, 1992, 33-year-old Daniel Ray Horning escaped from the Arizona State Prison in Florence. Horning had been serving four consecutive life sentences for aggravated assault, robbery, and kidnapping. He was also accused of killing and dismembering a man in Stockton, California, after being surprised while committing a robbery.

In the month following his escape, Horning's movements were a mystery. Then on June 25, he kidnapped a couple near Flagstaff and forced them to drive to the Grand Canyon. Along the way, he retrieved a shotgun that had been stashed away. After spending the night at the park, Horning attempted to kidnap a family of six in the parking lot of a store. But the effort backfired when the teenage son ran off, alerting everyone to Horning's presence. The Park Rangers gave chase, dodging Horning's buckshot.

The pursuit went on for miles. Then, all of a sudden, Horning slammed on the brakes, leaped out of the car, and escaped on foot into the park. The tactic worked: He got away. In the car, rangers found a note and cassette tape that outlined his plans to kidnap people and hold them hostage. In return for their lives, he wanted $1 million, his freedom, and the release of his convict brother from prison.

On June 29, Horning reappeared. He stole a station wagon and attempted to flee, but the Park Rangers had set up roadblocks. Horning ditched the car and fled back into the wilderness. A former Army reconnaissance specialist, he felt confident that he could disappear into the Grand Canyon and evade the police. And so he crept off into the parched land where only snakes, lizards, and scorpions thrived.

By this time, hundreds of law enforcement agents were involved in the case, including the Hostage Rescue Team. The HRT had been chasing Horning with dog teams for several days now. Initially, they had tried using infrared sensors aboard aircraft to find Horning, but the hot desert radiated so much heat—even at night—that they couldn't discern a rock from a human being. The dogs were much better: They could smell a scent for hours after a person passed by. HRT operators ran with the bloodhounds in full body armor for five to seven miles at a time, up and down the rocky canyons in pursuit of Horning. When the dogs wearied, a helicopter picked them up and replaced them with a fresh team. The hunt was constant, day and night. Over the course of 10 days, the HRT covered 80 miles in the desert terrain, driving an exhausted Horning ahead of them.

On July 4, Horning surfaced again. This time he captured two English women. After using them to get through police roadblocks, he tied them to a tree and left them behind. In his effort to escape, he attracted the attention of a State Trooper, who chased after him. Once again, Horning bailed out of the car and ran off into the canyons near Sedona. The officer considered pursuing Horning, but it was growing dark. The police and FBI decided to search for him at sunrise. However, around 10 P.M., a resident called the police saying that a strange man was drinking from his garden hose.

The HRT and County Sheriff responded to the call. After searching the area with bloodhounds, they found Horning hiding under the deck of a house. After a few hours negotiation, he was arrested and charged with attempted murder, armed robbery, and kidnapping.

A Profile of the HRT Today

The Hostage Rescue Team has had a rich and successful history since it was established in 1982. Some things have changed over the years, but many things have remained the same, such as the unit's commitment to high quality training standards and its selection of agents who are dedicated to saving lives.

The two-week selection process continues to place a tremendous amount of emotional, mental, and physical stress on the candidates. Most of the exercises performed during selection parallel actual cases the HRT has been involved with. For example, from the Horning incident, the HRT has incorporated a "dog run" exercise in which candidates follow a tracker across rough terrain and waterways for a number of miles. (Yes, *I* know how many miles the marches are, but I promised HRT I wouldn't reveal it.) These open-ended runs not only stress a candidate

Two HRT helicopters fly low and fast over a lake to drop off an assault element during a training exercise. Since speed and surprise are essential elements in any assault, the operators cling to the outside of the helicopter—riding the skids—so that they can deploy more quickly. The HRT has pre-positioned many of its helicopters and fixed-wing aircraft around the nation to speed up its response time to a crisis. *U.S. Federal Bureau of Investigation*

The HRT recently adopted a modified U.S. Marine Corps LAV-25 for riots and dangerous incidents where there is little or no protection for its operators, such as the 1996 Montana Freemen situation. The eight-wheeled, light-assault vehicle can withstand hits from 7.62-mm ammo. Six HRT operators and their equipment can fit inside the cargo area, three to a side. They enter the vehicle via a door-like hatch in the rear of the vehicle. A six-cylinder, turbocharged engine propels the vehicle along at 60 mph on the road. The 21-foot-long LAV is also amphibious, capable of moving at 6 mph in shallow water. *U.S. Federal Bureau of Investigation*

physically, but also mentally, since he never knows how far they're going.

Nothing is factored in for a person's size, sex or race during selection. It's a pass or fail environment. A candidate either does or does not do the job. That's all that matters. Over the years, three women have tried out for the team, but none have made it.

Those who make the team now go through a 14-week New Operators Training Course (NOTC). It is here that they learn CQB skills, assault and room clearing tactics, insertion methods, night patrolling tactics, and live-hostage rescue techniques. If they pass, they are either sent along for more specialized training (e.g., sniper school) or assigned to an HRT Team. All candidates are placed on a one-year's probation. The majority of today's operators have eight years of FBI experience and are in their mid- to late-30s. Many are married and have children. Less than half have had prior military experience. They serve

five to seven years with HRT before leaving for another position within the FBI. (There is a three-year minimum commitment to the team.)

Snipers receive training from both the FBI and the U.S. Marine Corps. Of the two, the eight-week USMC course is much more advanced. It focuses on things like concealment and covert movement, sniper hide construction and urban sniping techniques. Snipers are also trained how to be expert observers and how to survive in any environment for days on end. Although the average sniper shot is 75 yards, HRT snipers are trained out to 1,000 yards. This gives the snipers confidence in their skills, and it also gives the HRT the capability to do takedowns in rural situations, should it be necessary.

In 1996, Congress authorized the HRT to increase its strength from 50 to 100 operators. The addition of these men and women will allow the HRT to respond to protracted large crises, like the Waco Davidian and Montana Freemen sieges, or to several smaller events that occur simultaneously.

As for the tire shooting house, it was torn down after being deemed too antiquated. The walls—two tires wide and rounded—were not authentic enough. An operator who learned a tactic in the tire house had to reprogram himself for the 8-inch-thick straight walls found in the real world. Replacing the tire house is a new $6 million Tactical Firearm Training House. This state-of-the-art concrete facility is nearly six times larger than the tire house and features moveable walls, stairwells for various training exercises, a helipad, and a five-story tower for rappelling and climbing drills. Vehicles and aircraft mock-ups will be able to be placed inside the building where takedowns can be done in private. Lighting conditions can be changed, and closed-circuit cameras (including infrared) will be in place to film assaults for later analysis.

While this new building is being constructed, the HRT is using a temporary shooting house, known as The Maze (a.k.a. Hack's House). It is a 12-room structure that has rubber-matted steel walls to absorb the frangible bul-

317

lets used by the HRT for assault training. The rooms are filled with paper and steel targets. Mannequins and furniture are often used to add authenticity to the exercises.

The training done by the HRT is still as intense and continuous as it was in its founding days. Over the course of a month, operators may receive specialized training in linear assaults (e.g., planes, trains, buses), breaching, reconnaissance, night patrolling, rappelling, photography, trauma medical care, and other skills. This is in addition to their day-to-day firearms shooting and assault training. Preparedness is what allows the HRT members to deploy day or night to a crisis and carry out their mission in any weather condition. This was exemplified in 1996 when the HRT was sent to San Juan, Puerto Rico to conduct a high-risk arrest, and were then immediately redeployed to upstate Michigan for another mission. The team went from a balmy 95 degree paradise to an icy -35 degree arctic-like environment within a 12-hour period, changing their equipment along the way.

Who's Who

The HRT falls under the Critical Incident Response Group (CIRG), which is tasked with using its assets to resolve hostage-takings and sieges. It is comprised of several units that fall into two distinct divisions: Special Investigations and Tactical Support. Under the Special Investigations branch, there are five units: Abducted Children & Serial Killers Unit; Undercover Safeguard Unit; Investigative Support Unit; Crisis Management Unit; and Aviation & Special Operations Unit. The latter two play important roles in hostage situations.

The Crisis Management Unit (CMU) is comprised of negotiators and command post staff. The negotiators have years of experience, and often speak several languages. The CMU was formerly known as SOARS, which, as mentioned earlier, fathered the Hostage Rescue Team.

The Aviation & Special Operations Unit provides fixed-wing aircraft that are used for surveillance efforts. This includes the Nightstalker aircraft that are deployed with the HRT in crises to give them night vision capability from the air. These turbo-prop aircraft are equipped with FLIR (Forward Looking Infrared), high speed video, and high resolution cameras. Nightstalker aircraft were used in the 1996 Montana Freemen stand-off to provide aerial photographs of the area to the HRT for tactical planning purposes. (Yes, HRT was at Montana. They arrested the militia's leaders—Daniel Petersen and Leroy Schweitzer—before the siege began. They were chosen by FBI Director Freeh for this mission to minimize the risk of a potential shoot-out. The HRT also ran all the tactical operations during the siege.) The Nightstalkers are based in Washington, D.C., although there has been talk of deploying one of these sophisticated aircraft out on the West Coast to speed up response times in future crises.

Under the CIRG's Tactical Support branch is the HRT, SWAT Training Unit, and Special Detail Unit. The latter protects the U.S. Attorney General. The Hostage Rescue Team itself is comprised of a commander, deputy commander, and seven supervisors. Each supervisor is responsible for a particular scope of operation, such as breaching, training, and intelligence. The HRT's four assault teams are under one supervisor; its four sniper teams, under another.

Two assault teams and two sniper teams each comprise what is referred to as a "Blue Team" and a "Gold Team." These teams are on different cycles—a training cycle and a duty cycle—each of which lasts two weeks. During the training cycle, one team focuses on core counterterrorism skills such as CQB drills, room clearing, and breaching. Meanwhile, the other team is on the duty cycle, preparing for instant deployment. They may do protective details, conduct site surveys, or even undergo specialized training during their two-week cycle. By using this Blue/Gold concept, half the HRT is always ready to respond to an emergency.

An interesting arena within the HRT is the Tactical Helicopter Program, which provides the team with aircraft for transportation and tactical

Practice makes perfect, and the HRT practices every day to keep its counterterrorist skills honed. Here, two HRT operators practice doing an insertion via helicopter, shooting at targets (left) on the way in. The MD-530 "Little Bird" helicopter is popular with elite forces worldwide, due to its small size, speed and agility. *U.S. Federal Bureau of Investigation*

insertions. The HRT now has more than a dozen single- and twin-engine aircraft and helicopters, including the small, fast, and agile MD-530 "Little Bird." The HRT has prepositioned several of its aircraft at locations around the United States to ensure quick response times when a crisis arises.

Dialing 9-1-1

As the United States' premier counterterrorist force, the Hostage Rescue Team is deployed to hostage situations and sieges as they arise. It also participates in major public events, such as the Olympics and Presidential Conventions. In these events, they

The HRT has an arrangement with the U.S. Air Force to use USAF aircraft for deployments. This allows the team to be "wheels up" within four hours and on its way to the scene of a crisis. The Air Force provides C-130 Hercules, C-5 Galaxy and, shown here, C-141 StarLifter cargo aircraft to transport the HRT's palletized gear, Ford Explorers, armored vehicles, and helicopters. The C-141 can carry up to 89,000 pounds of cargo. *U.S. Department of Defense*

A rarely seen and precious gift given to HRT operators at the end of their tour of duty: an engraved ring with the HRT logo on it. The ring is purchased by the men in the unit and is presented to the departing team member at a going away party. For many operators, it's one of the most emotional moments in their lives. For years they have trained with the unit day in and day out, sweating and sacrificing themselves to save lives. *U.S. Federal Bureau of Investigation*

assist in thwarting acts of terrorism, as well as responding to any incidents that occur.

During the 1996 Olympic Games in Atlanta, the HRT visited all 45 venues and 38 training sites, mapped them out, and put them on computer. If a terrorist had taken athletes hostage, the HRT could have pulled up the blueprint and photos of the building and specific room on the computer and quickly created an assault plan. The team also prepared dozens of response options in anticipation of the more obvious terrorist attacks, including car bombings, hostage-takings in the Olympic village, and attacks against the nuclear reactor at the Georgia Institute of Technology. They rehearsed these assaults prior to the Games, to iron out all the wrinkles. In one exercise, "Olympic Charlie," they and other agencies had to deal simultaneously with a hijacking at the airport and a chemical gas attack in downtown Atlanta. The terrorists had driven a van filled with VX nerve gas through the city and crashed into a tanker carrying gasoline while other members of the group

held passengers hostage aboard a plane at the airport. It was the first exercise ever to be held by federal authorities involving the release of a poison gas at a public event.

While the Olympic Games were underway, the HRT and CIRG were on-call to immediately respond to any incident. An operations center located at the FBI Atlanta Field Office orchestrated their deployment and response.

If a terrorist incident happens in the United States, the local police and SWAT team are the first to respond. If they determine that the situation is more serious than they can handle, they call on the FBI for assistance. The FBI has a SWAT team at each of its 56 field offices nationwide. Supplementing this are nine enhanced SWAT teams of about 30 agents each that are located in the larger field offices such as New York City, Chicago, and Los Angeles. These nine teams have received special training from the HRT and possess enhanced equipment. It is their duty to rectify the terrorist situation if they can and, if they can't, to take charge of the scene until the HRT arrives.

In large crises, such as the Oklahoma City bombing and the Montana Freemen siege, the FBI has a special command post within its Washington, D.C. headquarters that directs operations until the situation is remedied. Established by Buck Revell in 1983, prior to the 1984 Olympic Games, the Strategic Information Operations Center is a secure suite of rooms staffed around the clock during major investigations. It has a conference room, galley and a command area that is filled with television monitors, fax machines, computers, secure telephones, and a secure videoconferencing system.

When attempting to remedy a crisis, the FBI uses all other methods before calling on the Hostage Rescue Team. Many unenlightened Americans do not understand that just because the HRT exists, it does not mean that it must be used, especially if the FBI does not have to use it. As Buck Revell points out,

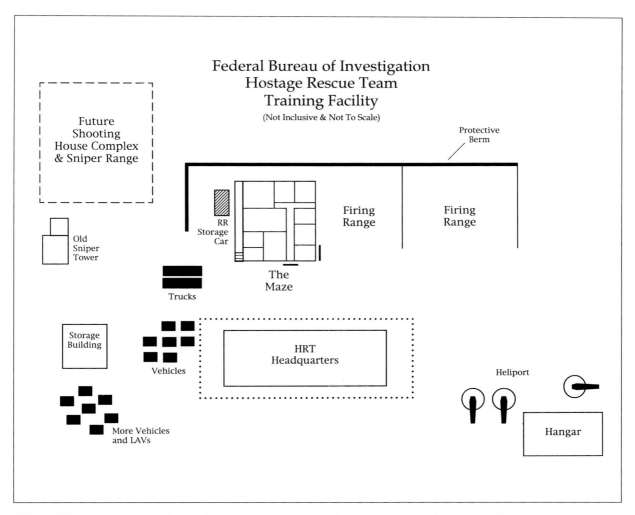

Federal Bureau of Investigation
Hostage Rescue Team
Training Facility
(Not Inclusive & Not To Scale)

Future Shooting House Complex & Sniper Range

Protective Berm

RR Storage Car

Old Sniper Tower

Firing Range

Firing Range

The Maze

Trucks

Storage Building

Vehicles

HRT Headquarters

Heliport

More Vehicles and LAVs

Hangar

"The HRT was never intended to be used as a first strike capability."

This is underscored by FBI Director Louis Freeh. "The HRT should not be used reflexively. I approach the use of HRT conservatively and seek independent assessments before it is used. Indeed, I cannot envision utilizing the HRT unless I am personally satisfied that it is necessary and appropriate to use it."

But when it is called upon, the HRT is ready to go. The members of this unit constantly prepare for worst-case situations. They understand that when they get the nod from the director to deploy, it's not going to be a cotton candy event. Somewhere in the United States, something has gone terribly, tragically wrong and their special skills are needed to save lives. As they don their equipment, they acknowledge the gravity of the mission ahead of them. They willingly go into harm's way because it is important to them to keep the United States free.

CHAPTER FIVE

The Shadow Stalkers: USMS Special Operations Group

> "In the normal course, we're not visible."
> —Lou Stagg, Commander, SOG

Alexandria is a small city located in the heart of the Creole State. Split by the Red River, the region surrounding Alexandria is dominated by pine trees, swamps, and critters of all shapes, colors, and sizes. It's difficult to believe that hidden among all the steamy marshes and scrub forests is the headquarters and training grounds of the U.S. Marshals Service's elite unit, the Special Operations Group (SOG). As local residents go about their work in Alexandria just a few miles away—down a dirt road that leads to a 40-acre complex—deputy marshals are firing Colt SMGs at targets, running obstacle courses, practicing dynamic entries, and learning breaching techniques in a classroom environment. Who would have guessed?

The Special Operations Group is the United States' oldest tactical team in the federal government, having been established in 1971—years before Delta Force,

"FREEZE!" The business end of a Colt SMG handled by a dead-serious SOG operator. The 9 mm uses the basic body and configuration of an M-16 rifle, but with a short and rigid telescoping butt. The SMG has a cyclic firing rate of 800 to 1,000 rounds per minute. It fires 20- or 32-shot magazines. *SF Tomajczyk*

SEAL Team Six and the FBI's HRT were even a thought in the back of someone's mind. When it was first established, SOG was used to respond to national emergencies and to counter civil disturbances, such as the seizure of Alcatraz Island and the occupation of the Twin Cities Naval Air Station just outside Minneapolis.

SOG's first major deployment occurred in February 1973, when members of the militant American Indian Movement seized the hamlet of Wounded Knee, on the Pine Ridge Sioux Reservation in South Dakota to raise awareness of American Indians' civil rights. The Special Operations Group was activated and more than 100 armed Deputy Marshals descended at Wounded Knee, along with dozens of FBI special agents and Bureau of Indian Affairs police officers. Both sides dug in. Within days, the hills were littered with bunkers and trenches as the negotiation process began to drag on. The siege, which piqued the world's interest, lasted 71 days before the captors finally surrendered to authorities. Nearly every night of the siege featured firefights between the Indians and federal officials, with thousands of rounds being fired. Two Indians were killed and U.S. Marshal Lloyd Grimm was paralyzed when a rifle bullet severed his spine; the great distance between the two entrenched parties prevented any further casualties. Although many SOG members felt they could retake the hamlet within hours by using armored personnel carri-

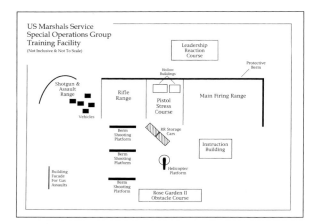

US Marshals Service
Special Operations Group
Training Facility
(Not Inclusive & Not To Scale)

Leadership Reaction Course

Protective Berm

Hollow Buildings

Shotgun & Assault Range

Rifle Range

Pistol Stress Course

Main Firing Range

Vehicles

Berm Shooting Platform

RR Storage Cars

Berm Shooting Platform

Instruction Building

Building Facade For Gas Assaults

Helicopter Platform

Berm Shooting Platform

Rose Garden II Obstacle Course

ers and tactical assault techniques, the unit was forbidden by the U.S. Attorney General to take down Wounded Knee. Instead, they were ordered to contain the situation and ensure that those who participated in the siege were arrested. Ultimately, a settlement was reached in May. The Indians were gathered up, arrested, and hauled away in buses, thus marking the successful end of the Special Operations Group's first serious involvement.

Since that time, SOG's mission has constantly evolved to match the needs of the times. It has moved away from managing civil disturbances and has learned how to vanquish the horrors of an ever-changing criminal element. Today, SOG is deployed to serve high-risk warrants, transport high-profile and dangerous prisoners, protect dignitaries and federal witnesses, provide security at federal courts, and apprehend dangerous fugitives (a.k.a. shadows). The latter role is the reason why the Special Operations Group is known by some as the "Shadow Stalkers." Fugitives from the law typically disappear into the deep shadows of our society to thwart apprehension.

Although it is not a dedicated counterterrorist team like the HRT or Delta Force, SOG does play an important role in the United States' war on terrorists. In any given week, the U.S. Marshals Service is responsible for about 23,000 unsentenced prisoners. Some of these are alleged terrorists and extremists who have either killed or threatened to kill innocent people. The Special Operations Group is responsible for guarding these purported tangos, so that their comrades don't attempt to free them. Recent notables under SOG's watchful eye included Timothy McVeigh (Oklahoma City bombing), Sheik Omar Abdel-Rahman (New York City bombing conspiracy), Ramzi Ahmed Yousef (Philippine Airlines bombing and World Trade Center bombing), and Theodore Kaczynski (Unabomber).

"I see SOG's mission in high threat terrorist type trials," says George "Ray" Havens, deputy director of the U.S. Marshals Service. "If we've got to move the Sheik and the people in the World Trade Center case from Springfield, Missouri, to Kansas City where they're going to be housed, that's a mission for a specially trained, specially equipped law enforcement group. That's a SOG mission."

SOG is also responsible for protecting the people that testify against terrorists so they don't end up on the bottom of some unnamed lake wearing cement boots. And, if someone makes a threat against a federal judicial official, SOG jumps in to protect them as well.

For example, during the biggest terrorism trial in U.S. history—in which Sheik Omar Abdel-Rahman and nine others were convicted, in October 1995, of con-

SOG operators practice two-man entry drills. SOG is organized around 12-man teams that typically use the "snake" formation to assault and clear a building of terrorists. The black outfit worn by SOG is just one of several uniforms in the team's closet. It is designed for night operations (i.e., camouflage) as well as to intimidate the "bad guys" so that they don't immediately respond to the team's threat. By the time they react, it's too late. SF Tomajczyk

Women comprise about 10 percent of SOG's strength. They undergo and endure the exact same training as their male counterparts. Note the SOG patch on this operator's shoulder (who, by the way, is an admirable marksman). The silhouette of the United States shows that SOG is a national team, the four regions identify the original organizational response structure (which is no longer used), the red-white-and-blue lightning suggests that SOG reacts patriotically and quickly to a crisis, the VI refers to the original six-hour response time that SOG adhered to (it's faster now), the stars identify the original location of SOG Headquarters and its training facilities (which have changed), and the dates—1789 and 1971—refer to the formation of the U.S. Marshals Service and SOG, respectively. This is one of the most difficult patches for collectors to acquire. Not even USMS staff can get them. *SF Tomajczyk*

spiring to wage a Holy War against the United States—members of SOG protected the judges and U.S. attorneys from possible attacks of retribution. The arrest and subsequent conviction of the Sheik, a well-known cleric, who was the spiritual leader of a militant Muslim group accused of deadly terrorist acts in Egypt, angered more than just a few people in the Middle East. A bombing attempt of the court room itself or a suicide machine gun massacre of court officials was not out of the question. Which is why SOG had plain-clothed observers stationed all over the building complex during the nine-month trial, as well as a heavily armed assault team waiting in a room ready to spring into action at the first signs of an attack. If somebody had been foolish enough to try anything, he would have been arrested within seconds.

Similarly, SOG was present at the World Trade Center bombing trial, which took place in 1994, prior to the above-mentioned "Holy War" terrorist trial. Four defendants were found guilty of the horrific 1993 bombing that claimed six lives and injured more than 1,000 people. They were each sentenced to 240 years of imprisonment without the possibility of parole. SOG ensured the safety of the witnesses and judicial officials during the trial, as well as thwarted any possible rescue efforts to free the defendants.

SOG was once again a shadow in the U.S. District Courts. This time, it was for Ramzi Ahmed Yousef, the alleged mastermind of the World Trade Center bombing, who was on trial. He was captured in Pakistan after a worldwide manhunt by the FBI. Upon his extradition to the United States, Yousef was put on trial and found guilty for a related terrorist act in which he and two others conspired to blow up 12 planes in 48 hours, killing 4,000 innocent Americans. (Yousef tested his idea by placing a bomb on a Philippine Airlines flight in 1994. The bomb exploded, killing a passenger and injuring 10 others.) Needless to say, Yousef and the others were found guilty. The 28-year-old militant was now being guarded by the Special Operations Group, while the World Trade Center bombing trial was in session.

A Close Look At SOG

The Special Operations Group is presently organized around four Teams, each of which is comprised of smaller 12-person teams. (Prior to 1996, SOG was organized around three Task Forces.) All tolled, SOG has upward of 100 operators, of which 10 percent are women. Most team members are in their 30s and many are married, some with children. Interestingly, none of the SOG teams is a dedicated, full-time unit like the FBI's Hostage Rescue Team. Deputy Marshals that have been accepted into SOG serve in district and field offices throughout the nation, remaining on call 24 hours a day for SOG missions. This is not to say, however, that there is no need or desire for a dedicated unit. In fact, USMS Deputy Director Ray Havens has a concept to create such a team at SOG Headquarters in Louisiana that will work and train every day to support the agency's mission. Havens envisions this core team being complemented out in the field by former SOG members, when necessary. For example, if SOG were to be deployed to Michigan for an operation, it could pull in six former team members from nearby field offices to assist with perimeter security, serve on entry teams, and so on.

Current SOG operators support Havens' vision for a full-time team. They understand the need for a team to train together all the time, in order to establish unit integrity and, more importantly, to ensure that everyone is prepared to dance the intricate choreography of an assault.

At any given time, one SOG team is on standby notice for deployment, with the other three teams being on call. This is similar to the way the Army's 82nd Airborne Division operates. The team remains on standby notice for about three weeks. If there is no deployment, they rotate to "in the hole" status while the other three teams assume higher levels of readiness.

If SOG is deployed, team members gather at the Tactical Center—SOG's headquarters—located at Camp Beauregard near Alexandria, Louisiana . . . that is, if time allows. Once at the Tactical Center, the operators hone their shooting skills and practice their assault mission before going wheels-up. However, if it's an emer-gency and they don't have time for this practice session, SOG operators travel directly to the crisis site and go on their experience and skills. Depending on the situation, SOG can be on location within a few hours. The team has its basic equipment palletized, ready to go at a moment's notice. It can be flown out by military or U.S. Marshals Service aircraft.

A basic assault team is comprised of 12 members, although it could be more or less depending on the mission. Lou Stagg, the commander of the Special Operations Group, works closely with the team commander to match the deploying team with the expected operating environment. As Stagg points out, a team may have to be deployed for longer than a week, so you might need to send more people so that operators get some down time. Similarly, an assault team may be in a situation that requires the use of four snipers to complement its normal crew. In the end, the situation dictates how many SOG operators are deployed and what special skills and equipment are provided.

So You Wanna Be a "Shadow Stalker?"

Becoming a member of SOG is no picnic. Only 10 to 15 percent of all applicants survive the selection process, which includes a series of interviews and 27 days of hellish training at the Tactical Center. In a recent class, 200 Deputy Marshals applied for SOG, 59 were accepted for training, and only 20 finished. Those statistics alone attest to the elite nature of the Special Operations Group.

Qualified Deputy Marshals are welcome to apply to SOG. The initial selection criterion is based on a deputy's physical skills, mental ability, background, and other factors. A numerical scoring system is used to make a list of possible candidates, from which several are invited to visit the Center for one-on-one interviews. SOG looks for mature, stable, and well-rounded candidates who are trainable, possess high skill levels in certain areas, and are capable of retaining perishable skills. Individualists, glory hounds, and hot doggers need not apply. Similarly, don't expect special treatment just because you happen to be a former Navy SEAL or SWAT team member.

"No one walks through the door," says Lou Stagg, pointing at the front of the Tactical Center. "I don't care what you were before you got here. You're starting off equal to everybody in those ranks."

Stagg admits that people from units around the world have indeed trained with SOG. Some have succeeded and others have failed. "It's a mind-set," says Stagg. "Some people can't adapt to it. They don't want to go through it again. They don't want to have to go back to the fundamentals."

After the one-on-one interviews, promising candidates must validate any skills they claim to have. For instance, if they say they can shoot a score of 90 percent, they have to prove it right then and there. Shooting certification from a District Office is not accepted by SOG. So braggarts beware.

Once the final candidates have been selected, they undergo a 27-day Qualification Course at the Tactical Center. It's essentially 27 days of immersion into pure, unadulterated stress. The course is designed to peak and ebb a candidate's emotions and physical abilities. Just about everything is done in a military-like manner. As a candidate, you never walk again. Instead, you march and move in formation. You are under constant pressure, 24 hours a day, to accomplish tasks while paying attention to the smallest of details. You have to shoot and perform and maintain discipline nonstop. The training itself lasts 15 to 17 hours a day, and is filled with physical exercise, obstacle courses, firearms training, field exercises, and assault tactics. You are given no guarantee that you'll get a full night's sleep. In fact, you're lucky if you get 60 minutes of shut-eye a day.

The stress and fatigue are used by SOG instructors to get a glimpse into your soul. How well can you hold up? What is your breaking point? Can you think clearly and function well under stress? Can you make good tactical decisions? Do you remain a team player or do you retreat and become an individualist? These are important questions that must be answered. SOG is a tight, even-keeled, and well-disciplined unit. It cannot allow one of its members to lose control while on a mission. To do so could jeopardize not only the success of the mission but also, more importantly, someone's life.

The rope climb that seems to never end. It is just one station in the 12-station Rose Garden obstacle course at SOG's 40-acre training facility in Louisiana. The 100-yard course is both stressful and competitive, with two operators racing against each other and the clock to finish within 150 seconds. Task Force Three Commander Wayne Plylar demonstrates good climbing technique using his feet to lock on to the rope so that he can easily reach above and pull himself upward. The Rose Garden requires about 80 percent upper-body strength to complete it. *SF Tomajczyk*

Unlike the Navy's famous BUD/S course for aspiring SEALs, SOG candidates are not paired up during training. Instead, they are placed into squads of 10 people. As attrition takes its toll, a candidate may be reassigned or merged into another squad. Internally, some people may naturally pair up because of similar backgrounds (e.g., two people with Special Forces training), but in the end, the entire squad is responsible for its performance. Everyone quickly learns to be a team player, trying to pull others to their level of ability.

The Leadership Reaction Course, a U.S. Air Force concept, is where SOG team leaders can see the tactical solving skills and interpersonal dynamics of unit members. Operators are given 10 minutes to solve a problem, such as the one shown here: getting across a water barrier without touching the red areas (or the water). There are 15 stations in the LRC, each with a unique problem to be addressed and overcome. In the end, team members tend to follow the advice of the most persistent and outspoken leader, not necessarily the strongest person. *SF Tomajczyk*

Observes Commander Stagg, "You have people that are striving to achieve on their own, as individuals, and to show their skills, so as to ensure their position in the unit, but at the same time, you see it become a team effort." Stagg says that it is typical for the training to start off as a group of individuals reporting in, then it slowly metamorphoses into a squad. By the end of the class, it's the candidates against the staff. "They get to the point where they're not going to lose one more person, regardless of what it takes."

There are essentially three ways for a candidate to leave the training cycle. First, a candidate can volunteer to leave, which is immediately granted. Second, an injured candidate can fail to finish the training. If this happens, he can reapply for the next session, but there is no guarantee of acceptance. And last, SOG instructors can remove a candidate if they feel he doesn't meet the criteria of what they are looking for. If a candidate leaves, nothing is put into his personnel jacket, and nothing is recorded at headquarters about his unsuccessful attempt. The reason for this is twofold: SOG doesn't want a candidate's failure to haunt him for the rest of his career as a Deputy Marshal, and SOG doesn't want to scare off future candidates from applying.

A Trip Through the Rose Garden

Most of the candidate training takes place miles away from the Tactical Center, out in the middle of a 13,000-acre Army reservation that is covered with pine forests. Here, hidden away from public view, is SOG's 40-acre training complex, which features several firing ranges, a helicopter sniper/rappelling platform, a mock city, an obstacle course, a leadership reaction course, a warehouse with moveable walls that is used for entry drills, a vehicle assault course, and a log cabin that is used for classroom training sessions. Much of this facility was built by SOG members over the years since they moved to Louisiana, in 1983. They built firing ranges, assembled the log cabin, and constructed berms. They also did a lot of improvising: two railroad cars serve as a storage shed for equipment.

One of the more unpleasant tasks SOG candidates have to endure is the obstacle course, which is located adjacent to the rifle/sniper range. Known sarcastically as Rose Garden II, this O-course is 100 yards long and has 12 stations that are guaranteed to make your upper body burn with exhaustion. Keith Erni, a SOG team commander, says that is deliberate. "The course was designed to require that you use about 80 percent of your upper body strength. Most people are weak in that area, and this is a good way to improve their strength. Strength and good technique are necessary ingredients to overcome the Rose Garden."

Candidates run the course in pairs against each other and against the clock. The course includes elevated logs to jump and climb over, 7-foot-high walls to scramble over, and a thick hanging rope to climb to the top of, 25 feet above. If you can do the full course in two and a half minutes, you're doing great. Most candidates, however, are fortunate to complete it in three to five minutes on the first try.

Drowned Rats

A unique training exercise that SOG candidates go through is the Leadership Reaction Course (LRC). Based on an Air Force concept and design, the LRC is a series of problems that groups of candidates must solve in 10 minutes, using limited resources. At SOG's training complex, the LRC is made up of about 12 stations, many of which have water barriers, steel tubing, and concrete walls. In one scenario, candidates are told to move a heavy ammo box—and themselves—over an 8-foot-high wall and then across a 15-foot-wide water barrier. Strung across the pool of water are five loosely slung chains. The candidates are to accomplish this task without touching either the water or anything painted red. Of course, just about everything is painted red, the chains are extremely wobbly, and anything that you could possibly use to your advantage is greased down so that you slip.

In another scenario, the candidates are ordered to cross a 25-foot-wide pool of water using just two boards—that together measure a total of 10 feet. In the middle of the pool are three vertical concrete posts that can be used. Problem is, only one person at a time can stand on them, and there are six people in the exercise. Needless to say, candidates get soaked falling into the water that they're not supposed to touch. By the end of the day, everyone looks like a drowned rat and are covered head-to-foot in slime. (Did I forget to mention that the water barriers are filled with stale, algae-ridden water in the summer?)

The purpose of the LRC is to give SOG team commanders the opportunity to witness the dynamics of a unit in action. Who is a leader? Who builds consensus?

SOG's primary firing range with five shooting distances. It is designed so that vehicles can be driven out on the pavement, allowing operators to practice movement and cover drills. The range can also be modified to include building facades, pop-up and spinning targets, etc. Low-light shooting drills are conducted in the evenings, with strobe lights being occasionally used to make "shoot/no shoot" drills more difficult for the operators. The tower in the middle is where the range master controls targets and the shooting tempo. *SF Tomajczyk*

How well do people work together? How good are their tactical solving skills? In the end, the unit members follow the strongest person. By strongest, I mean the individual who is the loudest and most persistent, not necessarily the most strong physically.

The lessons learned from the Leadership Reaction Course are so valuable that SOG Teams do LRC exercises during their normal training sessions held throughout the year.

Preparation for Deployment

When the Qualification Course finally comes to an end after 27 days, there are typically only about 10 candidates out of an original 60 or so still standing. After these survivors are assigned to a particular SOG team, they return to their District Office and resume their normal law enforcement duties. They don't meet or train with their new team until the unit's next scheduled training session, which is held at a minimum of every six months. When it arrives, all members of that particular SOG Team travel to the Tactical Center at Camp Beauregard. Then, for the next three weeks, they hone their shooting and assault skills.

This is not to suggest, however, that members of SOG Teams train only twice a year, because they don't. Individuals train on a regular basis at their District Office. And if their SOG Team is deployed, they not only benefit from the mission itself, but also from any training time they are able to take advantage of while out in the field. Keep in mind that training is not restricted to shooting a SMG on a firing range. Training also delves into many other topics, such as breaching techniques, rappelling, room entry tactics, first aid, and more. The foundation of many of these can be taught through manuals and audio-visual tools. During tenure with the Special Operations Group, there is always something to learn.

When SOG members get together with their teams at Camp Beauregard, the first few days are spent on the weapons range, shooting 9-mm Colt SMGs and Smith & Wesson .45 caliber Mod 645 (or .357 magnum) handguns at targets from various distances. The instructors start the training off slowly, so that team members can cement relationships with each other, as well as build self-confidence in their shooting abilities.

That all changes, however, with time. Perhaps the first indication is when the team is summoned for a low-light shooting exercise. The SOG operators arrive at the main weapons range after the sun has set. Then, under a strobe light's distracting flashes, the Shadow Stalkers have to shoot (or not shoot) at targets that spin around at them on the firing range. The targets are hidden inside the doorways and windows of a building facade. An operator has to decide—in a split instant—whether or not to shoot as he moves down the firing line. If the target is of a criminal wielding a gun, he shoots. If the target is a mother holding a baby, he restrains his fire. It's a stressful drill, and the flashing strobe light doesn't make it any easier.

For the remainder of their training session, SOG team members experience a wide variety of exercises and classroom instructions. For example, they may prac-

Realistic-looking targets used by SOG on the pistol and rifle ranges. Operators are trained to find a balance between speed and accuracy, and to shoot only hostile targets (i.e., those brandishing a weapon in a threatening manner). This means they have only a split second after seeing a target to decide whether or not to fire their weapon. Such control is vital on a mission, where a hostage's life is determined by the competence of the SOG operator. The target on the right shows just how accurate and consistent operators are in firing their weapons: The center has been chewed away. Indoor shooting can be done using a FATS simulator, which is found inside a nearby building. *SF Tomajczyk*

tice vehicle takedowns (it takes five to six armed operators to do it properly), helicopter insertions (the Army provides the use of its Black Hawk and Huey helicopters), and close-quarters battle drills (a mock town facilitates this). They may also do a two- to three-day field exercise in which they are inserted into the woods via helicopter and then have to stealthily make their way to a target miles away, conduct reconnaissance, and then do a takedown in the middle of the night, using night vision goggles, tear gas, SMGs, and flashbangs. SOG often uses a warehouse for this particular exercise. Standing three stories tall, the nondescript, gray-painted building features movable plywood walls inside that can be configured to match any type of structure. In fact, the warehouse is often used during real operations to mimic the blueprint design of the actual target, so that an SOG team can do dress rehearsal assaults before deploying on the mission.

The day I visited the warehouse, it was configured to represent an apartment building. Earlier, SOG Team members had assaulted the building from the outside, gaining entrance by breaching a rear door with explosives. Once inside, they moved swiftly through the small, furniture-strewn rooms toward their objective, shooting hostile targets with precision fire along the way. (The heavily pocked targets and mannequins attested to the accuracy.) I was told that SOG practices similar assaults in varying lighting conditions, as well as in gas environments, in which CS or CN tear gas is dispersed, thus forcing the assault team to wear gas masks. To be more realistic, instructors often move walls around without telling the team. This reflects the fact that buildings change from their blueprints over the years, as occupants add a closet here, close off a wall there, and move doorways to meet their personal needs. These type of surprises teach an assault team how to be flexible and how to quickly modify their takedown strategy.

Two operators demonstrate how a building entry is done on the Pistol Stress Course. They have been stealthily and fluidly moving toward the target, while covering each other, shooting targets and reloading their 9-mm Colts. The course features fences, gates, passageways, and obstacles (e.g. cars, mail boxes). Each building structure is color coded; a range master dictates which one the operators will assault, as well as which color-coded targets (red or blue) will be shot at. *SF Tomajczyk*

SOG operators also spend quite a bit of time on the Pistol Stress Course, where they move toward a target in pairs using parked vehicles, fences, and mailboxes as cover. As they approach the hollow buildings that makeup the course, they practice covering each other while shooting at hostile targets and reloading. During all this, instructors yell out which targets—red or blue—the Shadow Stalkers should shoot at. The Pistol Stress Course also serves as a decent-but-basic outdoor facility in which a six-member assault force can practice moving in "Snake" formation to an objective and then rehearse various room entry techniques, such as the Buttonhook and Crisscross.

Supplementing this training are exercises known as "Glass House" drills. In the real world, SOG doesn't always have time to build a scale model of the building they'll be assaulting, so they have to rely on other methods to practice their choreography. The Glass House is often used in these circumstances. It consists of putting tape on the floor or ground to represent the walls (albeit nonexistent) that make up the rooms and corridors of the target building. Then the assault team rehearses its entry technique, using the tape as a guideline.

For more realistic training, SOG visits its Urban Center, which is a mock-up of a small town. It is located a few miles away from SOG's main firing range, behind a barbed-wired security fence. When it was first designed, the Urban Center was intended to be comprised of several blocks filled with different types of commercial buildings (e.g., post office, grocery store, city hall, power company) and residential homes for SOG to practice its assaults on. However, due to the lack of funds, only one block of structures was actually built. The Urban Center is ideal for urban combat and close-quarters battle training. For example, a SOG team can fast rope from a UH-1 or UH-60 helicopter into the town, and quickly deploy to the objective where they establish sniper/observer teams and begin conducting reconnaissance. When an assault plan is finalized, the team then breaches the building (with or without the use of explosives), sends any tango on a visit to God, and rescues the hostages. Such training is invaluable in preparing SOG for the real thing.

It is unlikely that the Special Operations Group will ever finish building its Urban Center. There is a movement among Department of Justice agencies to consolidate training assets, so as to avoid duplication. "Duplication in law enforcement is ludicrous," says Ray Havens. "If I get a training building, another agency gets a bigger building, and another gets a training complex. This is how it has (traditionally) occurred, and I don't think it's cost effective." Havens points out that finishing the Urban Center isn't really necessary, since SOG can use Hogan's Alley at the FBI Academy in Virginia, or the so-called "Training City" at the Metro Dade Police Department in Florida. He does admit, however, that a drawback to using these other facilities is being able to work into the schedule.

Depending on how much money is in its budget, the Special Operations Group sporadically sends some of its teams to train at the facilities of other elite counterterrorist teams around the world (and vice versa). In the past, this included the facilities of Delta Force, SEAL Team Six, GIGN, GSG-9, and SAS. The military units only provide the use of their facilities, they do not directly train SOG members.

"The opportunities are always there," says SOG Commander Lou Stagg. "I can't identify any unit that is reluctant to try to learn something from someone else or expose themselves to someone else in the training environment." However, he does point out that you have to make certain that the training will, in fact, be beneficial to the team, given the constraints of budget and time. "Do I want to spend my time with a unit that's designed for one military purpose, when some of those skills would be good to know (but are not really applicable) to the civilian law enforcement role, or is it better to seek out another training source that better serves and mirrors the mission you have been assigned by your individual agency?"

Budgetary concerns and training appropriateness aside, another matter that SOG must take into consideration is whether or not there are enough personnel

A shootout at SOG's mock city, with the operator ideally using the car for cover. He is positioned behind the car's engine block, which provides ballistic protection, and he is crouched so that he can move up and down like a spring to fire his weapon without getting out of his shooting platform position. *SF Tomajczyk*

available to undergo the cross-training. Unlike military units, which are so large that a handful of operators are always available for training exercises, civilian law enforcement teams are generally so small that it is difficult to send teams off for training and still be able to respond to crises. People may be working different shifts, they may be serving collateral duties, or they may be involved with a task that supersedes training. Thus, it is difficult to pull enough operators together for extended time periods.

One interesting aspect of SOG is that it often provides tactical training to foreign law enforcement units under an MoU from the Department of State. The walls of the Tactical Center are adorned with plaques thanking SOG for its training efforts. Over the years, SOG has imparted advanced tactical skills to the Greek National Police, Bolivian National Police, Poland's Anti-Terrorist Squad, Philippine Naval Intelligence, and the Jordanian Public Security Police. Closer to home, SOG has also helped train the U.S. Border Patrol, INS, and

BATF Entry Control Teams. Most of these training sessions last four weeks and are conducted by SOG staff at its 40-acre facility.

Going Wheels-Up

When a crisis arises somewhere in the United States and SOG is needed to respond to it, the order for deployment comes either directly from the U.S. Attorney General through a request to the Director of the Marshals Service, or from the Director/Deputy Director of Marshals Service after receiving a request from a District Office. Either way, the Special Operations Group cannot deploy until it has received written permission from the headquarters directorate staff. Once the marching orders are given, SOG alerts the on-call team, which assembles at the Tactical Center. An advance team is immediately sent out ahead of the main body to begin conducting intelligence and prepare everything for the team's arrival.

Meanwhile, the Shadow Stalkers hone their shooting skills on the firing ranges and rehearse entry procedures in the warehouse, which is quickly configured to match the blueprint of the building they will be assaulting. If there is not enough time to reconfigure the ware-

What the well-dressed SOG operator is wearing these days: 30 pounds of weapons, ammo magazines, ballistic Kevlar helmet, tactical vest, radio, Nomex gloves, bulletproof vest, and tear gas. *SF Tomajczyk*

house, the assault teams go through Glass House drills. Not enough can be said for just how important it is that a team rehearse every minute detail of its entry choreography. Lives are at stake.

While this is going on, one or more of the available conference rooms at SOG Headquarters is turned into an operations center to coordinate all aspects of the team's deployment. Nearly every room of the building is loaded with telephone jacks, which allow command posts to be quickly established and expanded as needed. Simultaneously, palletized equipment is loaded into unmarked vans to be placed aboard military or USMS aircraft, and weapons (e.g., 9-mm Colt SMGs, H&K MP5s, sniper rifles) from SOG's basement arsenal are checked and made ready for use. Within hours, the team is ready to go wheels-up.

Adjacent to the Tactical Center is a large Army heliport that berths numerous UH-1 Iroquois and OH-58 Kiowa Warrior helicopters. (On some occasions, SOG has used unarmed Kiowa Warriors for scouting missions; its forward-looking infrared sensors are invaluable in tracking fugitives at night.) This grass-field heliport can be used by SOG to expeditiously deploy by helicopter to a nearby airport where larger aircraft are loaded and waiting to go. If a more private departure or arrival is needed, SOG can use the back parking lot of the Tactical Center as a mini heliport. Encircled by barbed-wire fencing, the lot is big enough for a UH-60 Black Hawk to land in. Over the years, this paved lot has seen visits from many elite units, including the Army's 160th SOAR.

Inside the Red October

Depending on the nature of the crisis that SOG is responding to, the deployed team may need a mobile command post at the scene. Prior to the 1996 Olympics, SOG had two Mobile Command Centers available to it: a 75-foot-long tractor trailer known as "Red October" (a.k.a. Big Red) and a 35-foot-long van known as "Blue November" (a.k.a. Little Red). The Red October, which got its name from author Tom Clancy after he walked through the vehicle and noticed all the red interior lights, is technologically the most advanced

Nerve centers for crises: Red October (left) and Blue November, high-tech mobile command posts. They are both equipped with conference rooms, galleys, weapons lockers, and state-of-the-art communication centers. If you look closely, you can see that a portion of the Red October's trailer expands to double width. Also, note the security monitor atop the Blue November. In 1996, the Red October was handed over to FEMA by the USMS, who found it too expensive to operate. *U.S. Marshals Service*

vehicle in the world. It stands 13 feet, 6 inches tall, weighs 85,000 pounds and is expandable to 22 feet in width using a hydraulic system. Inside, the vehicle features a security area, conference room, communications room, and a crisis room outfitted with TVs that can receive stations worldwide. The Red October also has a kitchenette that can prepare a five-course meal for 30 to 40 people for up to a month. The vehicle is so large that it cannot be airlifted, even by military aircraft. It takes two qualified drivers with special licenses to drive Red October to a crisis location (at four miles to the gallon). Every penny of the more than $1 million dollars that has been sunk into the Red October came from seized drug asset money, not taxpayer's dollars.

The Blue November arrived at the Marshals Service in 1994. This smaller vehicle has a communications center, conference area, galley, and a secured locker for weapons and other sensitive items. Blue November's communications capabilities include cellular phones, STU III secure telephones, VHF radio, satellite TV link, UHF/VHF air-to-ground radio, surveillance equipment (e.g., closed circuit television), TV monitors, satellite navigation system, VCRs, and computers. Externally, the vehicle has electrical outlets and hookups for additional telephones and satellite communications. The van can communicate with commercial aircraft and with any law enforcement agency in the United States. Unlike the Red October, Blue November can be transported by C-5 and C-17 aircraft, which allows it to be on site within hours.

Both the Red October and Blue November were present at the 1996 Olympics. The Red October was based at Dobbins AFB, and the Blue November was located in downtown Atlanta. Together, they served as mobile command posts and staging areas for the Marshals Service and SOG during the Games. After the Olympics concluded, the Red October was handed over to the Federal Emergency Management Agency. In spite of its awesome capabilities, the vehicle's gargantuan size and weight simply proved to be too difficult to deploy it in an expeditious manner during a crisis.

The Future of the SOG

The future of the Special Operations Group is bright. First and foremost, the current administration at USMS Headquarters is trying to more tightly define how the unit will be employed, so that it is not inappropriately used. To this end is Deputy Director Ray Havens' vision for a stand-alone, dedicated team that can train full-time in support of the agency's key missions. The administration is also trying to increase the amount of resources to support SOG. For example, SOG now has adequate training facilities and firepower, as well as state-of-the-art communications equipment. "We have some communications equipment now where I can set a briefcase on a table and communicate anywhere in the world," boasts Havens.

Havens is also a participant in a task force that is involved in declassifying military technology that could prove beneficial for the Special Operations Group. This includes less-than-lethal technologies that could be used to apprehend someone without seriously injuring or killing him.

Perhaps the only obstacle confronting the U.S. Marshals Service right now is its public relations image, which was shattered in August 1992, at a remote place known as Ruby Ridge. A team of deputy marshals was sent out into the mountainous region of northern Idaho to conduct surveillance of white supremacist Randall Weaver in preparation of serving an arrest warrant. The marshals unexpectedly ran into armed 14-year-old Samuel Weaver and a family friend—24-year-old Kevin Harris—near the Weaver cabin. Sam and Deputy U.S. Marshal William Degan were killed in a brief firefight that began when Sam's dog sniffed out the deputy marshals.

As Ray Havens points out, if Randall Weaver had simply gone to court as originally requested—like any other citizen—this incident never would have happened, and Weaver would have likely gotten either probation or a small sentence, since he had no previous criminal record. But

The famous star of the U.S. Marshals Service. It has been around since 1789 and is perhaps most often associated by the public with the "Wild West," during the days of Deputy U.S. Marshal Wyatt Earp (of OK Corral fame). *SF Tomajczyk*

the tragedy at Ruby Ridge did happen, and the Marshals Service is still paying the price. In the minds of some uniformed Americans, the Special Operations Group is to blame for the tragedy, even though the surveillance mission of Randy Weaver was *not* an SOG mission. (Yes, Degan happened to be the commander of Task Force 1 at the time, but he was the only SOG person at Ruby Ridge. He had been invited to accompany the other marshals in their surveillance efforts.) These same peo-

ple have also convinced themselves that the Special Operations Group is comprised of trigger-happy military commandos. This couldn't be further from the truth. Less than half the team's members have military experience and, more importantly, they are selected for SOG specifically because they *do* show restraint and clear-headedness in stressful situations.

"The facts are, when those guys went there (to Weaver's cabin), there was no way, shape, or form—there's not one scintilla of evidence—that they ever went there to do anything other than conduct an intelligence mission and make observations for an undercover operation. They were not planning to arrest that man," says Havens. "I don't know who fired the first shot. I just know that our people did the best job they could do under some very, very difficult circumstances. We've learned lessons from it, and we have a Department of Justice deadly force policy and rules-of-engagement that are now standard."

Considering all the successful deployments that SOG has made since 1971—literally hundreds of them—perhaps it's best to advocate for the unit, instead of blindly denouncing it. After all, the Special Operations Group does a tremendous amount of good for the United States. They protect our courts and federal witnesses from acts of terrorism, and they hunt down and arrest dangerous fugitives. Granted, in a free society, you can never protect every building and every person from harm, but the highly trained and versatile Shadow Stalkers certainly try.

CHAPTER SIX

Snuffing Out Super Terrorism: NEST and Other Elite Units

In 1975, the threat of nuclear terrorism almost became reality. An individual threatened to blow up the city of Boston with an improvised nuclear device if he was not paid $200,000. To prove that he was serious, he sent along some diagrams of his weapon to federal officials. Their seeming authenticity gave them much concern. At the time, the United States had no way to respond to such a threat. So arrangements quickly were made to pay the ransom, but the extortionist never picked it up. Was the bomb a hoax or did it truly exist? And if it was real, where is it today?

This incident slapped federal officials awake to the very real possibility of terrorists using nuclear bombs to achieve their goals. This also extended to the more likely scenario in which terrorists detonate a "normal" bomb

There are vast quantities of nuclear weapons and material around the world from the Cold War that terrorists can get their grubby paws on. In 1991, the terrorist group Islamic Jihad offered to buy a nuclear weapon from Russia's Arzamas-16 nuclear research center. In 1993, Iraq offered the same facility $2 billion for a warhead. Fortunately, none of these efforts succeeded. *U.S. Department of Defense*

that is laced with radioactive material like "hot" medical waste, which is much easier to acquire than weapons grade uranium. This type of device is known as a radiation bomb. (Had terrorists used this type of bomb at the World Trade Center in 1993, the effects would have been disastrous. Thousands of residents would have died from radiation poisoning, and downtown Manhattan would still be too contaminated to return to.)

And so the Nuclear Emergency Search Team (NEST) was created. Known as "America's Atomic A-Team" and "Nuclear Ninjas," this unit is part of the Department of Energy's Office of Emergency Response. NEST is tasked with finding and disarming nuclear devices, as well as providing technical support to the FBI, which has jurisdiction in cases involving nuclear threats. The unit is comprised of more than 750 volunteer scientists, engineers, and technicians from the national laboratories (e.g., Los Alamos, Sandia) and other agencies. Key components of NEST are located at the Nevada Operations Office, Nellis AFB (NV), and at Andrews AFB just outside of the nation's capitol.

Beware of the Boogey Man!

Nuclear terrorism is not farfetched. To build a small nuclear device, all a terrorist needs is two things: information and nuclear material. Bomb building information is readily available, which was underscored in the early 1980s by a Princeton

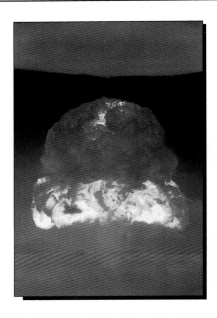

KEEPING WEAPONS OF MASS DESTRUCTION OUT OF THE UNITED STATES

The U.S. Customs Service stops terrorist tools from entering the United States, and prevents technology and weapons from being sent to hostile nations. To achieve this, customs has 6,000 inspectors who check people and cargo at more than 300 ports of entry, including international airports, seaports, and land borders. Supplementing this effort is customs' Office of Investigations, which has 2,400 special agents, marine enforcement officers, and air interdiction officers, along with 323 pilots and 300 intelligence analysts. Together, they work at plugging the terrorist pipeline.

For example, customs agents use high-tech sensors to locate nuclear materials. They have fixed X-ray equipment with radiation detection capability to examine baggage and bulk cargo, sensor-loaded vans that patrol borders, portal radiation detectors to check vehicles and container cargo, and radiation pagers to detect radiation on people. The latter device, which fastens on a belt like a beeper, is so sensitive that it sounds an alert on people who have had radiation therapy for cancer.

In the war against C/B agents, the Customs Service is exploring the use of chemical agent monitors (CAM) and back-scatter X-ray devices.

Customs has been successful in its antiterrorism efforts. In 1992, it thwarted the purchase of tactical nuclear weapons and weapons-grade uranium that was being sent to Iraq. And in June 1994, three New York residents were arrested for trying to ship nuclear-grade zirconium to Iraq (via Italy). U.S. Customs special agents seized 5 tons of the zirconium in a warehouse in the New York metropolitan area.

A scene that no one in the United States wants to see: the detonation of a nuclear device. Since 1975, there have been numerous nuclear terrorist threats but, fortunately, they have all been hoaxes so far. The Nuclear Emergency Search Team is the special unit that responds to threats and quickly determines whether or not they are real. This photo is of an 11 MT bomb exploding in an aboveground test (Operation Castle, Romeo Event) in 1954. LLNL

University student who designed a briefcase size bomb using public documents. This openness is further complicated by the thousands of unemployed Russian nuclear scientists, many of whom are willing to provide their knowledge of nuclear weapons design to the highest bidder.

As for nuclear material, an amateur only needs to get his hands on 18 pounds of 94-percent plutonium-239 (about the size of a grapefruit) or 55 pounds of highly enriched uranium. He can either steal it or buy it on the black-market. In 1994, more than 687 pounds of nuclear material was confiscated by police from traffickers worldwide. And that's only what they managed to catch. Plutonium fuel elements—which can be safely held, since they are not highly radioactive—come in disks that weigh a few tenths of a pound and resemble hockey pucks. They are easy to conceal in a pocket and walk out the door with.

Theft of nuclear material is increasing, especially since the collapse of the Soviet Union. In 1993, two fuel rods were cut off from a fuel assembly at the Chernobyl nuclear plant and disappeared. This, in

spite of the fact that the reactor building had high security. In 1995, 13 pounds of uranium—fuel from a Soviet naval reactor—was seized in Kiev. More recently, a Czech made arrangements to acquire 11 pounds of uranium a month from a Russian supplier for a client. The supplier promised they could give him 88 pounds of uranium immediately, and up to a ton in the long term. These are just three incidents of dozens reported in the past few years, and Russia is not alone. In 1994, 130 barrels of enriched uranium waste was stolen from a storage facility in South Africa. This demonstrates that theft can happen wherever nuclear materials are found.

In the United States, security is much tighter. For example, the Department of Energy employs some 4,500 guards to watch over nuclear weapons and facilities under its control. Many of these guards are former military (e.g., Delta Force, SEALs, Green Berets). Storage sites are protected by two continuous lines of intrusion detection sensors, as well as by imaging systems (e.g., closed-circuit TV, radar, infrared detectors), buttress perimeter fencing, lighting and clear zones. Additionally, huge concrete "King Tut" blocks are placed in front of bulk storage buildings; a forklift is needed to remove them. Tamper-proof magnetic switches and other intrusion detection devices are placed on all doors and windows of the facility. If anyone attempts to break in, the sensors notify a security control center, which is staffed 24 hours a day.

When nuclear warheads are transported, they are stored inside fireproof, coffin-like supercontainers that have security features to protect them from terrorist attacks. These containers, which can survive hits from 7.62-mm armor-piercing ammo, are transported by either a special vehicle (a.k.a. Safe Secure Transport Vehicle) or an armored nuclear weapons cargo train. Various military units (and, sometimes, the U.S. Marshals Service's Missile Escort Unit) provide armed guard over the warheads, as they are moved around the United States.

A rare look at NEST's shoulder patch. *SF Tomajczyk*

As you can see, it would be difficult for terrorists to get their hands on nuclear material in the United States, which is why they focus their efforts elsewhere.

The Threat Assessment Process

Since 1975, NEST has evaluated 110 threats and mobilized itself to respond to about 30 of them. Fortunately, all have been hoaxes. But who is to say that won't change with the next phone call?

When the FBI receives a nuclear threat, it passes along the information it has to DoE Threat Assessment Teams (NN-62). These teams, which are scattered around the country, are made up of scientists, weapons experts, linguists, and psychologists. At least three teams review the data and determine if the threat is valid and whether or not a critical mass can be achieved. They also decide whether the person has the resolve to use the weapon if it is real. In the end, the answer they give must be a definitive "yes" or "no." "Maybes" are not allowed. All of the teams must independently reach the same conclusion.

In September 1995, for example, the FBI was told that a Middle Eastern group was in possession of a Russian nuclear device. This weapon was supposedly located in the metropolitan New York area. The FBI passed the technical information over to the assessment teams, which determined the threat to be a hoax. In an earlier instance, however, NEST had to actually visit the site to determine if the device was nuclear. In that case—which occurred in 1991 in Sparks, Nevada—an extortionist had chained a device to a pole in a casino restaurant. NEST used its special equipment to look inside the box and figure out what they were dealing with. They determined that the device was harmless.

As part of the threat assessment process, the FBI and DoE run the terrorist's blackmail letter and any other available data (e.g., diagrams, messages) through a computer at Lawrence Livermore National Laboratory that compares this information with known published documents about nuclear weapons, including newspaper articles, scientific reports, and even spy novels. If the terrorists "lifted" a phrase from a book and used it in their extortion letter, the computer will quickly know it. This tells the FBI that the terrorists may not know what they are doing, since they are plagiarizing from a public source.

If a threat is deemed credible, the FBI asks the DoE for assistance from NEST. Alerted by an on-call duty officer, NEST immediately assembles its high-tech search and detection equipment. Much of this is already prepackaged for quick deployment. In fact, entire mini-laboratories can be wheeled aboard aircraft. The U.S. Air Force provides airlift capability for NEST. The team can be wheels-up in four to 24 hours, depending on the crisis and the type of equipment that must be sent.

Stamping Out Nuclear Fires

The first crucial task for NEST is to find the bomb. They divide the target city into a search grid and then use aircraft, helicopters, and vans to explore the area using gamma ray sensors and neutron sensors. These sensitive devices detect minute changes in natural radi-

NEST has two components: those who search for the nuclear device and those who disarm it. Here two searchers check out a stadium during an exercise. The briefcases they carry are actually gamma ray detectors that sense the presence of a nuclear bomb. When radiation is detected, an alarm is sounded in a small earphone worn by the searchers. The detecting equipment can also be carried inside innocent-looking backpacks and coolers, so as not to alarm the public. *Department of Energy/NOO*

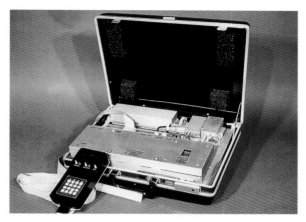

A close look at the "guts" of a gamma ray detector posing as a briefcase. *Department of Energy/NOO*

Scientists from the Remote Sensing Lab overlay radiation patterns onto aerial photographs and maps. The overlays show the different concentrations of radiation in the search area(s), and can indicate the presence of hidden nuclear material (e.g., uranium, plutonium) or a nuclear bomb. The radiation readings are taken by aircraft, vans, and/or search teams. *Department of Energy/NOO*

To find a hidden nuclear device, NEST uses fixed-wing aircraft and helicopters that are equipped with radiation detectors to quickly scan a suspected area, flying at low altitudes. If a "hot spot" reading is given, search teams and specially equipped vans narrow down the search until the bomb is found. This photo shows a MBB105C helicopter with a gamma pod strapped to its skids. The seats in the helicopter's cabin have been removed to make room for computers and other measuring equipment. All aerial surveillance aircraft are housed at the Remote Sensing Lab at Nellis AFB in Nevada. *Department of Energy/NOO*

A laboratory on wheels, ready to be placed aboard a plane and flown anywhere in the world. NEST has five cargo pods: photo lab, generator, video lab, communications lab, and a mechanical lab. This photo is of the photo lab, which comfortably seats one technician and provides that person with all the equipment needed to develop and enlarge aerial photographs and radiation-sensitive films. *Department of Energy/NOO*

ation that might suggest the location of the bomb. Supplementing this effort are NEST volunteers who carry radiation detection equipment (e.g., sodium iodide crystal detectors) hidden inside backpacks and briefcases. Armed with these sensors, they walk the streets searching for the bomb. They wear civilian clothes to avoid panicking the public or alerting the terrorists to their presence. As they search, they listen for an alert message that radiation has been detected. The message is broadcast from the sensing device to a wireless earphone hidden in their ear.

Once the bomb is located, things get tense. If the weapon is guarded, the terrorists first have to be removed from the equation. This task is accomplished by the FBI's Hostage Rescue Team. Depending on the situation, they use submachine guns and/or a high-adhesive foam to take out the terrorists. The resin foam, which was developed by Sandia National Laboratories, is fired from a special squirt gun. Sprayed at a terrorist's arms or legs, he will stick to himself and anything he touches. The backpack-mounted gun can fire multiple shots of the foam to 35 feet.

A high-tech gun designed to "slime" nuclear terrorists and protect the United States' nuclear arsenal. Developed by Sandia National Laboratories in 1992, this less-than-lethal weapon fires a super glue-like foam at terrorists, immediately disabling them. The 20-pound, shoulder-slung gun can fire multiple shots of the foam to 35 feet. The non-toxic foam is stored under pressure and expands 35-50 times when dispensed. Department of Energy SWAT Teams and the FBI's HRT have access to this new weapon. *Department of Energy/Sandia National Labs*

Once the terrorists are out of the picture, a special component of NEST enters the scene: the dismantling team. They have to disarm the bomb without making any mistakes or setting off any booby traps. Needless to say, it's not a task for the jittery or weak hearted. They often work with the Army's 52nd Ordnance Group (Ft. Gillem, Georgia) in disabling the device, especially if it is a military weapon or a sophisticated improvised explosive device. The 52nd has detachments all over the United States, which hastens the response time.

Robotic equipment is often used to take a first look at the bomb. These remote-controlled vehicles can be outfitted with video cameras, cutting devices and manipulator arms. Scientists and EOD personnel miles away can safely evaluate the device and figure out how to disarm it. Since most nuclear bombs require conventional explosives to start a chain reaction, NEST focuses on the trigger mechanism. Sometimes a carefully placed bullet can resolve the problem. In these instances, a rifle or 30-mm cannon is aimed at a specific point on the detonator. Then the bomb is enclosed within a 50-foot diameter tent that stands 35-feet tall. This tent is filled with a dense foam, which traps any radiation that may be released by a conventional explosion. When everything is ready, the rifle or cannon is fired.

In situations where a bullet is not appropriate, NEST volunteers dress in protective gear and enter the foam barrier. Once inside, they carefully disarm the nuclear devise by hand. Before fiddling with anything, they often pour liquid nitrogen on the trigger mechanism to freeze its electronics. It's safer that way.

Responding to a "Broken Arrow"

If there is a radiation release, or if a nuclear device is involved in an accident (e.g., train derailment, airplane crash), the Department of Energy's Accident Response Group (ARG) is called to the scene. Like NEST, ARG is comprised of volunteers from the national laboratories. This team, which is ready to respond within two hours, is trained in weapons recovery operations and in evaluating, collecting and reducing radioactive hazards. They use so-called "water knives"—a liquid abrasive jet of

Sometimes the best (and safest) way to examine a nuclear bomb is to use a robot. NEST uses a robot known as ATOM— a six-wheeled vehicle that is equipped with a manipulator arm and stereo video cameras attached to pan/tilt platforms. The cameras transmit their images back to NEST weapon designers so they can determine how to disarm the bomb. This photo shows a new reconnaissance robot, SARGE, being developed by Sandia National Laboratories. *Department of Energy/Sandia National Labs*

pressurized water and finely ground garnet—to make high-precision cuts in any material without causing heat or sparks. Such tools are used to cut into the fuselage of an aircraft or the trailer of a truck to retrieve the nuclear material.

ARG has several mobile labs that it can deploy to the scene from Lawrence Livermore and Los Alamos national laboratories. One such lab, known as "Hot Spot," includes two trucks with portable instruments and two trailers containing a sophisticated radiation-counting laboratory. It carries survey instruments for alpha, beta, gamma, and neutron radiation. Another mobile lab, "Ranger," is a van holding ground contamination survey systems that provide isodose plots indicating what's contaminated and by how much. A third lab is "Rascal." It analyzes air at the scene and adjacent areas for the presence of different types of radiation.

Since World War II, there have been 32 "Broken Arrow" incidents (i.e., an accident involving a nuclear weapon) that ARG has responded to. The last major accident occurred in 1980 when a Titan ICBM exploded inside a missile silo.

Every two years, ARG participates in a full-scale exercise to test the military's ability to respond to a "Broken Arrow" event. The most recent drill took place in September 1995, at the Naval Weapons Station in Yorktown, Virginia. The scenario revolved around a civilian plane that had crashed into a loading pier, which contained several nuclear weapons. The exercise lasted eight days and involved 1,600 people.

To assist with casualties of a nuclear accident or explosion, the Department of Energy has a Radiation Emergency Assistance Center and Training Site (REAC/TS) located in Oak Ridge, Tennessee. A response team can be deployed in an emergency, to assist in nuclear incidents. These teams are typically comprised of a physician, nurse, health physicist, cytogeneticist and radiobiologist. They are trained to perform medical and radiological triage, decontaminate people, assess radiation injuries, and determine the extent of radiation poisoning. Seriously ill patients can be transported to the Methodist Medical Center in Oak Ridge, which has a one-of-a-kind emergency room for treating nuclear injuries. REAC/TS also maintains a list of health professionals throughout the United States who are trained for radiation emergencies. These people can be called upon in a crisis to provide medical support.

Training for Disaster

Preparing for nuclear terrorism is a constant effort. NEST and other federal agencies routinely conduct training exercises whose scenarios anticipate the horrors that terrorists may one day inflict. For example, in "Compass Rose," federal agencies tested to see if a nuclear warhead could be stolen from a transport vehicle. The exercise was held in San Diego.

Several drills were run prior to the 1996 Olympic Games. In "Mirrored Image" (March 1996), NEST and nine other agencies participated in a scenario in which terrorists threatened to detonate a homemade nuclear bomb if a $3 million ransom was not paid. This weapon was made from spent nuclear fuel stolen from a military source.

Since NEST's creation in 1975, there have only been two full-fledged, multi-agency field exercises. This infrequency has come under criticism lately from Congress. The first exercise was "Mighty Derringer," which was held in 1986. The second was "Mirage Gold," which was held in New Orleans during the week of October 16, 1994.

In Mirage Gold, which involved some 1,200 players and cost $8 million to implement, the scenario went like the following. The New Orleans FBI Field Office received word that an informant was being held hostage by the Middle Eastern terrorist group Patriots for National Unity (PNU) at a safehouse near the airport. The FBI responded by staking out the building with its regional SWAT team, while deciding how to resolve the incident. However, it quickly became clear that the hostage's life was in danger, so the HRT assaulted the building around 3:30 A.M. The hostage was freed and the six terrorists killed. In the subsequent search of the building and interviews with the hostage, the FBI learned that the PNU intended to detonate a nuclear bomb in New Orleans.

Federal agencies descended on the city in an effort to find and disarm the bomb, as well as to capture the terrorists. Command posts of the participating agencies were located in various buildings at the Brown and Root Warehouse Complex in Gretna, Louisiana. The exercise ran around the clock, 24 hours a day, until 1:38 A.M., October 21.

NEST was deployed to locate the nuclear bomb(s). Using helicopters, vans, and street walkers, they began their search in earnest checking out buildings, residential areas, and even the Superdome. Meanwhile, the FBI hunted for members of the PNU. Through its investigation, the FBI was able to determine the various locations of the PNU around New Orleans, including the location of the terrorist leader, who was aboard a leased boat with four hostages.

On the morning of October 18, NEST sensors detected the presence of a nuclear bomb at the Bell Chase Naval Air Station. It was located inside a shed at the end of one of the runways. It was also guarded by three terrorists. Another nuclear device was found aboard the terrorist leader's boat.

At noon on October 19, the terrorists at the Naval Air Station left the site in a van and went to another safehouse. As soon as they left the airport, NEST and the 52nd Ordnance Group converged on the shed where the nuclear weapon was located. They began their analysis of the device, using photographs and X-rays to figure out how to safely disarm it.

On October 20, a decision was made to encapsulate the shed and bomb in a protective foam barrier, and fire a disabling shot at the bomb through the shed's wooden structure. It worked. The bomb was disarmed less than 30 minutes before it was scheduled to detonate. When the bomb didn't go off at the

Dense foam is used to contain radiation in case a nuclear device's conventional explosives go off. This foam is contained in a 50-foot diameter tent. Volunteers from NEST and the Army's 52nd Ordnance Group enter the foam wearing special suits and disarm the bomb. This photo shows the volunteers emerging from the foam after having successfully disarmed a nuclear bomb during a training exercise. *Department of Energy/LANL*

prearranged time, the terrorist leader ordered his henchmen at the safehouse to return to the airport and find out what happened. They did, and were arrested along the way.

As for the terrorist leader, he was taken down by DevGroup, which conducted a maritime assault on the boat. The four people being held hostage were subsequently set free, and New Orleans still stands today, unharmed.

Since Mirage Gold, the Department of Energy has increased the number of field drills it conducts each year, acknowledging the fact that skills dull if not put to use. The next major exercise on the scale of a Mirage Gold is scheduled for 1998, with similar exercises being held every fours years thereafter.

The Making of a Witches' Brew

Chemical and biological weapons are referred to as the poor man's atom bomb because they are easily made and cause widespread death. Their use by terrorist groups frightens officials, especially since the United States does not currently have a NEST-like team in place to track down and disarm these types of devices. The emergency response mechanism now consists of a hodgepodge of different federal agencies and military units. Officials know that it's only a matter of time before "bugs and gas" are used in the United States. Most C/B weapons can be made in a basement following Betty Crocker-like recipes and using store-bought materials. Over the years there have been several incidents of terrorists threatening to use witches' brew:

- In 1992, a neo-Nazi skinhead group planned to kill children in a Dallas Jewish day care center using cyanide.
- On Easter weekend in 1995, just days after the Oklahoma City bombing, a group threatened to release Sarin nerve gas at Disneyland in California. The FBI and other agencies responded to the threat, which eventually was determined to be a hoax.

The Accident Response Group (ARG) reacts to nuclear accidents, which are commonly known as "Broken Arrows." The team remains on constant alert, ready to respond within two hours plus flight time to the crisis site. This photo shows the ARG working on a military nuclear weapon that is located on a pier at the Naval Weapons Station in Yorktown, Virginia, during a September 1995 exercise. A civilian plane crashed into the pier, creating the emergency. There are five ARG elements in the United States, which are comprised of volunteers from the Department of Energy and the national laboratories. *Department of Energy/Sandia National Labs*

- In October 1995, four members of the anti-government Minnesota Patriots Council were convicted of planning to use ricin, a deadly toxin, to kill federal agents and government workers. Ricin, which is a derivative of the castor bean, is one of the most poisonous substances known. It can kill through inhalation or ingestion. The extremists, who joked about spreading the "government flu," had enough ricin on hand to kill 1,400 people.
- In November 1995, Larry Harris, an alleged member of the white supremacist group Aryan Nations, plead guilty to possessing three vials of *Yersinia pestis*, the organism that causes bubonic plague. Harris used a fraudulent EPA number and his company's state certification to illegally obtain the bacteria from a biomedical supply lab for $240. Untreated bubonic plague has a case fatality rate of about 50 to 60 percent.

- In December 1995, Thomas Lavy, an Army veteran and survivalist, was arrested after 30 federal agents—along with U.S. Army biological warfare experts and a small deployment from the FBI's HRT—raided the Arkansas farm he was staying at. They found 130 grams of ricin on the premises, which was enough to kill 30,000 people.

The Bugs Are Coming!

Biological warfare agents (e.g., anthrax, plague, tularemia, Q-fever) are more dangerous than chemical weapons because they can affect huge population centers. These agents are invisible, so you will never know that you are under attack until days afterward when people start dropping like flies. It would, in fact, be easy for a terrorist to fly over a city, release a biological agent and then disappear. In scenarios like this, it has been determined that 100 pounds of anthrax spores released upwind of a medium-size city of 500,000 like Des Moines, Iowa, would disable or kill half the population.

The doomsday cult Aum Shinrikyo understood the stealthy and deadly nature of biological agents. They conducted numerous experiments using anthrax and botulism, and even devised miniature anthrax dispensers that fit inside attaché cases. In 1992, in an effort to enhance its biological warfare capability, the cult sent a team of 40 to Zaire to acquire the deadly Ebola virus. The sect also purchased two radio-controlled drone aircraft from which to disburse biological agents.

The only documented case of a biological agent being used in the United States occurred in Oregon, in 1984. Two members of a sect produced and disbursed the bacteria that causes *Salmonellosis*, an intestinal disease, in restaurants in order to affect the outcome of a local election. Some 715 people became ill.

Don't let this sole case cause you to dismiss biological terrorism. There are hundreds of research labs, state health departments, and university laboratories nationwide that have "bugs" in their facilities. The organisms can be stolen or legally/illegally purchased, and then grown in a person's bathroom lab. After chemical warfare, biological warfare is the easiest type of terrorism for wackos to pursue.

Officials know this, which is why they are pushing so hard to create a national C/B response team similar to NEST. They are also conducting on-going exercises to prepare existing responders for a biological attack. In April 1997, for instance, FEMA sponsored "Ill Wind," a command post drill held in Washington, D.C., that tested the United States' response to a terrorist attack involving anthrax and chemical agents.

Technical Escort Unit

If federal and local agencies are unable to prevent a C/B attack from happening, requests for military help will end up at the Army's Technical Escort Unit (TEU). This one-of-a-kind team stands ready to be sent worldwide on short notice to detect, contain, limit the damage from, and clean up after an attack has occurred. It is also equipped to neutralize and dispose of toxic chemicals, munitions, and other hazardous materials. In fact, it was the TEU that cleaned up the hundreds of World War I chemical warheads unearthed in a Washington, D.C., suburb in 1991.

The TEU is headquartered at Aberdeen Proving Grounds in Maryland, with detachments at Pine Bluff Arsenal (Arkansas) and Dugway Proving Ground (Utah). The unit is comprised of 150 personnel: 19 officers, 63 enlisted and 68 civilians. They have all attended an intensive course to identify chemical agents, how to use decontamination equipment, and how to dispose of chemical agents. They also receive training in radiation safety, as well as in first aid and med-

The United States does not currently have a national team to respond to chemical and biological acts of terrorism. That fact frightens government officials, and it should. It is far easier for a terrorist to concoct a chemical or biological weapon in his basement—following Betty Crocker-like "how-to" manuals—and then release it in a subway station than it is for him to steal uranium and build a sophisticated, workable bomb. The United States needs to do something about this, and now. We're running out of time. *SF Tomajczyk*

ical management so they can treat casualties. On the technical side, team members learn how to operate chemical detection equipment, X-ray systems, gas chromatograph/mass spectrometers, and portable isotopic neutron spectroscopic devices. Additionally, those who specialize in bomb disposal are taught how to disarm C/B weapons.

According to Lt. Col. Timothy Madere, the TEU's battalion commander, each TEU member receives $60,000 worth of training when they first arrive at the unit, and about $20,000 worth of annual training thereafter. This training regimen is important because the team members must stay current on improvised weapon designs, as well as know how to use new equipment. Examples of the latter include state-of-the-art fluorescence techniques that can identify biological agents, and instruments created by Los Alamos scientists that can identify the composition of any chemical device without opening it.

The team regularly trains and works with the FBI and other agencies. For example, the TEU helped destroy Iraq's chemical munitions after the 1991 Gulf War, and it assisted the FBI in 1994 during its investigation of a possible U.S. link to the Aum Shinrikyo sarin gas attack in Tokyo.

The TEU is on-call 24 hours a day. It maintains two separate response capabilities. The first is the Chemical/Biological Response Team, which consists of 10 specialists that serve as the "first responders" of C/B incidents. They can be airborne within four hours. The second is the Alert Team, which serves as the

The "Fox" is a six-wheeled, amphibious NBC (nuclear, biological, chemical) reconnaissance vehicle currently in use with the U.S. Army and Marine Corps. In the event of a nuclear or C/B terrorist attack, it could be deployed to test the air and soil to determine the extent of contamination. In the event of a chemical or biological attack, it can identify the agent thereby making medical treatment more timely and accurate. The Fox is over-pressurized to protect its crew. It can travel at up to 65 mph and has a range of about 500 miles. *U.S. Army*

advance team for any follow-on TEU response team(s). The Alert Team conducts reconnaissance of the incident site, identifies the agents present, renders any explosive devices safe, and assists with small area decontamination. In the event of an emergency, the TEU can muster in 30 minutes (one hour during off hours) and can be airborne within four hours.

Caring for the Slimed & Dying

Let's face it: By the time you know that terrorists have launched a chemical or biological attack, it'll be too late. Most nerve gases are colorless and odorless, and the "bugs" of germ warfare are invisible. So when a terrorist attack occurs, who will take care of the thousands of casualties? Good question.

In the event of a chemical attack, firefighters and EMTs will have to be alert enough to put on their protective equipment first, before taking care of the injured, otherwise they will become casualties themselves. This was pointed out during an April 11, 1995, training incident in New York City in which nerve gas was released at a subway station. More than 100 first responders

were declared "dead" by referees after failing to recognize they were in a contaminated zone.

Treatment of patients begins at the scene, with EMTs giving victims of nerve agent poisoning shots of Atropine and Pralidoxime chloride, antidotes for Tabun and Sarin. Before patients can be taken to a hospital, they are decontaminated so that they don't pose a threat to the waiting nurses and doctors. This entails removing all their clothing and scrubbing them in DS2 or a bleach solution. Decon is accomplished by trained first-responders and military personnel wearing protective gear. In large disasters, the Army has a Chemical Casualty Site Team that can be deployed to provide on-site chemical casualty care training.

In the event of a biological attack, hospitals would take the brunt of it. Patients are going to run to local emergency rooms as they become ill, not knowing that they have been exposed to a germ warfare agent. Fortunately, most diseases are reportable to state health departments which, in turn, share their data with the Centers for Disease Control & Prevention in Atlanta. When they see the appearance of an unusual disease (e.g., anthrax) or a sudden and marked increase in a common disease (e.g., salmonellosis), the bells and whistles go off. So-called "disease detectives" immediately begin their investigation to figure out what is going on and try to stop any further spread of the disease.

Occasionally, a very deadly and highly contagious disease may surface (e.g., ebola). In these cases, the Army has an Aeromedical Isolation Team (AIT) that can be deployed. Comprised of physicians, nurses, medical assistants, and lab technicians, the AIT is trained to care for and transport people who are ill with an infectious agent. They use special isolation units called Vickers isolators to transport patients to a quarantine lab, where they can be treated without fear of having the disease spread to others. The Vickers isolators resemble Plexiglas torpedo tubes. The patient lies inside and the entire unit is carried by AIT members. The tube is under constant negative pressure so that the organism can't escape into the surrounding environment.

The AIT can be deployed worldwide on 12-hours notice using Air Force aircraft. At this time, the team can transport only two patients at any given time, due to the limited number of trained personnel and available equipment. However, the quarantine lab where patients are taken can accommodate 16 patients at Biocontainment Level 3, and four at Biocontainment Level 4. So like Noah's ark, AIT will move people two-by-two to the lab using their high-tech cocoons.

Metro Strike Teams

In either a chemical or biological attack, local hospitals can expect some medical assistance from one of the United States' 60 volunteer Disaster Medical Assistance Teams (DMAT), which are located at key cities around the nation (e.g., Boston, San Diego, Seattle). Of these, 21 are Level 1 teams, meaning they can mobilize within six hours with supplies and equipment for 72 hours of operation. However, DMAT is not equipped with chemical warfare protective gear. Hence, they cannot enter a contaminated area.

To address this problem, the U.S. Public Health Service is trying to create 18 so-called "Metro Strike Teams" that will be trained to assist in the medical management and public health consequences of C/B incidents. These teams, which will be based at major metropolitan areas around the United States, will be able to respond within 30 to 90 minutes with their equipment and medical supplies. The first Metro Strike Team of 30 members will be based in Washington, D.C. It and other teams will be comprised of a team commander, a medical director, physicians, pre-hospital care providers, and logisticians. To ensure that an MST is always available for deployment, each position will have two people assigned to it. This means there will be an aggregate roster of 60 team members.

Sending in the Marines

Supplementing the Metro Strike Teams' efforts in the military arena is the 350-member Marine Corps Chemical/Biological Incident Response Force (CBIRF), which is headquartered at Camp Lejeune, North Carolina. The unit was established in 1995 to improve the United States' ability to respond to C/B terrorist attacks, such as the one involving the Tokyo subway system. CBIRF responds to incidents at Navy and State Department facilities around the world. They identify threats, decontaminate areas, treat casualties, and bolster local hospitals' treatment capabilities.

Civilian authorities can request assistance from the CBIRF for incidents occurring at Olympic events or national political arenas. In fact, the unit was part of the security efforts at the 1996 Olympics. At this event, the unit tested a new piece of equipment known as the Medicam. This device, which looks like a pair of sunglasses, is worn outside a medical officer's gas mask. A small camera fastened to the glasses sends images of what the on-site doctor is seeing back to a medical person sitting in a specially equipped Humvee. A microphone and headset allow the two to converse, and a small screen inside the glasses permits the on-site doctor to see who he is talking to as he treats a patient. By using satellite technology, the picture and discussion can be broadcast worldwide, letting C/B experts assist in the diagnosis and treatment of victims.

CHAPTER SEVEN

Counterterrorism Weapons and Equipment

> "Counterterrorism forces have to be properly equipped to take down terrorists before they can cut hostages' throats or detonate a bomb. Going in with a laughable .22 or .38 will simply not do the trick, regardless of how evil you may look."—Anonymous

Counterterrorism experts learned an important lesson in 1977 when GSG-9 assaulted a Lufthansa 737 at Mogadishu Airport. The commandos forced entry through the plane's emergency exit doors and began taking down terrorists. In the cockpit, terrorist leader Mahmud took several hits from the point man who was using his .38 S&W Model 36. Although wounded, Mahmud was still able to fight back. He tossed two grenades at the commandos, which fortunately rolled under the seats before detonating. Becoming desperate, the point man grabbed an MP5 submachine gun and hosed Mahmud down with a quick burst.

What this incident taught CT units was, first, that they needed a larger magazine capacity than what a six-shot revolver offered. And second, they needed to use a weapon that was capable of "one shot, one kill." So,

The shotgun's drop-dead reputation can make even a dedicated terrorist think about surrendering. The weapon plays multiple roles in counterterrorism, from breaching doors to inserting tear gas into a building. This photo shows a Robar-modified Remington 870 defensive shotgun that is widely used by law enforcement agencies. *Robert A. Barrkman*

today, most eagles pack either 9-mm (for high capacity) or .45/.357 caliber (for knockdown power) handguns.

The FBI's Hostage Rescue Team uses a highly modified, semi-automatic, single-action .45 ACP that is custom-built by Les Baer on a Para-Ordnance frame. The 9-inch-long weapon features a frame-mounted ambidextrous safety, Commander-style exposed hammer, half-cock hammer notch, a high-ride beavertail grip safety, and a double-column magazine that holds 12 to 13 rounds of Federal's powerful 230-grain Hyda-Shok hollow-point bullets. It's an impressive weapon that is also quite accurate: It fires groupings no larger than 2 inches at 25 yards.

As mentioned earlier, the U.S. Marshals Special Operations Group uses the Smith & Wesson .45 and .357 handguns. Like the FBI, they, too, prefer Hydra-Shok bullets, but with a 185-grain load instead.

Among the military's elite units, the Beretta Model 92F pistol is widely used. The semi-automatic pistol holds 15 rounds of 9-mm Parabellum ammunition. The SEALs abandoned the 92F after they experienced problems with it, the most notable being catastrophic slide failure. (A popular saying heard in the NAVSPECWAR community was "You ain't a SEAL 'til you've eaten Italian steel.") They turned, instead, to using Sig Sauers, Heckler & Kochs, and even the old Colt M1911s. They also reportedly use a so-called

The .45 ACP custom built by Les Baer for exclusive use by the FBI's Hostage Rescue Team. Standard ammo is a 230-grain Hydra-Shok hollow-point bullet from Federal. *U.S. Federal Bureau of Investigation*

The new kid on the block: the USP .45 ACP from Heckler & Koch. It is in use with the elite units of the U.S. Special Operations Command. This particular USP is fitted with a detachable suppressor. It is ideal for those instances where silence is truly golden. *Heckler & Koch USA*

The U.S. Marshals Service Special Operations Group uses the Smith & Wesson .45 and .357 handguns, with 185-grain Hydra-Shok ammo. Operators, however, are permitted to carry another pistol brand as a back up; Sigs and Glocks are popular. *SF Tomajczyk*

"sub aqua" version of the Glock handgun, which is designed to be fired underwater. The pistol's polymer frame has a low magnetic signature—a definite plus when carrying out a mission near magnetic mines. And, for situations where a terrorist or hos-

tile dog has to be dealt with quietly, a suppressed .22 caliber Ruger pistol is used. It is jokingly referred to as a "Hush Puppy."

Today, the U.S. Special Operations Command issues the H&K USP .45 ACP. It features a special recoil reduction system, 12-round metal magazine, an oversized trigger guard for use with gloves, and it has a detachable sound suppressor and a laser aiming module. Other favorite handguns, at least among Delta Force operators, are said to be the Special Ops .45 ACP custom-built by Wilson, and the 9-mm H&K USP9 with 15-round polymer magazine.

The Marines' FAST and MEU(SOC) are using a modified M1911A1 .45 caliber pistol. This stainless steel sidearm features rubber-coated grips, an ambidextrous safety, high-profile combat sights, and an extra-wide grip safety for increased controllability (which aids in a fast follow-up second shot). Each pistol is hand-built by armorers at the Rifle Team Equipment shop in Quantico.

For backup handguns, the Sig Sauer P228 and Glock 17 are popular. In fact, the compact Sig P228 (9-mm, 10-round capacity) is used by the FBI, ATF, Secret Service, and DEA for special duty and concealment. Its larger brother, the P226 is the primary handgun of the SAS, FBI (excluding the HRT), and Navy SEALs. The P226 has a 15-round detachable box magazine for 9-mm Parabellum ammunition; 12 rounds for .357 SIG.

Many operators enjoy the Glock 17, which features a tough polymer frame. When this handgun first appeared, people laughed at its plastic design, saying that Mattel must have subcontracted the job. Unlike other pistols on the market that are double-action/single-action, there is no difference in trigger pull between the first and subsequent shots. This consistency aids in accurate shooting.

Submachine Guns (SMG)

SMGs are the workhorse of counterterrorism. With a squeeze of the finger, a terrorist can be convinced to stop what he's doing ... permanently. The submachine gun's compact size, large magazine capacity, and impressive firepower (not to mention all the goodies that can be affixed to an SMG, like a flashlight or laser aiming device) have made it beloved by assault teams around the world.

The undeniable champion of submachine guns is Heckler & Koch. The H&K MP5 series of SMGs is the chosen weapon of most of the world's elite counterterrorist forces, including Delta Force, Navy SEALs, FBI HRT, Secret Service Counter-Assault Team, SAS, GSG-9, and GIGN. Even the USMS Special Operations Group has MP5s in its arsenal to complement the 9-mm Colt SMGs they normally use. The weapon's accuracy is what makes it ideal for the precision shooting required in a hostage rescue operation, and its impressive firepower (800 to 900 rpm) lends itself to quickly sweeping a room, which is why the MP5 (most notably the MP5K) is referred to as a "room broom."

The Navy SEALs and Marine Corps FAST units currently use the 9-mm MP5N with a "Navy" trigger group, which features semi-automatic or fully automatic firing modes. It has a maximum effective range of 100 meters and shoots 800 rpm. With the retractable butt stock collapsed, the MP5N is only 19.3 inches long. The barrel is threaded to accept a sound suppressor. A mini flashlight can be affixed to the forward handguard (it is operated by pressing a switch custom fitted to the pistol grip). The MP5N takes 30-round magazines.

The FBI HRT has opted for the more powerful 10-mm MP5/10 SMG that features semi-automatic, two-round burst and fully automatic firing modes. At any range, the projectile fired from this weapon has nearly twice the muzzle energy of a comparable 9-mm, .40 S&W or .45 ACP cartridge. Although the operation of the MP5/10 is identical to the 9-mm MP5s, several improvements have been incorporated into the weapon's design, including a bolt catch device that holds the bolt group rearward after the magazine is empty. This alerts the operator to the fact that a new magazine needs to be loaded. (The last thing you want to happen is have an eagle point the weapon at a tango, pull the trigger, and hear the distinctive "CLICK" of an empty gun.) A unique "wet technology" sound suppressor fits the threaded barrel of the MP5/10. By adding 5 cc of water to this stainless steel suppressor, the SMG's report is lowered an additional 3 to 5 decibels. This suppressor can also be fired full of water without damage, making it ideal for maritime operations.

The impressive and hard-hitting 10-mm MP5/10 submachine gun currently used by the FBI's Hostage Rescue Team. The weapon features a 2-round burst trigger group and has a cyclic firing rate of 800 rpm. The lightweight and corrosion resistant synthetic magazine holds 30 rounds. *Heckler & Koch USA*

When concealment is necessary, elite forces turn to the compact 9-mm MP5K submachine gun, which was designed specifically for CT units. Perhaps the ultimate close-quarters weapon, the MP5K weighs only about 4 pounds and is less than 13 inches long. The weapon has a distinctive vertical foregrip, features 15- or 30-round magazines, and can be configured to fire single rounds, two- or three-round bursts, or full automatic. Its small size makes it ideal for covert operations and security details, which is why the Secret Service uses it when protecting the President. The weapon can be easily concealed under a jacket or in the glove compartment of a car. It can also be hidden and fired from inside a specially built briefcase.

Many CT forces use the 9-mm MP5SD submachine gun due to its integral sound suppressor. Unlike many SMGs, this one does *not* require the use of subsonic ammo for effective sound reduction. The MP5SD has a cyclic firing rate of 800 rpm. *STTU*

Think twice the next time you see someone with a briefcase! It could be hiding the compact 9-mm MP5K submachine gun. The weapon's trigger is conveniently located on the briefcase handle, as is the safety (button top left). The Secret Service uses this configuration when protecting the President and other VIPs. The MP5K (a.k.a. Room Broom) is a favorite among many CT units because of its small size and firepower (900 rpm). *Heckler & Koch USA*

Other SMGs used by CT units include the 9-mm Uzi, Ingram MAC 10, and 9-mm Colt assault rifle/SMG. The Uzi is popular with Navy SEALs, Israeli CT Teams, and GIGN. The Secret Service also enjoys it small size and firepower. In fact, Uzis seemingly appeared out of thin air during the 1981 assassination attempt of

President Reagan. The 9-mm Colt SMG is used by the U.S. Marshals Service SOG as their primary weapon, as well as by DEA task forces that go after narco-terrorists. The Colt uses the basic body and configuration of the M-16 rifle, but with a short and rigid telescoping butt. It fires 20- or 32-round magazines, and has a cyclic firing rate of 800 to 1,000 rpm.

The tiny Ingram MAC 10, which can be chambered for the .45 ACP and 9-mm Parabellum, is known for its high rate-of-fire. Firing at 1,090 rpm, a 30-round magazine is depleted in about 1.6 seconds. The weapon's accuracy, however, is another thing. Its performance beyond point-blank is so poor that many call it the "phone booth gun." In other words, you have to be in the same booth as the target to guarantee a hit. In spite of this, the MAC 10 is still found with Navy SEALs, Army Special Forces, and some federal agencies.

An unusual SMG is the 9-mm Spectre M-4 made by SITES SpA in Italy. Developed specifically for counterterrorism units, it is the only "double-action" sub-machine gun in existence. The M-4 is designed to be carried safely and brought into action instantly without requiring any safeties to be released or any cocking levers to be pulled. That makes it ideal for CQB and assaults. Measuring 13.7 inches long with its stock collapsed, the Spectre fires 30- or 50-round magazines (another unique feature), and has a cyclic firing rate of about 850 rpm.

Machine Guns

Machine guns are generally used only by national counterterrorist teams like Delta Force, DevGroup, and the FBI's Hostage Rescue Team. It is an ideal weapon to go up against a paramilitary group that's hiding in a fortified compound and is equipped with heavy armaments. Machine guns support CT operations by delivering a large volume of area fire against tangos from great distances.

Machine guns in use with CT units include the H&K 21, H&K 21E, and M-60E3 Light Machine Gun. These are all 7.62 mm, have a cyclic firing rate of 500-800 rpm, and generally have an effective range out to about a half mile or so. Before their mission was aborted, Delta Force intended to use the H&K 21 and M-60 during the April 1980 Iran rescue mission to secure their escape route. The SEALs presently use a stripped-down version of the M-60 when conducting inland patrol missions. It is used to deliver accurate, high-volume fire on targets at ranges beyond what the M-16 rifle can hit.

In the 5.56-mm category, several machine guns are appropriate for counterterrorism operations, including the H&K 23E and the M-249 Squad Automatic Weapon. The 16.3-pound M-249 has an effective range of 2,600 to 3,250 feet and fires 750 rpm. The weapon is so lightweight that a gunner can fire it accurately from the hip.

Shotguns

There are few weapons that capture a person's immediate respect more quickly than a shotgun. The knock-down power of the shotgun is matched by its

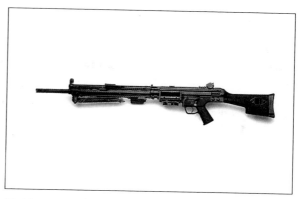

Machine guns, such as this 7.62-mm H&K 21E, provide CT units with tremendous firepower by delivering a large volume of area fire against terrorists. Such weapons are ideal for assaults against heavily armed paramilitary groups holed up in fortified compounds. *Heckler & Koch USA*

hyped reputation for being able to cut a person in half and/or destroy an entire room with a single round. Point a shotgun at someone, and they freeze. Although this weapon has been shunned by some in favor of SMGs, there is still a time and place for the shotgun's use in counterterrorism. For example, the shotgun is ideal for breaching locked doors (rifled slug or Shok-Lock round), projecting tear gas (ferret round), distracting terrorists (starflash rounds), concealing operations (smoke rounds), signaling (14,000 candlepower flare rounds), and disabling people without seriously injuring or killing them (rubber projectile rounds). The shotgun is also ideal for laying down firepower: A skilled shooter can fire five rounds in about a second, blanketing an area in a lead cloud.

Some of the favorite 12-gauge, semi-automatic shotguns used for CT operations include the H&K M1/M3 Super 90, Mossberg 500, Ithaca 37, H&K Benelli M-121, Remington 870, Franchi Model 12 SPAS, and the Robar customized 870. These weapons can have telescopic sights added to them to improve their long-range accuracy (up to 100 yards), and they can use magazine extension tubes to increase their firepower capability up to a total of 8 to 12 rounds.

The FBI uses a customized Remington 870 with a 3-inch chamber, a 14-inch barrel with a modified choke, a composite stock, Trijicon front sites, and several other features. The Secret Service also uses a customized Remington 870.

When concealment is needed, eagles use the sawed-off shotgun. It's short length allows it to be hidden under a topcoat, as well as to be used in tight spaces, such as aboard ships. Unfortunately, there are several drawbacks to using a sawed-off shotgun. First, it has reduced accuracy. Second, it has a reduced magazine capacity. Third, it has greater recoil and muzzle flash. And last, if the shotgun does not have a hand stop near the front grip or pump handle, the shooter can blow his hand off if he's not careful.

Assault Rifles

The assault rifle has been largely replaced by the SMG, simply because of the rifle's long range and excessive penetration. Neither of these characteristics is desired in the typical close-quarters environment of counterterrorism. If a rifle round misses its target, it will likely pass through the building and hit someone. However, like the shotgun, there *is* a time and place for assault rifles. For example, they are useful in giving a CT unit domination over a large area when extracting hostages from a terrorist occupied structure. Assault rifles are also ideal for perimeter security and counter-ambush operations. Furthermore, they lend themselves to cover large open areas like airports, maritime ports, and stadiums.

Assault rifles come in two calibers: .308 (7.62 mm) and .223 (5.56 mm). Heavy assault rifles (7.62 mm) used by counterterrorism teams include the FN-FAL, M-1A/M-14, and the H&K G3 series. Light assault rifles (5.56 mm) include the H&K 93, H&K 33, H&K 53, M-16A1/A2, Ruger Mini 14, FA MAS, Colt Commando, and the futuristic-looking Steyr AUG (Army Universal Gun) with its bullpup design. Most of these assault rifles have an effective range out to about 330 yards, fire 600 to 1,000 rpm, and have 5-, 20- and 30-round box magazines.

One shot, one kill. The sniper plays a vital role in remedying terrorist incidents by dropping a terrorist hundreds of yards away with a single bullet to the brain or heart. The Robar SR-90 is one of several state-of-the-art sniper rifles used by CT forces. The SR-90 is available in .308 Winchester or .300 Winchester Magnum. This rifle is topped with a 10x Leupold scope. *STTU*

Sniper Rifles

One shot, one kill. That's the motto of snipers, who take pride at being able to drop a tango from hundreds of yards away with a single bullet. To achieve this kind of accuracy, snipers rely on a high-precision rifle that is designed specifically for sniping. The most popular caliber rifle used for sniping is the 7.62-mm NATO/.308 Winchester (although the .300 Winchester Magnum is often preferred for longer range operations due to its greater velocity and energy). Most sniper rifles are customized to ensure their accuracy. For example, care is taken to make certain that the barrel's internal dimensions are uniform, that the rifling twist is maximized for the intended caliber and bullet weight, that the barrel is free-floating, and that the trigger breaks cleanly. Additionally, these rifles are equipped with sturdy bipods to create a non-vibrating platform, powerful scopes (e.g., Leupold Ultra M3 10x sniper scope, Hensoldt 10x40 telescopic sight), and adjustable butt stocks, cheek pads, and trigger shoes that can be adapted to fit the individual sniper firing the weapon.

Sniper rifles come as either bolt action or semi-automatic. The bolt action is ideal for precision shooting, with the semi-automatic serving as backup fire support. In counterterrorism, however, where rapid follow-up shots are often necessary, the semi-automatic sniper rifle (with a 5- or 20-round magazine) is usually the preferred choice.

Popular sniper rifles among elite CT forces include the Robar SR-60, Robar SR-90, Remington 700, M-21, M-24, M-40A1, FR-F2, Vaime Mk-2, McMillan M-86SR, H&K PSG-1, and H&K MSG90. The M-40A1 is a Marine Corps designed weapon built on a Remington 700 that is used as the foundation of the FBI's SWAT/HRT sniper rifles. It is topped with either a Leupold or Unertl scope. The rifle shoots groups of a quarter inch at 200 yards. The Secret Service builds its sniper rifles from the Remington 700, as well.

The FBI also builds sniper rifles on the McMillan A2 and Robar SR-90 stocks, using the Vari-X III Tactical 3.5-10 power sniper scope from Leupold. The scope's low power settings are useful in urban situations where wide field-of-view is often needed.

Both the Robar SR-60 and SR-90 are in wide use with numerous SWAT teams and domestic security agencies.

The Secret Service's Counter-Sniper Team reportedly uses the Vaime Mk2 7.62-mm rifle, as do some SEAL teams. Unlike other sniper rifles, the Vaime Mk2 was designed from the outset as a silenced sniper rifle for counterterrorist units. When firing a subsonic 7.62-mm x 51 NATO round, the Mk2 produces almost no recoil and makes about as much noise as a suppressed .22 weapon. The rifle fires a 10-round detachable box magazine, and has an effective range of about 200 meters.

Navy SEALs also use the McMillan M-86SR sniper rifle in both the .308 and .300 Winchester Magnum, equipped with a Leupold M1 Ultra 10x scope. They and Delta Force are also reportedly using Heckler & Koch's PSG-1 and MSG90, along with other state-of-the-art weapon systems. The MSG90 is similar to the PSG-1 except that it has a shorter barrel, features a more streamlined design,

has a harmonic stabilizer at the end of its barrel, and weighs 3 pounds less than the PSG-1.

Since sniping occasionally requires killing tangos at long ranges or disabling equipment such as aircraft and vehicles, CT snipers have turned to the powerful .50 caliber rifle. During the 1991 Gulf War, more than 200 McMillan M-88 .50 cal. sniper rifles (single shot, bolt action) were deployed to the Gulf for use by units that comprise the U.S. Special Operations Command, including Navy SEALs and the Army's Delta Force.

The 5-foot-long, 30-pound M-82A1 semi-automatic .50 caliber rifle from Barrett also saw action in the Gulf War, with anti-personnel kills being reported at 1,093 meters and an armored personnel carrier being disabled at 2,400 meters. The FBI's Hostage Rescue Team has the M-82A1 in its arsenal for special applications.

Firing a .50 caliber rifle is no picnic, even though a carefully designed double baffle, muzzle brake system absorbs most of the recoil so that it reportedly feels like firing a 12-gauge shotgun. However, one former Marine sniper who now trains elite units—including SEAL snipers—laughed when asked about the weapon's supposedly less-than-awesome kick. "Bullshit," he said adamantly. "Spend a day shooting this baby and you'll feel like you've been in a car wreck."

When you really have to reach out and seriously touch someone, nothing comes close to the .50 caliber sniper rifle, such as this Barrett M-82A1. The powerful .50 cal. is ideal for knocking out aircraft and vehicles, as well as terrorists at very long ranges (e.g., 1 mile or further). *Barrett Firearms Mfg.*

Special Weapons & Equipment

Assaulting terrorists and rescuing hostages requires not only highly trained and dedicated people, but also special equipment. For instance, flash-bang grenades (a.k.a. flashcrashes) are used to temporarily deafen, blind, and overwhelm a terrorist so that an assault team can safely enter a room before he can react. Such grenades, which were developed by the British SAS, typically produce a sound level of 175 decibels and a light level of 2.4 million candela when detonating. It's a mind-blowing experience for the terrorists on the receiving end.

Gas, such as CS and CN, is also useful in distracting terrorists. Counterterrorist units use either 37/38-mm gas guns or 12-gauge shotguns to launch ferret rounds filled with tear gas into a structure housing terrorists. Defense Technology of America has designed a futuristic-looking gas gun, the 37/38-mm L8 Multi-Launcher, which can unload six rounds of tear gas from its rotary magazine in three seconds. If you're an aficionado of Arnold Schwarzenegger, you saw a replica of this weapon in the movie *Terminator 2: Judgment Day*.

On some occasions, you simply don't want to use live ammo. Firing an SMG inside an underground nuclear missile silo, for example, is not always wise. In circumstances like this, operators rely on less-than-lethal technology. Such devices are intended to put you out of action, but not necessarily kill you. Examples of less-than-lethal

The L8 Multi-Launcher from DefTech fires six 37/38-mm tear gas rounds from its rotary magazine in an amazing three seconds. It's a great way to safely drive terrorists out of a building. *Defense Technology of America*

Baton rounds represent a less-than-lethal way to convince terrorists to surrender. The round is filled with five foam batons that have an effective range of about 100 feet. Wooden baton rounds are also available to CT forces, but they can kill if directly fired at a person, since the batons are heavier and less flexible than foam rubber. *Defense Technology of America*

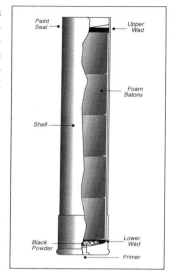

weapons include rubber bullets, baton rounds, bean bag rounds and sting grenades.

A baton round is a 37-mm, 38-mm, 40-mm, or 12-gauge round filled with 3 to 5 half-ounce foam rubber disks that disperse after being fired. The disks travel at about 320 fps out to a range of 100 feet. (Baton rounds filled with wooden disks are also available. But since they are heavier and less flexible than foam rubber, they can kill if directly fired at people. For this reason, they are "skip fired." That is, the gun is fired at the ground at an angle so that the disks ricochet toward the target. Wooden baton rounds are sometimes used by operators to break through windows of unoccupied rooms during an assault to distract terrorists' attention.)

A similar device to the foam rubber baton round is the "Stinger" round. It is the same caliber round, but filled with 42 rubber balls instead of disks. The 1.5-cm diameter balls travel at 280 fps out to a distance of 150 feet.

A Sting Grenade is a baseball-sized grenade filled with 180 rubber balls that are dispersed in a powerful 50-foot circular pattern. These grenades are not used when hostages are in the room, since serious injury can result. Sting grenades also come prepackaged with tear

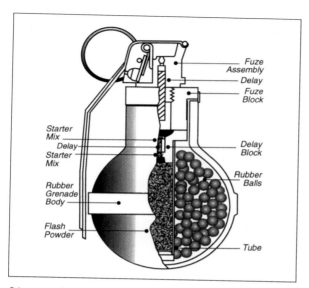

Labels on diagram:
Fuze Assembly
Delay
Fuze Block
Starter Mix
Delay
Starter Mix
Delay Block
Rubber Grenade Body
Rubber Balls
Flash Powder
Tube

Sting grenades can bring down anyone within 50 feet after detonation with their 180 rubber balls. Because of this, these grenades are not usually used by CT operators if hostages are in the same room as the terrorists, because the hostages could be seriously injured. A nastier relative of the sting grenade exists: it has CS tear gas mixed in with the rubber balls. *Defense Technology of America*

gas mixed in with the rubber balls. This makes for a real nasty weapon that makes everyone in a room miserable when it detonates. Assault teams must be masked before entering a room that has been painted by a sting grenade filled with active agent.

An interesting less-than-lethal weapon is a sound wave device that makes people become violently ill. The sonic apparatus emits certain frequencies that cause headaches, nausea, irritation, sweating, and even vomiting. It comes in various sizes, including a battery-sized device that can be covertly placed inside a terrorist's hideout. Within hours, he'll be too sick and distracted to fight effectively.

Ammunition

Unlike the military, which must abide by Geneva Convention protocols that dictate what type of ammu-

nition can be used on the battlefield, CT forces use whatever they want. Visit a CT unit's weapons locker and you'll likely find Black Talon, Hydra-Shok, and Glaser rounds. Of these, the Glaser Safety Slug has an amazing kill rate. Hit a tango in the arm, leg, or pinkie toe, and 90 percent of the time the resulting shock will kill him. The Glaser is a hollow point bullet filled with 330 mini-projectiles (#12 chilled lead shot) that are suspended in liquid Teflon. When the bullet strikes its target, the bullet disintegrates below the surface, releasing the shot in a cone-shaped pattern that destroys flesh and bone. This causes instant incapacitation.

Another "drop dead" round is the Law Grabber. It's a jacketed hollow point bullet that has a toothed tip. When fired, the bullet spins at 45,000 rpm, with its toothed point acting like a flying hole saw. This means that the bullet rapidly "drills" its way into a terrorist and then expands quickly, releasing its deadly energy.

For training purposes—especially in close-quarters shooting drills—the counterterrorism world relies on Simunition products. The most popular is the FX round (.38, .357, 9 mm), which has a plastic, pre-scored hollow bullet filled with a water-soluble red or blue marking powder. When the bullet hits, it shatters open and leaves behind a telltale splotch of paint. This helps confirm that a person has indeed been hit and by which side, the red or blue team. The FX round has enough sting when it strikes that it adds realism to the training. Operators quickly learn to keep their heads down and use cover during firefights.

The FX round can be fired from pistols, rifles and submachine guns, producing near-normal recoil. With a conversion kit, the round can also be fired from shotguns. The bullets are tactically accurate up to about 25 feet, which is ideal for CQB drills that take place in shooting houses.

Simunition also manufactures a so-called "vanishing bullet," the Greenshield round. Technically known as a frangible bullet, Greenshield ammo is a copper-polymer bullet that disintegrates into dust on impact, with no ricochet or splashback. The lead-free bullets come in .38, 9 mm, and 5.56 mm. The FBI's Hostage Rescue Team

One secret of counterterrorism is that it's not the weapon you use that counts, it's the ammunition. And CT forces have access to just about any type of ammo they want, from expanding hollow-points to Teflon and chilled-shot filled Glaser rounds. This photo shows an array of boattailed bullets (left to right): Sierra 168 grain, Lapua 185, Sierra 190, Sierra 220, .50 cal. 750 grain, spent .50 cal., and steel core of a .50 cal. *STTU*

The Simunition FX training rounds are ideal for close-quarters battle drills. The hollow bullet shatters open when striking a target, releasing a bright red or blue marking powder. Operators wear protective face and throat gear when practicing assaults using Simunition. *SF Tomajczyk*

Operators routinely wear 30 to 50 pounds of equipment when conducting an assault, which is why they must be in superb physical condition. These operators are wearing Nomex hoods, goggles, flame-retardant overalls, bulletproof vests, and multi-pocket tactical vests, which are typically filled with ammo magazines, first aid kit, mace, etc. Note that both men are carrying their handguns in a cross-draw position. This is unusual: most operators prefer to wear their handguns, extra ammo clips, and a flashbang grenade or two in thigh holsters. *STTU*

uses frangible bullets in its shooting house, The Maze. The metal walls of this facility are covered with a half-inch-thick rubber mat that allows the bullet to penetrate before crumbling into dust.

Because of the unpredictable nature of counterterrorism, CT forces often have to resort to using specialized ammunition to achieve certain tasks. For instance, when shooting through an aircraft's thick, cockpit windows, a non-jacketed round is used to prevent bullet fragmentation and injury to nearby hostages. Armor-piercing bullets are used to take down vehicles, heavy equipment, and aircraft. Incendiary bullets are ideal for starting fires, and frangible slugs are perfect for blasting open locked doors. The availability of specialized ammo to CT units is mind-boggling. You name it, they've probably got it.

And All the Rest

Dressing up for a takedown is an art unto itself. Today's CT operator wears 30 to 50 pounds of gear depending on the mission: Nomex balaclava and gloves, Nomex coveralls, shin pads, assault boots, Kevlar ballistic helmet, Bolle tactical goggles, load-bearing tactical vest (which holds ammo magazines, flashlight, radio gear and a first aid kit), thigh holster with pistol and ammo, throat microphones, flash-bang grenades and thigh pouch, submachine gun with sling, OC chemical spray, gas mask, knife, 90,000-volt stun gun, handcuffs or flex cuffs, chemical light sticks (visible light or infrared), and Kevlar bulletproof vest with an optional "chicken plate." Most tactical vests are designed to handle interchangeable sets of pouches and holders, so that the vest can be customized for a particular mission.

In addition to this basic outfitting, counterterrorism forces also use specialized equipment in various situations. The more commonplace items sent out into the field include: breaching equipment (hooligan tool, battering ram, jamb spreader, bolt cutters), explosives (shaped charge, C-4, detonator cord, ribbon cutting charge), mirrors, metal detectors, night vision goggles (Gen II, Gen III), grenades (smoke, stinger style), ballistic shields, extendible ladders, sound suppressors, glass punches, rappelling gear, diving gear, binoculars, surveillance equipment (cameras, microphones, borescopes, recording devices, fiber optic devices), chemical agent detectors, satellite communications equipment, sniper gear (drag bag, mat, spotting scope, ghillie suit), laser designators, lock picking guns, and more. One unique item is a small electronic device that can open nearly every brand of garage door. It is used to achieve covert, non-forcible entries.

CHAPTER EIGHT

Takedown!
Training and Tactics

> "Any action taken against terrorists must be swift,
> forceful, and aggressive."
> —Anonymous

Speed. Surprise. Violence of action. These three concepts are at the heart of counterterrorism. Every elite team strives to achieve these when assaulting terrorists. Hit them hard. Hit them fast. And do it in such a way that the tangos are shocked and unable to respond effectively.

To acquire this capability, CT forces constantly practice takedowns, doing various entry tactics and CQB techniques. They practice in shooting houses, in abandoned buildings, on trains, aboard ships, and in planes. They do it during the day, in the afternoon, and under the cover of darkness. They do it in the deserts and in the mountains, as well as in rural towns and in huge cities. And they do it in all weather conditions: rain, fog, snow, sleet, and oppressive heat.

BLAM! Stun grenades are designed to temporarily blind and deafen hostiles into submission. Here, two stun grenades filled with magnesium particles explode. It is not unusual for such devices to start fires. To prevent a terrorist from throwing a flashbang back at the assault team, the grenade usually has a very short fuse, no longer than 1.5 seconds. *STTU*

A four-man and six-man assault team crouched at the ready to take down a house during a training drill. As is commonplace, explosive breaching charges have been set at two entry ways, allowing the teams to simultaneously enter at different points. Note the use of the shields by the point men, to protect their men from the blast wave and debris. *STTU*

American counterterrorist teams each have their own training facilities: The FBI HRT has its training complex at Quantico; Delta Force has its Special Operations Training center at Ft. Bragg; DevGroup has its training complex at Dam Neck; and the

CT forces routinely train in low-light conditions, where it is difficult to quickly identify hostiles from friendlies. Combative Concepts, Inc., is one of several private organizations that trains elite units in low-light shooting tactics. Here, a CCI instructor demonstrates one way to shoot and scoot in the dark. He's using the modified crossed wrist method with an assault rifle and a larger-than-normal flashlight. *SF Tomajczyk*

No, it's not a Star Trek laser gun, though it does look like it belongs to the twenty-first century. It's actually a paintball gun that is widely used by CT forces to practice close-quarters combat shooting drills. The paintball magazine (absent in the photo) affixes to the tube in front of the Red-dot sight. *SF Tomajczyk*

Marshal Services' SOG has its 40-acre Tactical Center in Louisiana. These complexes are typically made up of firing ranges, indoor shooting houses, situation rooms, rappelling towers, sniper ranges, linear targets (e.g., buses, planes), mock urban town centers, and obstacle courses. They are hidden from the public so that assault tactics cannot be witnessed, and so that any sudden preparations a unit makes to deploy on a mission do not tip off the terrorists that an organized response is underway. By its very nature, counterterrorism must be cloaked in secrecy.

A less publicized training facility, which is home of two quasi counterterrorist units, is the James J. Rowley Training Center in Beltsville, Maryland. The two units in question are the Secret Service's Counter Assault Team (CAT) and Counter Sniper Team (CST). They are deployed with the President to protect him from assassination attempts. The CST, which draws its members from the Uniformed Branch, works with the President's advance team to identify potential sniper hiding spots along a motorcade route or in a particular area or building, and then keeps an eye on them to eliminate any sniper that may appear. CAT is responsible for thwarting and reacting to armed assaults made against the President. They fight the assailants while the Secret Service's close protection detail rushes the President out of harm's way. This unit, which was created after the 1981 assassination attempt on President Reagan, routinely sits in a room or vehicle within seconds of the President, armed and decked-out in their assault gear. The leader carries two radios: one that connects him with the tactical team, and the other to talk with the President's protection detail.

All of the United States' CT forces cross-train at each other's facilities, as well as at other complexes around the world (e.g., GSG-9, GIGN, SAS) and those that are privately owned. With regard to the latter, many units receive training from such organizations as Combative Concepts, Inc., Specialized Tactical Training Unit, Thunder Ranch, Gunsite, Thor International, and the Mid-South Institute. These facil-

Live-fire hostage rescue drills are the closest a CT unit can get to the real thing. Volunteers (in this case, a woman) are tied up and placed inside a shooting house. CT forces enter the structure, move room to room engaging terrorist targets, and then rescue the hostage. If an assaulter bypasses a target, he cannot turn around and engage it. If he does, he will be shooting in the direction of his assault team. *STTU*

ities commonly provide training in advanced assault tactics, high-risk entry methods, close-quarters combat shooting (e.g., rapid aimed fire, point shooting, aimed quick kill, double tap, multiple target indexing), barricade takedowns, low-light shooting techniques, explosive breaching, and sniping.

The Mid-South Institute of Self-Defense Shooting is perhaps the best-known and most innovative shooting school in the United States. Located at Lake Cormorant, Mississippi, and founded by world-class shooter John Shaw, the facility features 22 ranges and two shooting houses on 40 acres of land. One of the shooting houses (6,000 square feet) has 28 rooms that 2-, 4- and 6-man assault teams can run through, while shooting at moving hostile targets with live fire. Mid-South also has a military drop zone approved for parachute operations, as well as an adjacent 2,500-foot runway that can be used for airborne-related tactics. Since its inception in 1982, Mid-

South has provided training to Delta Force, DevGroup, FBI HRT, Secret Service CAT, USMS SOG, 160th SOAR, and a host of other elite units including the British SAS.

Military CT forces often conduct joint training exercises in major urban areas of the United States. For example, in June 1995, units from Ft. Bragg and Ft. Campbell—reportedly Delta Force and the 160th SOAR—descended on four Pittsburgh, Pennsylvania, sites to conduct a nighttime rescue operation using night vision goggles. Nine helicopters (six OH-6A Cayuse and three MH-60 Black Hawks) flew over Pittsburgh and inserted commandos, who fast-roped to their objectives. The commandos then used explosive charges to gain access to the buildings in which the hostages and terrorists were housed. Although the drill went smoothly, it alarmed many residents who were not aware that a training exercise was going on. Several, in fact, thought the city was under attack. Similar drills have been conducted elsewhere

Live-fire drills are an important way to keep one's shooting skills honed. Here, an operator armed with a H&K MP5SD practices using effective cover (a truck trailer) to shoot at targets. It is not unusual for members of some elite CT forces to shoot 2,500 rounds a week. *STTU*

Hi there, mind if we drop in? Rappelling is often the easiest and quickest means to reach terrorists hiding in some areas of the building. Whenever possible, assaults are done by working from the top of the building down toward the first floor. *STTU*

and they change their approach direction so that the terrorists aren't able to figure out where they are. In some rooms, two men will enter; in others, four. And still others, six or more. Sometimes the men will enter simultaneously using the buttonhook entry, or one at a time using the crisscross or X entry technique. On occasion, a room needs only to be cleared by a "high/low" combination, in which one operator kneels with his SMG, while the other stands directly over him. Each man can quickly check half the room and safely engage any terrorists without fear of shooting his partner. (If the kneeling man stands up suddenly, his head safely pushes the standing man's SMG up and out of the way.)

Mouseholes are another way for a team to avoid predictability. Using shaped charges, the assault team can blast small holes in the internal walls of the building and move from room to room. This not only shocks the terrorists, who typically are guarding the

hallways but, more importantly, it means that the assault team follows the path it wants to, not what the building's layout dictates.

If an entry team of four or more men assaults a room, the third man in the Snake often wears additional protective body armor. This is because terrorists can usually react and start firing their weapons at the assault team by the time the third man hits the doorway. Hence the third man can only hope that either the flash-bangs stun the terrorists long enough for the first two team members to drop them, or that the terrorists have terrible aim.

When clearing a room, there is a specific routine operators follow. First, they dominate the room by moving to positions that allow them to overwhelm the terrorists with interlocking fields-of-fire. Second, they eliminate the threat as quickly as possible. Third, they control the situation and secure all personnel with either handcuffs or plastic tie-ties.

Two CCI instructors demonstrate the high/low stack method of clearing a room. The pair will simultaneously pivot outward to their right to clear the far corner directly to their left inside the doorway. As they do so, their weapons will sweep across the inside of the entire room. If any terrorists are waiting inside, they'll be quickly taken down. *SF Tomajczyk*

Explosive caulk was used to cut a "mousehole" in this wooden door. Mouseholes, which are often used in inside walls, allow an assault team to pick their own path through a building instead of relying on hallways that might be booby trapped. Assault team members wear goggles to protect their eyes from the smoke and debris that results from the door charge's detonation. *STTU*

Fourth, they search the dead to ensure that they are dead and no longer pose a threat. Often an "eye thump" is done to see if there is any deep pain response in an unconscious person. Fifth, they search the room to determine if there are any other potential threats to the team. And last, they evacuate the hostages and prisoners.

The reason for handcuffing everyone is because an assault team doesn't have the time to sort out hostages from terrorists playing "sheep." That task is left to follow-on teams. The assault teams' primary mission is to swiftly eliminate the immediate threat before hostages are killed. And that typically entails a "double-tap" to a terrorist's head.

A key aspect of counterterrorism is to dominate the situation. Chokes and strangles are two ways to subdue hostiles when killing is not permitted. A choke prevents the assailant from breathing, whereas a strangle cuts off the blood flow to the brain. In this photo, a choke hold is being practiced on a volunteer. If the choke is held 30 to 90 seconds, the person will go unconscious. Note the operator maintaining control of the weapon, so that if it is fired no one will be hurt. *STTU*

The easy way to assault an aircraft: Use a luggage conveyor belt at night to run up and open the main hatch. When doing this, the assault team has to keep in mind that the plane's weight from fuel, luggage, and passengers can cause the door's height above the ground to change. Often a team will attempt to open the hatch only to discover that they can't; the conveyor or ladder is blocking it shut. *STTU*

Linear Assaults

The second most common takedown scenario involves what is known as a linear target: buses, planes, and trains (including subways). All of these targets are narrow and very confining, offering limited space to move around in and almost no protective cover for the assault team. (A terrorist, for example, can shoot an operator at the rear of an airplane from the cockpit doorway.) These targets are also difficult to sneak up on, since passenger windows usually run the length of the vehicle. Furthermore, they offer few natural entry points. A train has two doors; a bus, one. The average plane has two doors and perhaps two to four emergency exits. For all of these reasons, linear assaults are innately dangerous and require special skills to accomplish successfully.

The United States' CT forces practice assaulting all types of linear targets. With regard to aircraft, they do takedowns at remote areas of airports using several different types of aircraft. They study the aircraft and airport operations so they can plan assaults based on various contingencies. For example, they learn where an aircraft's blind spots are so they can approach the craft without being seen. They learn the location of hatches and what warning lights on the control panel in the cockpit are lit up if a hatch is opened. And they learn where the "soft spots" on the fuselage are located, in case an explosive entry is needed.

In a typical terrorist hijacking of an aircraft, sniper-observers are placed around the aircraft. Those on the left side are typically labeled "Papa 1, Papa 3," and so on, while those positioned on the right side are labeled "Sierra 2, Sierra 4," and so on. Each sniper-observer has a specific portion of the plane that they are responsible for. For instance, Papa 1 and Sierra 2 both watch the plane's cockpit area. Papa 5 and Sierra 6 usually are assigned the wing

A close look at a bus takedown. Several assault team members attack the doors while others use step ladders to get to window height where they can shoot at terrorists. Linear targets, like this bus, are difficult to assault. There are few natural entry points and all the windows allow the terrorists (and sympathetic hostages) to see you coming. *STTU*

area. Papa 3 and Sierra 4 keep an eye on the space between the wing and cockpit. Each sniper-observer relays information to the command post about what the terrorists are doing.

As the assault team(s) moves into position—usually approaching from the rear of the aircraft where a natural blind spot exists—the snipers provide cover for them, just in case the team is spotted. When the assault is initiated, the snipers are often used to surgically kill, in a synchronized manner, as many terrorists as possible that are visible in windows and open doorways. They use non-jacketed bullets, so that nearby hostages are not injured by fragmentation as the bullet passes through the window and/or fuselage.

In some instances, snipers are used to disable the aircraft, to prevent it from taking off. In these cases, the .50 caliber sniper rifle—such as the Barrett M-82 .50—is ideal.

As the operators storm the plane in several places at the same time—often tossing flash-bangs ahead of them to stun the terrorists—they yell at the passengers to duck. The quarters are so cramped inside a plane that it's easy for passengers to be hit by bullets as the terrorists panic and spray their SMGs down the length of the plane; many planes are only about 15 feet wide inside. (In some cases, snipers will be ordered to fire into the upper third of the aircraft to encourage passengers inside to get down. This is done at the very beginning of an assault, and also serves as diversionary fire.)

Yo, ho, ho and a bottle of rum. How 'bout some lead instead? Two operators practice boarding a ship and taking down terrorists on the deck. CT forces must be prepared to respond to terrorist incidents in any environment, including the maritime arena. *STTU*

If all goes well, the assault is over within 30 seconds or so, with the last gunfight usually being held in the cockpit where the terrorist leader has barricaded himself.

Ship Takedowns

Ship hijackings are relatively rare, and for a number of reasons. First, the huge size of a passenger ship requires a large terrorist assault team to take control of the vessel and then guard the hundreds of hostages that are taken. Getting that many terrorists aboard the ship in the first place can be a difficult logistics problem. Second, once terrorists are aboard, there is no easy way for them to escape if they change their mind. They're surrounded not only by water, but also by military and police forces. And third, a ship is too large to defend against a determined assault done by counterterrorist forces.

Yet, the United States' elite teams—most notably DevGroup—train for ship assaults. One of the first things done before doing a takedown is to collect intelligence. The ship is shadowed by satellites, aircraft, and boats, and blueprints of the vessel's layout are acquired from the ship's owners. If a sister ship exists—and often they do—the CT team will visit it to practice their insertion technique and assault tactic.

Because of the lack of cover at sea, assaults are usually done under the cover of darkness. Helicopters carrying sniper teams and assault teams fly low above the ocean and approach from the ship's stern. Helicopters carrying the snipers arrive first, positioning themselves on either side of the ship at a 45- to 60-degree angle to the assault team that fast-ropes onto the stern. This prevents sniper bullets from ricocheting into friendly forces. (Assault team members also wear either glint tape or infrared chem sticks so that the snipers do not mistake them for terrorists.) The snipers take out any hostiles while providing intelligence data (e.g., terrorist locations, booby traps, weapon types, clear routes) via radio to the assault team.

Sometimes, assault teams do not use helicopters as part of a takedown. Instead, they rely on raiding craft with silenced engines to quietly approach the ship from astern and then climb aboard. In other instances, the assault team uses SCUBA or mini-subs to stealthily approach a ship either at night or during daylight. As covered in an earlier chapter, this tactic was considered by Navy SEALs to resolve the *Achille Lauro* hijacking in 1985. In all of these cases, the assault teams use extendible painter's poles and/or caving ladders with hooks to climb the ship's hull.

Regardless of how the operators get aboard the ship, once they hit the deck, they move in a "Train" formation, quickly clearing rooms and corridors of terrorists and hostages as they head for the ship's bridge. The two-man clearance technique—in which two operators enter a room and split left and right staying 18 inches off the wall—is most commonly used by assault teams due to the small size of the compartments. The operators run about three-quarters of the way down the wall, shooting any armed terrorists they encounter in their sphere of influence. Prisoners are secured to the ship; each operator typically carries enough gear to fully secure six prisoners.

Large compartments, such as the mess hall and crew lounge, are cleared by four men instead of just two. While the four operators clear the room, the breacher and point man continue down the passageway to the next room. Here, the point man maintains security and the breacher prepares for entry. When the four assault team members catch up to them, the room is breached. This fleet-footed choreography continues room-to-room, deck-to-deck. The assault formation itself changes as the team encounters L-shaped corridors (one-man assault), T-shaped corridors (two-man assault), cross-shaped corridors (three man assault), internal stairs (one man assault), external stairs (four man assault), and the ship's bridge (four- to six-man assault).

Once the assault of the ship's bridge is completed, follow-on forces land aboard the ship to deal with the hostages and any wounded personnel. Meanwhile, the bowels of the ship are cleared of terrorists. The vessel's communications room, engineering compartment, and steering room are guarded after being cleared so that a lone terrorist straggler is not able to somehow circle back and do any damage. When the internal clearance is finished and all the detainees are accounted for, the assault team extracts.

The amount of time required to take down a passenger ship depends on several things, including the size of the ship, the number of terrorists aboard the vessel, and the determination of the terrorists to fight the CT forces. Regardless of whether it takes 10 minutes or 10 hours, the result will likely always be the same: the demise of the terrorists. The motto of counterterrorism, "Speed. Surprise. Violence of action" ensures it.

CT forces routinely secure hostages and prisoners with handcuffs or, in this case, tie-ties. Made of nylon-reinforced plastic, the unbelievably strong tie-ties have to be cut off to be removed. *SF Tomajczyk*

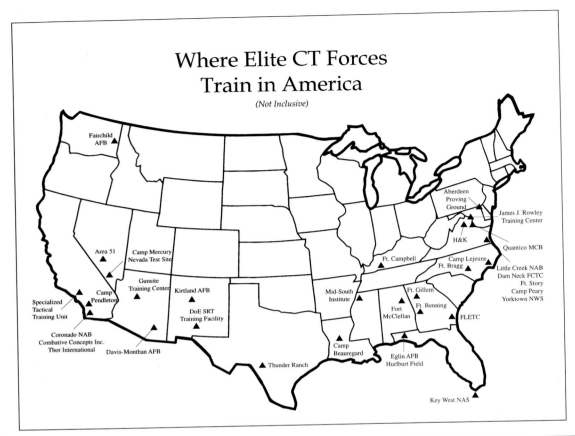

Where Elite CT Forces Train in America

(Not Inclusive)

Fairchild AFB

Aberdeen Proving Ground

James J. Rowley Training Center

H&K

Quantico MCB

Area 51

Camp Mercury Nevada Test Site

Ft. Campbell

Camp Lejeune
Ft. Bragg

Little Creek NAB
Dam Neck FCTC
Ft. Story
Camp Peary
Yorktown NWS

Gunsite Training Center

Kirtland AFB

Ft. Gillem

Specialized Tactical Training Unit

Camp Pendleton

Mid-South Institute

Fort McClellan

Ft. Benning

FLETC

DoE SRT Training Facility

Coronado NAB
Combative Concepts Inc.
Thor International

Davis-Monthan AFB

Thunder Ranch

Camp Beauregard

Eglin AFB
Hurlburt Field

Key West NAS

Training for Tomorrow

The United States is now at an important crossroads. Terrorism has stained our soil and the chances of that stain growing larger in the future are quite good. There is an undercurrent of dissension not only among extremists overseas, but also among our own citizens. People want change and are now more willing then ever to resort to violence to force their ideas of change into reality. As long as this continues, we will have a need for highly trained, special elite teams to resolve crises, in extremis situations, and terrorist actions.

Fortunately, units like Delta Force and DevGroup stand ready to emergencies abroad, and the FBI's Hostage Rescue Team is poised to resolve incidents here at home. In fact, HRT has begun to be more proactive in its approach. The HRT and the FBI's Critical Incident Response Group (CIRG) recently established open

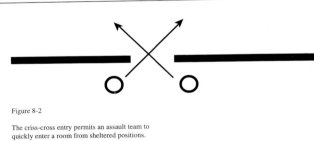

Figure 8-2

The criss-cross entry permits an assault team to quickly enter a room from sheltered positions.

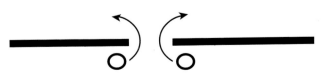

Figure 8-3

The buttonhook entry allows two assault team members to simultaneously enter a room providing, of course, that the doorway is wide enough.

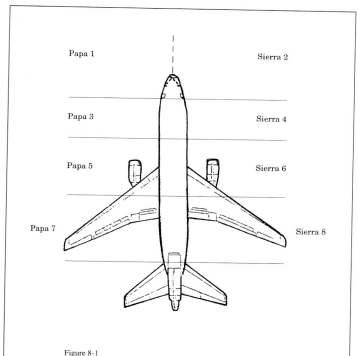

Figure 8-1

Sniper-observer team locations that would typically be positioned around a McDonnell Douglas DC-10, three-engined transport. Firing positions can be moved to reinforce a particular area of the plane that is heavily used by terrorists or tht is to be used by the assault team to gain entry.

of negotiations. The potential for escalation of this situation into a bloody war-like crisis involving other militias sympathetic to McLaren was effectively defused.

This kind of communication/negotiation process is likely to become more heavily used in the future. Many law enforcement agencies are, in fact, expanding their capabilities in this arena. However, when talk is cheap and the wackos of the world resort to body counts and bombs, we can all take a deep sigh of relief knowing that America's elite counterterrorist forces are at hand. These highly trained and specially equipped men and women willingly walk into life and death situations for one reason: To save lives.

communication with many militias and extremist groups throughout the country so they can lower tensions before things get out of hand and result in bloodshed.

This tactic proved to be invaluable during the April 1997 standoff in Fort Davis, Texas, in which Republic of Texas leader Richard McLaren and his followers refused to surrender after a warrant had been served for McLaren's arrest. He was wanted for failure to appear in court in a dispute over bogus liens and other illegal papers he filed in the name of the Republic of Texas. The HRT and CIRG were in communication with key militia leaders around the United States throughout the crisis, relaying messages in an attempt to defuse the situation as well as reassuring the militias that the HRT was not gearing up to respond. McLaren surrendered peacefully to local law enforcement officials after a tense week

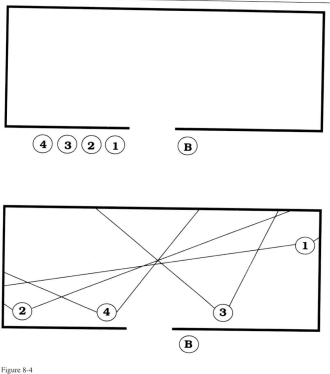

Figure 8-4

This figure shows a fairly standard four-man entry. After the breacher (B) forces open the door, the lead man in the "Snake" or "Train" crosses the room to opposite corner, taking control of most of the room. The second man buttonhooks through the doorway and heads for the corner. The third man follows the leader; the last man in the stack, the second man. Room clearing can be done in as little as seven seconds. The lines represent sectors-of-fire for each operator. In small rooms, only two men are used.

GLOSSARY

ARG: Accident Response Group, a DoE volunteer unit that responds to nuclear accidents. See also NEST.

ATA: Anti-Terrorist Assistance, a program operated by the State Department to train foreign law enforcement agencies in counterterrorism techniques. The U.S. Marshals Service SOG provides the tactical training at its Tactical Center in Louisiana.

ATAC: Anti-Terrorist Alert Center. Located in Washington, D.C., and operated by the Navy, the center monitors terrorist activities worldwide and sends out alerts of impending attacks.

Bang: Slang for a flash-bang grenade.

BATF: Bureau of Alcohol, Tobacco & Firearms, a federal agency that controls the movement of these three controlled items, as well as explosives.

Bent Spear: Codename for a nuclear weapons incident. See also Broken Arrow.

Black Talon: A lethal, hollow-point bullet that fragments into claw-like shards upon impact.

Blow and Go: Phrase used by CT units in reference to dynamic entries; you blow the explosive charges and immediately enter the building through the breach or hole.

Broken Arrow: Codename for a nuclear accident. It is much more serious than a Bent Spear. See also Dull Sword.

BUD/S: Basic Underwater Demolition/SEAL training. A 26-week basic training course at Coronado, California, that all SEAL candidates must endure and pass in order to be considered for the SEAL teams.

CAM: Chemical Agent Monitor, a device that detects chemical warfare agents, such as sarin and soman. It is typically set up along a perimeter, downwind of a potential gas release to warn of an attack.

Canary: Slang for a hostage.

CAT: U.S. Secret Service's Counter-Assault Team.

C/B: Chemical/Biological.

CBDCOM: Chemical & Biological Defense Command, an Army command whose units respond to chemical and biological incidents.

CBIRF: Chemical/Biological Incident Response Force, a Marine Corps unit.

Chicken Plate: Slang for the ceramic or steel disk that fits inside a bulletproof vest. The plate, which is positioned over the heart, is designed to withstand hits from high-caliber bullets.

CIRG: Critical Incident Response Group. A component of the FBI that oversees the deployment of the Hostage Rescue Team and negotiators to crises.

CR: Designation for a tear gas agent that can penetrate a gas mask filter that normally will stop CS and CN tear gas. CR is used against terrorists equipped with gas masks.

Crow: Slang for a terrorist. See also Tango.

CST: U.S. Secret Service's Counter-Sniper Team.

CTC: Counterterrorism Center. Staffed and operated by the CIA, the center monitors the whereabouts and actions of terrorists worldwide.

DevGroup: Development Group, the new name for SEAL Team Six.

DoD: Department of Defense.

DoE: Department of Energy.

DoS: Department of State, a federal agency that deals with terrorism involving Americans outside the continental United States.

Double Tap: Two aimed shots fired in rapid succession at a terrorist to ensure that he does not pose any further threat. See also Mozambique.

Dry Hole: An empty room or structure.

Dull Sword: Codename for a situation in which a nuclear weapon malfunctions or is damaged, and could result in detonation or radioactive contamination. See also Bent Spear.

Eagle: Slang for a good guy (i.e., counterterrorism operator).

EOC: Emergency Operations Center.

EPIC: El Paso Intelligence Center. Operated by the DEA, EPIC tracks and interdicts the movement of drugs, aliens, and weapons. Numerous federal agencies participate at EPIC, including the FBI, Secret Service, and Customs Service.

FAA: Federal Aviation Administration, a federal agency that is responsible for terrorist incidents that occur aboard U.S. aircraft.

FAST: Fleet Antiterrorist Security Team, a Marine Corps unit.

FBG: Flash-bang grenade. Also referred to as "bangs" and "flashcrashes."

Ferret: A finned plastic capsule (12 gauge, 37 mm) that contains tear gas. The ferret has a blunt front end that is scored; it bursts open on impact, releasing the gas. Ferrets can penetrate 3/4-inch plywood barriers at 100 feet.

Frags: Fragmentation grenades.

Frangible Ammo: A copper-polymer bullet that turns into dust when it strikes a target, resulting in no ricochet or fragments flying back at the shooter. Frangible ammo is used by CT units for CQB drills.

Funny Platoon: Nickname for Delta Force's all-female detachment, which conducts recon and collects intelligence for the team.

GIGN: Groupe d'Intervention de la Gendarmerie Nationale, France's elite counterterrorist unit. Among GIGN's accomplishments were the rescue of a school bus of children that was hijacked in Djibouti by four terrorists in February 1976, and the assault of an Air France jetliner that was hijacked by Algerian terrorists in December 1994.

Glaser Round: A high-velocity, prefragmented projectile produced in a soft point, round-nose style bullet. Nearly 100 percent of available energy is transferred to the target, resulting in massive trauma. The Glaser round gives a 9 mm the same stopping power as a .44 magnum.

Glass House Drill: An exercise in which an assault team practices assaulting a target using tape on the floor to indicate the location of walls, doorways, furniture, etc. Glass house drills are done when an assault team doesn't have time to build a scale mock structure of the target.

GSG-9: Grenzchutzgruppe-9, Germany's elite counterterrorist unit. GSG-9 retook a hijacked Lufthansa 737 with 91 persons aboard that had been hijacked by terrorists in October 1977. The assault occurred at Mogadishu Airport; no hostages were killed.

HAHO: High Altitude, High Opening. A parachute insertion technique used to thwart detection by hostile forces on the ground. Parachutists jump out at 20,000+ feet, deploy their chutes, and quietly drift to the predetermined landing site 25 to 50 miles away downwind from where they initially jumped out of the plane.

HALO: High Altitude, Low Opening. A parachute insertion technique in which the parachutist falls to about 2,000 feet above the ground before deploying his parachute. HALO minimizes the time you spend floating down in your parachute, which is when you are most at risk from enemy observation and fire.

Head Job: Slang term meaning to be shot in the head.

HEU: Highly Enriched Uranium.

HRT: Hostage Rescue Team, an elite FBI unit that responds to terrorist and similar high-risk incidents.

Hydra-Shok: Lethal hollow-point ammunition manufactured by Federal Cartridge Company. Many CT forces use Hydra-Shok ammo, including the FBI's HRT and the U.S. Marshals Service's SOG.

IND: Improvised Nuclear Device (i.e., a homemade nuclear bomb).

INS: Immigration & Naturalization Service, a federal agency that prevents the illegal entry of individuals into the United States.

Jedi: Nickname for members of DevGroup, after the movie Star Wars.

JSOC: Joint Special Operations Command. A component of the U.S. Special Operations Command headquartered at Pope AFB that oversees the employment of DevGroup, SFOD-D, and 160th SOAR.

Kicker: Nickname for someone on an assault team who is responsible for kicking open a closed door.

Little Bird: Nickname for an AH-6 or MH-6 helicopter used by the HRT and military CT forces for assaults and covert insertions.

MEU/SOC: Marine Expeditionary Unit—Special Operations Capable. A specially trained and equipped Marine Corps unit that conducts unconventional warfare and hostage recovery.

Mob: Nickname for DevGroup.

Mousehole: Nickname for a small, round-shaped breach made into walls and/or doorways with explosives. CT assault teams use mouseholes to move room to room in a building to avoid hallways (which are often booby-trapped or covered by weapons fire), as well as to surprise tangos.

Mozambique: Slang for firing two bullets to the chest of a terrorist and one to the head. This ensures that the tango is permanently out of the picture. See also Double Tap.

NCA: National Command Authority. The top-level of America's military chain-of-command, which consists of the President and the Secretary of Defense.

NEST: Nuclear Emergency Search Team, a DoE unit that locates nuclear devices and weapons. See also ARG.

Night Stalkers: See TF-160.

Non-Lethal Weapons (Less Than Lethal): Weapons designed to injure, stun, distract, confuse, etc., rather than kill a human being.

NVG: Night Vision Goggle.

OC: Oleoresin Capsicum, an inflammatory tear gas made from red peppers. The hotness of OC is based on the capsaicin content of oleoresin. The unit of measure is called a Scoville Heat Unit (SHU). Pure capsaicin is 15 million SHU. Spray containers used by CT units have 5 percent OC with 2 million SHU. OC causes immediate and temporary blindness, as well as induces choking, coughing, and nausea.

Operator: General term for a member of an assault team, as opposed to a supervisor or commander.

Parrot: Slang for a person who has not yet been identified as a friendly or a bad guy. Hence, he is an unknown.

Plink: A single discriminating shot, usually a bullet to the head.

Ranch: See Wally World.

Room Broom: Nickname for a compact submachine gun, such as the H&K MP5K.

SAS: Special Air Service, Great Britain's premier CT unit that gained world attention in 1980 when it recaptured Princess Gate from terrorists who had taken over the Iranian embassy in London (Operation Nimrod).

Scuba/HALO Physical: Nickname for the thorough medical physical given to candidates applying to Delta Force.

SEAL: Sea/Air/Land, one component of the Navy's Special Warfare Command that is tasked with special operations. The acronym also jokingly stands for "Sleep, Eat And Live it up!"

Semtex: A Czechoslovakian plastique explosive that is popular with terrorists.

SFOD-D: Special Forces Operational Detachment-Delta, which is more popularly known as Delta Force.

Shadow Stalkers: Nickname for the USMS Special Operations Group. It comes from the fact that the unit hunts dangerous fugitives (a.k.a. shadows), as well as waits in the shadows of federal courthouses during high-profile cases to thwart terrorist attacks.

Shoot and Scoot: A phrase that aptly describes how an assault team clears a building or structure: They find the bad guys, shoot 'em, and then quickly move on to the next room or area.

Shooter: Nickname for the members of an assault team who are responsible for shooting hostiles. See also Kicker.

SIOC: Strategic Information Operations Center, a specially equipped suite from which the FBI directs major investigations (e.g., World Trade Center bombing, Montana Freemen siege).

Slime: Slang term meaning to be gassed with a chemical agent.

Snake: Nickname for a six-man assault formation that is used to clear a building.

SOG: Special Operations Group. 1) In the FBI, SOG is responsible for covert intelligence gathering. 2) In the U.S. Marshals Service, SOG is an elite unit that deploys to high-risk situations, such as escorting terrorists to and from federal courts.

SRT: Special Reaction Team. In the military, a specially trained unit that reacts to and resolves special threats, such as terrorist acts and hostage taking. Organized under a squad concept, the ideal SRT is comprised of nine members.

Stockholm Syndrome: When hostages begin to empathize with their captors and turn against their rescuers. Named after a 1973 incident that occurred in Stockholm, Sweden, in which two suspects held four clerks hostage for 131 hours after an aborted robbery. When an assault team attempted to release them, the hostages shielded the suspects with their bodies. One hostage later married one of the suspects.

SWAT: Special Weapons and Tactics, a unit that is trained and equipped to handle special, high-risk incidents (e.g., barricaded suspects, snipers, armed encounters). Most law enforcement agencies and military bases have SWAT teams.

Takedown: An assault on a target.

Tango: Slang for a terrorist. So named after the military's designation for the letter "T" (Tango) in the phonetic alphabet. See also Crow.

TF-160: Task Force 160, which is also known as the 160th Special Operations Aviation Regiment (160th SOAR). It is an elite Army unit based out of Ft. Campbell, Kentucky, that engages in covert operations and ferries Delta Force and other special operations units around. The 160th SOAR is nicknamed "Night Stalkers" because it does most of its work at night.

Tie-Tie (Flex Cuffs): A lightweight and flexible 22-inch-long plastic band that is used to handcuff someone's wrists or legs. The keyless tie-tie is so strong (tensile strength of 370 pounds) that it can only be removed by cutting it off with a knife or a pair of clippers.

Trick: To modify and/or customize a weapon.

Uncle Fester: A person who publishes/shares information on how to make chemical weapons.

USCS: United States Customs Service, a federal agency that prevents the illegal entry of substances, weapons, etc.

USMS: United States Marshals Service

USSOCOM: United States Special Operations Command. A unified command established in 1987 and headquartered at MacDill AFB in Tampa, Florida. It has overall operational command of military special operations forces. See also JSOC.

USSS: United States Secret Service.

Wally World: Nickname for Delta Force's new, multimillion dollar, special operations training facility at Ft. Bragg. (The original Delta Force HQ was located at Ft. Bragg's old stockade and was known as "The Ranch" because of the propensity of some operators to chew tobacco and wear cowboy boots. When Delta moved to its new facilities, the name came along with it.)

Willy Peter (WPs): Nickname for a White Phosphorus incendiary grenade.

Index

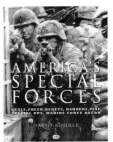

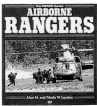
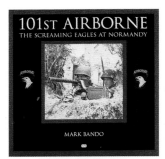
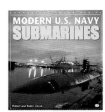